LATIN AMERICA: WORLD IN REVOLUTION

BY CARLETON BEALS

Latin America: World in Revolution
Cyclone Carry: The Story of Carry Nation
Nomads and Empire Builders
Brass Knuckle Crusade: The Great Know-Nothing Conspiracy
House in Mexico
John Eliot: The Man Who Loved the Indians (Book Club Choice)
Adventure of the Western Sea: The Story of Robert Gray
Taste of Glory
Stephen F. Austin: Father of Texas
The Long Land: Chile
Our Yankee Heritage:
  The Making of Greater New Haven
  The Making of Bristol (Barnes Foundation Award)
  New England's Contribution to American Civilization
What South Americans Think of Us (Collaboration)
Lands of the Dawning Morrow
Rio Grande to Cape Horn
Dawn Over the Amazon (Book Club Choice)
Pan America: A Program for the Western Hemisphere
The Great Circle
Glass Houses
The Coming Struggle for Latin America
America South
American Earth: The Biography of a Nation
The Stones Awake
Fire on the Andes
The Story of Huey P. Long
Crime of Cuba
Black River
Porfirio Diaz: Dictator of Mexico (Guggenheim Fellowship)
Banana Gold
Con Sandino en Nicaragua
Mexican Maze (Book Club Choice)
Destroying Victor
Brimstone and Chile
Rome or Death: The Story of Fascism
Mexico: An Interpretation

Carleton Beals

LATIN AMERICA: WORLD IN REVOLUTION

GREENWOOD PRESS, PUBLISHERS
WESTPORT, CONNECTICUT

Library of Congress Cataloging in Publication Data

Beals, Carleton, 1893-
    Latin America: world in revolution.

    Reprint of the ed. published by Abelard-Schuman,
London, New York.
    Bibliography: p.
    1. Latin America--History--20th century. I. Title.
F1414.B42 1974   980'.03   74-9631
ISBN 0-8371-7598-4

Reprinted with the permission of Abelard Schuman Ltd.

Reprinted in 1974 by Greenwood Press,
a division of Williamhouse-Regency Inc.

Library of Congress Catalog Card Number 74-9631

ISBN 0-8371-7598-4

Printed in the United States of America

CONTENTS

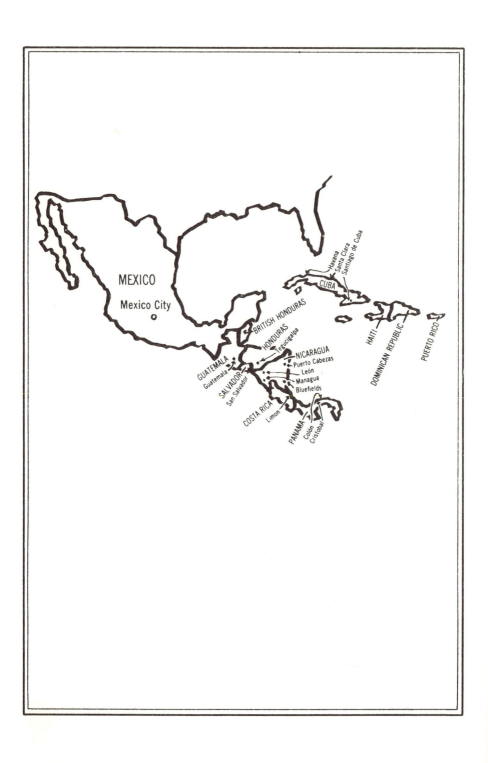

1 ⃝ THE TALE OF TWO REVOLUTIONS

1

Mexico 1911. May 21. 11:00 p.m.

The purr of motor-cars creeps through the unpaved, unlit streets in the frontier city of Ciudad Juárez in Mexico. Headlights shine on the closed customs house. Far off sounds the *Alerta* of a rebel sentry of the forces of Francisco Madero, spearhead of a nationwide uprising against the thirty-year dictatorship of Porfirio Díaz.

Already Díaz's federal troops, driven out of the border city, have fled also from Torreón to the South. There, low elements, pro-revolutionary, sacked the city and murdered two hundred Chinamen — hated for their greedy monopoly of retail trade. Colima near the Pacific fell to the rebels, May 20. Next day far-south Acapulco and historic Chilpancingo were surrendered; the day after, the revolutionists moved into balmy Cuernavaca to the north — only a cat's meow from the national capital. They were smothered in flowers by the delirious throngs. Defense of Tehuacán, the Puebla spa, collapsed. The whole country was surging up in revolt.

Eighty-year-old Porfirio Díaz, sick in his Cadena Street mansion in Mexico City from an infested jaw, with a high fever and in excruciating pain, was sending telegrams to the whole world reiterating his determination to hang on. But close supporters, including his vice-president, Ramón Corral, had already fled from the country; others were trying to make deals with the revolters.

His own last-minute representative authorized to dicker with them — Supreme Court Justice Francisco Carbajal — this night of May 21, stepped from his car in front of the dark Juárez customs house to greet three shadow-like men: Ernesto Madero (uncle of the liberator); political writer and médico, Emilio Vásquez Gómez; Yucatán editor, José María Pino Suárez. Behind, rebel soldiers stood at attention. Matches were struck in the dry hot air, flickering on dark intense faces and glittering eyes. A stub of candle was produced, a document spread out. It provided for an armistice.

The conditions were sternly simple. Díaz and his vice-president, Corral, were to resign at once; bearded Francisco de la Barra, foreign minister, would assume the provisional presidency to hold October elections. Most Díaz governors were to be replaced. The document bore the revolutionary slogan: "Effective Suffrage; No Re-election" (which still appears on every government communiqué).

This was Mexico's political Magna Carta. The economic Magna Carta, the 1917 Querétaro Constitution — the first of its sort in the world's history — would cost much more war and bloodshed. It would be drawn up defiantly under the menace of John Pershing's bayonets and in disregard of threatening notes from Washington, trying in vain to halt the threat to foreign oil properties.

These two documents represented Mexico's "second independence." A new era had begun.

Mexico City. May 23.

Jubilant crowds swirled through the streets of the capital, from the great Zócalo and the National Palace to the tree-studded Alameda and out to the wide, handsome Paseo de la Reforma; they swarmed into the ivory-and-gold sessions of the Congress, creating panic; they shouted into the faces of the Presidential Guards at the Cadena residence. Business houses hastily ran down their iron curtains, turning the main streets into narrow canyons of stone and steel, where wide sombreros bobbed along and *guarache* sandals shuffled like a storm of autumn leaves. Shouts arose:

"Death to Porfirio!"

"Down with the Tyrant!"

"Death to the Gringos!"

"To hell with the Yankee Cabrones!"

"Viva Madero!"

"Viva Pancho Villa!"

"Viva la Revolución!"

Mexico City. May 25. Midday.

Minister de la Barra stood beside Díaz's bedside with the latter's resignation to be signed.

The hero of a hundred battles groaned hoarsely, "I came into my seat in a storm of bullets. That is how I shall depart."

Even as he spoke, mobs howled outside, a window crashed into splinters, firing echoed across the flat roof-tops, and bullets ricocheted down the narrow streets.

Porfirio's family pleaded with the aging, agonizing dictator to resign. Doña Carmen, his wife, insisted. The Papal Nuncio added cajolery. Finance Minister José Ives Limantour, a brilliant Machiavellian well-known in the banking circles of the world and who had already made several financial deals with Gustavo Madero, the liberator's undulating brother, peremptorily demanded that the dictator resign.

Not until midnight did Díaz capitulate and sign with shaking hand. At once he was sneaked out of the house, to be escorted to Vera Cruz by General Victoriano Huerta — a heavy-set, brutal Indian-type soon to betray the country — to leave for Paris on the *Ypiranga*.

Deep in the night and all night and all day, the churchbells began ringing, booming out the glad tidings of the end of the dictatorship, the triumph of the people. Exultant townspeople, in spite of sporadic shooting, began painting out old street signs, daubing them with the names of revolutionary heroes: Francisco Madero (the main street), Pino Suárez, Abraham González, Filomeno Mata.

The world's first social revolution of this century had taken over the country. The first great setback for colonialism, imperialism, dollar diplomacy, had occurred; the first serious check to the southward thrust of dollars and Marines. The Mexican revolution set off the cycle of world-change in this century — a chain of social convulsions that have since rocked most of the planet. Soon came the upheaval in China, fermenting against European imperialism ever since the Boxer revolt. Events in Mexico triggered a whole series of upheavals in Latin America and led to counter-revolutions, a number aided by U.S. Marine invasions of Nicaragua, Honduras, Haiti, the Dominican Republic — a policy of containment by force that did little to contain and which ruined our good name everywhere.

For the continent-wide forces of national independence and economic liberation steadily gathered volume. The conditions which brought about the Mexican revolution, present also in most of Latin America, have grown more acute everywhere; today they portend massive continental upheaval.

2

The Mexican revolution would be prolonged, a terrible anguish; birth pangs are followed always by tearing and blood, and blood would flow in rivers. The movement would grow and deepen, would acquire volume and power. Outside meddling merely prolonged the agony, confused the issues, fed the rivers of blood, but turned the will of the people to steel. All over south Mexico, the peasant revolt of Emiliano Zapata drove out the *hacendados*, seized land, burned and pillaged and rejoiced.

The rule of the murderous Rurales, the highest paid law-and-order thuggery in the world, was over. So ended serfdom and feudal monopolies, the domination of the Church and large landholders, of foreign ownership of railroads and oil.

Thus was the ancient Indian system of communal *ejidos* reborn, thus were the doors of education opened, and new rights for peasants and workers established.

Presently part of the new birth was the splendid outburst of some of the greatest modern painters in our century — Diego Rivera, José Clemente Orozco, David Siqueiros.

Vera Cruz. July 2, 1911.

Filomeno Mata, heroic editor of *Diario del Hogar,* who had suffered many years of torture in Díaz's prisons, died at the age of sixty-four.

Mexico City. July 2, 1961.

(Fifty years later.) Seventy-five-year-old Filomeno Mata, Jr. (also an editor and staunch defender of freedom) and sixty-five-year-old David Siqueiros (Mexico's greatest living painter) for a whole year had been caged in cells at the National Penitentiary because they had formed an organization in behalf of scores of political prisoners and labor leaders crowding the jails under the present López Mateos administration.

Mexico City. March 10, 1962.

They were sentenced to eight years each, in a dirty courtroom with broken windows, for the nebulous crime of "social dissolution."

And so history swings full cycle. Once more U.S. entrepreneurs are swarming into Mexico, getting lush concessions. Once more the U.S. press, true to form, hails and praises the oppressor, President López Mateos, now nicknamed the "little hunchback Porfirio" — *"Porfirito jorabito"* — as the great leader of "democracy." Once more the Church is creeping back into power, baldly flouting the constitution, raising up violence and disorders in the name of a false "anti-Communist" crusade. A new robber baron era is swinging into high gear, and the palaces of the nouveaux riches, sheathed in pink tezontle lava like the Spanish palaces of old, have transformed the Lomas of Chapultepec — Grasshopper Hill — into the Nob Hill of the southlands.

And so the Díaz super-state is edging back: labor leaders and teachers are in jail, editors who love freedom are in jail, and painters — the glory of the Revolution — are in jail. The poison of power and injustice seeps in everywhere; step by step, the new

Dictatorship is being erected — this time in the name of Boom and Progress, of Technocracy and Democracy. And so, out of this Mexican back-eddy, inevitably, Revindicating Revolution Number Two is also gathering momentum.

3

Cuba. 1958. December. 10:30 p.m.

The Associated Press, blithely accepting a last-minute handout of the Batista government, informs the world that the Fidel Castro revolutionists have been crushed in Santa Clara, the key city of central Cuba.

At Camp Colombia, overlooking Havana, Dictator Fulgencio Batista already knows the game is up; the plane for his flight abroad is warming up. Two days previously, he had sent his two youngest children to New York.

He sits, stolid, dark-faced, staring at the big new electronic board with lights indicating the cities still held by his crumbling U.S.-trained army. One by one they are flickering out; the darkness grows.

He sits listening now to the receiver of his new island-wide electronic intercommunications system, a gadget recently installed with the aid of his U.S. military advisers.

Already he knows of the treachery of his high generals. Eulogio Cantillo in Oriente Province, who commands the bulk of the army supplies, tanks and planes, and the flower of the forces, has been making unauthorized deals with Fidel Castro (whom he will also betray). Cantillo has also made a secret pact with General Alberto Chaviano (brother-in-law of Defense Minister Francisco Tabernilla Dolz) and others to oust the dictator, kill opponents and set up a military junta. Already Batista knows of the secret visits behind his back of Cantillo, the treacherous Tabernilla military clan and other army conspirators to the U.S. Embassy.

Earlier in the month, U.S. Ambassador Earl Smith — so Batista has related in his post-revolutionary *Respuesta* — had given the dictator a veiled suggestion he get out, had even discussed where he should seek asylum. His first refuge was to be Spain;

after a few months he would be granted a haven in the United States. This promise, if made, was never kept.

Ever since 1934, Dictator Batista had served the United States and its private interests well, far better than he had the Cuban people, who had been driven under the lash, tortured and murdered. Their mutilated bodies had been hung up in the public places or tossed out in the public streets. Agrarian leader Antonio Guiteras had been murdered on a lonely Matanzas shore. My good friend, Octavio Seigle, was burned alive in his automobile. (Later his killer became one of the favored C.I.A. trainers of ex-Batista forces for the invasion of Cuba in 1961.)

At the behest of the U.S. Embassy, Batista in 1934 had kicked out his comrade-in-arms, Dr. Ramón Grau San Martín, and had installed Carlos Mendieta — of the same party as fallen dictator Gerardo Machado — as president, in an orgy of blood and murder. Riotous, sanguinary years dragged by until the days of the Castro revolters in the Sierra Maestra of Oriente.

For example, time will never blot out the spectacle late in 1957 of those twenty-seven mutilated bodies of boys dangling from the plaza trees in Holguín in blind military retaliation for the assassination of a brutal army officer, or those thrown into the weeds of the Havana suburbs itself or left on the main streets with eyeballs gouged-out, fingernails torn-out, ears cut-off, testicles cut out, flesh burned deep.

These things the U.S. press did not talk about; the dutiful little sergeant who had come to own great hotels and apartment houses in New York and on the Gold Coast of Florida, was adulated at home and by the U.S. press, and his hand-picked assassins were decorated by U.S. officials. For he had kept a peace of sorts, a semi-peace, the peace of the graveyard, in behalf of the great U.S. sugar plantations and utility companies, kept it with bayonets and terror — while luxurious apartment houses rose in Havana, while roulette wheels of U.S. gangsters and of the Las Vegas empire spun on every other corner and in every municipality in the land, while all Havana became a vast brothel, and the night-clubs, pornographic movie houses owned by U.S. gangsters, labor-leaders, mayors, cabinet ministers, displayed their nude rhumba dances and sex perversions. Boom, progress, democracy! Business, graft, political corruption, lavish ostentation, and dollars — a glittering superstructure erected on

the back of barefoot, half-starved peasants. Such was the great
U.S. sugar plantation! Such was Cuban Democracy! Progress!

But now, at the end of 1958, the brutalities behind the silks
and satins were becoming known. The faithful little dictator had
become expendable — so it was believed in Washington — and
at least, belatedly, arms shipments to him were cut off. In any
case he was doomed. In two years of fighting, a dozen fanatics
in the mountains of the east had grown to thousands, and little
by little his power had been eaten away. His U.S.-trained troops
were caught in ambush, fled, defected, died. His U.S. planes
and the napalm bombs destroyed whole towns, but the revolt
grew. The tanks, all the fine equipment, were now useless to
hold down the people any longer. It was a defeat for Batista.
It was a defeat for the U.S. military mission, which advised the
dictatorship until the last hour. A colossal bit of bungling, unmatched until they staged the Bay of Pigs invasion of April 1961.

Now the last hour was here. The final curtain would be rung
down — a matter of hours, now. Over the fancy intercom system at Camp Colombia, the dictator listened in on the incredible events in Santa Clara — as point after point was stormed.
His planes, bombing, strewing napalm, turned men, women and
children into chunks of charcoal. But the rebel forces moved in
relentlessly through the flames and the carnage.

If Santa Clara fell, Batista was lost, all was lost.

Already he knew of the capture (by purchase and by bullets)
of the "million dollar" train, sent to succor the city with the last
of his munitions and men. For it, the bottom of the supply barrel
had been scraped in Havana. Already the dictator suspected,
and presently was to know, the commander of that train, Flor-
entino Rosell, had been bought out by "Che" Guevara, the young
Argentine doctor commanding the Santa Clara attack; already
Rosell had fled on his private yacht to the arms of U.S. immigration officials.

Now at Camp Colombia this fateful night, the dictator was
plugged in to the last government hold-out position in the be-
leaguered sugar-city — the Santa Clara police barracks. At the
very height of the attack, he listened in on the ugly quarrel between the last-ditch military commandant, General Joaquín
Casillas Lumpui, and the chief of police, each believing he had
the sole right to give orders.

Batista listened to the hoarse commands, the shouts of the soldiers crying out for surrender to the enemy. He listened to the dull boom of cannon, the rat-tat-tat of machine guns, the screams of the wounded. Listened to the final arrest of the officers by their own soldiers. On the great board the light labeled Santa Clara went dark.

A few hours later, Batista and his wife were flying east over Guantánamo — that U.S. naval base seized long ago by force and fraud and flimsy papers, symbol of an earlier imperialistic era, still stubbornly held as a bulwark of perpetuated imperialism — on over the Windward Passage, over Haiti where death stalked under the dictatorship of "democratic" François Duvalier, kept in power only by U.S. bayonets and dollars — to seek asylum in that other great "democracy" of the Free World, that of hangman Generalísimo Almirantísimo Rafael Leonidas Trujillo, "Benefactor of the Fatherland." Malicious rumor said that Batista had to shell out a million dollars to Trujillo for the privilege. Quite a bite, if true, but only a postage stamp for the fallen Cuban dictator, the orphan who had ridden from rags to riches on the backs of his people.

That same night of the flight from Camp Colombia, treacherous defense minister Tabernilla, his eyes bulging with terror, his face hollowed with horror — so a news photo shows him — and a group of panic-stricken fellow-officers seized another plane at gun point and flew deep into the United States.

4

Havana. January 1, 1959.

Sunrise over the Guanabacoa Hills. The warm early light flooded the ancient Spanish walls and the new shining skyscrapers, the tall, blue-windowed U.S. Embassy which loomed on the beautiful Malecón Esplanade — with its swarms of attachés and employees, technicians, commercial agents, labor nuncios, good-will enterprisers, cultural and information emissaries, T-men, narcotic snoopers, F.B.I. agents, C.I.A. agents and Marine Guards. The sun glittered on the lofty Havana Riviera Hotel, the most magnificent on the continent, and on great

crowds roaring jubilantly through the narrow, stained streets of
Old Havana.

The great wave that had started in Mexico, that had ebbed
and risen and ebbed all over Latin America, had risen again,
to burst in full power over the little island of Cuba and its seven
million long-suffering people.

Even before the first morning light had struck through the bars
of ancient, hill-perched Principe Castle, the thousands of in-
mates knew that Batista had fled, and ten thousand relatives
of the prisoners already milled about outside crying out for the
freedom of their loved ones. The prisoners screamed their de-
light at the news, they pounded their tin cups on the pavement
and the bars, they shook their bars in a deafening roar of iron
and lungs — a thousand political prisoners, some of them deep-
scarred with torture, and several thousand thieves, footpads,
rapers, thugs and murders. They shook the bars, they broke
the bars. Their fingers reached out and seized guards and took
their keys; they swarmed free into the corridors, freeing everybody, shouting:

"Death to Batista!"

"Death to the Tyrant!"

"Death to the Yankees: *Hijos de la Papaya!*"

"Viva Fidel Castro! Viva Fidel! Viva Fidel!"

(Exactly twenty-five years before this, on another New Year's
dawn, I, too, had seen the sunrise over Guanabacoa Hills from
behind the iron bars of Principe Castle. I knew that maze of steel
cages, those slimy ancient corridors, that stench of excrement
and unwashed bodies, the thousands of prisoners of despair.
With the Minister of Justice, I had been helping to get released
three hundred political prisoners thrust there by Batista. Once
more in 1959 I thought over the many miseries and tragedies of
this past quarter of a century in the great U.S. sugar plantation
known as Cuba — all the age-old miseries of Principe Castle.)

But this morning, though the front gates had been thrown
wide, none of the prisoners went out, even though the sunlight
of God flamed gloriously on the stones outside. With that strange
Latin love for formality, etiquette and legal niceties, they were
patiently waiting until a judge could be awakened who would
issue an *order* for their release. Even after it arrived, two murderers refused to leave their cells. "We would be brought back
again in a few days," they explained.

The warden — a general — cowered, broken and despairing, in his office, his service revolver at the ready on his desk. He sat there in a dark daze, unaware of the passing hours, his face running with sweat, his lips moving silently. Thus the newspaper reporters found him. At first he was scarcely able to speak. Then he straightened up.

"As a soldier I could not betray my trust and free those prisoners. But as a man I could not shoot them down. I could not turn the machine guns on the thousands outside, all the women and children crying out for their loved ones. I simply could not do it. I came in here to be alone, to think for a moment, to blow out my brains."

By then, prisoners were embracing their loved ones who had surged inside. They were burning their striped uniforms on the stone floors and putting on ordinary civilian clothes.

But the political prisoners marched out arm in arm, proudly wearing their prison-stripes as symbols of suffering and honor, singing the Song of the Revolution, that lilting, blood-tingling melody that had come down with the veterans from the Sierra Maestra. On their sleeves they wore the new red-black armbands embossed with the white M-26 insignia, "Movement of the 26th of July." That was the day in 1953 when the first small group of revolutionists, led by Fidel Castro, had attacked the mighty Moncada Barracks in Santiago — most to become the first martyrs of *The Revolution*.

Long before the prison-striped heroes reached the central plaza, the avenging crowds had completed their smashing, and olive-green revolutionary militiamen stood guard over the scenes of destruction. Every gambling casino in the city, except those in the three largest hotels, had been gutted. In all the downtown streets smoldered big heaps of broken roulette and dice tables, sheets of green felt, broken red, green and blue chips, busted bottles, slot machines, cigarette machines, tables, chairs, leather sofas, oil paintings of naked women. These smoking remains of the vice-ridden city dens and brothels had been the joint property of U.S. gangsters (several on the top F.B.I. wanted list), of the mayor of Havana, of cabinet ministers, labor leaders, of Batista himself. They represented part of the golden plunder, over and beyond that sucked out of Cuba each year by the great U.S. sugar plantations and public utilities. The joints were all wrecked now. Carry Nation never did a more thorough job of smashing in her wild hatchet forays across the United States.

The Havana crowds also smashed the heavily subsidized newspaper of Senator Rolando Mansferrer — the ex-Communist who maintained a powerful secret organization of thugs (to assassinate enemies of the Batista dictatorship) which, even several days after the victory of the Revolution, staged an assault on the Máximo Gómez business block in the central plaza. He, too, escaped to the United States with a pile of gold, and now struts around Miami with armed guards.

The Havana crowds this January 1, 1959, ripped out the parking meters (a private graft of the nephew of the dictator and an irritating reminder of U.S. mechanized culture). They ripped out the telephone coin boxes (for they knew of the $300,000 graft paid over to Batista and his henchmen in connection with recent rate-increases). They were still smarting from that elaborate ceremony in the National Palace when the grateful company had presented the dictator with a solid gold telephone, a ceremony attended by Ambassador Arthur Gardner — even though he had had to walk across the marble pavement scarcely dry yet from scrubbing out the blood of murdered student martyrs of a few days before.

The excited dancing crowds burned the furniture from the fashionable Vedado home of Eusebio Mujol, head of the great Cuban Labor Federation, who had become one of Cuba's top multi-millionaires, owner of big plantations, owner with gangsters and corrupt officials of gambling casinos, cabarets, hotels, newspapers and at least one radio station. He, too, escaped to the United States, to Washington, where he promptly became an adviser on Cuban affairs to that great liberty-loving organization known as the AFL-CIO, which at once began issuing lying blasts against the Cuban revolution — as it had previously done *in favor* of the Batista dictatorship. It had been allied with the Batista confederation, never once had protested when the soldiery took over the labor offices in behalf of this same Mujol, never once protesting when drum-head emergency courts railroaded hundreds of striking electrical workers to Principe Castle.

Already rebel leaders "Che" Guevara and big blond Camilio Cienfuegos were racing their forces to take over the Havana barracks and public buildings. Also to Havana came racing

Fauré Chamont, with the Student Federation rebels of the Escambray Front in hills close to Havana, who had never wholly accepted Fidel's leadership. They seized the National Palace, the University and the chief army arsenal. Here was a portent of dangerous division, of serious trouble.

5

Santiago de Cuba. January 2.

Fidel Castro, following his secret deal with Cantillo and subordinates, led his forces into the capital of Oriente Province without bloodshed — directly to historic Moncada fortress, scene of the early July 26 assault. There he promised a great crowd that he would convert the barracks into a modern school center.

Practically every man, woman and child of the 165,000 inhabitants of this hot eastern city swarmed on into the plaza between the palace and the cathedral.

There at 1:30 p.m., flanked by Archbishop Monsignor Enrique Pérez Serrantes, Castro told of the exploits and hopes of the revolution and installed Judge Manuel Urrutia Lléo (who had tried to save the lives of prisoners at the time of the Moncada assault) as provisional president. Urrutia would serve for his day and hour — until the revolution became too radical for him — whereupon Fidel, master of the new Cuba, would send him home again in silence.

But for now, Urrutia was packed off to take over the National Palace. He had to pace the Havana airport for many hours until Chamont and his men were finally pried loose from the Palace — with promises. (Chamont was given $100,000 and was sent off to Red China; became ambassador in Moscow.)

Urrutia entered a city in the throes of a general strike — that had been called hastily by Fidel from Santiago — to try to prevent a last minute seizure of power by the Smith-Cantillo military junta, still hoping to save the Batista system. The streets were mountains of stinking garbage, fermenting in the hot sun, alongside the piles of refuse from gambling dens, streets strewn with the broken glass from smashed windows of "Batista" enterprises.

There were no police now, only a few patrolling July 26 militiamen, yet, strangely enough, overnight Havana had become a more orderly city than at any time during the long years of the dictator's administration.

Castro set out on his week-long triumphal tour of the island for his final climax of victory — his entry into Havana.

Havana. January 9.

Fidel was due! All Havana swarmed into the streets — a million people — to greet the hero. My car was corralled and stalled, inundated by people, people, people, on the great Malecón Esplanade, close to the Castillo de San Salvador de la Punta.

The Malecón is one of the splendid sea avenues of the world, comparable to the Copacabana of Rio, the Malecón of Montevideo. It represents one of the more pleasant efforts of the engineers of the first U.S. military occupation. It has since been extended well beyond Miraflores and Marianao.

There I waited on the ramparts of the sea-wall, just out of reach of the tongues of white ocean-spray. Across the harbor rose the high-flung solid walls and deep-cut parapets of ancient Morro Castle and the yellow Cabaña Annex; near them towered the vulgar, clumsy white Christ put up at the behest of Batista's second wife; the white dome of the National Observatory; the tall lighthouse, its black ball and yellow-blue striped flag announcing clear weather, but not really telling of the splendor of this golden shimmering day. Nearer at hand on the Malecón was the heroic equestrian statue of Liberator Máximo Gómez and, back of the National Palace, the enormous garden plaza, blazing with flowers, at this moment was jammed with a half-million cheering people. The flat roofs all about were black with people. They clung to lamp posts. They straddled the branches of trees.

At this point on the Malecón, the gracious tree-shaded Prado comes in. It was likewise black with people unable to crush into the Esplanade along the sea. Beyond them rose the Sevilla Biltmore Hotel and the white dome of the Legislative Palace, a dull imitation of the Washington capitol, put up a long time ago with incredible graft by that earlier Washington pet, Dictator Gerardo Machado, paid candidate of the Cuban Electric Company.

The whole Malecón is solid with people as far as the eye can reach, far out in the Vedado and Marianao. They carry placards, wave red-black M-26 banners or the Cuban lone-star flag. Arms are full of flowers, and now and then there is cheering, frequently the singing of the national anthem or the Song of the Revolution. The multicolored throng merges into distant blackness beyond the U.S. Embassy, the soaring many-hued apartment houses, the lofty Habana Riviera. They are gray masses under the arcades, but vivid in the open sun and on the seawall — until they fade into a sea of sun-haze almost as blue as the placid Caribbean itself.

It is the people's day. Few times in history has a hero ever received a greater mass demonstration. All Havana is here, blind with emotion.

The morning hours wheel by. The crowd waits patiently. Now and then police-cars and motorcycles, commandeered by the new people's militia in olive-green, try to keep a lane open down the center of the Malecón, and the people, hoping that this heralds the approach of the hero, stir; they stand on tiptoe or seek better vantage points. Now and then groups, sometimes school-children march hither and yon through the briefly opened passage-way. Gradually, as the hours float by, the flowers in the arms of the spectators wilt.

News filters through that Fidel has been detained beyond Guanabacoa, that he is talking to the people there, that he is going to have lunch there. People shift on their tired feet, wait patiently, on and on. Except for a few who have had the foresight to bring sandwiches, nobody here will eat. Every bar and restaurant in the city is sealed up tight. Not even street-venders. This is too great a day to bother making a few pennies. For what? Is not this the day of the millennium — heaven on earth? Tomorrow everybody will eat. Tomorrow the woes of the world will be wiped out. Today they swallow only the manna of new hope that sifts down softly on the golden wings of this sun-drenched day.

But what does Castro really plan to do? What does the revolution really mean?

6

Castro has played his cards close to his chest, not disclosing his intimate plans. He has been holed up in the Sierra Maestra, reading Montesquieu between ambushes, now and then trying out his telescopic rifle. Mostly he has remained silent behind his big new beard. He has repudiated all coalitions of the exiles, recognizing only the July 26 Movement. Its pronouncements have been vaguely "democratic" — generalized statements about schools, justice and land reform — typical demogogic hogwash. Standard. The sort of double-talk one gets from Washington but hardly the voice of authentic revolution. Castro did not talk. But today he will talk — and keep on talking, talking, talking — and acting.

There was, of course, Fidel's address to the military court at his Moncada Barracks trial in 1953, one of the great utterances of our age. In it, he told of the long-suffering history of the island, the heartless exploitation of the people, particularly by foreign corporations, the land monopoly that had to be broken, the independence and new freedom that had to be won. But that speech was scarcely available until well after the revolution.

Now, this New Year's day, only Castro, and perhaps not even he, knows what the future may hold. He is in command of all Cuba now.

There were plenty of signs that he had courage, that he was indomitable, that he would never be swerved. There was also evidence that behind the revolutionary lines he had put into effect a provisional land decree, had given land to peasants, had even shot several landowners, that this battle-time decree of the Sierra would be polished up and issued soon as the law of the whole land.

But he himself was born into a rich land-holding family, still owning broad acres. Would he strip his own family? And would he dare touch the great U.S. sugar plantations and their idle lands, that sometimes stretched from sea to sea, and restore ownership to the Cuban people? If he did not, the revolution would be a farce. It would wither away, it would fall into the dust of a bitter memory.

If he did dare, then the might of dollar diplomacy and economic aggression (and, as it turned out, military force also) would be reaching for his throat. There is never any easy road for a popular revolution. The road that lay ahead of Cuba and these cheering multitudes would be rocky.

7

A roll of human thunder rose like a mounting wave. At last
Fidel was entering the city. From far off the deep-throated rum-
ble came, like a roaring mating animal of the forest. It reached
the Malecón, down where it starts near the shipping piers:
Grace, United Fruit, Ward — scarcely a Cuban name in the lot.
The wave came rushing on toward where we stood, a great rising wall of sound. Soon the tongues of ocean spray and the lick-
ing tongues of mass emotion leapt at us, engulfed us in choking
delirium.

Jeeps bang past, more beards now, olive-green uniforms not
so clean now, soiled with the sweat and dirt of recent battles.
Then armored tanks, snorting, grinding, rattling.

"Fidel! Fidel! Fidel!"

Big beard and all, he comes. He is smiling, waving his hand
now and then, one arm about his small son, this day also in olive-
green with an M-26 red-black band. Fidel comes not on the traditional white horse, but in the open turret of a tank, herding a
whole fleet of tanks that only yesterday were supplied by the United States to Batista's brutal army; little tanks, big tanks, monster
tanks, with mighty caterpillar treads from which the macadam of
Havana would be long in recovering. Even disabled tanks on
trucks, one so big it is carried by two trucks. But there are also
several home-made tanks, born of desperate ingenuity, strange
Wizard of Oz contraptions, dented with many bullets. And out
of the turrets, all of them, wave the beards of veterans, the beards
of the revolution. Boys, some no more than thirteen, unable to
grow beards, have let their hair grow long so that they look more
like girls. The veterans, the fighters, the heroes spout out of every
turret, they are sprawled on every inch of the outside of the
tanks, miraculously pasted there like cats. They are crammed
into jeeps and cars and trucks.

And there really are girls — in olive-green shirts and black
skirts, lying on the tank plates, riding the jeeps, their clothes
soiled and torn, streaked with the sweat and blood of battle.
They grip their rifles or submachine guns with a curious fierce-
ness, still at the ready, as if not quite sure that the battle is really
over, that the victory has been really won. They are fired with the
ideals of a free Cuba. Some are the sweethearts or wives of men

who have been tortured by the Batista soldiery, or have themselves been tortured. They have fought in the Sierra Maestra, in
Bayamo, in Oriente, in Santa Clara.

This is really a new Cuba! This — for better or worse — is a
long way from the traditional life of the soft, seductive shel-
tered señoritas of the middle class.

The veterans roll on! They roll on in a storm of red flowers.
But this is no spit and polish parade beloved by generals. This is
war, suddenly turned into victory and peace. This is the revolution. This is the revolution on the march — the last armed march
until the repelling of the criminally lawless C.I.A. invasion at
the Bay of Pigs in April 1961.

There is something beautiful, pathetic, in the unbelieving eyes
of some of these country boys, turned into men and veterans
overnight, as they gaze with amazement at the delirious crowds,
with amazement and vast pride at the great golden towers of this
splendid capital, their capital now, which most of them have never even seen before.

Camp Colombia. January 9.

Fidel Castro, after a brief look-in on President Urrutia at the
Palace, swept on to Camp Colombia, the military center, where
he had called all the people for a rendezvous of victory.

Camp Colombia was first established by the U.S. military
forces after the Spanish-American War, and from that vantage
point, General Leonard Wood dictated the new Cuban constitution and the Platt Amendment, converting Cuba into an imperialist dependency, not a free nation as had been promised. He
would not allow an "i" or a "t" to be changed in the imposed document of Cuban "freedom," which kept all real controls in U.S.
hands, while a swarm of North American carpetbaggers — the
inevitable villains of every war — bought up ruined sugar estates
and other properties for a few cents on the dollar.

Again in subsequent armed invasions, the Marines and soldiery
of the North occupied Camp Colombia — 1906, 1909, 1912,
1917, 1919. Whenever the U.S. soldiery were not there, it was
the seat of Cuban army power, controlling the destinies of the
country — for sixty years of pretended democracy and independence. Now it belonged to Fidel Castro and his rebel militia.
For what purpose?

At Camp Colombia there had occurred a number of early fights for control of the rich island. There Batista staged his "shower bath" revolution and his subsequent coups. But the generals were gone now. They had fled in fright— braid and medals and swishing tails — from the sinking ship of dictatorship. No, not all. A few hide-outers would be captured and die before the firing squads of the revolution.

No, not all. The U.S. military missionaries, who had lost the battle along with the Batista forces, settled back in their comfortable apartments, waiting hopefully for the Castro betrayal of the people, waiting for their new day of power with Castro, waiting for the usual quick betrayal by Latin American revolutionary leaders. (As has happened with Betancourt in Venezuela, with Figueres in Costa Rica, with Haya de la Torre in Peru — lately, with Frondizi in Argentina and Arosemena in Ecuador.)

But this very day they are in for a bad shock. For when Castro addresses the great multitude which, after waiting for him all day has trudged out, an ever growing river of humanity, miles and miles to the military camp, he tells them not merely of the trials of the revolution, but asserts that this is Cuba's first real *Independence* — political and economic. This is the definite end of imperialism, of colonialism, of alien ownership of Cuba. And he speaks precisely of military matters: Batista's beaten army will be completely disbanded — from soldiers to generals. And the U.S. military mission?

"Nothing it taught the Cuban Army had any value, it merely assured the triumph of the Revolution." In a few days the U.S. generals, colonels and majors will get their walking papers and swarm over to Haiti, to bolster up another shaky dictatorship — having learned nothing whatever.

And Castro adds, "The Revolution has not produced one general, nor will it . . . Within a few days we shall use our military planes to rain down shoes, clothing, food, toys and pledges of land reform on the poor peasants of Oriente who stood by the Revolutionary forces in the darkest days so faithfully and courageously. Our planes will be symbols of love, not of terror."

He promises to convert the barracks on the land into schools. (And has done so.) He promises to convert Camp Colombia into a great school center for ten thousand children. "From this day on, it will be renamed Camp Liberty."

(This work was about half-completed when it was bombed by

the planes on the eve of the Bay of Pigs invasion. Terror again — this time against the school-children of Cuba in the name of "freedom and democracy" — by a supposedly superior, civilized land.)

At this moment in his "Camp Liberty" speech, doves fluttered around his shoulder, and one lit on his shoulder. Doves of Peace!

Dramatic showmanship, but not new in the history of the world. Did he have corn in his ears like Mahomet? It was a trick used also by Dictator López de Santanna of Mexico long ago, and by Sam Houston when he went to Texas — except those two gentlemen enticed *eagles* to their shoulders.

8

And so the revolution came to Cuba. It is a culmination of the rise of new forces, of new violences in the name of liberty; first in Mexico; then it has roared on in one form or another, mostly without success, bringing fresh betrayals, into most of the countries of long-enslaved Latin America. The story is written all over the continent with a powerful moving finger: Sandino in Nicaragua (assassinated); Allessandri, the Lion of Tarapacá, in Chile; Getulio Vargas of Brazil (a suicide); Gaitán of Colombia (assassinated); Germán Busch (a suicide); Villaroel (hung to a plaza lamp post) and Paz Estenssoro in Bolivia; Perón in Argentina; Arévalo and Arbenz in Guatemala; Haya de la Torre in Peru; Betancourt in Venezuela. In one form and another such leaders (though most soon betrayed their trust), and the masses behind them, have symbolized the aspirations of the long-suffering exploited people of Latin America. They have been the rolling thunder of freedom long denied, a freedom still denied in nearly all Central and South America.

9

Latin America is one of the great geographical, zoographical cultural areas of the globe, occupying a territory three times the size of the United States. By the end of the century it will have 600,000,000 people. It is a majestic, vital new force in the world.

The rise of that civilization, the liberation of its people cannot be halted, not for long, by dollars or bayonets, by do-good aid or by force, by puppet dictators or outside propaganda. For the industrial revolution, at long last, pounds on the door; on its heels comes the atomic revolution — the new age of electronics.

People thirst for freedom, economic justice, for national independence — things never really known or had. It is part of the revolutionary Zeitgeist of today's world. The giant is inevitably awakening. Such is the message of history. Before long these people will shape their own destinies, not as satellites, not in accordance with the sterile goals of the Cold War or the wishes of Washington or Moscow but in accordance with the necessities of their own history and culture, their own hopes and passion. They will carve out their own deep channels.

Liberation will assume myriad forms. All we can be sure of is, whether we like it or not, the continent south of us is on its way now to a new destiny.

2 ◯ THE MOVING FINGER OF HISTORY

1

Long before Madame Marie Curie, sheepmen in Patagonia used to kick aside chunks of black pitchblende. Andean Argentina is rich in uranium, stuff of modern war and death, still not greatly mined.

Higher up in the mountains, the llamas munched grass between outcroppings of shiny coal — vast deposits never utilized until after World War II, when Argentina, Chile and Brazil installed steel mills.

In 1674 a muleteer, crossing the Andean crags to Salta, picked up a curious lustrous stone — stibnite, source of antimony, and it sat for years on the town-clerk's desk as a paperweight. Several hundred years went by before it began to be mined profitably.

Early last century, a Scotchman in the northern Chilean desert noticed vines growing exuberantly from a heap of excavated whitish earth, and the nitrate industry was born — to bring so much wealth to a few Chileans and the Guggenheims, so much grief for the country and its people, so much war to the world. The first vessel to go through the newly built Panama Canal was loaded with Chilean nitrate for the battlefields of Europe.

Not until Chile's floating steel-mill at Talcahuano became a reality, did the marble of icy Skyring Gulf in the Straits of Magellan become important, not till then did electric shovels scoop out the rich iron deposits near northern Coquimbo.

The aluminum industry is fairly new in the world; only recently were the super-rich bauxite deposits in British Guiana exploited, and already the political and social destinies of that long-neglected colony have been altered by an awakening of the people, the rise to power of the new People's Party, led by Cheddi Jagan, demanding full independence.

Paraguay has enormous iron deposits, but no steel mill. It could become the core of a great South American industrial complex. Instead, it is ruled by a dictator, Alfredo Stroessner, whose cruelties have driven 300,000 Paraguayans into exile. The majority of the people are worse off than in the day of early Jesuit concentration camps, where Indians were taught to be Christians — and slaves.

Only a small share of Latin American resources have ever been utilized. That little amounts to hundreds of billions of dollars annually, but it has never properly benefited the people. In Mexico, ragged beggars still sit on top of the rich Guanajuato silver mines, which have poured forth fantastic wealth for four centuries: wealth to create millionaire hidalgos, but not homes; wealth to build magnificent churches, but not schools; wealth to sheathe banquet chambers, but not to feed the hungry. For centuries it provided its Royal Fifth for the pomp and luxury of the Spanish kings — such rulers as Mad Juana and the obese gourmand, Charles the Fat. It filled the coffers of the Vatican. But the beggars are still there, hands outstretched in the Guanajuato sunshine.

Incredibly rich in resources, the southern world is a long-plundered continent. Though so undeveloped, for four centuries the quick surface wealth was drained off by Spain and Portugal — imperialist lands steeped in medieval darkness, to this day ruled by cruel dictatorships.

The first gold from the Americas — the gold of temple ornaments and priceless art objects melted down by the Conquistadores of Hernán Cortés — still encrusts the ornate ceiling of Santa María Maggiore in Rome — a process of plundering the New World that was not reversed until the hoarding in Fort Knox. But Latin America got none of it back.

For centuries European descendants of Hernán Cortés, without ever seeing America, reaped vast profits from Mexican estates improperly given to the Conquistador by the Spanish Crown. Not until late in the Mexican revolution were the Pignatelli — that noble Italian family of Marqueses — obliged to hurry to the New World to try to recover their confiscated properties. And failed. Their only achievement was to discover the lost bones, so they claimed, of their famous ancestor. His name is still anathema to Mexicans.

2

If mining provided bonanzas, land monopoly *was and is* the chief citadel of wealth and power. For not even after Independence (1810-1823) did the New World win immunity from looting — from within and without. Independence freed the slaves, gave Indians and mestizos equal citizenship rights, eliminated the Peninsulars (Europeans) from government and army posts (though not from the Church), established "democratic" constitutions modeled on that of the United States. But the movement soon became a Counter-Revolution. The Creoles (Europeans born in the New World), aided by Church and Army, seized power and preserved largely intact the whole structure of feudal colonial society. Thus there was no economic basis for the new representative system: votes became bayonets, bayonets became votes — still true for the most part. The New World was reconquered — by its own brutal armies.

Independence also brought — increasingly so — what Latin American historians call "The Second Conquest" or "The Second Colonialism."

"The Second Colonialism" has been the seizure of territory and the economic and political incursions by foreign powers, which soon set up a capitalist alliance with the feudal reaction, an alliance that over the century has grown more powerful and deadly. It was never more powerful than today — 1962. Today the enormous resources of U.S. corporations and of the U.S. government are directed implacably in the false name of "freedom and progress" — to strengthening all reactionary forces. Our policy, while talking of "reforms" and "planning", seeks above all else to maintain the status quo. Mostly it is a stagnating, unprogressive, self-defeating policy. As one Latin American has put it, the Alliance for Progress is "much Alliance but little Progress."

The looting went on. The new republics were continuously stripped — even as today — by their own corrupt generals, churchmen and hacendados, the principal ruling groups, and by outside speculators and corporations. Wealthy landlords hoarded their plunder or shipped it overseas. Great chests of gold and silver continued to go to Rome, and the Vatican still gets a larger revenue and income — also fabulous bequests and inheritances — from down there than it derives from the prosperous United States.

In each country the Church waxed fat. In some — as in Mexico before the Juárez Reform — it came to own more than half of all cultivated land; in many, as in present day Ecuador, it is the largest single landholder.

The generals, too, became big landholders. And so the old Creole families held on to their patrimonies and expanded their acreage.

In Mexico as late as 1923, before land-distribution got under way, large haciendas occupied 80 to 99 percent of some states. Many big plantations there still flout the laws, particularly in the south; and generals and politicians grab land in violation of the statutes. Once more, in the guise of land reform, the present López Mateos administration has been ousting peasants from their *ejidos* or communal lands and incorporating the areas into larger plantations — all in the name of "the Revolution." Some ejected peasants have been given larger farms elsewhere — but worthless arid acres, with the promises of irrigation and improvements, promises not fulfilled.

Vast estates in Chile, reaching from the top of the Andes to the edge of the sea, are still owned by the direct descendants of the Conquistadores who received them free as Crown grants. There, too, under the guise of "an agrarian reform law," thousands of peasants are being driven onto the highways from lands they have tilled for generations, and the hectares are grabbed up by politicians and hacendados and U.S. corporations.

The process of spoilation is even worse in Peru. All over the country the Army and plantation guards and hired APRA *búfalos*, or strong-arm gangs, have been moving in on the age-old Indian communities, driving the peasants off in bloodshed, burning their homes, their villages, their crops — seizing the lands in behalf of large owners *(gamonales)* and foreign corporations — such as Cerro de Pasco, the Peruvian Corporation, Grace and Company, the Gildermeisters.

At the same time, the U.S. taxpayer recently shelled out $23,-000,000, and will shell out much more, for "agrarian reform" — not reform at all, but a dubious "resettlement" to move some thousands of highland families off their ancestral lands down into the hot jungles to become peons on the new large sugar estates of favorites of the Prado regime — people doomed, physically unable to adapt to the lowlands, dumped there without proper health, protection or schooling.

It is the cruel process of Porfirio Díaz in shipping peons to the Yucatán henequen estates at $65.00 a head. Peruvian peasants in a few years have lost more land by far than has been doled out to them in those forlorn frontier jungles; while an aftermath has been the take-over by the military junta of Pérez Godoy, when the July 1962 elections fraudulently tried to impose Haya de la Torre, head of APRA, as president.

Colombia is worse. More land is being stolen than the proposed agrarian reform legislation (expected to cost the U.S. taxpayer at least sixty millions) will provide. That pseudo-reform will hand over the worst land, arid land, jungle land, undeveloped land — for which the hacendados never dreamed of getting good money.

In Venezuela President Kennedy, visiting Caracas in December 1961, went through the staged ceremony of delivering a title for nineteen acres to a peasant. Just who was he fooling? Kennedy flew in for twenty minutes to a "show-place," but mostly the nineteen-acre plots are in the highlands, near-worthless lands, mostly without water, unable to sustain a farmer; or else are remote in jungles, without adequate transportation, schools or medical care.

Locally the "reform" is known as the "Siberian land rush" — but shaky Rómulo Betancourt, who, like the late Frondizi in Argentina, has become a Washington yes-man and a prisoner of the Church and Army, has to be held up as a symbol of "the democratic way." He is scheduled to get $600,000,000 in the next year or so — the biggest slice of the Alliance cheese. Could oil have anything to do with it?

All over Latin America, land-monopoly of more recent vintage has been built up from outside, adding the additional curse of absentee ownership. Taking advantage of U.S. military occupations, disturbed conditions, periodic depressions, dictator concessions, many of these vast holdings have been acquired for a song by U.S. adventurers and corporations.

Mr. Randolph Hearst, among other Americans, once became the owner of 7,500,000 acres in Chihuahua, Mexico — for a bag of peanuts. But the revolution confiscated them for the benefit of everybody concerned. Naturally Mr. Hearst exercised his noble right of "freedom of the press" to scream "Communist" and to publish forged documents.

The United Fruit Company got hold of Cuban lands, originally snapped up by U.S. carpetbaggers during periods of military occupation — for two bags of peanuts. These holdings, too, have been lost.

In Guatemala, President Jacobo Arbenz enforced a new agrarian law, dealing chiefly with idle lands, but attempting to reduce over-large unused holdings. Much of the banana land, held for speculation, had been secured previously for little or *nothing* from an obstinate Congress ringed by the bayonets of previous dictators. When one grant also gave the United Fruit Company absolute monopoly over Guatemalan ports, several oppositionist newspaper editors had to be murdered.

But Arbenz did not get far in his plans of liberation. Till 1954 dollar diplomacy, utilizing the then new instrument of international intrigue and counter-revolution, the Central Intelligence Agency (C.I.A.), raised a false smoke-screen of anti-communism, staged an invasion, bombed cities (incidentally, a large British steamer was sunk), and tossed the president out. Dictatorship was reimposed — the evil back-tracking regime of pipsqueak Carlos Castillo Armas (assassinated) and Manuel Ydígoras, a regime which, long after the murder and firing-squads of the immediate take-over, is still slaughtering protesting Guatemalans in the public streets and in the hills and mountains. Merely two years ago the Somozas and Ydígoras were saved for a day and an hour by rushing U.S. battleships to the coasts. The anger of the people simmers and boils, is ready to overflow again.

A similar bloody, but unsuccessful, armed invasion of Cuba, also promoted, trained, supplied, paid-for by the C.I.A. and the Pentagon, was launched against the Castro government in April 1961 — an even more flagrant and bloody violation of Inter-American treaties, the U.N. charter and international law.

In the face of discontent, hatred and inevitable revolution, large U.S. land-holding is still expanding in many parts of Latin America: the Nelson Rockefeller companies in Venezuela, Brazil, Ecuador and elsewhere; King Ranches in Cuba (lost now), Argentina, etc.; meat-packers buying *estancias* in Argentina, Uruguay and Paraguay; United Fruit in Honduras, Ecuador, and Panama; Grace and Company, Cerro de Pasco and others in Peru. Copper and nitrate companies in Chile have taken over large additional tracts; vast acreages have been acquired in Mato Grosso deep in Brazil's interior; cotton lands, by the cattle, cotton and other concerns; 40,000,000 acres in Paraguay's Chaco to U.S. oil companies; vast oil acreages in Bolivia; rich coffee lands in Oriente, Paraguay.

These alien enterprises, though they bring in improved methods, are operated within the feudal set-up originally imposed by force by the Spanish Conquest. In some instances, especially around the Caribbean, the newer techniques have merely duplicated the inhumane features of much of California's large land-holding — the use of miserably remunerated, itinerant labor.

In Cuba, the great foreign sugar-plantations utilized a large work-force during the *zafra* or harvest, for a dollar or so a day; then the men and their families were kicked off during the "dead" season to beg or starve in the towns and cities, for there was little or no industry to take up the slack. At all times, at least half of Cuba's natural work force was unemployed — a situation bound to bring revolution — as it did.

3

Most large estates in Latin America are backward, lack equipment and scientific methods. They avoid the purchase of modern machinery, which, since it must be imported, is doubly expensive; so are replacement parts. Gasoline, electricity, skilled labor are expensive, whereas the cost of peon labor is infinitesimal, a few cents a day. Thus the hacendado makes few improvements, except in his own Casa Granda, or ranch house, which is often palatial. He builds few roads or schools. The peons are mostly without medical or dental care, although in recent years in a few countries, education and medical care of sorts must now be provided — e.g. Perón's *Ley de Peón* in Argentina. Except that there these provisions were no longer enforced by the subsequent "democratic" regimes, for the latifundistas and the generals are now back in the saddle, arrogant and relentless.

Except for foreign markets, the haciendas attempt to be self-sufficient. They tend to become little independent kingdoms within a kingdom. Often in the Andes, as in Ecuador and Peru, they have their own police, judges and prisons; they control both local and federal officials, police, army officers, mayors, judges, inspectors — and often the president himself, always a large landowner. The same in Cuba before the revolution. In Honduras, various presidents have been lawyers of the United Fruit Company, the gross annual income of which has exceeded the national revenues.

Hacienda workers are not really citizens but subjects of the hacendado. In Argentina, prior to the new electoral law enforced by Perón, they could rarely vote; the hacendado would ride into the polling booth with a list of their names and announce: "420 votes for Fulano de Tal."

Some day-week-month labor is hired, at wages rarely exceeding a dollar a day, more often a sixth of that, and share croppers and tenants are obliged to give part time to the hacienda, even provide equipment, tools and animals. As far as possible, a permanent labor force is maintained: by serfdom (the *yanacones* of Peru), by debt enslavement, or by granting crude prehistoric houses and a small plot of ground. This last system is, of course, more humane than, for instance, the seasonal labor system of the alien sugar plantations in Cuba, prior to the revolution.

And so the whole feudal structure operates *against* modernization. Only close to cities are some improvements made and slightly better wages paid.

This system has been viable — and for centuries — for with a degree of internal diversification, the hacienda is nearly self-sufficient. When things go wrong the peons can, in a pinch, feed themselves. When international prices drop, there is little need to buy outside commodities or gasoline or machine-parts. Wages can be cut or postponed.

Resistance to improvement or change by the land-holding class is natural. Since before the nineteenth century, the hacendados have comprised a privileged ruling group, far above the poor and ignorant. Their lives are pleasantly varied: part of the year riding over their great estates, playing cowboy, staging barbecues and fine balls, hunting and fishing; at other times, living an elegant life, often at the cost of the government as diplomatic, consular or special representatives, in Paris, Madrid, Rome, more lately in New York and Washington. They are gracious, well-educated patrons of the arts, often philanthropists — as the Larco Herreras in Peru — and they help to set literary and aesthetic tastes, though today they have little sympathy with the more virile modern painters and writers. The chasm between old and new is widening.

Even were the hacendados imbued with the psychology or the desire to adapt to the new modern world, they are too hamstrung by economic realities to be able to lift themselves or their countries out of the twilight of colonialism.

They are blinded, too, by generations of class-rule. Ex-President Enrique Camilo Ponce of Ecuador, a clerical reactionary and wealthy landowner, a very clever stuffed shirt, told me he could see no need for agrarian reform, no need for any change in the serf system. Oh yes, a little more pay since the peasants felt the lack of modern gadgets; perhaps a bit more education, but not much, they had no need for it. They should not be spoiled — or allowed to organize. His attitude is almost the same as that of certain British governors three centuries ago in the American colonies, who saw nothing wrong with the indenture system (seven-year serfdom) and believed education was dangerous. It merely made people uppish. (This is also the attitude of the Church in Latin America. Education should be wholly under its control — for the selected few.)

Despite all the injustices, the feudal land system did work for centuries. It provided a balanced social organization. After "independence" it grew less stable and is now cracking under many pressures.

Not for long now can it survive the impact of modern industry, of urbanization, the rise of an independent industrialist class, the rise of labor and peasant movements. Certainly it cannot meet the food needs of the unprecedented population growth now occurring or the rise of the great cities: Mexico City, 4,000,-000; Sao Paulo, 4,000,000; Buenos Aires 7,000,000. Most capitals now have over a million people and are growing fast. The cities have to be fed — even if only crumbs. Soon 600,000,000 people, with a high percentage of young people, will find no room on the land. Naturally, they are going to make room — and not by piddling "reform" which will merely aggravate the situation.

For the typical old-style plantation is as outmoded as the slave plantation in the South of the United States — so resistant to inevitable economic change it brought on one of the world's worst civil wars; in Latin America, the same violent struggle is almost inevitable. Here, too, the land-systems of the southern continent are approaching a dead end. Traditional land-use is doomed. The dilemma, of course, is formidable, almost insurmountable. The old is too old and the new is not quite strong enough yet to impose itself.

4

The petty types of land-reform — or rather resettlement — envisaged by the Alliance for Progress, may prove more dangerous than helpful. Even these innocuous improvements (?) are bitterly opposed by the very people to whom the money is being given. This so-called program mostly permits big owners to get paid for their worthless land — a windfall for the wrong people and a cruel chantage for those supposedly helped. In any case, a limited number of small proprietors, unable, with what they are given, either to be self-sufficient or to compete with the commercial crops of the large haciendas, are at the mercy of unscrupulous middlemen. This sort of piddling half-way reform runs counter to the urbanization and all new industrial trends. As a result, in countries with rich lands, food has to be imported for the growing cities.

Indeed, the Alliance for Progress solution is *less modern, more reactionary, than the dying but stubborn hacienda system.* Our program is largely based on the concept of the self-sufficient family farmer, which, though once a fine if limited way of life, is no longer feasible in an industrialized society and to the extent that it still exists, in the United States and Latin America, provides no decent existence.

Ironically, too, the money is to be handed over to the very elements, the land-holding politicians, who have no interest in, but hate, land-reform, and who will not countenance basic solutions. They will not promote except with lip service even minor land reforms. We are setting the wolves to guard the sheep. Moreover, our "food for peace," which hurts native agriculture, goes mostly to speculators, haciendas and U.S. corporations, for profiteering.

Some time ago, Pedro F. Marotta wrote that Argentina's limited prosperity was due more to its vastness than to intelligent land-use, that its failure to progress was due to land monopoly, estates with millions of acres, sometimes only twenty or thirty thousand of them cultivated.

Luis F. Heysen pointed out, well before World War II, that the large, backward landholder, utilizing only a fraction of his vast acreage, was "a survival from medieval times through 120 years of the Republic and is a perennial menace for the economic future of the country."

Though the southern country has almost as much potential land for farming or pasturage as the United States, as early as 1868, the great Domingo Faustino Sarmiento wrote that already the Republic was doomed, for the immigrant could not find "a palm's hand of territory."

Argentine land enclosures continued. In 1879 by means of the Campaign of the Desert, which slaughtered thousands of pacific Indians and peasants and burned their homes, 40,000,000 hectares, 100,000,000 acres, of state lands and smaller free holdings were seized. These owners remained on the margin of progress; they did not promote development, yet by the activities of commercial-minded Buenos Aires, the building of railroads and other social improvements, these new proprietors were "converted into millionaires without their expending the slightest effort . . . converted . . . into a real oligarchy."

In Buenos Aires Province alone, in spite of much new small truck-farming, 70 percent of the land is still held in big plantations and ranches. And "the Argentina Pampa, so fertile, is a beautiful Venus de Milo without arms . . . . Large landholding is what chokes it." Two hundred thousand proprietors — some owning more than a million acres — control a fifth of Argentina's *entire* area.

Land monopoly has sent seven million people, a third of the nation's population, into greater Buenos Aires; and the government has been unable to provide them with water, housing, toilets, sanitation, electric light, street-paving, transportation, schools or hospitals. At the beginning of this century, the once beautiful city had abolished all slums, was ahead of the world in urban planning; now, in this year 1963, its ditches run with human excrement and sewage; the whole city stinks to high heaven! Now that the military, prodded on by the U.S. mission, have taken over once more, the down-spiral will be worse.

Certainly not until Juan Perón's *Ley de Peón*, were halfway decent wages and living conditions, paid vacations, proper food, schooling, or medical care instituted for the peasants. For the first time in history they were allowed to vote and to organize — a new era for the countryside.

Yet not enough. For little land was expropriated; the basic power was not altered. So the gains were soon lost by the bloody, "democratic," U.S.-backed dictatorship of General Pedro Aramburu, then of the puppet Arturo Frondizi — tied hand and foot to the military, the landholders, the Church and the U.S.A.

Since World War II, Argentine land seizures by wealthy owners have continued. The barbed wire has reached far up among the sliding stones of the Andes, far down into the peat bogs of Tierra del Fuego, far north into the Chaco, far northeast into the rich Mesopotamia. The abuses are worse than ever — as a visit, particularly to Jujuy, Salta, Misiones, Tucumán, will quickly reveal.

All this monopoly has come about in Argentina, not as a result of the gradual demise of laissez-faire and free enterprise and the rise of monopoly capitalism as in the United States; it existed before the rise of industrial concentration; it existed before the Republic was founded. It strangles further national development. Its answer is military rule, and, with the newest concessions to U.S. capital, once proud Argentina has been converted in a few short years into a sort of Banana Republic.

5

Since Pope Alexander's famous bull *Inter Coelera* of May 4,

1493, which gave the Catholic monarchs of Spain and Portugal dominion over all New World conquests and territories, the Church, except for short interludes, has remained an integral part of government rule. In Mexico, Argentina, Peru, Ecuador, everywhere, the prelates have been part of the land-holding aristocracy; they have been landholders and, as such, have set their faces stonily against land-reform or modernization — as they still do.

The recitation of such facts does not constitute an attack against the Catholic *religion;* quite the contrary. But apart from its spiritual obligations, the Church is deeply involved in the things of Caesar; besides conducting Mass, celebrating confessions, officiating at baptisms, christenings, marriages, it is a massive business corporation, owning much land, in some places banks and businesses. It is an economic and political enterprise of powerful proportions, of which even the U.S. Steel corporation could be envious.

The Church to a considerable degree shaped the destinies of the colonies; later on, the early republics. For 240 years, the Inquisition — the Gestapo of colonial and imperialist rule — tortured prisoners by tearing out their tongues; confiscated properties, lashed or burned offenders in the public places. The institution was elevated into an organized police-terror instrument, Nazi style, for maintaining colonial rule, ecclesiastic feudalism and theft of land. Indians were converted at the point of the sword, or shipped off to the living death of the mines, or slaughtered.

Yet in some respects, the Catholic Church in Latin America was kinder, often more generous, than were the New England Puritans, who also did a good deal of branding, ear-cropping and eye-gouging and proved their Christianity by stealing the native hunting grounds and killing off the aborigines. Hence in Latin America the majority of the people are still Indians and mestizos.

The Church grew fabulously wealthy. The prelates earned as much or more than even the high-paid U.S. aid experts now also "helping" the people. Except for the lower clergy, the hierarchy fought the Independence movements bitterly. Not until victory was at hand did the Pope begin lauding the great chiefs previously excommunicated: Sucre became "Illustrious," and it was "Thank God for the glorious Bolívar." And the archbishops helped see that power was put safely into the hands of the devout, wealthy, land-holding Creoles. In many instances they themselves took over the reins of government directly; if not, they promptly staged a Te Deum for each new caudillo.

They remain the shadow behind the heads of state, have been close at the elbow of Frondizi, of Prado, of Ponce, of Ydígoras, of Stroessner, of the latest gun-boat government of the Dominican Republic (a priest is a member of the Junta). An American embassy can stop the passage of a labor law, as in Bolivia in 1942 (the result, the Peñaranda government toppled, and the gates of revolution were really opened), but the Church can get more direct results. A government fell in Peru in 1934 when it was excommunicated for passing a divorce law. The hierarchy was able to round up a military general in Argentina to toss out Perón when the latter broke violently with the Church (or vice versa?). It has made and unmade government after government in Ecuador. In some countries civil suits cannot be brought against any member of the clergy, only in ecclesiastical courts.

Read the novels of Ecuadorean Jorge Icaza, or the *Gold Serpent* by Peruvian Ciro Alegría, or *Santa* by Federico Gambóa, or the fine novels by Carlos Fuentes, Mexico's contemporary writer, or almost any Latin American novel, to get the intimate picture of how the local priests exploit and cheat but "comfort" the poorer villagers and the peasants.

Go to lofty, lovely, poverty-stricken Quito atop the Andes, but don't expect to get a night's rest. Ecuador is officially dedicated as "The Republic of the Heart of Jesus," and Church bells begin booming and pounding at 4 a.m.; they keep it up all day and late into the night. Two or three times each week great throngs of the pious sing hymns and carols in the central plaza long before daylight. But their Jesus is not the Prince of Peace any more than ours is. Fascistic pro-church groups make periodic raids on villages to attack peasant protestors.

During the colonial period, the Church had all education in its hands; even now in some countries there are more church schools than public schools, as in Peru and Paraguay. Credit must be given for the Church's early scholarship; it founded great universities a century before Harvard. But they never educated the people (after four centuries illiteracy is as high in most countries as in Central Africa). They taught the workers to build clean, beautiful temples, some of which are architectural gems for all the centuries, but not how to build comfortable, clean homes or to know the elementary rules of personal hygiene. Three centuries of colonial rule, a century and a half of life under the republics, and still the feudal Church rulers have not managed to teach the mass of the people to read or write — without which no true votes can be cast, no new industry can be built. In most of the continent the illiteracy rate ranges from 60 to 90 percent. Even in Argentina, education has been going backward not forward — its people are tobogganing down to the banana level. Compare this with Castro's Cuba. With limited resources, but universal enthusiasm, illiteracy was wiped out, not in four hundred years, but in exactly *one year,* and except for a few thousand aged and sick, everybody was taught to read and write.

The Holy Alliance for Progress (AFP) believes that it can appreciably reduce illiteracy in about ten years by its program of "gradualism." Finally after a year of grave deliberations, it has tentatively proposed to grant $80,000,000 to $150,000,000 for education in nineteen countries, or at least $4,210,000 per country. Since there are approximately 150,000,000 illiterates in Latin America, this will mean $1.00 a head — not enough to get anybody through "A.B.C." New York, with a population of seven million or so, spends nearly a billion a year, and the sum is inadequate, and some of its school buildings are ancient rat-holes. Just who is kidding whom? Illiterates are accumulating faster in Latin America than the AFP can unmake them — even were the effort sincere.

The large sums of U.S. taxpayers' money, now being handed over to Catholic agencies and schools in Latin America, is not to help the people, but on the contrary, to maintain the Church as a ruling power, to halt progress, to promote the empire of private investment. Recently, $3,000,000 of U.S. taxpayers' money was handed over to the Peruvian Catholic charity organization; millions to a Catholic radio station in Colombia for Cuban C.I.A. agents to attack Cuba.

6

Militarism was the power instrument in the Spanish colonies.

After Independence the armies, sometimes led by ex-Spanish generals such as Agustín Iturbide in Mexico, took over. In the early chaos and turbulence, the importance of the generals as rulers increased tremendously. The laurels of the great armies of liberation soon withered, and the applause of the people died away as bitter conditions developed.

Nearly all the countries were near ruin after ten to twenty years of armed struggle, and in some, as in Chile, even after Independence, devastation still went on eight years longer as the Spaniards, hanging on to Chiloé Island (the Quemoy of the South), sent bandits and hirelings to raid and rob and burn the countryside. It was difficult to build up new world commerce outside of the empire — though some prior contacts had been made by smuggling. It was difficult to get the fields planted again, or to start industries, or to maintain peace. Before any of these things were accomplished, the countries were re-occupied *by their own armies,* and the countryside was repeatedly pillaged by bands of hungry soldiers.

The General rather than the Spaniard became the new symbol of oppression; the Army, the institution to be feared, from that day to this — doubly so now, with lavish American aid — the worst evil of political and social life, a hungry cancer everywhere. We fed that cancer $30,000,000 in Brazil in 1960. A president whom we didn't like, Janio Cuadros, was kicked out. Only by popular demonstrations, the anger of numerous governors, a last minute split in the armed forces themselves, and by strikes was a military take-over prevented. In Peru, where more than $20,000,000 was to be given out in 1962, the Army took over in July. All this military build-up is in the name of "continental defense." Who is fooling whom?

It is a booming business for the arms industry in the United States, already bursting at the seams. It has been estimated that 92 percent of the U.S. military aid money and the funds spent by the local governments is spent in the United States. The cancer has grown and grown until it is breaking the backs of the southern lands. By 1957 U.S. military aid totalled $32,000,000, and local expenditures are automatically expanded even more. In that year the South American countries spent $927,000,000. By 1960 when our military aid to the southern lands totalled $67,-000,000, their expenditures rose to $1,400,000,000 according to

Rodney Arismendi in his *El Plan Kennedy y la America Latina*. This means that the southern countries are now expending in the non-productive enterprise of war more than they will receive under the Alliance for Progress in aid for social welfare.

U.S. aid during these post-war years has greatly enlarged the Army's political role, and this throw-back has slowed down or blocked normal economic and social evolution. It has blocked the liberation of the peoples. Argentina, indeed, has been cast right back into the days of the early caudillos. Not long ago ex-President Eduardo Santos of Colombia cried out to the American government to stop arming the Latin American armies. The Army in his country in the past ten years has slaughtered 300,000 people, has stolen land and estates, looted and plundered the countryside. Santos remarked, "Our countries are militarily occupied countries — occupied by our own armed forces."

The Republics came to belong to the Generals in an intimate personal-property sense: the marble halls, the broad acres, the moneys of State. As Oscar Efrén Reyes wrote of the Ecuadorean army: "The majority of the chiefs dispose of the funds in their charge as though they were for their personal benefit... The defrauding of the nation [by] ... fictitious enlistments, sinecures *[piperas]* ... grafting with barrack repairs, uniforms — the altering of price and quality." The chieftain is "the master of lives and property" with absolute power over whatever "feudal domains the government hands over to him." And — very much as a modern U.S. corporation head uses company employees -- so the officer "uses the soldiers any time to labor on his own property or those of his friends." (This, of course, is not wholly unknown in the U.S. Army where many soldiers become flunkeys of the top brass.) In all Latin America, government posts, contracts, concessions, moneys, commands, are spoils for the greedy military class — from lieutenant to general. In Ecuador the Army, at the behest of a U.S. officer who flew down from Panama to persuade Ecuadorian troops and officers to threaten revolt, early in 1961 forced President Arosemena to break relations with Cuba.

Under Batista, the Cuban colonels automatically got the national lottery graft — and each week appeared with their little bags to cart off 10 percent of the take. The chief prizes were awarded to upper echelon generals and politicians.

To increase chances for graft, army officers everywhere often have deliberately provoked local populations to desperate insurrection — and profit even more by suppressing it, at the same time becoming more indispensable to the government.

Many years ago, after crossing the lofty Sierra Madre mountains in Sinaloa and Durango in Mexico, I stumbled one evening into the outskirts of the village of Milpa Verde and, after a "Quien viva?," was taken by soldiers to local headquarters.

The colonel told me, "You were lucky. The Villistas — the men of Pancho Villa — are going to attack us tonight, and I gave orders for every outsider to be shot on sight."

The Villistas began their assault before daybreak, and firing went on all that day. People went about their usual business calmly. Women walked to the river with ollas on their heads right through the bullets to get water from the river. There they washed clothes just as though the battle was not going on.

No one seemed to get hit, though a vast amount of ammunition was burned up. That evening a truce was arranged with the Villistas. They were permitted to occupy half the town, but were to clear out the next morning. That night both bands got drunk together and galloped up and down the streets, shooting at the stars and shouting, *"Mueran los Gringos."* (I was the only Gringo within five hundred miles.) A deal was made: the next morning the Villistas went off loaded with guns and ammunition they had bought from the Federals. And so war and banditry went on in that uptorn corner of the country, and the bearded President Venustiano Carranza seemed unable to pacify the land. His hold steadily weakened.

It is always possible in Latin America that bullets bounce back to kill those who hand them out, as the French red-legs found out in Mexico when they spent a year trying to capture Vera Cruz and Puebla. U.S. arms sent to Mexico and Nicaragua ended up in the hands of Sandino and killed many Marines.

Weapons — U.S. machine guns, bazookas, rifles, bullets and finally tanks and airplanes given Batista in Cuba — were captured or bought by the Castro rebels in the Sierra Madre — at least a whole train-load for a million dollars — and these same weapons (falsely labeled Russian at the last minute by the Washington propaganda offices, as were those obtained by Sandino twenty-five years earlier) then killed the C.I.A. invaders at the Bay of Pigs. (The antiaircraft and submachine guns were, of course, mostly Czech weapons.)

The weapons now being used by guerillas in Guatemala and

Ecuador are not of Cuban origin, but U.S. materials of war, handed over to dictators for alleged defense of the continent, or else from the stores of the United Fruit Company plantations, accumulated, according to government claims, at the time Arbenz was overthrown in 1954.

As Juárez said when he put down Díaz's first revolt — and before passing from the scene — in words describing the present unjust pattern of most of Latin America, now everywhere abetted by U.S. military missions:

"The militarism of other days again raises its hateful standards ... Its purpose is to destroy the work consolidated in fourteen years of immense sacrifice and to take us back into the days when a revolution signified only a change of personnel in power ... For added mockery, it invokes the constitution."

This, indeed, is the story of Argentina in 1962, one-hundred years later.

It is the story of present-day Paraguay, of Ecuador, of Peru, of Colombia, of Venezuela, of all Central America (except possibly of Costa Rica), of Haiti, of the Dominican Republic — even with its provisional U.S. gunboat government, sweetly labelled "Democratic."

7

Such is the medieval social structure of Latin America. That system has come to the end of the road, in spite of the desperate efforts of the privileged classes and the United States to perpetuate it. Every dollar of the Alliance for Progress money buttresses up the anciens regimes, perpetuates them a bit more; but this misdirected effort deepens the revolutionary upsurge. The will for independence and popular liberation grows stronger. Our "gradualism," hitched to our false propaganda, our money, our military missions, our subsidies to the Church, may hold back the tide for a few brief years, but the debacle by such tactics of damming up normal social change will be far worse, far more catastrophic. Our dollars, creating new intolerable stresses, actually are promoting more communism than does Soviet propaganda. We, not the Russians, are its chief promoters.

As Colombian ex-President Eduardo Santos has put it, decrying U.S.-promoted militarism: "What we would defend against communism would be our own freedom but if we have already been stripped of them, we have nothing left to defend. It is thus that the gateway to communism is thrown open by the anti-Communists."

For the spirit of liberty, aroused during the independence wars, has never died, and new forces are at work. The struggle that followed the throwing off of the Spanish yoke, all during the first century of Independence, resulted in an instability usually misinterpreted by more fortunate countries as indicating the people of the new republics were unfit for self-government. Actually the peoples rarely got any chance for self-government, were struggling to obtain it. The guns were in the hands of the caudillos, who rushed in and out of the governing palaces in response chiefly to the behests of the Church and the large landholders.

Thus the popular struggles were extraordinarily sterile, for they consisted chiefly in trying to enforce idealistic paper constitutions unrelated to realities, to gain or retain the rights of popular suffrage and civil liberties, in a futile struggle because of the utter lack of economic liberties among the people, lack of health, lack of education. Hence the angels of reform were always dancing on the head of a pin, as today with the Alliance for Progress. José Martí, Cuba's great independence leader, put it in this wise: "A country which wins political liberty without winning economic liberty will end up by losing all liberty; but a people that wins economic liberty can go on to win its political freedom also." Actually neither political nor economic freedom can ever be separated. That is something the present-day Latin American is beginning to understand.

In only a few countries have elections acquired any validity. Mostly they are a prerogative of the privileged and serve to maintain the rule of the feudal minority. When the show-down comes, as in this year 1962 in Argentina, and the people do speak, their will is respected only so long as it goes along with the interests of the ruling elite, and particularly of the armed forces. The day comes when the only exit is via revolution.

Long before this, from the eighteenth century on, the beginnings of the industrial age and the new commercialism brought terrible wars and revolutions to Europe. Both the American, the French and the Latin American Independence revolutions were

symptoms of the new capitalism, which aggravated relations between states and created strains and stresses within. The Civil
War in the United States saw the conquest of the feudal Southern aristocracy, which was blocking internal development, by
the industrial North. That this tremendous change can come to
Latin American without similar upheavals seems unlikely — because feudalism is still so entrenched, yet so unstable as pressures increase, so unable to meet the needs of the near future.
Upheavals have already occurred; more are on the way.

Industrialization is even more difficult for the under-developed southlands than it was for England or the United States.
European capitalism had a relatively simple problem: it required the partial or complete destruction of feudal order,
methods and social relations, the demagogic control of the new
uprooted masses flooding into the cities and simultaneously the
conquest of overseas markets and colonies. In the United States
it was even easier — there were only a few vestiges of feudalism
on the eastern seaboard which was otherwise an open frontier,
with vast resources to be plundered and developed.

For Latin American industrialization, so belated, the obsta-
cles are far greater. It is not merely because of the battle with
feudal institutions, but because in colonial areas capitalism joins
with feudalism and attempts to preserve it. New Latin American
industry as yet can enjoy few export markets, and since purchasing power in a backward agrarian system remains so low, it is
apt to be strangled in the cradle. At the same time, new industry must simultaneously compete with that of the advanced efficiency techniques, the low-cost articles, of mass-production
countries — the great powers. All these headaches come at a time
when labor movements spring full-bodied and militant into the
arena — something the first industrial nations did not have to con-
tend with for a century or more, not until capitalism had become deeply rooted and fortified.

Obviously, the countries to the South will continue to sit on
their dung-heaps if they depend on the traditional laissez-faire,
or free enterprise, or foreign capital, to bring about new consumer goods industrialization. "Free enterprise," even in advanced industrial countries, has always meant a state-private alliance: favorable tariffs, free land and mineral grants, special
subsidies, tax favors, plus battleships and wars to open up frozen

markets abroad, viz. Perry's tour to Japan and Smedley Butler's to Nicaragua; purchases of armaments, now grown to such proportions that nearly all industry is an adjunct of the military and would otherwise collapse — as was the case in Hitler's Germany.

The inevitable solution in the semi-colonial southlands has been for the newer independent native industrialists to seek their own alliances in the armed forces and try to take over the state.

The newer system of economic independence and colonial emancipation — if it may be called that — and of state-private initiative, first appeared in Mexico under Plutarco Elías Calles about 1926, when the monolithic National Revolutionary Party was created. The generals and caudillos were brought under control and converted into industrialists rather than parasitic gangsters. Calles himself became a manufacturer of light-bulbs, auto-tires and other goods. His successor General Abelardo Rodríguez became a multi-millionaire entrepreneur.

A curious alliance was formed between organized labor and peasants with the new native industrialists. Presently Lombardo Toledano was making a ten-year pact with manufacturers not to strike against "Mexican" industry. "Build up the fatherland first!" Any strikes were directed against foreign enterprises — with the customary slogan of "Yankee, Go Home." Capital export taxes were fashioned; rail, shipping and tax rebates were given to home-grown, not foreign-owned, industry; new protective tariffs were enacted, and then a 51 percent Mexican ownership of all industry was enforced.

In Brazil Getulio Vargas operated in more direct style. If he decided a chemical factory was needed, he advised private industry, offering tax and other benefits. If there were no takers, he proposed a mixed government-private enterprise; if there were still no private takers, he went ahead as a government undertaking. His slogan was "Get what Brazil needs as quickly as possible," and the great São Paulo industrial complex of today is in good part the result of his genius, energy and policies. He had no silly rigid theories such as those held by big business on the one hand, or Communists on the other. Proof of the pudding was in the eating.

Various similar systems looking toward industrialization and increased production were launched, such as the government-financed Fomento Corporation of Chile, with its mixed enterprises, so successful but now stymied by U.S. meddling and our imposed "Austerity" program.

The extreme example, up until the Cuban Revolution, was the Juan Perón revolution in Argentina. The country then began reaching toward the Calles solution in Mexico twenty years earlier! Neutralism, economic autarchy, labor-native-industry alliance. He bought out British and U.S. public utilities, threw out British treaties controlling Argentina's industry and tariffs, which even prevented highway building. At the same time he promoted a peasant movement to curb the large landholders, the wheat and cattle barons; he created a national sales monopoly to handle major agricultural crops and sucked out most of its profits to gain capital for starting new industries on joint government-private initiative.

At the same time he was thus able to face up to and get favorable terms from the joint U.S.-British meat buying consortium that had been bleeding Argentina so badly. It was government versus government, but the U.S. press and a great many Argentinians saw nothing improper in the U.S.-British government agency; they shouted "Fascism" and/or "Communism" at Perón. (Fashions in libel, as in everything else, change with the times.) Perón pushed a pre-Nasser type of nationalism and neutralism, pro-industrialist, pro-labor, pro-peasant. He failed partly because his timing was wrong in the march of international events, and then at the end when he backed water by trying to return to the U.S. fold by giving away the country's oil reserves, he lost his own following at home.

After his downfall production seriously declined, thanks to the new regime's policy of giving a free hand to the *estancieros,* to the international traders, and the favoring of foreign investors at the expense of the native industrial class. The return of full power to the military meant an anti-labor policy and the suppression of peasant organizations. The austerity program imposed by the International Monetary Fund at U.S. behest has hit the poor and causes continued unemployment and stagnation. It has pushed Argentina steadily backwards and has led to the loss of capital, deflation and economic decline. By 1962 Argentina had just about reached bottom.

But new forces are reshaping the continent. The industrial revolution and the world-shaking electronic revolution knock on the doors. The population explosion is shaking all the nations. Piddling projects for housing or schools, petty land resettlement undertakings, food for peace — these do not create new productive power. These merely build up more costly permanent overhead and debt the countries cannot afford. For the past ten years, the productive capacity of the countries has not kept pace with this growth. A price-squeeze on raw materials as compared to manufactured goods has broken the backs of the people. Yet the demand for goods, for comforts, for a decent living grows daily more insistent. Two hundred million people — and there will be nearly six hundred million by the end of the century — are no longer willing to exist on less than a few hundred dollars a year income. The Alliance for Progress cannot possibly solve this.

Perhaps nobody can solve it, and so the people themselves will act. Latin America is a world in revolution. There is no longer any turning back.

On April 8, 1962, Mexico's leading novelist, Carlos Fuentes, known throughout the continent, was supposed to discuss the Alliance for Progress with the Assistant Sub-Secretary of State Richard N. Goodwin, in charge of Latin American affairs, but at the last minute Fuentes was denied permission to come to the United States. The loss is ours. What he had to say was important not merely for the Department of State but for every American. He could not be heard here; no one in the United States is likely to read his words. But already they have been published from one end of Latin America to the other.

At the close of his proposed talk, he states:

> "Please, Americans, look beyond the intellectual provincialism of the Cold War. Look where we wish to go; we men of the underdeveloped world, hungry and revolutionary ... We are different from you ... Do not be provincial. Try to understand the world's diversity ... We wish to coexist with you as loyal friends, not as sick slaves, badly fed, ignorant ... And we wish to liberate you from a fate worse than that of the slave: that of master.
>
> "Understand it well: Latin America does not intend to be

your backyard. We are going to enter the world ... The
first measure of cooperation is for you to know enough to
respect the revolutionary change at work in our peoples
... Latin America knows its road. Nothing, my North American friends, is going to stop these 200,000,000 people."

3 ◯ THE FIRST DECADE — 1910 TO 1920

1

The centenary independence celebration in Mexico, September 15-16, 1910, which coincided with the Dictator's eightieth birthday, was Porfirio Díaz's last magnificent gesture. Twenty million pesos provided splendid arches, decorations and fireworks.

The festivities climaxed many enterprises: the establishment of an insane asylum, the laying of the cornerstone of the San Gerónimo Atlixco jail, the opening of the Tacubaya seismographic station, the start of a statue to George Washington on Plaza Dinamarca. The only sour note, shortly before the event, was the pelting of Díaz's house with oranges and stones.

To the lavish ceremony came plenipotentiaries and notables from all the world, expenses paid and given the right to send cables free to their home countries. The King of Spain sent back the uniform of Liberator Morelos. The French, whom Díaz had fought so valiantly at Puebla and elsewhere, returned the keys of Mexico City.

Illuminations, floral arches, receptions, music, dances, special

opera and theater presentations, Belshazzar banquets, dedica-
tions, memorials, military parades, historic pantomimes,
speeches and more speeches! A vast allegorical procession de-
picted Mexico from Montezuma to Emperor Iturbide. Every
window and balcony blazed with color, flowers, brocades, rugs,
rich hangings. Not even a latter-day Hollywood movie of a Roman orgy has ever surpassed the golden reality of those two last
days in Mexico.

Major events were presided over by the aging dictator, his
gold-braided uniform bedecked from collar to hem on both sides
with so many jeweled decorations from the potentates of
the world he could stand erect only with an effort.

Endless orations and articles touted Díaz as the greatest hero
of Mexican history, of all America, the colossus of the modern
world. He was "the Prince of Peace," "the Unparalleled Patriot,"
"Father of the People," "Creator of the National Wealth and
Greatness." Such were phrases by U.S. and other newsmen —
in between champagne lifting.

Said Ambassador Henry Lane Wilson — affiliated with the
worst Republican machine elements and powerful U.S. interests — "The celebration closed with the impressive ceremony of
the Apotheosis, followed by a magnificent ball, over which the
President and Mrs. Díaz presided with real dignity and ceremony
. . . Díaz was crowned the Savior and Ruler of Mexico. . . . "

The ballroom, enlivened by a 150-piece orchestra, had 20,000
electric stars on the ceiling and among the red roses. Twenty
carloads of champagne were consumed. Five hundred pictur-
esquely costumed lackeys served caviar and smoked salmon and
poured "oceans of wine."

The Palace privileged were dancing over the volcano of a
starving, enslaved Mexico. But Daniel's *Mene, Mene, Tekel Up-
harsin* was smothered under flowers and banners. The best
people did not believe that volcano could ever erupt — not with
Díaz's gaudy, big-sombreroed Rurales who "shot first and inquired afterwards" — but mostly never inquired. Not with more
and more Yankee dollars flowing in, people then not yet knowing
that on the tide of dollars and alien enterprise, the red fire of
revolt and war always comes flaming. The tide sweeps away the
old walls, breaks the habits and traditions of men. In a feudal
society, dollars are always revolutionary messengers — messengers more effective than all the "Red agents" of communism.

The more dollars, the tighter the controls, the sooner the blow-up.

It was not yet so apparent. All production and trade statistics showed the fantastic "progress" of the country, and so quakes of discontent went unheeded. And why not? In thirty odd years, the national budget had increased from 20 to 100 million dollars. The number of pieces of mail handled had grown from 5 to 192 million. No industry had existed when Díaz arrived. Now there were textile mills, sugar-refineries, iron and smelter plants, paper mills, soap factories, breweries. Gold and silver production had increased from 25 to 160 million dollars. Naturally the gold and silver, also the mining profits, went abroad, but enough was left to pay the twenty-five-cents-a-day wages and modest taxes.

Progress in production really was impressive. Railroads had been built. President Lerdo de Tejada, whom Diáz overthrew, once remarked, "Poor Mexico with the United States so close and God so far away!"; and he had opposed granting railroad concessions through the northern deserts to connect with U. S. lines, predicting it would lead to the loss of still more of Mexico's territory to the greedy, expanding country to the north. But railroads had been pushed into many places, from Rio Grande far south to the Suchiate River on the border of Guatemala. U.S. Ambassador Thompson had wangled big concessions that permitted him to set up both the U.S. Banking Company and the Pan American Railroad Company.

While these bright developments marched ahead, agriculture languished in feudal self-sufficiency and peasant bondage — unable to provide the expanding urban centers with food, so that cattle, corn, wheat, and other foodstuffs had to be imported at high prices the half-starving people could scarcely afford. And so, in spite of the glitter, there was poverty and groaning and unrest.

2

Sometime before the Centennial, Porfirio Díaz had betaken his near eighty years to the international bridge at Juárez to greet President Howard Taft.

A huge electric sign on the Mexican side read "WEL-COME," except the "W" had blacked out, leaving "ELCOME" —

"He eats." The starving, barefoot peasants, in white "pajamas," looked at the sign and at barrel-bursting Taft, and shrugged. "He eats," there was no doubt about it.

Taft's amiable interchange on the bridge was to secure the renewal of the lease for the U.S. naval base on Magdalena Bay — the Gringos always wanted something. But for once Díaz could not fill the outstretched hand; popular fury at having a U.S. base on Mexican soil (there are secret ones now, God help us!) had risen to such pitch, Díaz had to refuse. This led to a certain coolness, and U.S. officials showed less zeal in persecuting anti-Díaz elements on U.S. soil. Hints of the prolonged evils and abuses of the Díaz dictatorship at long last were beginning to seep into the U.S. press. Also, John Kenneth Turner, friend of the much-persecuted Magón brothers, wrote *Barbarous Mexico;* and it sold well.

But the hint of coolness was not merely on the U.S. side. Early in November 1910, Mexican Arturo Rodríguez was lynched in Texas, in the noble fashion of that civilized commonwealth, whereupon angry mobs filled Mexican streets shouting, "Death to the Gringos!" Pro-Díaz Ambassador Wilson believed these unprecedented demonstrations were deliberately provoked by the authorities "to divert public attention from growing discontent." Certainly the Mexican police, never before at a loss to club and murder, seemed unable to cope with the three-day outburst of hatred. U.S. flags were burned, U.S. businesses and the subsidized *American Herald* were attacked. Members of the American Club saved their quarters, guns in hand behind impromptu barricades, and one American citizen in Guadalajara saved his life by shooting three rioters.

As usual, the great-hearted U.S. public was shocked, wondering how savage Mexicans (from whom we had already seized half their country and still hold a part awarded to them by international arbitration) should be so ungrateful for all the U.S. investments and civilizing efforts. They still wonder — about similar events all over Latin America — more frequent now, for the plunder today far exceeds that of those days in 1910. Except, disorders can now be shrugged off as "Communist-inspired" — as General Marshall did in Bogotá, as Richard Nixon did in Venezuela, as Puerifoy did in Guatemala.

But under Diáz, trouble-makers were being handled well.

Conspirators Flores and Ricardo Magón and other busybodies had been periodically jailed in the United States at the Dictator's behest. Madero was safely ensconced in the San Luís Potosí calaboose, and, prior to the October elections (on the heels of the Centenary), 60,000 Anti-Re-electionists were rounded up and put behind bars to insure a truly "democratic" plebiscite.

Aquiles Serdán, companion of Madero's campaign tours (Madero by this time had escaped to the United States), editor of the paper *No Reelección*, went home to Puebla, disguised in woman's black dress. "I'm taking my wife her widow's outfit," he told a friend with cheerful premonition.

The ubiquitous Díaz secret-service police, the Army, the gendarmerie descended on his home. He fought from behind barricades. The chief of police was killed. So were Aquiles and his brother — the first prominent martyrs of the revolution-to-be. His blood was to rise up into ̇10,000 warriors. It is always so — something people in power never learn.

Thus Mexico in 1910 saw the last touches put on the perfect feudal super-state, based on terror and slavery allied with U.S. corporations and the State Department. The elections were "free," yet no one dared speak openly, not even in whispers. The ubiquitous gendarme tapped the shoulders of men who paused on the street to converse. Only U.S. citizens were above the law.

The elite rolled down the fashionable Paseos in French motorcars, and poor souls in *guarache* sandals and pajamas found themselves lodged in the calaboose if they entered main streets. In some places, they could not even come into town to sell their wares unless dressed in European garb.

3

Serfdom reached its cruelest proportions. George McCutcheon McBride, in his *Land Systems of Mexico*, classic study of the Díaz period, revealed that in every state, except Baja California (a territory) and Tamulipas, 95 percent or more of the rural population owned no land or property, and in the great agricultural state of Oaxaca, only two-tenths of 1 percent owned land. Except for a few hundred people, everybody else was a tenant or a peón, and 80 percent could not read or write. No schools, no hospitals, not enough food.

The landowner could maltreat his peons with impunity, throw them on to the road, sell them off to the slave plantations of Yucatán at $65.00 a head — where they often worked with chains on their legs. He could beat them, brand them, kill them. *Jus primus noctis,* first night with all brides, was the landholder's right.

American owners, who had acquired vast tracts, conformed to this pattern. As Turner wrote in *Barbarous Mexico:*

"Americans [also] work the slaves — buy them, drive them, lock them up at night, beat them, kill them . . . all over the tropical section of Mexico, on the plantations of rubber, sugar-cane, tropical fruits — everywhere you will find Americans buying, imprisoning, killing slaves."

It was all "Scientific." The new rulers of Mexico were "Científicos" — eggheads who followed the positivist doctrines of Auguste Comte — a Mexican version of technocracy which in more industrial nations has since become synonymous with mechanical fascism — the apotheosis of the robot society.

Progress, not human beings, ruled the roost. Plus self-enrichment. This Científico clique included leading editors and professors, ministers, senators, governors, bishops, bankers, landholders and industrialists. The elite! The power elite. It included the brilliant cynical polemicist, Francisco Bulnes, leader of a fake senate opposition party. Behind them, were the San Rafael Paper Company, in good part American-owned, the Tobacco Trust (El Buen Tono), French-owned; the great untaxed Pulque Trust; the great U.S. corporations and the U.S. Embassy. They webbed every transaction. Not a street was paved, or a sewage system installed, even in the smallest village, without the O.K. of the state governor, who, as chief of the public-works soup kitchen, dished out the concessions to the Científicos who, after taking a deep cut, often passed them on to U.S. corporations. To be a governor was to own a kingdom and become a millionaire. The governors ran gambling houses (forbidden by law), brothels, cabarets. They were the vice-lords of the land and had absolute powers to jail and kill.

Lush concessions were ladled out to them and to foreign capitalists in the name of "Progress and Science." The entire southern half of Lower California went to Luis Haller, who sold it to a U.S. colonizing company; 7,500,000 acres in northern Mexico to two Científicos,who handed it over to Randolph Hearst; the copper resources of Sonora went to Colonel Greene. Land and mining concessions to U.S. interests in the Yaqui Indian region deprived them of river lands and led to savage warfare that cost the dictator 50,000,000 pesos and lasted well on into the revolutionary period; immense rubber concessions (via the Científico law office of Joaquín Casasus) went to the Rockefellers and Aldrich (Ambassador Wilson was his tool) and ruined poor towns. Quintana Roo was divided among a few companies, which led to revolts and massacres. In most localities the *ejidos* were enclosed by the nearest great landholder. In Morelos the Atlihuayán hacienda in Yautepec was created by the seizure of the *ejidos* by Governor Pablo Escandón. The robbed people appealed to Diáz, who wept over their misfortunes and restored a small, worthless portion! One hundred and forty-five million acres were given away to twenty-eight personal favorites of Diáz. Three hundred million acres were sold for two cents an acre, and much of it resold to American corporations for a song. Valuable oil and mineral resources were turned over to U.S. and British corporations, including the Guggenheims, who tried to put the wealthy Madero family out of the smelter business.

Even the employees on the railroads — except for the track-mending peons — were Americans — Gringos — and often the conductors, unable to speak Spanish, could not help passengers.

The Church, once the principal landholder of Mexico, had also become a big owner again. The Benito Juárez Reformation, in the sixties, after driving the French out of Mexico and executing Emperor Maximilian on the Querétaro Hill of Bells, had stripped away Church lands and had tried to implant small land-holding under a free system. Since the lower classes had had no experience and could not compete with larger units, this merely made possible the swift building up of huge new estates; and these new feudal rulers — even more rapacious than the Church — went on to break up the Indian communal *ejidos* which had survived four centuries of Conquest. Thus the entire rural population was quickly wrenched out of its age-old cooperative communities and reduced to peonage.

Even so, what Juárez had left Mexico was an imperishable dream of human liberty. Díaz was the counter-revolution — in the name of the revolution and freedom. His thirty-year rule destroyed all personal liberties, substituting the organized super-state, which handed over a large part of the country to foreign enterprise, creating thereby a curious alliance of native feudalism with alien capitalism — still the customary pattern in most of Latin America.

It was, in short, the inauguration of the industrial revolution — not by Mexicans but by foreigners — the new era of big business and monopoly capitalism *from abroad*, grafted on to the feudal nightmare of backwardness, peonage, illiteracy, diseases and cruelty, all intensified because of the vast indigenous, culturally submerged population, progressively reduced to serfdom. The new Díaz slogan, which at the start had been "less administration and more liberty," soon became "Bread or the Cudgel" — *"Pan ó Palo."* But most of the bread — and all of the cake — went to the Científicos and foreigners. The club was for the people.

4

In spite of dictatorial controls, toward the end of Diáz's rule a few great books were written which revealed the workings of his system — some of them, ironically, by leading Científicos, books such as Julio Guerrero's magnificent *El Génesis del Crimen in México* (1901). Federico Gambóa wrote *Santa*, the sentimental but, for the respectable, shocking story of a prostitute. "I won fame and money by a fallen woman," he told me. Francisco Bulnes brilliantly debunked Mexican history and acidly attacked all liberal tendencies; Salvador Quevedo y Zubieta, though a subsidized tool of the Dictatorship, in his excellent novel *Camada* exposed the venality and corruption of the medical profession. Heriberto Frías in his novel *Tomochic* described the brutality and orgies of an army campaign against northern mountain Indians; José López Portilla y Rojas, who though a sympathizer with the hacendados, nevertheless painted a tragic picture of the life of the people in his *Parcela*.

Just before the downfall, everybody was reading Francisco I. Madero's *The Presidential Succession* (1911), devoted to political reform, but with some attention to the need for agrarian and economic changes. It formed the basis for his Plan de San Luís Potosí, which succinctly set forth the proposals of the armed revolt that followed.

The slogan that soon took hold of all the rural population and swept across the dry rubble of national despair in a roaring flame, was, of course, "Land, Water and Schools." The peasants had little interest in political reforms. Palaver about "democracy" left them cold. They were willing to follow any leader — which accounts for the great popularity of Pancho Villa and Emiliano Zapata — who struck down the power of the hacendados.

Landlessness, illiteracy and misery became the powerful moving force behind the revolution. Another fundamental cause was the economic invasion by the United States, the impact of dollars and outside capital — the industrial awakening which thrust through sleepy feudal ruralism, allied itself with that feudalism, yet inevitably cracked it apart. This, plus the irritating special privileges to foreigners, helped disrupt the century-old fabric. It brought revolution to Mexico sooner than elsewhere in Latin America, where conditions for the most part were as bad or worse — and it came nearly seven years before the Russian upheaval.

The Madero program promised to "re-establish the dignity of the constitution" and embraced "effective suffrage and no re-election" as a guiding democratic principle. State and local autonomy were to be respected and the rule of the cruel *jefes politiques*, the *caciques*, or local bosses, was to be ended. The very fact that *cacique* was an Aztec word, that in the sixteenth century it was absorbed into the Spanish language and provided the aptest expression yet discovered for feudal bossism even in the mother country, indicated that here was an institution that would not be abolished by the stroke of a pen.

Madero, himself a vegetarian and a spiritualist, free of all the vices, felt impelled to outlaw alcoholism and gambling. But "Mexicanization" of the railroads struck a more basic note. So did his doctrine of equal rights for Indians, though this had theoretically been established when the Mexican Republic was born a century earlier. Land for the poor was his most basic proposal, and here was the real nub of his problem. Here, if he attempted

to accomplish something, he would find himself pitted against
the powerful land-holding class and the Church. The Díaz system had not been uprooted; the privileged had suffered from
the counter-marching but were still the major power-group.

Only a strong revolutionary government dedicated to complete agrarian reform could hope to transform the country, and
unless it did, the regime would be whittled away, it would sick-
en and fall by the wayside.

Madero's program was tame enough considering the century-
old evils that needed attention, and the forces against any basic
change, even minor changes, were, of course, overwhelming. The
visionary Madero did not know how to implant his reforms, and
since any and every reform, however mild, hurts somebody's
pocketbook, it was not sufficient to wave a wand or use cajolery.
He simply did not know how to start his program operating. Nor
did his selfish family; they wanted him in power, but they also
wanted his efforts to be baulked.

Thus the forces against him were overwhelming. Besides his
own political inexperience, he was faced with (1) the rapacity
of his own family, whose pillaging of concessions and public
funds damaged his reputation; (2) the military plotting of such
generals as Bernardo Reyes and Félix Díaz; (3) the General
Orozco counter-revolution backed by the Terrazas family and
other big landholders; (4) the plotting of American Big Business; (5) the open antagonism and secret plotting of the American Ambassador, Henry Lane Wilson, with close corporation
tie-ups, who strove to precipitate intervention; (6) the antagonism of the American government, which at critical moments
sent threatening notes, mobilized border forces and later on even
invaded.

5

The resultant national disintegration, in good part due to
President Madero's failure to institute land reform, played into
the revengeful purposes of foreign and domestic reaction. His
inadequate plan of land distribution was promptly abandoned;
instead he exhausted his financial resources by attempting to sub-
due Emiliano Zapata with an army under General Huerta! Madero was soon isolated, the stage set for the coup d'état of the

bloody Huerta, paladin of the super-state tradition, in a white-guard reign of terror. His take-over was arranged *in the U.S. Embassy,* and Ambassador Henry Lane Wilson and American business interests moved heaven and earth to have him recognized by the White House.

No amount of recognition or non-recognition could have saved Huerta. The forces of the agrarian-libertarian-democratic revolution of Madero were gathering strength for a further advance upon the State. The banner of revolt was promptly raised by Don Venustiano Carranza, aided by the picturesque Villa, a strange mixture of bandit, dictator, and social-reformer. Behind Carranza and Villa were rallied the small farming class of the north, the dispossessed Indians, the small business man, even elements of American capital fearing for their investments when Huerta proceeded to reward the *British* Pearson interests.

In the subsequent Carranza-Villa split, American capital and the State Department — with typical short-sightedness, perhaps duped by so many romantic newspaper stories about him — got behind Villa! But the more determined, serious, revolutionary elements, with few exceptions, backed Carranza, and presently, after Villa's Columbus raid, we were put in the ridiculous role of having to send Pershing into Mexico to try to hunt down our erstwhile protégé!

Carranza was an ex-Porfirio governor, and it is doubtful if he was ever heart and soul with the revolutionary movement. He did accept the open support of the more radical elements during those precarious days when he was bottled up in Vera Cruz and his future seemed uncertain. He gained three influential supports: (1) the financial backing of General Alvarado in Yucatán who, it is said, sent him 20,000,000 pesos from the treasury of the state-owned *Comisión Reguladora del Mercado de Henequén;* (2) the sympathy of Labor crystallized into *batallones rojos;* (3) and the military genius of Obregón, who drove Villa north from Celaya into the Durango cactus. Carranza soon betrayed all three.

6

The highlight of the revolutionary era was the 1917 Querétaro

Constitution, written in the shadow of the Maximilian gallows on the Hill of Bells. The constitutional convention faced the glitter of General Pershing's invading bayonets, and even as it labored, the State Department began bombarding Carranza with dire warnings that the revolutionary and social provisions, particularly nationalization of the sub-soil, were not acceptable. Already dollar diplomacy had helped create chaos and bloodshed. More would occur.

The constitution, as finally adopted — though much of it was paste-potted from the legal systems of all nations — was more enlightened and revolutionary than any similar document in existence. Its weakness as of the earlier more "democratic" constitutions of the continent was that few organized popular forces existed to make its provisions effective. That was to mean violent struggle for years but it still became a beacon light for the oppressed not only of Mexico but of the world.

It went well beyond the 1857 constitution in its curtailment of Church power. Though it guaranteed religious freedom, ministers and priests were forbidden to vote or participate in politics, celebrate religious acts or wear their habits outside of churches, could no longer control schools, charitable institutions, asylums, hospitals, or foundations devoted to scientific research or the dissemination of knowledge. Convents and monasteries were abolished. All Church property was "nationalized," churches could be used only by government license.

Property ownership provisions were equally far-reaching. All subsoil mineral and oil rights were nationalized. "Communism," shrieked the Hearst papers. Merely a restitution of ancient Spanish statutory provisions, retorted the Mexicans.

All communal lands enclosed since 1857 were ordered returned to their original owners. Each state was given the right to determine the maximum amount of land any one person or corporation could own. The excess could be sold in small parcels on long-term payments. The constitution forbade monopoly, and specially revoked any and all government contracts celebrated since 1876, which created such. Foreigners were permitted to acquire ownership in lands, waters, or in concessions to develop mines, waters, or oil-fields only by special government contracts that forbade appeals for diplomatic protection under penalty of immediate forfeiture.

The labor clauses were extensive and precise: the eight-hour day (seven hours at night), six-day week, minimum wage, equal pay for equal work, payment of wages in legal currency, limitation of overtime to three hours, double pay for overtime, social insurance, workmen's compensation. Employers in remote places and on haciendas had to provide good housing, public markets, and schools. Sanitary conditions and safety appliances had to be maintained. The right to organize and to strike was guaranteed, lock-outs were permitted only in case of excess production — something Mexico had never known. Arbitration and conciliation became compulsory. Wage-claims were given precedence in all bankruptcy proceedings. Three months' pay was awarded to discharged employees plus (by later regulations) one month extra for each year of previous employment.

These provisions, and other pledges, were never put into operation during the Carranza government: no real land and labor reform, no expansion of the school system. The more enlightened constitutional provisions were ignored or misconstrued; many still are. Few *ejidos* were returned, even in the face of court decrees; land was not distributed, except in certain states, then was forcibly torn away at the first opportunity; labor not only did not receive protection accorded it by the constitutional code, but unions were persecuted. The educational budget was steadily curtailed, thousands of schools closed. The slogan of "Mexico for the Mexicans," one of Carranza's strongest early rallying calls, came to mean "Mexico for certain Mexicans" — for a small vicious military clique, which, cloaked behind noble phrases, plundered the country.

An era was inaugurated comparable to our own post-Civil War carpet-bag period. The honest revolutionary elements (the more decent leaders, such as Generals Obregón, Calles, Alvarado) were forced out, or deserted the Army for the plow and the loom, leaving professional militarists in control. Carranza's favorite, General Barragán, chief of Carranza's staff and military ruler of Mexico, was an upstart of less than thirty years, who filled perfectly the shoes of the aristocratic tradition, swaggered around the capital with a gold-headed cane and women of ill-repute, who came to own a string of mansions on the fashionable Paseo de la Reforma. General Urquizo, Acting Secretary of War, was a bestial, unscrupulous, and universally hated autocrat. General

Diéguez, former governor of Jalisco, used several million pesos from the federal government allocated for education to build a private railroad from Guadalajara to Lake Chapala.

One general shot the tiles off the Don Quixto room in the fashionable Hotel Regis for sheer amusement and to demonstrate his lawless power. Another general of "the gray automobile scandal," who captained a gang of house-robbers, was sent on a special mission abroad until all human evidence of his activities could be eliminated.

The *Diario Oficial* is befouled with immense grants of oil, timber, mining and agricultural properties made to these men or their agents in violation of the new constitution.

Such was the character of the Carranza military party, which lived from the fat of the land, padding pay-rolls, marauding, looting the countryside, destroying commerce, commandeering railway rolling stock, promoting disorders to insure a continuance of their public thievery, until the people, as in Díaz's time, came to fear the federal soldier more than the bandit.

No money was left for constructive undertakings. The pitifully few schools of the Díaz regime were closed until, at the time of Carranza's fall, large residential suburbs of the capital, such as Mixcoac and Tacubaya, could not boast a single elementary school; five-sixths of those in the city itself were closed. The teachers in the institutions remaining open, and the professors of the national university, worked for part pay and on occasions for no pay, and were ridden down by the soldiery when they protested — as today under López Mateos.

The military tried everywhere to crush the incipient labor movement. *Casa del Obrera Mundial,* the first serious attempt of Mexican workers at organization, was suppressed. Scarcely an important strike occurred that Carranza's Secretary of State, Manuel Berlanga, did not send federal soldiers to shoot down the workers or invoke the treason act. Workers were forced to sneak into the fields, as in the days of old Russia, to hold their meetings.

Carranza tried to foist into power as his successor Ignacio Bonillas, Mexican Ambassador in Washington, contemptuously called *"Meester"* Bonillas because he knew more English than Spanish and favored the U.S. Bonillas was touted as a civilian and was to end the rule of the generals and caudillos. Actually the government party, so loudly denouncing militarism, was being run by Generals Murgía, Barragán, all the most notorious army grafters.

The more revolutionary forces backed General Alvaro Obregón of Sonora. He was put under house arrest in Mexico, on charges of plotting insurrection. He escaped, circulated the plan of Agua Prieta, and rallied behind him the Yaquis of his native state, the labor and peasant forces, the vast majority of the people.

A strong supporter, as Carranza well knew, was General Alvarado of Yucatán, backed by the *Liga de Resistencia del Partido Socialista*, with 100,000 members, led by the "Socialist" apostle Felipe Carrillo. They tore away the opulence of the Church, put the Indians on the land, opened schools on every hacienda, gave the Indians free medical attention, instituted alcoholic prohibition and birth control, founded cooperative stores.

Naturally the United States Government and the McCormack company wanted its war henequén,' of which Yucatán had a world monopoly, cheaper. The United States Food Commission fought the Yucatán Henequén Reguladora at every turn, holding up its ships in United States ports, multiplying frictions, threatening to blacklist the Yucatán Government.

Carranza moved in the Army, and Yucatán was swept by guns and fire. The peons were driven from their acquired lands at the point of the bayonet. Their cooperative stores were pillaged and destroyed. In July 1919, machine guns were turned on the defenseless people of the town of Muna. Over 1,000 members of the Liga de Resistencia were killed, murders celebrated by the flogging of one hundred Indians naked in the plaza of Motul, the home town of Felipe Carrillo.

Election day arrived. Pedro Llugo, a young school teacher, sent by the governor to the village of Tekit as an election inspector, had his head cut off by the soldiery, who stuck it on the ballot-box as a warning.

Next, federal troops moved in on Sonora and, on April 10, 1920, that state, under the governorship of Obregón's supporter, Adolfo de la Huerta, aided by General Plutarco Elías Calles, seceded from the United States of Mexico.

7

Obregón's "Revindicating Revolution" when he took over in

1920 cut the Army down to 50,000 men, drastically reducing
the military budget, giving land to ousted elements and providing tractors, plows, telephones, seed, rifles, schoolbooks.

Under Minister of Education, José Vasconcelos, primary schools
were opened even in remote Indian outposts. By 1922 more than
a million pupils were back in classrooms. Preparatory schools
and the University were reshaped, better to serve students and
the public, and a vast program of book publishing was undertaken. Painters were put to work on frescoes in the public buildings, and the art movement, that soon became the greatest glory
of the revolution, got under way. (Now, under López Mateos,
painters are put in jail.) The land program went ahead, *ejidos*
were restored; industry began expanding once more. The Revindicating Revolution under Obregón wrote a bright page.

The long controversies with the oil companies and the Church
burst into open warfare. The subsequent agreements between
Ambassador Dwight Morrow of the House of Morgan, and Obregón's successor, President Plutarco Elías Calles, at the much touted ham-and-egg-breakfast conferences at Chapultepec Castle,
were certainly better than war, which was what Secretary of
State Frank Kellogg threatened. Calles held out against the full
demands of the oil companies, Morrow was still able to save face.
The Mexicans got the essence of their theoretical demands; the
companies got the oil.

The most serious betrayal involved in the talks was Calles'
agreement to expropriate no more lands unless they were paid
for with cash on the barrel, rather than in bonds as heretofore.
Later, the State Department tried unsuccessfully to put this
across in Cuba. In Mexico it spelled, for some years, the death-
knell of the agrarian revolution.

Ambassador Morrow, i.e. the U.S. government and the bankers, began busily solving, or seeming to solve, not only Mexico's
international relations, but all her domestic affairs: the Church
dispute, the henequén question, industry, finances, the national
railways. Calles and Morrow ripped the heart and soul out of
the revolution. But the revolutionary generals themselves had
become rich entrepreneurs; Calles himself had acquired wealth
and plantations and factories by unsavory methods, all in the
name of "socialism" — socialism on a platter.

The real "Revindicating Revolution" fought back, gradually

gathered new momentum, and, after the assassination of Obregón and the sordid interlude of the Presidencies of Portes Gil, Ortiz Rubio, and Abelardo Rodríguez, gained new momentum. This put General Lázaro Cárdenas into office, not by war, but by orderly electoral process. Mexico, in spite of all the antagonistic efforts and the hostile schemes of official Washington, was gradually building up fuller independence and a more stable order based on wider justice, more sensitive to the popular will.

Cárdenas added to that peace and stability by his vigorous fulfillment of the Revindicating Revolution: the rapid renewal of the agrarian problem when 40,000,000 acres were distributed, the expropriation of rebellious foreign oil companies, the nationalization of the railroads, an active pro-Indian policy, the first real battle against illiteracy, the stimulation of rural development and industry — all this was carried out under Cárdenas, the most important leader produced by the Revolution and today one of the idolized leaders of a free America.

Today under López Mateos, who has followed a brutal anti-labor policy, who has struck down civil liberties right and left, who has abetted the new use of the church to influence, who has permitted the assassins of peasant leaders and others to go unpunished, who has thrust the leading painter of the country, David Alfredo Siqueiros, in jail for years, many of its fundamental achievements have been destroyed. Mexico once more stands at the crossroads and unless civic rights are restored and respected and the steady destruction of the great land reforms halted, another revolution will be the unfortunate answer.

4 ◯ YANKEE GO HOME

1

One man, above all, during the first half of this century, stands out as the hero of the twentieth century independence struggles: César Augusto Sandino of Nicaragua. He fought the invading U. S. Marines for nearly seven years — from 1926 to 1932. In the end they left, after staging a "democracy" election, leaving Sandino and his little force bloody but unbowed. It was, to say the least, a moral defeat for the U.S. military and for U.S. prestige. His long persistent fight marked the ending of our military invasions not only of Nicaragua, but of Haiti and the Dominican Republic.

Depression plus the growing storm of anger throughout Latin America, demonstrations, burning of U.S. flags, smashing of Embassy windows, bitter parliamentary resolutions, trade embargos, a 14 percent drop in trade, and worse to come, made a changed policy imperative. Sandino's heroic lonely battle fired the imagination and conscience of the entire continent. He proved, as did Fidel Castro later at the Bay of Pigs, that it was possible for a determined Latin American patriot, a freedom fighter, to stand up against powerful outside aggression.

Sandino was, of course, called an "outlaw" and a "bandit" — the usual epithets for anyone fighting for his country against a power invader. The same epithets were hurled at Abd El Krim of the Riff revolt in Morocco and, for that matter, at George Washington in the Thirteen Colonies. Sandino retorted in a letter to a Marine officer calling for his surrender as an "outlaw" that the only outlaws in Nicaragua were the Marines — an interchange not published in the U.S. press.

Except for a few small independent journals, the U.S. press failed to give an honest account of the struggle, let alone its significance. How could it be otherwise? The representative of the Associated Press was Irving Lindbergh, High Commissioner of Nicaragua, who made Nicaragua pay the claims of bankers and others arising from revolutions the United States itself had provoked; the representative of the United Press was Clifford D. Ham, collector of customs, who saw to it that the bankers and creditors were paid off.

But in spite of smear propaganda, not all could be concealed, and to this day the Nicaraguan invasion leaves a bad odor in the nostrils of liberty-loving peoples. It created enduring distrust of the United States in all Latin America. It created a new, evil U.S. tradition. It bred revolution.

U.S. intervention began in 1909 when a quarrel developed between Secretary of State Philander C. Knox, a corporation lawyer, and Liberal Party President José Santos Zelaya. He had dominated Nicaragua since 1893.

Earlier, as a busy beaver for U.S. interests in China, and particularly Manchuria, Knox had thoroughly messed up our Far Eastern policy in a way that cost us our good name and was one of the causes of the Chinese revolution. He now plunged us into irreparable mistakes in Nicaragua.

Nicaragua, the largest of the Central American countries, about the size of England, then had a population of less than a million. On the Atlantic banana coast, a large Negro population, mostly imported from Jamaica, was cut off from the white-mestizo Pacific coast and the capital, Managua, located halfway between the Liberal city of León and the Conservative city of Granda, on enormous Lake Nicaragua.

The northern mountain region, Las Segovias, where Sandino came to operate, was largely peopled by mestizos and Indians who, ever since Conquest days, had remained fiercely jealous of their independence.

The only means of crossing the country, other than by air or by travelling on horseback over mountains and through dense jungles, was via the San Juan River on primitive barges, whose departures were heralded by conch-shells; first to Graytown, then by tiny coast vessels to Bluefields or to Puerto Cabezas on the far northern coast.

The mountains, jungle and Atlantic coast were exploited by American corporations engaged in raising bananas, cutting mahogany and mining copper and gold.

Punitive American intervention had occurred in the 1850's when the Walker filibuster expeditions took over, thanks to rivalries between trans-isthmian U.S. steamship companies — shortly after the California gold-rush. Later on, a savage bombardment of Graytown by a U.S. battleship, for a petty reason, razed the town, killing men, women and children, and left a baleful memory.

Under Liberal President Zelaya, who took over in 1893, the tempo of development was quickened. He promoted transportation, mining, lumbering, coffee production and education, but also handed out monopolies to himself, to his clique and to favored foreigners: contracted unsound loans, issued large amounts of paper money. His was a personal dynasty — similar to, though less cruel, than that of Gómez in Venezuela, Trujillo in the Dominican Republic, the present Somoza dictatorship in Nicaragua. By 1907 he began trying to unify Central America, threatening force if necessary. The United States and Mexico (later squeezed out of Central American affairs) imposed — at least on paper — a policy of compulsory arbitration of disputes by creating the Central American Court of Justice.

Zelaya, increasingly irritated by U.S. meddling, cultivated other international ties. He bypassed the New York bankers and celebrated a large loan deal with the British Ethelburga banking syndicate; he was accused (likely false propaganda) of making secret overtures to the Japanese to build a canal. Then he cancelled the concession to the La Luz and Los Angeles Mining Company. Diplomatic exchanges grew bitter.

According to noted Venezuelan writer Horacio Blanco Fombona (later court-martialled by Marines in Santo Domingo), Knox was the chief stockholder of the La Luz company; his nephew was the Bluefields manager of the mining company, who happened to employ a twenty-five-dollar-a-week clerk, one Adolfo Díaz.

State Department opposition to any Latin American government always starts guns popping from the bush, even where money is not involved. In this instance, Governor Juan J. Estrada of Bluefields, capital of the mid-east coast province, was bribed and raised revolt. He was financed by $600,000 provided by said clerk, Adolfo Díaz. General Emiliano Chamorro, to become one of the puppets of later Marine intervention, arrived to help out.

Soon after, Zelaya executed two North American soldiers of fortune, captured while dynamiting the San Juan River for the rebels. This so aroused Philander Knox's righteous wrath that he broke off relations (December 1, 1909) and praised the Conservative revolters as representing the Nicaraguan people, for whom Knox's heart now bled profusely.

Zelaya resigned and fled to Mexico, after turning over his government to his legal successor, Vice-President José Madriz, probably the most respected man in the country.

But U.S. interests had too much money involved in the revolt, and Knox was determined to wipe out the existing establishment and completely destroy the Liberal Party, even though the country was overwhelmingly liberal in sentiment. The government, however, still had an army and resources, and soon Estrada and his men were cooped up in Bluefields, surrounded by overpowering federal forces.

U. S. battleships ready on the scene made Bluefields a "neutral zone" and landed Marines. The government forces, unable to maintain a prolonged siege in the surrounding jungles, were obliged to retire. Madriz had to resign. He turned over his sash of office to Estrada. The U.S.-backed rebel was in the saddle.

But the State Department made doubly sure it would collect its pound of flesh. Minister Thomas C. Dawson of Panama was rushed down on a battleship and forced Estrada and his government to come aboard and there sign away Nicaragua's independence on the dotted line. Not merely dollar diplomacy, but gunboat diplomacy. For the next fifteen years about all any Nicaraguan executive could sign were pieces of toilet-paper that blew in the windows from the Embassy, the U.S. Marine barracks, and the offices of New York bankers.

The immediate conditions imposed on Estrada were: "legalize" his seizure of power by naming Adolfo Díaz vice-president and, calling a constitutional assembly, accept a high commission of two Americans and one U.S.-named Nicaraguan, answerable to the Secretary of State; settle all U.S. and other claims against Nicaragua (mostly due to the revolution we ourselves had promoted). Most claims were steals based on dubious losses or expectations of grandiose future profits. Those of Nicaraguans were mostly pressed by political favorites, several even based on "mental or moral anguish."

Estrada had also to install Clifford D. Ham as collector of customs, and arrange for a $15,000,000 loan with Seligman and Brown Brothers (fiscal agents for the United States Mortgage and Trust Company).

The New York bankers also took over all undistributed moneys of the Ethelburga loan — at a falsely pegged exchange rate that netted them nearly $400,000. Altogether, wrote Rafael de Nogales, who witnessed many Nicaraguan events, the various refunding costs alone "amounted to considerably over forty percent of the existing foreign debt of Nicaragua."

These financial arrangements and claims — the Castrillo-Knox convention — were so filthy that even the U.S. Senate turned them down in one of its rarer moods of integrity.

Still, with State Department approval, the bankers cooked up a quickie loan of a million and a half and took over 51 percent control of the National Bank and the national railroads. (Part of the indoor sport of the next few decades was buying and selling these two institutions at low cost for the bankers and a high price for Nicaraguans.)

Through currency manipulation and a so-called austerity program — similar to those we are now imposing on all Latin America — prices and profits were increased, wage increases were blocked, and people were reduced to greater misery. Customs duties had to be increased 150 percent. Small business was ruined. Only U.S. speculators and the bankers profited.

The Constituent Assembly was packed by Emilano Chamorro's conservative faction; and when President Estrada tried to assert his rights, the U.S. minister forced him to resign in favor of Vice-President Adolfo Díaz. And so Knox's mining company and its two-bit clerk had come to rule the whole roost. Dollar Diplomacy had won.

Our Minister reported secretly to the State Department, "The sentiment of an overwhelming majority of Nicaragua is antagonistic to the United States." Well! Well!

The Constituent Assembly named General Luis N. Mena provisional president to succeed Díaz at the end of his term. With the blessings of the Embassy, Díaz suppressed the Assembly and ordered Mena's arrest.

2

Inevitably revolt flared. At once, on August 3, 1912, Díaz asked for U.S. intervention. The following day Marines were landed and deployed to police Managua and the railroad.

Even so, the rebels captured key railroad points, including such large cities as Masaya and León.

Brown Brothers demanded additional protection for their half-owned railroad, and Major Smedley D. Butler was rushed up from Panama with reinforcements that presently totalled 2,700 men.

The same hypocritical formula was used as is today in South Vietnam, that the Marines — accompanying Nicaraguan troops everywhere — would not fight unless fired upon. The U.S. forces stormed into Masaya and León, and other points which the Díaz forces had been unable to take. Rebel chief General Mena was obliged to surrender to Admiral H. S. Sutherland. Insult was added to injury when the United States officially declared that all this bloodshed lent "strong moral support to the legally constituted government for the people of Nicaragua."

As for the destruction of U.S. property — the protection of which was one of our excuses — U.S. intervention had resulted in the destruction of more U.S. and Nicaraguan property than in any previous revolution. U.S. General Feland — later in charge of the forces against Sandino — told me years afterward in the Athletic Club of Columbus, Ohio: "American property in Nicaragua was never in any danger until after we intervened. We had no business being there."

The Nicaraguan government — i.e., our own puppet government — had to squeeze Nicaragua in order to pay for all losses. Little or nothing was left for schools, public health or economic progress.

And so our sneak aid to revolutionary disorder in behalf of a mining company had led to full intervention and bayonet rule. Since "democratic" appearances had to be preserved, an honest bayonet election, with U.S. Marines guarding the sacred polls, was celebrated. Nearly all citizens were disenfranchised. In the liberal center of León, second largest city in the country, only eighty persons were allowed to vote. Throughout the country Díaz received all of 4,000 votes — "honestly counted" — in a population of 800,000, and was duly seated "legally" in power.

Díaz's government was bankrupt again, and he had to beg for more money. He received some small aid, for which the bankers now took over the direct management of the National Bank and handled all government revenues — with the sanction of Secretary of State William Jennings Bryan.

Economic crisis deepened as war in Europe cut off Nicaragua's market for coffee and other goods. Soon the government could not even pay its employees. New revolt flared, this time headed by haters of U.S. intervention and of the usurous bank deals. But by driblets of U.S. money — mostly, however, by Marine bayonets — puppet Díaz managed to hold on for four years.

Another bayonet-occupation election was held. The candidate was "strong-arm" Emiliano Chamorro. It was a pay-off. As minister in Díaz's cabinet, he had put over the canal deal we coveted — "steal" would be a more appropriate word. The Marines did not even permit the Liberal candidate, Dr. Julián Irías, inside the country to campaign, and Chamorro was duly eased into office in January 1917. Whether the United States taught the Nicaraguans how to hold a "democratic" election, or whether our officials by this time had learned the know-how from the Nicaraguans, we shall never know.

The name "Chamorro" became synonymous with nepotism. In his government, thirteen important officials — several cabinet ministers, heads of the armed forces, the police chiefs of Managua and Corinto, bore the name Chamorro. Several were young irresponsible wastrels. Swarms of relatives of his wife also held fat jobs.

I once met a "spark-plug inspector" on a road project, who had a government car and earned a fabulous salary. "What are your duties?" I asked.

"Oh, I ride out and look over spark plugs on the equipment and order them replaced if necessary. Uusually I do it on Sunday because that way I can give my whole family a nice outing."

This pay-off to Chamorro and his buzzards was chiefly for the canal rights — the infamous Bryan-Chamorro treaty. For $3,000,-000 and in violation of the treaty rights of Costa Rica, Salvador, Honduras and Guatemala, Chamorro had given the United States a hundred-year option to construct a canal (to follow the San Juan River, where Costa Rica had inalienable navigation rights); and ninety-nine-year leases for naval bases on Great and Little Corn Islands (also claimed by Colombia, which was not consulted) and on islands on the Pacific side in the Gulf of Fonseca, the joint property of three countries, none of which except Nicaragua was consulted.

This treaty would not have passed except that the Nicaraguan congressional building was surrounded by U.S. Marines with naked bayonets. According to Nogales, the treaty was read only in English, which few Senators understood. And so was put over a treaty that grossly violated the rights of all Central America, not to mention the rights of the Nicaraguan people themselves.

The injured countries took their protests to the Central American Court of Justice — whose decrees *we* had made binding on all the countries. It ruled against Nicaragua. The treaty violated rights guaranteed in the 1858 Canas-Jerez treaty, the 1888 Cleveland award, and the 1907 Central American treaty (U.S.-made). Neither Nicaragua nor the United States paid the slightest heed to this decision, and the "Oficina de Paz" — as Guatemalan writer Rafael Arévalo Martínez called it in his satirical book — folded up. A bright experiment in international concord came to an ignominious end — went right down the drain.

But when the hard-pressed Nicaraguan government tried to collect the $3,000,000 mess of pottage, the State Department said, "Nay, nay, Pauline." *Nicaragua did not get one red penny of the spoils.* As Sandino later said to me in San Rafael: "From that infamous treaty, Nicaragua did not get enough to give each Nicaraguan a tin of sardines and crackers. Better that they would have at least had one meal out of it."

The State Department arbitrarily decided the money had to be used to pay off the arrears on the old Ethelburga loan (much of which the country had never seen or smelled), now owned by the New York banks, and the Brown Brothers loan. Even a modest request for $100,000 to start three schools was ignored.

At the last moment — as the government foundered for lack of funds — it was allowed to draw half a million dollars from current customs revenue sums (which also belonged to the bankers) to meet urgent payrolls. For this — since all canal rights and moneys had been stolen from it — the government had to turn over the remaining 50 percent equity in the railroad and the National Bank stock to the same bankers.

In October 1916, another Marine election installed Chamorro's uncle, Diego Chamorro, as his successor. Diego died in office October 12, 1923, and Vice-President Bartolomé Martínez assumed office. (By then the United States was also intervening in the Caribbean and in Honduras, and had customs control of Salvador.)

W. W. Dodds was sent down to draw up a brand new election law, which was forced on the reluctant Nicaraguan Congress in special session.

An alliance was then patched up between Conservatives and Liberals (hoping to get a wedge in the door after so many years): Carlos Solórzano (Conservative) and Juan B. Sacasa (Liberal), for president and vice-president, were the candidates.

The new government was thus a U.S.-imposed coalition, the ever wet dream of all U.S. negotiators in moments of crisis abroad, always a result of prior blundering (as now in Laos) and ever a prelude to worse disasters. Coalition, forced on any land by outsiders, is a comic-store cigar that always blows up and makes the face look worse than ever.

The new Nicaraguan Congress (after voting itself a 50 percent salary increase — the usual austerity procedure, even in the United States) declared the elections fradulent, but the United States recognized the new administration. The Congress also threw overboard arrangements by U.S. fiscal adviser Jeremiah W. Jenks for a half-million dollar loan, as being "impractical"; also a $5,-000,000 loan to pave streets and build sewers — a steal by U.S. carpet-bag contractors. It did adopt the U.S. proposal to establish a constabulary force, under a U.S. officer, who would enjoy incredible privileges and pay.

3

The Marines pulled out, except for an embassy guard, amid universal jubilation — August 1924.

But the Army had not been disbanded. It remained in charge of two brothers of the president's wife, so prospects for the new "non-political" U.S.-imposed law-and-order corps did not seem overly bright. Not long after, when Solórzano — in accord with the election pact — appointed a well-known Liberal to the cabinet, one of his wife's brothers, Alfredo Rivas, led a hundred soldiers to shoot up the official reception, and arrested all Liberal Party guests.

Emiliano Chamorro then seized the army fortress, Tiscapa, above the city. Vice-President Sacasa fled. Solórzano was in on the whole double-cross, but from time to time Chamorro lobbed a few artillery shells at the Palace, and sent 2,000 men to bring back Sacasa, "dead or alive." Sacasa escaped to Washington, and Solórzano soon had to resign.

Though the State Department was peeved that its doll house coalition had collapsed, and refused to recognize its previously obliging servant Chamorro (even though he now offered to sell back again the railway and national bank at bargain rates), it gave Sacasa, the legal successor, a crude brush-off.

He went on to Mexico, where President Plutarco Elías Calles, happy to put any spoke in U.S. plans, helped him with arms and money.

Liberal revolters seized Bluefields on the Atlantic side. As before, it was declared a neutral zone. But on the insistence of Clifford D. Ham (playing ball with Chamorro despite nonrecognition), the Marines tossed the Liberals out of the port.

Meanwhile, provided with Mexican military supplies (which greatly angered our State Department), Sacasa set up the "legal" government in Puerto Cabezas on the northeast shore in a few shacks belonging to the Bragman's Bluff Lumber Company. Mexico at once recognized it as the "constituted government of Nicaragua" and began shipping arms to both coasts.

Washington managed to oust Chamorro, but ignored Sacasa's legal claims and on November 11, 1926, installed its old faithful mining clerk, Díaz — by this time the most hated man in all Nicaragua — as president. He was promised a quickie $300,000 loan, a $6,000,000 loan to follow.

"Dollar diplomacy in its basest form," cried opponents. Díaz came back with charges that Mexican aid to Sacasa represented a "world-wide Bolshevik plot."

"A shameless subterfuge!" retorted the Mexicans, and shipped in more arms.

Two weeks after Sacasa set up his government, Admiral Latimer landed Marines and sailors in Puerto Cabezas and at Rio Grande, where guns and machine guns and 2,000,000 rounds of ammunition were seized and sunk in the sea. He blockaded the port, took over the radio stations to prevent Sacasa from communicating with the outside world, and ordered him and his government out of Puerto Cabezas within six hours. He refused to leave.

Various Sacasa generals escaped the U.S. military dragnet and struggled through the jungles to raise revolt in the interior. In the dead of night, young General Sandino dredged up some dumped supplies at Rio Grande under the noses of the Marines, and paddled up the Cocos River to raise revolt in the Segovias. Everywhere he was successful; everywhere he was supported by the people.

In spite of U.S. gold and U.S. bayonets, the Liberal revolt grew. More "neutral zones" had to be established. "Not intervention," nervous Nellie Kellogg told the Press with a straight face, "just places where no fighting is allowed."

General Moncada, with plenty of arms and ammunition, moved steadily toward the capital. As the situation degenerated, the United States readied 4,500 men for new intervention to try to keep the hated Díaz in power.

Even the conservative, pro-clerical *La Nación* of Buenos Aires called our invasion of Nicaragua and our policies toward that country "an injurious attitude toward the ideals and sentiments of international justice professed by all civilized nations," and denounced Coolidge in no uncertain terms.

Protest mass meetings were staged from Buenos Aires to Paris, from Punta Arenas to the Rio Grande. The Costa Rican Congress threatened to hold up banana contracts with the United Fruit company until justice was rendered to Nicaragua.

In answer, President Coolidge hotly denounced Mexican aid to Sacasa, and Kellogg lashed out at Mexico's "Bolshevistic activities."

But few people were fooled. Nicaragua, thus raped, became the "Little Belgium of our Hemisphere." Not until another colossal blunder, the C.I.A. Bay of Pigs invasion of Cuba, did such a mighty wave of anti-U.S. feeling sweep the continent and surge on around the globe.

As Nogales put it, "Nicaragua is not, as some people believe, a local affair, but one which involves the fate of all the governments of Latin America."

Sacasa, still holed up in Puerto Cabezas, a virtual prisoner of the Marines, managed somehow to get statements out. He dubbed U.S. "dollar policy toward Nicaragua" for the past two decades as "not a ... policy beneficial to the Americas as a whole, but ... for the exclusive benefit of a certain group of banks."

On March 6, 1926, Senator Burton K. Wheeler told the Ford Forum in Boston: "The Kellogg-Coolidge policy has led to armed intervention in Nicaragua in behalf of an American-made puppet-president foisted upon the people against their own will for the simple reason that he is ready at whatever cost to Nicaragua to serve the New York bankers who for seventeen years have been mercilessly exploiting Nicaragua under the aegis of the State Department."

H. Ofilio Argüello, Sacasa's counselor at Puerto Cabezas, summarized it: "Nicaragua ... the past sixteen years has gone back at least a half a century. Public schools . . . throughout the entire country have been closed wholesale.... Money formerly devoted to public instruction is used to subsidize Jesuit and parochial schools . . . . Concessions of utterly ruinous character have been given to powerful American concerns, which have merely exploited the natural resources of the country for their own benefit without any advantage whatsoever to Nicaraguans."

He added, "The State Department, throwing American honor to the dogs, recognized Adolfo Díaz as president of Nicaragua. To do this, it had to violate the spirit and the letter of a treaty it had sponsored ... a constitution which it had sponsored, had to lend itself to all manner of legal trickery and political chicanery ... The overwhelming majority of the people of Nicaragua ... jointly despise that ... little Victrola dog [Díaz] listening to his master's voice.

"The State Department ... when it failed to get away with the raw deal ... began rushing warships and marines and bombing planes to . . . carry out its cowardly program of bluff and bully-ing!"

Coolidge solemnly announced the United States "was not in-tervening in the internal affairs of Nicaragua."

But Adolfo Díaz, secure behind U.S. bayonets, with U.S. dol-lars in his pocket, formally thanked the U.S. armed forces for having "averted the horrors of Bolshevism."

He was far from saved. Already on February 6, the Liberals attacked the important Pacific Coast center of Chinandega. Aft-er days of bloody fighting and victory, they were driven off by aerial bombardment from U.S. mercenaries, a terrible slaughter that left hundreds of civilians, men, women and children lying mutilated in the streets. Half the city was burned down. It was Nicaragua's pro-Franco Guernica, as savage and inhuman as the Nazi-Fascist bombardment later in Spain.

More Marines were rushed in, and the British sent a cruiser to Corinto — at secret U.S. request, it was claimed, so that the Monroe Doctrine could in turn be used as an excuse for shoving in more than 5,000 Marines. A large supply of arms was rushed to Díaz in return for notes bearing 6 percent interest. General Henry L. Stimson hurried down armed with extraordinary pow-ers as Coolidge's personal emissary.

By then both Díaz and the Marines faced complete debacle. In all the campaign the government, even though bolstered by the Marines, had not won a single important engagement and the rebels, with a major army of veterans, were now poised on the threshold of full success. General Moncada, at the head of his victorious army could not be prevented from taking Managua — a coup that would arouse hilarity.

4

For the moment Stimson's big problem was to save face, also U.S. concessions and financial arrangements. This meant that temporarily, Díaz, too, had at all costs to be saved. But he was realist enough to realize that an about-face had to be made, that the Liberals simply had to be allowed to take over the country.

He had three Sacasa emissaries brought by battleship from Puerto Cabezas and laid down the dictum to them that Sacasa had to recognize Díaz as president and disband the Constitutionalist government. The three emissaries left in a huff of hot words. Stimson then followed the procedure of pro-consuls since time immemorial and sought out the head of military force — Moncada. A conference was set up at Tipitapa a few miles from the capital and from Moncada's outposts.

First he delivered an arrogant ultimatum. "The President of the United States has determined to supervise the elections of 1928 . . . The permanency in power of President Díaz . . . is considered indispensable for this plan and will be insisted upon . . . The forces of the United States will be authorized to take charge of the arms of those who shall give them up . . . and to *disarm by force* those who refuse to comply."

But the bitter pill was sweetened. Moncada's force would immediately receive generous supplies of food and clothing. Moncada would be paid $10.00 for every rifle turned over . . . On his side, Díaz promised to take no reprisals and issue a general amnesty. Freedom of the press would be permitted, and Liberal party governors would be appointed for the six provinces then controlled by the Constitutional Army. This promise was never kept.

The real sop was a U.S.-supervised election the following year, with the tacit understanding that Moncada would be a candidate and receive U.S. support. It meant he would be the next president.

Moncada, after one pathetic statement on May 4, that a million inhabitants could not fight a rich, powerful, armed nation of 120,000,000, capitulated.

It was a grand double-cross all around. The United States was double-crossing her pals, the Conservatives; Moncada was double-crossing his officers and the brave men who had toiled through swamp and jungle overcoming incredible odds. He took from their lips the sweet honey of victory — to ice his own cake.

From this time on, Moncada breathed no word of criticism of the U.S. invaders. He lavishly praised the Marines and U.S. officials and the United States. He got hold of a religious medal, sawed off the image of the Virgin, and reconditioned it as a "medal of peace" to pin on the chest of Admiral Latimer aboard his flagship in a groveling ceremony of adulation.

Sacasa, too, did a little double-crossing — after it was tacitly agreed he would be the president to follow Moncada — provided he folded up shop in Puerto Cabezas and endorsed, too, the Moncada-Stimson agreement, thus playing Judas Iscariot with those who had sacrificed and worked for him.

Nicaragua certainly needed peace. But did this insure peace? Was it a peace that any dignified Nicaraguan could accept?

Stimson rejoiced at the "end of the insurrection." On May 15, four days after the final surrender ceremonies at Tipitapa, he advised the State Department that he had already received 6,200 rifles, 272 machine guns and 5,000,000 rounds of ammunition. Even the terrible bandit "Everest Cabulla, guerilla chief of Chinandega, has agreed to turn over his arms."

"Peace in Nicaragua" headlined the U.S. press, and lavish praise was heaped on Stimson. One paper, however, did suggest that it seemed "more like the peace of the hawk than the dove."

It was all premature. On May 16 — the following day — Cabulla boldly attacked U.S. Marines, and an officer and a Marine were killed. Shortly after this, he did agree to parley with a Marine officer about laying down his arms. The parley was held, and after he delivered his side arms, he was treacherously murdered by the officer with his own revolver.

Another rude shock was to come. Young General Sandino, instead of delivering his arms at Jinotega, gathered together his clans and moved on to his native town, San Rafael del Norte, closer to the mountains. He controlled the country from there on north and soon began attacking Marine outposts.

"I consider Moncada not only a traitor but also as a deserter who passed over to the enemy," Sandino told the press (not published in the United States). "Nobody authorized him . . . to enter into secret treaties with the enemy in the name of the Constitutional Army, and especially with the invaders of our country."

Sandino's first attack came to Ocotal, where supplies were captured. He was finally driven out by bombing planes. Exaggerated claims were made in the U.S. press that they had killed three hundred rebels. Actually only a handful of Sandinistas were killed. The bulk of the dead were civilians, including women and children.

Once more Díaz was favored with a loan, and once more the entire stock of the National Bank and national railroads were mortgaged to the New York bankers. But the shadow of Sandino, "the outlaw," darkened the smiles and the hand-rubbing.

5

For nearly seven years, Sandino kept up the grueling, unequal struggle. The story of his resistance was suppressed so far as possible, but Marines were ambushed and killed, towns were taken, and through the back-door of Honduras, he managed to send out accounts of his operations, his proclamations, his plans — and the news spread to all Latin American and the entire world.

"A flea-bite" one commentator called it. But, as Rafael de Nogales remarked in his fine book, *The Looting of Nicaragua*, "even a flea-bite in an elephant's ear is likely to cause infection if not properly treated." The United States had no medicine except force and money. The elephant's ear did get infected and began to swell and swell.

In 1928 General Feland told me in Managua, "I'd have to have 50,000 men to get rid of Sandino, and even then it would be mere good luck, a mischance or a betrayal by one of his own followers. The 5,000 men I have are barely enough to keep communications open and man key garrisons."

All those years the good name of the United States went down and down. Its military abilities suffered ridicule; Sandino emerged as the hero of the Americas. He kept on until the Marines left in 1933; then, as he had promised, laid down his arms.

By then the Great Depression was blighting the world.

5 ◯ THE DEPRESSION YEARS: SOUTH AMERICA

1

The great U.S. Depression brought tragedies and violence to all in the Western Hemisphere, to every home and every country. But some beneficial changes, too.

Chief among those for Latin America was President Herbert Hoover's announcement of the proximate withdrawal of Marines from Nicaragua, Haiti and the Dominican Republic.

In Mexico the reforms of Lázaro Cárdenas were carried out. Chilean upheavals brought many tears and salutary changes: labor laws, new industry, benefits to the people — and a new national philosophy. In Peru, student leader Haya de la Torre, who ten years before had launched the Popular Revolutionary Alliance of America (APRA), came back to Peru in a whirlwind of mass popularity and for ten more years (before, in the hope of winning power, he betrayed all his principles) reoriented the political life of his people.

The handwriting of the Great Depression was on the wall as early as 1928 — for in that year trade between the United

States and Latin America fell off appreciably. But the drunken whoopla of boom prosperity was blind to all indications that the bubble was about to burst. Everybody looked through the roseate spectacles of grab and spend. After the bubble did burst in 1929, foreign trade plummeted, shaking the economies of the entire globe. Trade with Latin America dropped to levels of the early century, and governments toppled like cards before a puff. Never was it brought home to the southern countries so humiliatingly how utterly dependent they were on outside markets. Mostly the generals took over.

But new attitudes and philosophies also took hold. All stressed the necessity for independence, autarchy, self-sufficiency.

In Argentina, hit by a military coup and a series of corrupt bayonet elections, conservative economists worked on a comprehensive national rehabilitation plan. It was absurd for such a great country to depend for its prosperity almost entirely on the export of half its products whose prices were determined in London or Washington. It must promote the production of goods in which Argentina was deficient — foodstuffs, oils, minerals, steel, manufactured products. The country had to become more self-reliant. It had enough resources to emerge from the existing colonial subserviency to the imperialist powers. This program became known as the Pinedo Plan, when it was pushed through Parliament in 1940 by the then Finance Minister, Federico Pinedo.

It was largely this plan which Perón attempted to put into effect, but with added safeguards for labor, the peasants and social reform — and to a degree succeeded. Above all, it proposed to recover foreign investments, to stop the outflow of Argentina's money and wealth, and limit or control future foreign investments.

Naturally these views and practices were fought bitterly and long by the U.S. government, in the end successfully, with, as it is now so evident, financial and political catastrophe.

But prior to all this, the country was hit by the 1930 military coup of General José F. Uriburu, "who brought relief to the well-born" faced with popular revolt. It was a swift coup and a deadly regime. First, the general distributed seven million pesos among his fellow officers. Military victory and loot are usually synonymous.

It was a landholder-Catholic blow at the hated regime of Radical President Hipólito Yrigoyen, and it had popular support because of Yrigoyen's late-hour corruption and oppression. But the real bug in the woodwork, some whispered, was the fact that Yrigoyen had just celebrated a secret deal with the Soviets for petroleum — this and Hoover's personal spleen, when Yrigoyen — always anti-American — had practically insulted the newly elected U.S. President on his visit two years before. The oil deal is said to have spurred Uriburu to act.

By 1920 U.S. corporations had invested in Argentina not over $46,000,000. But within four years, Americans owned $145,000,-000 merely in state and municipal bonds— an amount to increase rapidly as the vast loan-racket carried on by leading U.S. banks became a continental chantage. By 1924, according to Robert W. Dunn, investment in meat and industry had grown to more than $100,000,000. *Barron's Magazine* of March 17 put the grand total at $250,000,000. Though this was still only about 12 percent of Britain's stake there, the United States already controlled most of the meat-packing and meat exports. As early as 1920, Argentines controlled only 10 percent of this major export item. In all some 190 big U.S. companies were at work in Argentina and busily expanding their holdings.

Uriburu's political tactics are important, for they were followed almost precisely by the firing-squads of General Aramburu, following the downfall of Perón in 1954 — another great "democrat" according to the State Department. Similar Uriburu tactics were pursued by the Army in the 1962 ousting of Arturo Frondizi.

After a period of terror and torture, and in spite of bayonet control of the ballot boxes, two years later Yrigoyen's Party, the "dishonest" Radicals who had "perverted" the constitutional system, were overwhelmingly elected. Uriburu promptly voided the elections, outlawed the Radical party, just as the military have now outlawed the Peronistas — and duly elected his own pet, who was also the white-haired boy of Washington, General Agustín P. Justo.

2

Great Depression events in Chile were even more dramatic.

After all, Argentina could always sell its meat to Great Britain
— for that country had no cattle industry, as had the United
States, to menace the market — and its meat was by all odds
still the finest in the world. Wheat sales might be undercut by
Canada and the United States; sheep sales by Australia; but meat
was gold.

In contrast Chile's copper and nitrates (already hurt by syn-
thentic production in Germany) were riding a leaky boat that
threatened to be submerged completely. A League of Nations
report showed Chile was harder hit by the depression than any
other country on earth.

Actually, depression had hit badly as early as 1920, in the aftermath of World War I, and there had been little recovery. In
the elections of that year, Arturo Alessandri, the son of an Italian immigrant become wealthy, from the nitrate port of Iquique
in Tarapacá Province, roared across the northern desert, through
the Vales of Paradise and the southern rain country, shouting
the woes of the middle-class, the unemployed nitrate and copper workers, the sorrows of the exploited *rotos*, the ragged ones
of field and mine. "The Lion of Tarapacá" was a big man, shag-
gy-headed, and his mighty voice was a great cataract of eloquence. He was easily elected president.

For four years he battled against further collapse, as synthetic nitrates ruined Chile's major industry and drove hordes of
workers into the cities, unemployed and starving. Blocked by a
reactionary Congress, he could do little, but in 1924 he won a
majority and pushed through a labor law modeled on those of
Mexico and Uruguay: recognition of free unions, collective bargaining, health insurance, abolishment of child labor. But he was
unable to meet army payrolls or find work for the unemployed
and by mid-year he was tossed out by bayonets and fled to Italy.

A military junta soon handed over its powers to Colonel Carlos Ibáñez. Presently, Socialist colonel Marmaduke Grove seized
power.

In the kaleidoscope of shifting power, Carlos Dávila, former
ambassador to Washington, also a Socialist, briefly became president. The word "Socialist" was too terrifying for Washington,
which withheld recognition.

The U.S. ambassador was a close personal friend of Dávila,
and he moved heaven and earth to convince the State Depart-

ment that the new president was not going to shake down the pillars or confiscate U.S. properties. It was hard sledding, but one day he rushed to the Palace, his face glowing.

"Don Carlos, they're going to recognize you tomorrow."

Dávila took his head in his hands. "My dear friend, what, oh what have you done? Get on the wire at once and tell them not to do it."

"But Don Carlos . . . "

"Three days from now I'll be out, *caput*, no longer president."

As chaos spread, Alessandri was called back from exile. For six months he wrestled with trouble heaped on trouble, but pushed through a new constitution, modeled on that of Mexico but milder. The powers of eminent domain over private property were greatly expanded. Church and State were separated, and subventions to the former were to end within five years. Religious tolerance was permitted.

Alessandri was ousted again in October 1925 by Ibáñez, who installed rich landowner Figueroa Larrain as provisional president. Unable to curb Ibáñez's brutal suppression of civil rights and the press, and his railroading of labor leaders into island prisons, Figueroa soon resigned, and Ibáñez ruled in his own right.

He was hailed in the United States as the "epitome of democracy." Washington was breathing easier. The era of so-called Socialists seemed to be over, and the lure of "the Strong Man" enabled New York bankers to sell millions of bonds to gullible investors — $300,000,000 in nigh worthless bonds, money which strengthened Ibáñez' dictatorship.

He poured cash lavishly upon the army and increased officers' pay. Costly public works — railroads, port facilities, irrigation, power projects — took up the employment slack. To revive the nitrate industry, he set up the new Cosach Company — owned jointly by the Chilean government and private investors, chiefly the Guggenheims, a scandalous, fraudulent, stock-watering scheme. It soon went down in collapse and with it Ibáñez.

By then the Great Depression had hit Chile an almost mortal blow. There was no more U.S. money with which to splurge; trade fell off alarmingly, bond payments could not be met, government employees were dismissed right and left, and great mobs of unemployed and students rioted in the plazas. In July 1931, Ibáñez escaped by the skin of his teeth to Argentina.

Two years of wild disorder and increasing misery resulted. In December 1932, Alessandri was back in office. He had become an out-and-out conservative now; his cabinet, made up wholly of Conservatives, was ruled by Gustavo Ross, a wealthy landowner and industrialist, hated by the masses. The Radicals (the big center party of industrialists and middle-class) also withdrew their support. The Left, to which was now added a strong Communist party, grew turbulent.

The prospect was gloomy, it was downright black. Mineral production had dropped to half that of even 1927. Nitrate production to one-twentieth. Government revenues to an eighth. Public employees went unpaid for months on end. In 1932 only forty-two automobiles were imported, compared to 100,000 in 1929.

Actually Ross was a great financier and patriot. He instituted more basic reforms than any previous leftist regime, reconstructed the whole edifice of the economy. Modern Chile is his creation. A realist, he was not bothered about the economic theories that still bemuse the world — capitalism, free enterprise, socialism, communism, fascism, but drove ahead toward economic recovery. By 1937 he had balanced the budget and had redeemed a fourth of Chile's bonded indebtedness by slyly buying up lands in the open market, for a few cents on the dollar — a practice that, when perpetrated by indebted governments, is considered immoral by all bankers. He reorganized the whole nitrate business, taking a fourth of all profits for the government. He further alarmed U.S. interests by nationalizing the British-owned trans-Andean railway, and he brought blackmarketing charges against U.S. foreign power corporations, accusing them of illegally exporting profits, and forced them into a new combine, one-third of earnings to go to the government, one-third to rate reductions and the final third to stockholders. A similar super-state consortium was forced on the copper companies.

Electric power output was doubled by 1937, and Chile began turning out shoes, textiles, glassware, soap, paper, cement, plumbing fixtures, electric light bulbs.

In 1936 Alessandri put down a railroad strike, brutally, and the Popular Front rallied the country against Ross's candidacy for the presidency. On the eve of elections, ubiquitous ex-Dictator Ibáñez, aided by "Nazi" strong-arm gangs, tried to seize power. The revolters were smashed. Ironically, the new Fascist elements then joined the Popular Front. Left-wing Pedro Aguirre Cerda won by a small majority.

He was in for a stormy time. But Chile's situation steadily improved. His great Corporación de Fomento — Development Corporation — was to write a new history in Chile's independent industrial growth.

3

The Great Depression changed the history of Brazil. President Washington Luiz Pereira de Souza (1926-30) of the São Paulo coffee dynasty imposed as his successor a close associate in the King Koffee Klub, Julio Prestes. This was in violation of the unwritten tradition that the Executive office had to rotate between São Paulo and the mining state of Minas Gerais. At once Getulio Vargas put himself at the head of the *mineiros* and the hard-riding *gauchos* (cowboys) of his home state, southern Rio Grande do Sul, where he was serving as governor. He utilized the usual slogan that elections had been rigged. Before it developed into nation-wide civil war, a group of army officers and politicos seized Rio de Janeiro, blocked the seating of Prestes, and installed Vargas in the National Palace.

Vargas, born in Rio Grande do Sul in 1883, was then forty-seven, with a varied and romantic career already behind him. He had been a cowboy, studied at Jesuit schools, joined the Army as a private, then studied law, "because to be eminently successful in Brazilian politics, a man has to know the people, be skilled enough in the art of war to be able to talk back to the generals and colonels, and also be a lawyer."

Installed in the Palace, he played man against man, group against group, state against state — a superb and cunning politician. Gilberto Freyre described him as "silent, introspective, subtle, realistic, distant, cold ... telluric, instinctive, fatalistic, proud, dramatic."

He inherited economic catastrophe. Over-production of coffee (which provided 70 percent of Brazil's exports and revenues) coincided with world economic collapse. By early 1929 coffee grade "Rio No. 7" was down to 15 cents a pound, not enough to pay the costs of production; by 1938 it was down to 5.25 cents with enough in warehouses to supply the entire world for a whole year.

Brazil's hard-hit finances could not bear the high costs of storage and subvention. Payment on the foreign debt alone, not to mention profits shipped out by foreign investors, called for the export of $200,000,000 worth of goods a year, five times Brazil's favorable balance of trade in boom years. Now the favorable balance was wiped out entirely for years. Trade deficits and debt charges kept mounting. All the Koffee Kings were going bankrupt, ditto the commission men, ditto merchants, and unemployment rose like a scummy tide in all the cities and on the land. Coffee was dumped into the sea, coffee was burned, great pyres of pungent smoke all over São Paulo — a symbol of the hot grills of human hunger, starvation and death.

National despair permitted Vargas to obtain extraordinary dictatorial powers: control of all state and municipal governments, censorship of the press, a free hand to deal with the economy — and with the army. He did not bother holding elections, and in July 1932, hard-hit São Paulo revolted and was backed by rebels in other states. It took three months of hard fighting to restore order.

He bent then sufficiently to call a constitutional convention, which he controlled from A to Z. It set up a corporate Fascist state, but did provide labor and the peasant gains and granted women suffrage.

But the following year, barracks revolts occurred in Rio and in Pernambuco. Vargas conveniently called this military disaffection "Communist" and put the country under martial law.

Indeed the revolt was tied in with the Aliança Nacional Libertadora, affiliated with Moscow, and headed by the young officer Luiz Carlos Prestes. He finally led revolting forces on an incredible march of 5,000 miles through the jungle to refuge in Bolivia.

Trouble also came from the extreme Right, the Integralista Green Shirts, led by a strange fanatic, Plinio Salgado, who believed in fascism and the Fuehrer principle, anti-Semitism and Sun Worship. He was subsidized by Nazis, wealthy German São Paolo industrialists and the German Embassy. With the slogan "God, Nation and Family," his Green Shirts, wearing Green-Sun arm-bands, were initiated into Sun Worship rites. They came to number several hundred thousand, many were from leading families and — like the Birchites in the United States today — gained secret adherents in the army, navy and government offices. Soon Vargas found use for them.

Though constitutionally ineligible to succeed himself, he called for elections in 1933. He listened disgustedly to the droning old-line politicians; their phonograph disc talk was remote from Brazilian realities, devoid of meaning for Brazil. He disbanded Congress and declared martial law, warning the country against the "Communist threat."

Salgado nobly offered him 100,000 armed followers to protect the Republic. Vargas accepted their support, helped them set up elaborate Rio headquarters. In November, he set aside the constitution and declared the Estado Novo — a Fascist coup against his own government. Salgado was in honored attendance at the ceremonies. His Green Shirts marched proudly.

Vargas absorbed a few of them into the regular forces, then sent Salgado to go climb a tree.

Or so he thought. Some time later, Integralistas and army units attacked the Palace one dark night, overpowering the guards. Vargas in pajamas, his wife and daughter in night gowns, rifles in hand, ran from window to window firing at the attackers and actually held out till loyal troops arrived.

His self-written constitution for the Estado Novo gave him the right to rule by decree until such times as the new document was ratified by plebiscite (which he never called) and a new Congress elected. This document gave him the right to appoint every governor, every major, every judge in the country. It was complete iron-clad personal dictatorship.

Blandly he told a New York correspondent, "A Fascist government? By no means, this is a super democracy. By abolishing all parties, I have made it possible for all citizens to come direct to me."

The new constitution was not wholly without merit. It gave labor new rights, established the eight-hour day, limited night work hours, abolished child labor, provided medical care for sick workers and expectant mothers. The slogan of the new document was "Brazil for the Brazilians," and theoretically the State assumed ownership of all national wealth and property.

Vargas put in an "American front" as Foreign Minister — the

able, wily Oswaldo Aranha, ever yes-man for Washington and much doted over by Cordell Hull. At the same time, Vargas amused himself by sending birthday greetings to Hitler and Mussolini. By this adroit cat-mouse game he pried $300,000,000 out of Washington, in those days an unprecedented sum.

With this as a booster, he was able to bridge economic disaster, also to suppress newspapers and jail editors, throw thirty thousand political opponents into jail, and in general make a mockery of U.S. claims that he represented noble democracy fighting Hitlerism. His Minister of War was dull, pompous General Enrico Dutra, an out-and-out pro-Nazi. His chief of staff was the brilliant Brazilian nationalist, Góes Monteiro, one of the most outspoken pro-Nazis on the continent. Both were decorated by Hitler for their "valued services . . . to Germany."

Vargas was roundly criticized for his barter deals with Germany, as are makers of barter deals with the Soviet Union today. But it was excellent business that helped pull Brazil out of the red. Such deals bypassed costly banker's financing and brought a better price for Brazil's coffee, cotton, tobacco, vegetable oils and citrus fruits. Brazil became the biggest citrus fruit exporter in the world. By 1937 Germany was selling Brazil twice as much as Great Britain and, just before the war, surpassed the United States. By the time war cut off needed outside products, Brazil, no longer so dependent on coffee, was in better shape to survive and grew industrially faster than ever.

Vargas I, the astute and conniving international poker-player and the slippery opportunistic dictator, had as his Siamese twin Vargas II — his alter ego — patriot and nationalist, striving to build up his country, to diversify production and to industrialize.

As the booming war years rolled up ever bigger trade figures, the country bounded ahead. By 1943 industrial production was forty-three times as great as in 1907. With the help of several hundred thousand Japanese immigrants, he made Brazil over into a cotton-growing land, some 4,000,000 bales per year, and a textile exporting country. They also started a big silk industry. In five years he upped paper-production from a few thousand tons to half a million tons annually. All sorts of new products were turned out, production in all lines greatly expanded: rubber and electrical goods, tire making, leather products, plumbing tools, machine-tools, chemicals, cement, drugs. By the end of World War II, Brazil was exporting radios, adding machines, electric stoves and refrigerators, metal goods, steel office equipment, metal tubing, electrical supplies, chemicals, drugs.

Vargas followed no theories in this effort. Like Ross he disregarded the clichés, which for him were not for guidance but for the tic-tac-toe game of politics. His motto was "Get things done."

He searched for and exploited new mineral fields: diamonds, quartz crystals, lead, vanadium, manganese, molybdenum. He discovered nickel deposits and started exploiting them. U.S. corporation geologists said Brazil had no oil. He got other experts and started drilling, bringing in the first wells. Pretty soon it was being said that most of Brazil floated on oil.

Brazil already had several small steel plants — it has a fourth of the world's high-grade iron ore — but in 1941 Vargas set up the government-owned National Steel Company, wangled money out of the Export-Import bank which previously had refused to loan money for government enterprises of this nature, and started the mighty Volta Redonda steel mill halfway between São Paulo and Rio.

Swamps were drained, highways (some through virgin jungle), railroads, airfields, new cities were built. Vast Tennessee Valley projects were worked out, five such for the great São Francisco River, which would have created a whole new empire of farm and factory production; but the powers-that-be in Washington would not finance government establishments competitive with U.S. utilities.

For the first time in history, Brazil ceased to be almost solely a coffee-exporting country, merely a provider of raw materials and jungle products; it drove toward a rounded economy on all fronts.

Vargas made many crooked political turns as the years went by; he shifted alliances time and again. He lost power and regained it. Material progress was great, but social justice and political evolution languished. No change was made in the feudal land structure, except that a new class of industrialists arose, as did strong labor unions.

But increasingly toward the end, he moved steadily closer to the people, to the common man. He founded the Labor Party, and, regardless of his demagogy, he was the maker of modern Brazil. He refused to consider Brazil a colony or a slavish satellite of U.S. policy. Thus he was the maker, also, of the bold new nationalism, the neutralism and universal internationalism, later followed by Cuadros and Goulart.

4

Everywhere in Latin America, Depression changes were startling. The retraction of U.S. government and corporate pressures helped bring about greater — and healthier — independence and initiative. All too often the new regimes were a reimposition of the old-time ruthless trio of feudal power — church, landowners and army — to block progress and human rights; yet even such regimes, in order to survive in a difficult period of deflation, had to join the march of promoting industrial growth. It became a case of do or die.

Uruguay had long languished in backwardness, its people in misery, its governments broken by disorders and military coups. But after 1907, it shook off its lethargy and gained some stability. Yet as late as 1920, 96 percent of the utilized land was in enormous stock-raising estancias in the hands of several hundred ruling families. People were serfs or else they crowded into Montevideo and other cities. Nor has this aspect of life changed much since then. Even today an area said to be as large as the total cultivated area of Japan is owned by twenty-three families, a vast domain with few roads, no schools, no stores, no health care, few signs of civilized institutions. Until the end of the first term of the great president José Battle (1903-7), who rallied the middle class and the new immigrants against the reactionary landholders, all agriculture was backward. The illiteracy rate was still over 50 percent.

Battle widened the political base and created a well-organized liberal wing in the ruling Colorado Party. He then had to fight to control the country. The *Blancos*, controlling fully a third of the nation, angered by his reforms, went to war, and it was a hard and bloody civil conflict.

During his second term (1911-1915), he won the backing of the workers and peasants, but lost entirely the support of the richer Colorados, who seceded to form the die-hard Riverista Party. He fought to set up a *Bundesrat* type of government, such as that in Switzerland, where he had visited for two years after his first term, believing that would end the curse of caudillismo and militarism.

But not until two years after he left office was he able, through constant editorializing in *El Día,* to get his new constitution adopted: a Congress elected by proportional representation, a nine-member council, with jurisdiction over education, health finance, commerce and industry; free elections, freedom of the press. Cornerstones were: compulsory free education and university education (for the first time) for women; freedom of labor to organize and strike, the eight-hour day, minimum wages, old-age pensions, accident insurance.

But he opposed land reform, saying that new industry would automatically reduce the size of big estates. On the other hand, he forced through tariffs to protect national industry and prevent "foreign economic imperialism," and promoted governmental participation in new enterprise. "Competition" in industry, he told Congress as early as 1911, was not "invariably something desirable nor is monopoly necessarily to be condemned . . . . The modern state unhesitatingly accepts its status as an economic organization. It will enter industry when competition is not practical, when control by private interests vests in it authority inconsistent with the welfare of the State . . . when the continued export of national wealth is considered undesirable."

In 1928 a government packing plant was opened, and today all packing plants are run by the government. A state-owned mortgage bank and a state insurance bank in competition with private enterprises were set up, and by 1934 the government was doing two-thirds of the fire insurance, three-fourths of the life and marine insurance, and all the workers' compensation insurance. The government took over the entire nation's light and power business. In 1948 all railways were taken over from the British. These "Socialistic" tendencies discouraged new foreign capital, but in 1936 the *British South American Trade Journal* said British investors had no complaints: "The return is, and practically always has been, relatively greater than in any other country in Latin America."

The Great Depression broke the back of the Liberal movement. In 1931 a coalition was set up similar to that now controlling Colombia, of the more reactionary Colorados and Blancos, the latter led by the arrant pro-Nazi Luis Alberto de Herrera. He elected Gabriel Terra, who dissolved Congress and the nine-man Council, restricted the press, roughhoused the oppositionists, including the Communists, and ruled by decree. He forced through a new constitution that concentrated all power in the executive.

In 1938 he arbitrarily imposed his brother-in-law Alfredo Baldomir as president. But the latter, in sympathy with the Liberal-Socialist tradition of Battle, restored the previous constitution and the nine-man governing Council, lifted the controls off the press, permitted free elections and guided Uruguay through the more prosperous war years on the Allied side.

5

Peru was racked by its own peculiar miseries. It is a country whose ruling caste has peculiarly rancid, Spanish conquest ideas. It was freed from Spanish rule by the Argentinean San Martín and the Venezuelan Simón Bolívar, not by its own efforts. It has never had a bona fide popular uprising.

Actually there are three Perus, the Europeanized coast (with Lima as the seat of all power in the country), the Indian highlands (seat of the ancient Inca Empire), and the vast jungles to the east. The coast still represents the spirit of the original Spanish Conquest which broke the Empire. It still rules, even though after Independence it has never been able to match the greatness or justice of Incan days.

There is a fourth intermediary Peru, the border land between the part European coast and Inca land — the mestizo belt of the highlands, around the 5000-7000-foot level. A humorous difference is revealed by the anecdote that the creoles — people of pure European descent — in Lima, the capital on the coast, rush when there is trouble into their homes and barricade their doors and windows; whereas the mestizos or cholos of beautiful Arequipa, the little city under the towering majesty of snow-clad Misti, rush into the streets, guns in hand, shouting, "Whom are we fighting for now?"

The first upsurge of Peruvian wealth and ruling-class prosperity came with the guano period, a gift of the birds not of man, and the nitrate period, a gift of the rainless desert. The up-rhythm was broken when Spain, taking advantage of the U.S. Civil War, tried to reconquer Peru, causing a long war from 1862 to 1866, during which Chincha Island, the richest guano deposit, was seized.

Once more, considerable expansion followed — this was when the fantastic San Francisco embezzler Henry Meiggs, relative of Minor C. Keith, founder of United Fruit, built the railroad over the Andes, the highest in the world, provided with oxygen for passengers. It was a colossal steal, though the road got built.

As Peru's great writer, Manuel Gonzáles Prada, put it: "He built many bridges and tunnels in the Andes, but wrecked many homes and reputations in Lima." Meiggs had a great harem of the most aristocratic ladies and girls in Lima. In the corrupt spirit of guano enrichment, the people were willing — as the same author remarked — to throw themselves "into the sewer if at the bottom they had glimpsed a golden *sol* (Peruvian dollar). Husbands sold their wives, fathers their daughters, brothers their sisters." Since the Limeñas are the most beautiful women in South America, likely a good time was had by all — or some.

The bubble popped again with a disastrous bloody war (1879-83) when Chile (backed by England) tore away rich nitrate coast lands of both Peru and Bolivia, which was sealed up without access to the sea. Chilean forces marched into Lima, quartered troops in famous San Marcos University, pillaged every wealthy home and finally imposed a humiliating peace.

Peru sank into miserable backwardness from which it has scarcely emerged, in which the British Peruvian Corporation, Grace and Company and other foreign speculators gobbled up the richest resources. The Peruvian Corporation, in return for assuming Peru's national debt, took over the steamship line on Lake Titicaca, all the railroads, and was to get 3,000,000 tons of guano for sixty-six years, the free use of seven ports and a subsidy of $400,000,000 payable over thirty-three years.

The continuing misery of the land saw the rise of Augusto B. Leguía, President from 1902-1912 and dictator from 1919-30. His dictatorship plus his need for heavy financing provided the entering wedge for the inrush of U.S. capital and loans, and the pushing of the British to one side (though the Peruvian Corporation still remains powerful).

At that time the New York bankers were actually forcing money down the throats of all South American dictators and painting rosy pictures of the future to gullible U.S. investors. They even bribed southern rulers to accept money. Leguía's own son, among others, was bribed $415,000 (a commission?) to put over a huge loan. The lone Embassy secretary who warned the State Department of irregularities and the unsoundness of the venture, was drummed out of the service.[1]

It was a Porfirio Díaz plunder era, in which Leguía, his family and favorites stole millions of acres, in which powerful American corporations received lush concessions — such companies as Cerro de Pasco (copper, and other metals), the Canadian Corporation, Standard Oil, and W. R. Grace and Company.

The original founder of the Grace dynasty had started nearly a hundred years earlier as a ship's chandler in Valparaiso, using armed thugs to promote his business. They raided ships in harbor, shanghaied crews, and stole the supplies, which would then be sold back to the plundered vessels. Even U.S. naval vessels were not immune, and a scandalous Congressional investigation forced the outlawing of the concern. (Today the executive of the present powerful company heads up President Kennedy's business committee to promote business investments in Latin America in connection with his new Alliance for Progress. The name "Grace" is going to irk a great many Latin Americans.)

There is no doubt that Leguía's peace of the sword, like that of Díaz, had advantages; the country enjoyed much material expansion. Nothing attracts officials and private money and praise to a Latin American country so much as strong dictatorship. Leguía did promote considerable education — mostly in the hands of the Church. Lima, up until the time of President José Bustamante (1946), had only three public schools, so Peru has remained the most backward of the South American countries with respect to public education and still has an extremely high illiteracy percentage.

Leguía imposed a Liberal constitution (1920), but he ignored it from the first day, trampled on the bill of rights, censored or

1. This seems to be the historic process where Peru is concerned. Thus two honest employees of the U.S. Aid service in Peru, who exposed the colossal graft and mismanagement there, were broken several years ago, being unable thereafter to secure any employment in any department in Washington; other honest men involved were forced to resign, or were hounded, while the wastrels, thieves and cover-up artists have been protected and promoted.

closed down newspapers, filled the jails with political prisoners, and shut San Marcos University down as completely as when it had been occupied by Chilean invaders. Iron rule was maintained by police and army. Leguía re-elected himself twice in a wholly illegal fashion, yet no ruler in South America has ever been more praised and adulated in U.S. publications. But his grave was dug even before the Great Depression — when he was pushed into it.

The pioneer spade-work for the regeneration of public life had been done by Manuel Gonzáles Prada, a writer who died in 1918, the year before Leguía started his dictatorial period. Gonzáles Prada wrote, "No honest man can engage in Peruvian politics. It means traveling through a sewer, and he will be fouled up whichever wall he touches." In his *Prosa Menuda,* collected and published in Buenos Aires in 1941: "In Peru there exist two great falsehoods: the Republic and Christianity. We talk about civil liberties, but most Peruvians have no security in their freedom or their lives. We talk about 'Christian charity' and consent 'to the crucifixion of a race. Our Catholicism is an inferior paganism, without greatness in its philosophy or magnificence,' and 'our form of government should be called a continuation of the Conquest and Viceroyalty.' "

His writing influenced the cripple, José Carlos Mariátegui, who died at the age of thirty-five in 1930, the last year of Leguía's rule, and whose publications — especially *Siete Ensayos de Interpretación de la Realidad Peruana* (Seven Essays of Interpretation of Peruvian Reality) — in 1928 are by all odds the greatest, most penetrating economic and political studies ever to come out of Peru. Mariátegui was a giant in all Latin America — great for his clarity, power and vivid style. He was a Marxist, but without dogma. He did not use Marxism as a rigid yardstick, but as a springboard for creative interpretation of Peru's social and political forces. He saw the ruin of Peru, all the injustices, as due chiefly to land monopoly, *gamonalismo* (rule by the large latifundists), and to the Church and Army which represented perpetual political disaster: its blundering wars and the failure to utilize the available resources of land, people and geophysical potentialities.

Mariátegui delineated the conflict between the old feudalism, with its slaves (*yanacones*) of the Sierra, and the newer, commercialized, exporting haciendas of the coast and deep rich inner valleys, which were being rapidly absorbed by foreign corporations, using miserably paid day labor. He predicted the continued seizure and eventual extinction of Indian land communities (something now being carried out brutally on a big scale with the aid of troops and APRA hoodlums, the Búfalos). He also saw the hypocrisy and folly of isolated land settlement, the sort of reform now being pushed with U.S. money throughout Latin America. "Whereas the Indian Comunidad can still display some stubborn resistance to expanding monopoly, the small holder was and is helpless."

Such reform was tried in Leguía's day, while he and his cronies were stealing millions of acres. Reform of this sort was and is tolerated, sometimes welcomed by the latifundistas, for it represents no change in property structure, no menace to their power.

"It offers them," remarked Mariátegui, "the opportunity to sell properties little or poorly utilized and infertile at high prices." Such lands, paid for outright by the government and turned over to peasants on long-term payments, cannot provide even self-subsistence, let alone enough to keep up payments. Some regions have never known a money economy. "Invariably the large landowner takes back such land for almost nothing."

The "Indian problem" is really an agrarian problem. "The supposition that the indigenous problem is an ethnic problem is nourished by the most rancid repertory of imperialistic ideas . . . The degeneracy of the Peruvian Indian is a cheap invention of the petty lawyers of the feudal Round Table." Charitable help, education and other ameliorative devices have never helped the Indian. "He will reach his true stature only by his own mass organization and by putting an end to land monopoly."

Again Mariátegui refers to the petty plans of settlement in small holdings. "Such types of small holdings, regardless of present bitter exploitation, represent a step backward, not forward. It was and is an attempt to preserve existing injustices, not to solve the land problem."

Before me are the copious underlinings in the copy of his book that he dedicated to me "in homage," October 1, 1929. It is a temptation not to present his profound and animated views about education, the new student movement, the Church Problem, Regionalism and Centralism, and Literature — to name a few chapters.

6

In the realm of practical politics, the chief disciple of Gonzáles Prada, who later took over — and diluted — the ideas of Mariátegui, was the Trujillo student leader, Victor Haya de la Torre. He was twenty-four when Leguía seized power, and he and his followers soon faced army cudgels. He was forced into exile in 1920 and traveled for years in Mexico, the United States, Western Europe and Russia.

In 1924, in Mexico, Haya founded APRA (Alianza Popular Revolucionaria Americana). By the time he was able to return to Peru in 1930 he had whipped up a big following throughout the continent and in his own country especially.

Haya was a strong "anti-imperialist," who denounced Yankee financial penetration and wanted the Panama Canal internationalized. But he believed that no movement, openly labeled "Communist," could succeed because the United States would crush it — as it has tried to do in Cuba — and he himself was against the doctrine of the dictatorship of the proletariat.

His views brought him into conflict with the Communists. Julio Mella, the Cuban student leader exiled in Mexico (later assassinated there), wrote an impassioned pamphlet against Haya and his organization.

Haya was worried and asked me to moderate a face-to-face meeting with Mella. Both men were handsome. Mella was a young sun-god. Haya was stocky, with massive face and big nose. Both were supremely articulate and brilliant. Both knew all the literature on the subject.

If they found some common ground in their programs, there was no agreement whatsoever about tactics. Haya's approach was more eclectic: a compound of communism, democracy, the Mexican agrarian revolution and European socialism — pretty fuzzy, but his eloquence made everything sound logical. He favored nationalization of industry and land, the revindication of the rights of the Indians as equal citizens. He was anti-militarist, anti-Church and anti-imperialist.

He argued that the proletariat was small in all the countries, that anything labeled "Communist" would be struck down by the United States, that the countries were still too weak and undeveloped to be independent, but that a nationalist position could win backing from nearly all groups in society. He was essentially a politician and a compromiser.

Mella, Communist to the core, considered the class-struggle and the dictatorship of the proletariat as sacred as virgin birth. "Why lead the people out of one swamp to lead them into another?" he argued.

"We have enough enemies to fight, so why fight each other?" Haya finally said.

"Your kind are our worst enemies," retorted Mella, with true Communist intransigence. "The future must tell the story."

It did in part. Haya in due time went back on all his principles, until the day came when he was a favorite of the U.S. Embassy which had once considered him a dangerous Communist. But Mella can give us no record. Shortly after this meeting he was assassinated by agents of Dictator Machado of Cuba.

The interchanges grew in virulence. Haya's first lieutenant, Manuel Seone (vice-presidential candidate in 1962), came out with *Creole Communists*, charging that the parties in Latin America were made up of elite intellectuals remote from the masses, who merely used revolutionary doctrines and the party as stepping stones to good posts in the bureaucracies, then became turncoats. Many had done so, and many more were to do so. The supreme example, of course, is Rómulo Betancourt, President of Venezuela. But Haya and Seone found they did not have to be Communists to turn their coats inside out.

In spite of Communist opposition, Haya's movement took deep root in Peru, especially among middle-class elements, students and the intelligentsia. In a short time it was, though soon outlawed, the most powerful party in the country. A few unions were attracted.

Leguía at once began persecuting all Apristas, throwing them into jail or deporting them. Each persecution raised Haya's stature, and to his followers he became a demigod. But he was attacked more ferociously than ever by the Communists, also by landowners, by foreign capitalists and the press at home and in the United States. In Peru, he was bitterly assailed by *El Comercio*, mouthpiece of the Civilistas (who correspond to the

Científicos of Mexico, but are less intelligent). The movement continued to grow. Cells were organized in shops and business, labor unions, government offices and among younger army and navy officers.

The underground propaganda plus the Great Depression did Leguía in. His whole edifice of apparently impregnable power collapsed overnight. True democratic elements could not stomach his terrorism. Fanatic nationalists were infuriated by his 1929 compromise on Tacna and Arica, his pacific settlement of the Leticia controversy with Colombia, and his cowtowing to U.S. financial interests. Anti-clericals, readers of the great Peruvian writer long dead, Francisco Paula de Vigil, denounced his favors to the Church and his political appointments of members of the cloth.

The coup de grace was the sudden tumbling of prices for copper, oil, cotton, sugar. The Great Depression.

Revolt was led by the semi-barbarian caudillo, army officer Luís Sánchez Cerro, who lost three fingers when he seized the barrel of an enemy machine gun and turned it about to fire at government forces. Leguía, who tried to flee, was pursued out to sea, taken off a ship headed for England and imprisoned on an island off Callao, where he died in 1932. Haya returned to the country to talk to vast, cheering, handkerchief-waving crowds.

Elections were held in 1931. Haya was a candidate for the presidency. There is no doubt that the Apristas won overwhelmingly, but bayonets did the final counting. Sánchez Cerro announced himself elected.

Haya could have raised massive revolt and thrown the dictator out, but confident that he would win peacefully the next time, he refused to plunge the country into civil war. Nobility or cowardice, whichever it was, he lost his one golden opportunity. When a group of Apristas did revolt a few years later, they were easily crushed. When Haya ran again in 1962, his glamor had become badly tarnished.

Sánchez Cerro's terrorism made that of Leguía seem gentlemanly. All political activity, all debate, most newspapers were silenced. Thousands, including Haya de la Torre, were jailed, chained to the walls in the Panóptico, the big red fortress near downtown Lima. In Trujillo several thousand Apristas were mowed down. The country shuddered in stunned silence.

To quiet internal murmurs Sánchez repudiated Leguía's settlement with Colombia, raised the flag of "patriotism" and sent
troops to Leticia to seize the disputed territory by force. Mostly
silenced, many Apristas volunteered in order to get hold of arms.
Then, in April 1933, Sánchez Cerro was assassinated — undoubtedly by an Aprista.

General Manuel Oscar Benavides took over the presidency —
chiefly because he happened to be nearest the National Palace
at that moment. He was a massive, bull-necked creature with
a hoarse voice and a pompous manner.

He came to terms with Colombia and governed reasonably
well with good ministers from 1933-39: promoted public works,
encouraged education and sanitation, and set-up equitable labor
legislation. Haya and other Apristas were released. But their activities soon aroused Benavides' wrath. The low-priced cooperative restaurants they set up were considered conspiratorial centers. The party was outlawed by a regulation forbidding all "international parties."

However, Haya celebrated a secret conference with the dictator, promising the Apristas would not revolt provided elections were held, even though his party was outlawed. Theoretically Haya was still being hunted by the police, and even though
he slept in a different house every night, he went about openly
and waved pleasantly to policemen supposed to apprehend him.

But other prominent Apristas fled. The notable critic, Luis Alberto Sánchez, escaped to Chile where he became head of the
prominent publishing house of Ercilla. A newspaper man on the
suppressed Aprista daily, *La Tribuna*, Ciro Alegría, was hiding
out, starving and anxious to escape abroad. I translated several
articles for him and sold them to the *Christian Science Monitor*.
The payment was small, but the Peruvian *sol* was inflated, so it
was enough for him to make his way to Chile also. Later he wrote
the remarkable Farrar-Rinehart prize-winning novel, *Broad
and Alien is the World*. No novel in Spanish or English provides
a better, more poignant picture of life in Peru.

In the 1936 elections, Aprista backing elected an obscure candidate overwhelmingly. Benavides, as Sánchez Cerro had done, as
the army men did later in Venezuela and in Argentina in 1962
against the Peronistas, refused to recognize the outcome. He
stopped the ballot counting midway and had Congress name him

president for three years more without elections. Persecution of Apristas was stepped up, and Haya and many others were deported.

Humorously enough, the Communists, really an "international party," were not molested. They represented no immediate political threat, and the leaders received fat jobs under the dictatorship. It was a shortsighted effort to divide popular forces, but the Communists hated Haya more than the dictatorship. Even more humorously, the military, the rightists, American business men and the U.S. Embassy were still unable to distinguish between Aprismo and communism. Of the two they feared Haya's party worse, for it had a big mass following, and Haya had not yet begun currying favor at the Embassy.

In the new elections in 1939 Benavides' official candidate, Manuel Prado, son of an ex-President who had sold out during the nitrate war, a typical "Gente Bien" plantation aristocrat, made a pre-election pact with the Apristas, guaranteeing them full civil liberties. He was easily elected. Haya, with a free hand now to rally his followers, saw his way greased into the presidency. Ambition became more important than principles, and he began reneging on his entire program. The World War gave him his excuse. The Apristas should spend their energies fighting nazism, not bickering with enemies at home; they should stand shoulder to shoulder with the Big Brother to the North. He dropped his Panama Canal plank, his nationalization and agrarian planks; he put his pro-Indian program on ice, and made overtures to the Church, the Army, U.S. business and the U.S. Embassy. He helped settle strikes against the Cerro de Pasco corporation and pushed the granting of an oil concession to a U.S. company.

When I visited Peru in 1946, I had long talks with Haya. He had grown obese, less *simpático*. He now had a new grandiose dream, the beautification and rehabilitation of Lima, the capital. His desk was littered with blueprints and projection sketches. More vital things, it struck me, called for money and effort.

Though in 1945 Haya had not been a candidate, he could still rally 100,000 people to shout themselves hoarse. He backed José Luís Bustamante, a liberal, ineffective man, who agreed to give the Apristas a share in the cabinet.

For a time the Apristas really threw their weight around. The Búfalos, the APRA strong-arm gangs, smashed up opposition newspapers, through only yesterday they had stood for the fullest freedom of the press. They schemed to get full control of Bustamante's government.

But the assassination of the editor of a virulently anti-Aprista newspaper, *La Prensa,* (apparently it was a crime of passion) was believed to have been done by the Apristas; the scandal shook all Peru, leading Apristas were called in by the police investigators and held for days. Presently, an ill-planned, abortive revolt of some dissident Apristas and a few sailors and soldiers, who seized the Callao forts in October 1948, brought about the outlawing of the Apristas once more and paved the way for the seizure of power by General Manuel Odría.

Haya took refuge in the Colombian Embassy, where he had to remain until 1954. All leaders fled into exile again, for the new dictator was implacable. He had vowed to uproot the movement completely.

When Odría finally had to abandon his dictatorship ten years later because of illness and Manuel Prado was re-elected with hidden Apra support, Haya returned to reopen his daily paper, *La Tribuna,* and take up political intriguing where he had left off.

Today Haya pontificates incessantly, his moral bankruptcy is complete, but he can still move large sectors of public opinion.

Today he is the protégé of the U.S. Embassy and foreign investors; he himself has forgotten, except for lip-service, the needs of the Peruvian people, never more abused than under Prado's semi-terroristic government. The Aprista Búfalos, the armed thugs maintained by Haya, have even been hired out to plantation and corporation owners to break strikes or drive Indians out of their communal lands, with cries of "anti-communism."

According to *La Política* of Mexico (June 15, 1962), Haya "placed himself at the service of United States interests, with an excellent monthly salary for the work he did in organizing the so-called Congress of Freedom and Culture, set up by the Washington government, and which, to hide its real significance, maintains luxurious headquarters in Paris on Rue de la Peninière 23."

Numbers of APRA bigwigs have remained loyal because the party is still a road to bureaucratic preferment. Thus Luís Alberto Sánchez, the leading writer and intellectual of Aprismo, in May 1961 became Rector of San Marcos University. His duty is to suppress pro-Cuban and other students by Aprista strong-arm methods.

Such is the deplorably sad end of what promised to be a great movement of freedom for the Peruvian people. Today it is merely a faint echo of stunted New Dealism, serving to befuddle the people, to maintain the power of the military and big landowners, the Church and foreign corporations. And, of course, to befool visiting American liberal writers, who listen to Haya's golden eloquence and who hope they will get a nice juicy personal plum out of the new Alliance for Progress.

In 1962 Haya ran for president again. In spite of the declining strength of APRA, the confused political line-up seemed to make his victory possible. He brought in a Cuban, an exiled Batista man, to edit La Tribuna, and the country was overrun with anti-Castro Cubans campaigning for him. It was clear that he was the chosen C.I.A. candidate and was getting the support of U.S. money. He was known as "Our Boy."

In the elections there were seven candidates, including two out-and-out Leftists (Communists are outlawed), one Socialist and one ultra-clerical. None of these was expected to get many votes. The Catholic Party (Christian Democrat) candidate, Hector Conejo, was scarcely in the running. The avowed Left candidates, César Pando (The National Liberation Front), Alberto Ruiz (Social Progress Movement) and Luciano Castillo (Socialist Party), had little chance. Their meetings were broken up by police and soldiery. They got no space in the larger newspapers and no time on the radio and other news outlets "mostly controlled," according to La Prensa, "by American companies."

The two serious contenders were Fernando Belaunde Terry (Popular Action Party) and Manuel Odría, the former dictator, representing the ultra-conservative forces.

Rightist Fernando Belaunde, a brilliant intellectual and writer, had been barnstorming throughout the country to the remotest village in the Andes for several years, had made many promises and had become very popular. His leading backers had me to dinner one April night in 1961 and tried until three in the morning to convince me that Belaunde was the right man to be made president. They talked eloquently of his organization, techniques and personality. I kept coming back to his program. What did he stand for? The answers were flimsy, and when I kept on insisting, one broke out angrily, saying, "You can't expect him to give away his hand at this stage. Did Castro tell his program when he was in the mountains of Oriente?"

The comparison startled me. But this was not a civil war. It was presumably an election, or going to be one. Perhaps there was something mysterious behind the cautious Belaunde front. During the campaign he did announce that if elected he would recognize Castro's government, later took it back.

But would it be an election? Seventy-five percent of the people, for literacy or property reasons, are not allowed to vote. Elections are therefore a hypocritical game indulged in by the elite, the politicians, the Army and a few of the urban proletariat.

Obviously the whole election was a farce. Even before the voting day, *El Comercio*, one of the most conservative dailies in all South America, had said, "The campaign has not been honest or clean. . . . There are pernicious plans afoot to distort the electoral results by means of a gross mechanism of fraud on the part of APRA and with the complicity of the authorities and the electoral officials."

Furthermore, even before the voting, the head of the Navy, the Chief of General Staff, and the Commandant in Lima jointly announced they would seize power "if there should be a leftist triumph." For them, of course, Haya is still a leftist not to be trusted. They prefer Belaunde or even Odría. Odría threatened also to seize power by force if the elections were rigged.

In the count, Belaunde began forging ahead, Odría was in third place. But the vote from the chief province controlled by APRA, La Libertad, was withheld until the last, and when it came through, it was solidly for Haya, putting him slightly in the lead, but by a mere 14,000 votes. Since he did not have a third of the total vote, the election would have to be thrown into Congress. There the Apristas and the government had a majority, and the Apristas still exulted — even though in view of general disenfranchisement, Haya had a bare 7 1/2 percent of the potential votes of the population.

The crowing by the Apristas was premature. The Army alleged that Aprista frauds were committed in ten of the twenty-two electoral departments. It alleged that the U.S. ambassador had grossly meddled in the elections on behalf of Haya.

A week before Prado's term was to expire, the Junta, led by

General Juan Pérez Godoy, took over the rule of the country. They announced that honest elections would be held within one year, that no member of the Junta would be a candidate. After a few days civil rights were restored, all parties allowed to function. A long-standing telephone strike was amicably settled. (By December 1962, all leftists and some rightist groups were practically outlawed, hundreds of arrests made in the dead of night.)

The Apristas, controlling the general confederation of labor, called a general strike. It fizzled out before it started. Pérez called in the leaders, listened to their grievances, promised to meet all just demands. He agreed to inaugurate public works to take up the unemployment slack, announced he would wipe out the slums of Lima.

Mr. Kennedy, after consulting with Ambassador Loeb, refused to recognize the new regime, though this violated the provisions of the Bogotá agreements, and cut off all aid.

General Pérez remarked mildly, "At least we would see that it reaches the people, which thus far has not happened."

We had not hesitated to recognize the corrupt and shameless military regime in Argentina, finding an excuse in the fact that it wore a tiny fig leaf of "constitutionality." In addition, its economic affairs were controlled by Alvaro Alsogaray, who secretly, behind the back of Congress, had *unconstitutionally* given away the oil rights of the country to U.S. corporations and was every inch our "yes-man."

Was it because we wanted to pry something out of Peru and saw this means of doing it? The grapevine says that the Pentagon had been having some trouble getting secret military and atomic bases.

In the *New York Times* (July 12, 1962), its able correspondent Tad Szulc remarked about President Kennedy's attempts to run the internal affairs of Peru: The U.S. had cast itself in "the role of tough policeman of Latin American democracy . . . the most significant turn in the hemisphere policy since the nice plum of the Alliance for Progress sixteen months ago." The skeptic might ask, "What democracy?" He might ask, "What new policy?"

Then, in mid-August, he recognized the Pérez military crowd and resumed aid. It remains to be seen whether Pérez granted what was secretly demanded or whether the previous corruption and waste in our aid to Peru comes to an end. In any case none of all this has much to do with democracy or the needs and welfare of the Peruvian people.

7

Ecuador, a Church-ridden country with the lowest standard of living in South America, an annual per capita income of less than $80.00 (much less for the bulk of the population), is dependent upon low-priced exports and high-priced imports. When the bottom dropped out of bananas, sugar, coffee, rice, cacao, the bottom dropped out of government also. From 1930-44, the country had fourteen different presidents — most imposed by force.

The trouble had begun ten years earlier when the United States had sent in a so-called austerity and financial mission, and its efforts had balanced the budget but had wrecked Ecuadorean economy. Ten years of disorder followed; by 1930 no economic resilience was left, only worse disorders.

Colombia, still smarting from the 1903 seizure of Panama, had sunk into dictatorship, defeatism and misery, though it was one of the richest lands of the continent, with resources matched by few. Bitterness toward the United States was great, is still great. Secretary of State William Jennings Bryan's olive-branch of a belated $25,000,000 conscience money payment partially straightened out relations. But this was still considerably less than the $40,000,000 we paid for the worthless franchise of the defunct French Company merely for canal rights, and on top of that Panama was lost. The word "Panama" has since become a common Spanish synonym for "steal." (Bigwigs in U.S. politics and business got windfalls.) Actually the U.S. taxpayer's money was merely a bribe to obtain oil concessions — millions of acres. The secret papers were all ready for signing when the money was finally voted by the U.S. Congress.

Considerable U.S. money began coming in from Standard Oil, Royal Dutch, United Fruit, City Service Company, gold and platinum mining concerns, a meat packing company. The shady Samuel Insull interests also spread tentacles over the land, getting hold of public utilities. In a short time U.S. holdings jumped from a few millions to $100,000,000, and many Colombian bonds of dubious worth were peddled to U.S investors. Naturally this sudden influx (being repeated now on a bigger scale in

the sixties) brought the usual fever-flush of apparent prosperity — little islands of gold began shining in a leaden feudal
economy, without much benefit for most Colombians.

The country's greatest native enterprise was coffee-growing;
by 1920 it supplied a fourth of the world's finest mild coffee. But
in 1929 the price dropped down around the shoes. A major disaster. In the economic confusion, the Conservative Party split,
and the Liberals, the more progressive wing of the oligarchy,
peacefully took over in 1930.

President Olaya Herrera managed to fill out his term, then an
authentic New Dealer, President Alfonso López (1934-38), lib-
eralized the 1886 constitution, established rights of eminent domain and guaranteed Labor "the full protection of the State."

In Venezuela, aged and bloody Vicente Gómez, friend of foreign oil companies, managed to hang on as tyrant until his death
in 1935. It was discovered he had looted $100,000,000 — still in
the country, and how much more deposited from abroad? — for
which more than a hundred offspring, legitimate and illegiti-
mate, clamored for a share. At his death jubilant demonstrators
filled the streets of Caracas; some fell before police bullets, and
one wrote "Freedom" with his own blood on the sidewalk.

Order was re-established. The people were too cowed and
beaten down to stage renovation. But as war approached, the
country floated on a sea of black-oil prosperity — at least prosperity for the elite. Though the overall income is the highest in
all Latin America, the Venezuelan people were, and are, close
to being the most underpaid and miserable of all Latin America.

Panama, after some disturbances, turned to a more liberal
course when hit by the Depression. President Harmodio Arias,
one of the few patriotic executives the country has ever had,
wangled considerable increase in canal payments, won other
concessions, worked on plans to develop the interior, worked
for the recovery of the property of Colón, the second-largest city,
mostly owned, outside the Zone, by the U.S. government; gained
concessions for Panama employment and better wages on the
Canal Zone and against the Gold-Silver system — nice names for
wage and racial discrimination exercised against Panamanians
and Negroes.

6 ◯ THE DEPRESSION YEARS: MEXICO AND MIDDLE AMERICA

1

Ever since 1889 Costa Rica had been peaceful, with normal elections, and it had more teachers than soldiers. It was considered a model for possible orderly prosperous existence in Central American countries. Partly, this may have been due to the fact that, except for the vast United Fruit Company holdings, rural property was relatively fairly distributed. The only interruption in this placidity came in 1917 when Federico Tinoco seized the Presidency, throttled the press and took repressive measures.

At bottom it was a feud between the United Fruit Company and a U.S. oil company. The feud brought machine guns into the Chamber of Deputies, sent congressmen ducking under their chairs and even under their beds at home from hails of bullets. The companies were bidding high against each other for votes, and whichever side a congressman chose or didn't choose, he was likely to be shot up by some gang of paid thugs. But no oil

was found and, after two years, democratic processes reassert-
ed themselves: Tinoco had to get out.

Costa Rica, chiefly an exporter of coffee and bananas, was
subsequently hard hit by the Great Depression, but an attempted
reactionary coup in 1932 was easily suppressed, and the civilian
and constitutional tradition was maintained.

The Great Depression saw the withdrawal of U.S. forces from
Nicaragua. The justifiably prolonged revolt by Sandino seemed
to have won its objectives. Within a month after the last Marine
pulled out, he laid down his arms, trading them for land on the
Cocos River, seed and implements and school houses.

U.S. withdrawal left an unstable situation, for the Moncada-
Sacasa governments, branded as "yes-man" governments for the
United States, had no internal prestige. The intervention had
been hailed by the usual obedient newspaper praise as having
taught the Nicaraguans democracy. It had created a non-par-
tisan National Guard (paid semanticists claimed this was not an
army) to uphold that democracy. Actually no basis had been
laid. No schools had been erected, few promised roads had been
built, health measures had not gone far beyond areas held by
U.S. troops; the people were illiterate, unemployed, starved.
But the budget had been balanced, debts had been paid — while
economic stagnation made prospects bleak.

What prosperity existed before the Great Depression, paradox-
ically, was largely due to the spending for army food and supplies of the invading five thousand U.S. troops and officers. Thus
troop withdrawal, however necessary, was a further blow. It
came at a time of coffee collapse, the drying up of the market
for lumber abroad, decrease in banana shipments.

No alien rule is ever just. Beside the economic consequences
of withdrawal, a power vacuum was left. It could not be filled
by democratic organizations, which had not been allowed to exist. It could be filled only by the National Guard we had trained,
pledged never to interfere with politics. But the Guardia had
to intervene. The country was left wholly at the mercy of the
Guardia and the man we had installed to run it — General Anastasio Somoza.

One of his first black deeds, before taking over the government, was the assassination of Sandino and his young brother.
Sandino had come to Managua as the guest of President Sacasa
to talk over the problems of demobilization.

But President Sacasa did not have the courage to punish the murderers, who went about the city proudly displaying the personal property and ears of the victims.

Somoza soon took over and instituted one of the cruelest and greediest despotisms known in the Americas. He seized no U.S. property, instead ambassadors and officials became his business associates. Repeatedly he obtained moneys and investments from the United States. But he seized all native property of any importance, the finest haciendas in the land, took over businesses and set up personal monopolies.

Had such methods been carried on to benefit the people, he would have been branded "Communist," and the Marines would have gone back in. But since it was solely to maintain the Somoza clique and friends in luxury and power, he was glorified in the U.S. mass magazines. Paid publicity agents took care of his relations with the free press. He rode high and handsome for twenty-five years, until an assassin's bullet struck him down.

His son Luis (backed by his brother who was head of the National Guard) took over power. After faking a war-like expedition against Honduras and jailing or driving out all opponents, chiefly by means of a trumped-up trial of alleged assassins of Anastasio, he held a "democratic" election. The Somoza dynasty still rules Nicaragua.

2

Honduras, a beautiful country — jungles, fine valleys, magnificent mountains and lakes — is largely a fief of the United Fruit Company, which long had a bigger local income than the national government, and numbers of United Fruit lawyers have been president. All during this century, even before the Great Depression, Honduras was turbulent except for the six-year rule of able President Francisco Bertrand. Early in the thirties, General Tiburcio Carías Andino seized power, but was balked by temporary U.S. intervention. A battleship conference off Armapala imposed a puppet president, General Vicente Tosta — who had neither the ability or strength to run the country — in the false name of "legality," and in 1933, with U.S. prestige, interference and influence waning in the area, Carías boldly took over and held power until 1948.

In 1946, for the third time, I revisited Tegucigalpa, the capital, at that moment under martial law; heavy military patrols, jailings, tortures, violence. Carías was a gigantic man weighing well over 200 pounds, all hard bone and muscle, who sat rigid and erect, his powerful hands on his spread knees, and answered me with heavy grunts. Glib explanations were given me by his leading minister, Carlos Izaguirre — who had just published an enormous two-volume novel, *Bajo el Chubazo (Under the Drizzle)*, of considerable merit.

Much relieved when the talk was over, the dictator amiably took me to the third floor of the Palace to show me his canaries.

The tiled corridor beside the patio balustrade was filled with canary cages, and the dictator's eyes filled with gentle love. He cared for those canaries with his own hands, grieved like a doting mother when they were sick or died. He had fought in civil wars for a quarter of a century, had killed hundreds, perhaps thousands of men — and enjoyed killing men — but he cooed like a child over his sweet canaries. The applicable psychiatric terms are well known.

Salvador, the smallest and most densely populated country on the American mainland, is a volcanic land. Earthquakes occur almost daily, and every year or so railroad tracks have to be moved out of the way of lava flows.

Its indigenous inhabitants are mostly Pipiles (Nahuatl), cousins of the Aztecs who invaded and settled here as early as the twelfth century. Today it is a mestizo country, but dominated by a few Conquest families, the "Koffee Kings." Germans bought land and by World War I had enough influence to keep Salvador neutral, whereupon, quite illegally and ruthlessly, the United States blockaded the country.

In 1913 a leading coffee family seized control and ruled, not too badly, for the next seventeen years. When the Great Depression broke in 1930, the coffee market went up in smoke, and the government was taken over by brutal General Maximiliano Hernández Martínez, who made his decisions in consultation with occult powers and had all street-lights painted blue to cure an epidemic. He slaughtered six thousand protesting peasants, calling them "Communists."

In 1960 a military junta took over. It favored Cuba, the United

States refused to give aid, and it was soon replaced with another junta, which deported, jailed and killed students, professors, leading citizens. It broke with Cuba, lauded the Alliance for Progress, and got prompt help from the Inter-American bank and the United States.

Early in 1962 its head, Colonel Julio Adalberto Rivera, ran for president as candidate of a party of his own devising. No other parties, Right or Left, would put up candidates. Even so he toured the country assiduously, using army helicopters, and received the unanimous vote of the few who did vote. His methods have paralleled those of Batista, and he has the generous aid of U.S. agents and money.

Guatemala is one of the loveliest lands on earth — slim, tall mountains, jungle coasts, great rivers, handsome lakes. I once called it "a four-leaf clover." It is divided into four main regions: Los Altos, the northern, salubrious highland region populated by Quiché Indians (90 percent of the country's entire population is Indian), the lower coffee country, the coastal jungles and hot country devoted to sugar and bananas, and the Central African type of region, the northeastern Petén, with almost impenetrable jungles. The Caribbean shore has mostly Negroes, imported from Jamaica for the banana industry. The stem of the clover is high Guatemala City, with its dream of a spring climate. Guatemala's worst blights have been earthquakes (which have destroyed three capitals), malaria, the United Fruit Company and dictatorships.

Throughout most of its independent history, it has been ruled by long-term dictatorships, with savage disorderly interludes. From the time of independence from the Central American Confederation (set up when the Spaniards were driven out), it was lorded over more or less continuously for a quarter of a century by Rafael Carrera, an illiterate, cruel Indian of talents. American Consul John Lloyd Stevens, one of the great chroniclers of the region, described him in 1839 as "five-foot six inches in height, with straight black hair, an Indian complexion without beard, who did not seem to be more than twenty-one . . ."

He was followed, after disorders from 1865-71, by Justo Rufino Barrios, who ruled for fourteen years. One of the better Liberal leaders of Central America, who did much good (and evil) for Guatemala, he was consumed, and eventually destroyed, by his ambition to recreate the Central American Federation by force.

A rabid anti-clerical, he attacked the Church, deported the Jesuits, the archbishop and bishops, suppressed convents and monasteries, forbade priests to wear clerical garb on the streets or teach in schools or hold religious processions. Civil marriage was made obligatory. He broke the Church's political power, though it is now being restored by U.S. money and the present dictator Ydígoras.

Power was taken over in 1898 by one of the cruelest, most corrupt dictators, Manuel Estrada Cabrera — much adulated in the United States — who laid the cornerstones of United Fruit power in the country, which in turn was influential in bringing in the Rockefeller Foundation to clean up the worst in sanitary conditions.

Estrada stole most of the property and resources and moneys of the country, but was driven out in 1920 by an enraged people when he pocketed funds sent from all over the world for relief from the terrible earthquake that destroyed half the capital and killed so many people.

When the Great Depression hit the country, after some disorders, power was seized in 1931 (until 1944) by Jorge Ubico, a ruthless dictator highly favored by the United Fruit Company, Washington, and the U.S. press as a great progressive leader. He put up a front of impeccable honesty, punished government servants (whom he did not like) when they were caught stealing. He carried out — with U.S. aid — public works and built a few roads.

United Fruit received new concessions and cemented their monopoly control on all ports.

3

Mexico weathered the Great Depression better than most Latin American countries, chiefly because of its agrarian reform, its incipient native industrialization, and its wider economic base, which made it less dependent on exports of low-priced raw materials to the shrinking market of the United States. Except for the revolt of General Saturnino Cedillo, the "last of the revolutionary caudillos," who had been driving the peasants off their new lands, Mexico suffered few Depression disorders and

Cedillo's revolt was quickly suppressed. The country forged ahead. The trend was back to basic revolutionary principles.

Lázaro Cárdenas (1934-40), the greatest of all the leaders, carried the revolutionary process ahead, completed much of Obregón's Revindicating Revolution. Taking up again where the Calles-Morrow agreements had stopped economic evolution in its tracks, he distributed more land than all prior revolutionary regimes combined.

Even the Church grudgingly admired him, for though he enforced the religious laws, he stopped all flagrant attacks on them and their churches. Abruptly he dismissed his Minister of Agriculture, Tomás Garrido, ex-Governor of Tabasco, when the latter's Red Shirts manhandled Sunday worshippers in the suburbs of Coyocán.

When the oil companies refused to abide by a labor board decree and shut down operations, Cárdenas expropriated their lands, wells and business offices and started a new era of economic independence. The National Labor Board had found that, beginning with 1924, real wages had decreased 23 percent while profits, in spite of depression, had increased 17.82 percent.

The oil companies wielded much pressure and spread adverse propaganda, blocked shipments of oil equipment and replacements, refused to ship or buy Mexican government oil. But Cárdenas hired free-lance tankers and got the oil out — to Japan, Germany, Europe. He was criticized sharply for dealing with the totalitarian powers (though our policies made it inevitable); but F.D.R.'s New Deal was not disposed to quarrel with him, and he won the play.

March 18, the day of the oil expropriation, is still celebrated in lavish official and popular ceremonies as "The Declaration of Mexican Economic Independence."

Money was always lacking, and though graft and dishonesty were checked better than under any previous regimes, many officials and outside speculators dug their fingers into the till. Sadly enough, one of the worst was Cárdenas' own brother, who became a millionaire.

But even Cárdenas' enemies came to praise his honesty and integrity. All Cárdenas' measures were directed toward improving the lot of the peasants and workers, ergo he was savagely denounced by the U.S. press.

When ex-President Calles could not stomach the new reforms and stirred up trouble, Cárdenas sent a messenger to Calles' estate near Mexico (acquired by shady methods) to inform him he was traveling to the United States immediately. Calles' only baggage as he mounted the plane was a copy of Hitler's *Mein Kampf.* He was chuckled into oblivion.

One of Lázaro's first acts was to allow every citizen to send a telegram free over the nationally-owned telegraph lines setting forth any grievances or proposals; if the proposals were good, he promised they would be carried out; if the grievances were valid, they would be rectified.

Cárdenas traveled the country constantly, even to remote villages, set up his offices at a table in the central plaza and received delegations of farmers, miners, factory workers all day, sometimes all night. A school? The orders were given. A teacher? He appointed one at once. A doctor? They got a doctor. A water-system? The engineer set out from Mexico City within hours. Nor did he ignore personal sufferings: a new leg for a revolutionary veteran, hospital care in the nearest city. A boundary dispute? He called in the opposite party and secured a signed amicable agreement then and there. He stands as the greatest figure in the Mexico of our century.

4

The lifting of the nightmare of the twenty-year U.S. military occupation of the Dominican Republic and of Haiti, the end of alien terrorism and money-draining, created great hope there and all over Latin America (a hope that now seems ridiculous) that the era of U.S. imperialism, armed aggression and dollar diplomacy had come to an end, that henceforth the good-neighbor policy was to rule.

It was premature. Under Truman, economic penetration increased. Political coercion increased, got worse under Eisenhower. Ahead lay the invasion of Guatemala. Ahead lay the 1961 invasion of Cuba. There was the flourishing of military power over Panama in March 1959 at the time of the silly rowboat invasion. Military missions were planted in nearly all countries; secret bases were secured. In late 1960 battleships were rushed to shore up the endangered Nicaraguan and Guatemalan dictatorships. Battleships were rushed in 1961 to back up secret diplomatic pressure to see that the right kind of government was installed in the Dominican Republic and that the power structure of Trujilloism remained intact.

In 1934 after a bayonet election in Haiti, labeled democratic, in which the people and even high officials were loath to participate, we withdrew from the Black Republic, leaving some excessively costly public works and roads built by the long-abandoned corvee or forced labor system on a more brutal and illegal basis than in old days.

In 1914 the United States sent the gunboat *Machuas* to Haiti, landed sailors, seized $500,000 in gold from the National Bank of Haiti and carted it to the National City Bank of New York. In July and August the following year, Marines were landed, and the Haitians' Congress named as president General Philippe Sudre D'Artiguenave, an elite, near-white mulatto of the most hated exploiting group, after he had given assurances, according to Admiral Caperton, that he was favorably disposed to all U.S. demands. In August the Marines began seizing all customs houses and their funds. A treaty ratifying U.S. political and financial control was forced through Congress by bayonets, withholding salaries and other threats.

In 1917, a constitution made in Washington was sent down for ratification. When Congress refused to adopt it, that august body was booted out in the traditional way of all Latin American dictators (made even less palatable when done by outside invaders).

The chief new constitutional stipulation, violating a hundred years of constitutional life on the island, was to permit white foreigners to own land. This, according to the U.S. Senate McCormick Hearings, was chiefly at the behest of two U.S. corporations, one supplying the U.S. Navy with castor oil, the other wishing to grab sugar lands. When Congress refused to act, a referendum on foreign ownership of land was presented to the voters who were told that abstention would be "an unpatriotic act against U.S. occupation." As the voters filed in past the Marines they were handed a white slip saying "Oui." The "Non" voting slips were not even untied. There were, all told, only 300 votes against the measure on the entire island. These, the Haitians deemed, were cast by the Marines themselves, to give the results a better appearance.

All these good deeds had caused a blind revolt in which the

Marines ruthlessly slaughtered 2,000 men, women and children — according to General George Barrett's report, 2250 by June 30, 1920. The chief leader of that revolt, labeled a "Caco bandit," was assassinated in the most obscene manner by a Marine.

The first serious protest about Marine brutalities was made directly to the State Department by a U.S. missionary, L. Tom Evans. When he got back to Haiti he was arrested, all his papers seized, and held incommunicado in a narrow cell for thirteen days. He was taken by a navy officer before a Negro judge who was terrorized into convicting him for rebellion and attempted escape. This, however, was reversed by a higher court. Presently, H. Upschitz, a naturalized U.S. citizen, who made charges against the Marines, was deported and when he returned was murdered.

The McCormick Senate Hearings disclosed that under martial law and harsh censorship the story was a dreary one of Marine drunkenness, disorders, rape, theft, and wanton, indiscriminate killings, of prison tortures, beatings and burnings with hot irons. The editor of the *Courier Haitian* was fined $300 and sentenced to hard labor for eighteen months for printing an article about a Haitian police beating.

The U.S. officers and men introduced race bigotry and segregation. Even upper-class Haitians were excluded from customary cafes, restaurants and hotels.

After much brutality, the occupation officials arranged for Puppet President Number Two, another elite mulatto, the odious Louis Borno, who was inaugurated May 15, 1922. In 1930 Borno was induced to resign and turn the office over to Stenio Vincent, a third elite mulatto, who would presumably hold free elections.

Though we withdrew in 1934, a financial mission practically ruled the land until 1941 when all foreign obligations had been liquidated. No money was left for education during the occupation or for years after.

Vincent, who stayed on without election until 1936, continued some of the worst Marine abuses, suppressed the press, jailed editors, writers and others, including the leading poet, Jacques Romain. The people sank into worse economic misery than before our original invasion. It was only a matter of time until the 3,000-man Guarde d'Haiti, which we had set up, would take over the reins of power. Today, under illegal president François Duvalier, Haiti probably has a worse dictatorship and more misery than at any time since the Marines left. The government has been financed and kept in power by U.S. aid and the Pentagon. In 1962 monetary aid was suddenly held up when Duvalier refused to discharge a number of alleged Communists.

In the Dominican Republic the story is paralleled, except that the U.S. Navy, when it took over, governed directly, without setting up a puppet government. Official orders read: "Military Occupation," "Military Government," "Military Law." The occupation carried on ruthless fighting, jailed or killed the outstanding intellectuals, writers and artists, closed down newspapers, roughed up honorable citizens, perpetrated wanton killings in the main streets. A Spanish priest, as Melvin Knight mentions in his admirable *The Americans in Santo Domingo,* spent five months in the infamous calaboose of Samaná for praising the efficiency of the German Army in a table conversation — this long before the United States entered the war.

The U.S. Senate Committee Hearings of 1921-22 are crammed with a sickening accumulation of the most incredible and horrifying brutalities, perpetrated by a country that was preparing to fight the Kaiser to make the world safe for democracy.

But the sentencing by a military court of the leading poet, Fabio Fiallo, to three years of imprisonment for criticizing the occupation, gave the United States a black eye everywhere in the world. A flame of protest swept over Latin America.

Finally the Great Depression, plus the New Deal, brought withdrawal of U.S. forces.

The inevitable happened. The man we had installed, who came to head our newly created National Guard, Rafael Leonidas Trujillo, an ex-cattle-thief, post-office hi-jacker, assassin, took over and ruled with murder and torture and theft. He, his family and a few cronies grabbed all the best land, moved in on all business and trade and set up monopolies of every consumer product from salt to girls in the white slave trade. Many were imported from Europe and provided with diplomatic passports to prevent police molestation, and shipped to every New World country. A pimp rose to the head of this activity; he married high, became a diplomat and world figure.

Trujillo's bloody hand reached out to foreign lands. At least three leading exiles, two of them my friends, were assassinated in New York. The police there were never able to solve these crimes but, at the behest of the Dominican consulate, were ever ready to arrest and persecute Dominican exiles on every possible occasion. Other leaders were murdered in Cuba and Mexico.

The kidnapping of Columbia University professor Dr. Jesús de Galíndez from New York, the subsequent murder of a U.S. pilot on the island, and the disappearance, "suicide" or murder of prominent Trujillo police and army officers followed in an effort to cover up. American and Dominican witnesses mysteriously vanished or died. The case has never been cleared up. The last indictments made by a grand jury have been quietly quashed. It is said that very high officials were indirectly involved, that it would mean public disclosures of F.B.I. and C.I.A. activities on behalf of the dictator.

The names of some of those patriots, though some were long ago killed by Trujillo, are still on the State Department's Black List — and are not allowed to go back to the Dominican Republic on any U.S. plane or vessel from any part of the world, a ban clapped on after Trujillo was assassinated. Many patriotic Dominicans are still forbidden to go home lest they prove troublesome to the present "gunboat" government.

Trujillo's worst crime was to slaughter, on October 2, 1937, some 10,000 Haitians. Some of these had been brought into the country in violation of Dominican laws by the U.S. occupation, in behalf of newly acquired U.S. sugar plantations. Others were squatters in the western wilderness, who had tried to escape the terrors of U.S. occupation in Haiti. Others were occupants of a strip of territory along the borderland, in an area given to the Dominican Republic by a U.S. settlement of the disputed line. The bodies of these Haitians were piled mountain high and destroyed with gasoline, in the style of Ignatius Donnelly's picture in *Caesar's Column*, or taken down to the sea in army trucks, dripping with blood, to be fed to the sharks. *Trujillo directed this wholesale murder in person!*

This horror was kept out of the U.S. press; can one doubt that it was other than by official orders? I tried to tell the story, but no periodical was willing to print it. I was "biased." It was "exaggerated." But these Haitians were Haitians, and the Haitian government, despite its dependence on Washington, wanted recompense. These Haitians were Catholics and Christians, and the Haitian hierarchy was disturbed.

Not until Trujillo got uppish, refusing Washington's pressure to make some amends, was the full story finally leaked. It appeared in the *New York Tribune,* with big headlines, on November 10, 1937, almost as though it had happened the day before. Then there was a scamper by the other papers and magazines to make up for lost time. My own article was then published by *Current History.*

In the end, of course, Trujillo was merely slapped on the wrist, obliged to pay $750,000 to the Haitian government — and we provided much of the money to pay it. We established the great moral principle that the life of a Haitian is worth $7.50. All the Haitians could do was mutter in their beards and be happy they received anything. Those murdered by our Marines were not worth even that much.

And so, Trujillo's government was blessed and tucked back under our protective wing until the day in 1961 when he was assassinated. Trujillo blithely strutted behind a velvet curtain of adulation — provided by American ambassadors and Madison Avenue publicity firms. Even U.S. Senators were on his payroll. Former Senator Hamilton Fish received $50,000 which he explained to the income tax people was for business operations, not income. Franklin Roosevelt was in his hire. Even a one-time socialist lawyer and promoter of civil liberties, Morris Ernst, was hired to make an "objective" cover-up of the kidnapping of Dr. Galíndez.

One close associate, decorated by Trujillo, was De Lesseps Morrison, former mayor of New Orleans, who now serves as Kennedy's representative on the council of the Organization of American States. He has been responsible in good part for punitive measures and for the Punta del Este deal against Cuba.

5

After the Great Depression broke, Cuba briefly took the road of new freedom.

That island — owned lock, stock and barrel by U.S. corporations, with a starving population 50 percent unemployed — was under the heel of the cruel ten-year dictatorship of Gerardo

Machado. He had been president of a U.S. utility subsidiary, and the parent company had put up half a million to get him named president.

It was a time of disaster. Depression had begun there ten years earlier than in the United States — after the so-called post-war Dance of the Millions, when sugar finally had plummeted to near worthlessness. Cubans were literally starving. During "the dead season," after the *zafra* had been harvested, at night, in Havana — as in every other city on the island — in all the arcades around the central plazas, along the Prado and the Malecón, slept heaps of starving, ragged people, men, women and children. Prostitutes in swarms, many naked, unable to afford a decent dress, stepped over these poor folk, opening their coats to show their wares to any passing male. That was Cuba, under Machado, under U.S. ownership, under U.S. tutelage.

Naturally terror ruled the island — shootings, dynamitings, death, murders, torture and prison — just as in the final years of Batista's more recent rule.

Gradually some of these horrors leaked out. They could not be forever hidden. Gradually Machado, as later Batista, became too much of a liability, became expendable — especially after F.D.R. announced the Good Neighbor Policy, a New Deal for Latin America also.

Ambassador Sumner Welles was sent down to kick Machado out. As is customary in such undercover jobs, Welles went to the Army behind the Dictator's back (just as Ambassador Smith consulted with army leaders behind Batista's back a quarter of a century later). Machado was done.

The stage was set. The dictator hurried to a plane per schedule; the provisional government, named by Welles, was installed. It was headed by De Cespedes, an honorable man, unrelated to organized students, the professors, the workers, not even the middle class, but willing to oblige.

The last thing Machado did, before entering his plane, was to phone the head of the utility corporation that had befriended him: "I am going now. Watch out for your properties."

The mobs roamed Havana streets; they looted and burned the homes of the Machado cabinet ministers. But the city soon settled down, as the new puppet provisional government took over the Machado police and army apparatus; this was part of the deal.

But the island was honeycombed with the secret revolutionary A.B.C. terrorists, a middle-class group headed by Martínez Saenz, an employee of the National City bank. Like the Italian strong-arm middle-class Fasci, it was against Labor and against speculators, but had less nationalistic flavor and no patriotic pride. It was organized into independent seven-man cells, so the police were unable to crack its secrets. One prominent A.B.C. member was the leading writer, Jorge Mañach.

The A.B.C. head in the Army was court-stenographer Sergeant Fulgencio Batista, an orphan educated by Protestant missionaries, a cane-cutter, a day-laborer, a railroad worker who had fought his way up against great odds. He was a short mestizo type with an engaging personality. Probably he had some Negro blood and blood of the Mayas, who were brought over in the late colonial period from Yucatán to work as slaves on the sugar plantations.

There occurred, one night in September 1933, what has become known as the "Shower-bath Revolt." Batista assembled the non-coms at Camp Colombia to petition for better housing, club-facilities, shower-baths. Word came that all the petitioners were to be arrested in the morning. Batista gathered his clans, entered the fine officers' homes and seized all the officers in the camp.

Not until then was he aware he had overthrown a government. Hurriedly he sent out a call to Dr. Grau San Martín, a National University professor, who headed the revolutionary student and faculty organization fighting the dictatorship, and a government was set up consisting of students, professors and A.B.C. elements. To win more public confidence in the new government, especially from the United States, a conservative banker was routed out of his bed in the dead of night. He refused point-blank to serve, but was dragged from his couch, amid the screams of his wife, and taken to Camp Colombia. He served a few days, then resigned.

Ambassador Sumner Welles was livid that his well-laid schemes were smashed. He refused recognition to new provisional President Grau San Martín, and thirty U.S. battleships were rushed to Cuban waters — perhaps as an expression of the Good-Neighbor policy. All through the Grau administration a cruiser remained in Havana harbor with its naked guns pointing up O'Reilly Street.

Welles stubbornly opposed every reform and tried to protect the officers when Batista released them. They holed up under his wing in the National Hotel, issued anti-government proclamations, conspired, until Batista boldly turned his artillery on the lofty edifice.

Welles fought such things as Grau's mild minimum wage, $1.00 a day, new labor legislation, the efforts of brilliant Antonio Guiteras to institute land reform.

Peasants began occupying estates. In several instances U.S. managers were put under house arrest. Welles was especially wrathful about a light company strike and Grau's decrees reducing light rates, at that time the highest in the world.

At the Embassy, when asked about this, his neck muscles grew more rigid than usual, and the blood mounted into his wooden face. He told me sternly that those rates had been set during the first U. S. occupation — thirty years earlier — that Cuba had agreed to recognize all arrangements made under that military occupation and, unless permitted by the U.S. government, could make no changes in the rates.

He had been a little helper of the First National City Bank of New York when he had served during the Dominican military occupation. He was now also looking after the proper people. Later, rate reduction actually benefited the light and power company by stimulating wider consumption.

Batista was Welles' bête noire. The Ambassador was determined to overthrow the Grau government. He inaugurated what is known in Cuba as "the era of garage diplomacy," meeting clandestinely in garages, tennis courts and such places with the heads of the secret A.B.C. terrorist group. He was in love with the whole A.B.C. personnel, and wished to have them set up a coalition government with Carlos Mendieta as president. Mendieta was head of a dissident wing of deposed dictator Machado's Liberal Party, an inept stuffed shirt, utterly dull, but dutiful to American wishes. So he impressed me when he took me to the Havana Yacht Club for lunch.

Under continued U.S. pressure, conditions grew more difficult. The economy was worse than ever, and none of Grau's tepid measures were helping much. Guiteras' land program offered fu-

ture promise, but his timid fellow cabinet ministers held him
back. Meanwhile U.S. guns remained pointed up O'Reilly Street.

On a twilight early in January 1934, Batista walked me across
the Camp Colombia drill grounds to the reviewing stand. We
talked there. He deplored political parties and Congress but said
these annoying institutions were necessary — much as Mussolini
once said he would not suppress parliament "because the people
need their little toys." Batista finally told me: "No government
can survive in Cuba that does not have United States government support." He had no love for Welles, but Welles wanted
Mendieta to be president, and Welles wielded the fists of money
and battleships.

Batista felt it might be a workable arrangement. Mendieta had
some political following, and with an A.B.C. coalition and supported by the armed forces, a stable government might result.
"Grau has to go," he concluded. "Even if he were an archangel,
the United States will never recognize him." What did I think of
this?

It was the rankest betrayal. Batista was stabbing his closest
comrades in the back.

After a bit I said, "I'm glad I am leaving Cuba for South America in a few days and that I will not be here to witness this sell-
out."

His face tightened, he said good-bye coldly. I was not to see
him again until the general strike period of 1935, more than a
year later, when his regime was almost tumbled from power.

Soon after I reached Peru, Cuban army airplanes dropped a
few bombs "made-in-the-U.S.A." on the Havana Palace. The
Grau forces held out in a few police stations but were soon overrun. Grau resigned, turning the government over to my friend
Colonel Carlos Hevia — "The Flower of Three Days" — to establish a chain of apparent "legality," so dear to U.S. emissaries.

And so Mendieta was duly seated in the presidency — for two
stormy years of police and army brutality, bombs, overt terrorism and killings — police brutality worse than that under Machado. It was a foretaste of the long night of oppression ahead
for Cuba.

One of the first signs of army rule was when Batista moved in
with troops and ruthlessly crushed the electrical workers' strike
with jailings and deaths. The high rates were restored.

Young Guiteras was hunted down on a lonely Matantzas shore and murdered, and the immediate danger of an agrarian revolution was ended. The peasants were driven by bayonets off the lands on which they had squatted. Cuba, if still an uproarious place, was once more safe for foreign corporations and the "Sugar Trust."

The nature of the New Deal and good neighborliness became clear. Four men in F.D.R.'s Cabinet, including the Secretary of the Treasury, had big Cuban sugar and utility holdings or were direct agents of companies with such holdings.

Part of the inside deal was that Mendieta would be recognized immediately (done within four days) and that the Platt Amendment would be repealed, thus abolishing U.S. tutelage over Cuban finances, diplomacy and ending the right of armed intervention. But a secret clause expanded the acreage at the Guantánamo base and provided more privileges there. Cuban sovereignty was still a maimed thing — just an expression on paper.

Welles never could unbend his stiff aristocratic neck to Batista, but his successor, Jefferson Caffery, positively drooled over the little dictator, considered him the wonder boy of the century. Caffery was a rice-grower from Louisiana who soon put Cuba out of the rice business. He made the sage, solemn remark: "If the white man fails in Cuba, we will fail everywhere in the world" — and added, "Guess you'd better not quote that."

The White foreigner — the Yankee — did not fail — not yet — and Cuba was sent down the road of twenty-five more years of ugly dictatorship — until that last day of 1958 when the little Napoleon headed over the sea to refuge in the Dominican Republic. Not till then did Cuba win its first true independence.

For how long? Has it, instead, merely become a Soviet satellite? Not exactly, but it is now definitely part of the Socialist bloc. It enjoys Soviet, Czech, Polish, East German, Hungarian, Rumanian, Bulgarian, Egyptian, Indian, Indonesian, Chinese trade and aid, plus a few crumbs thrown by Yugoslavia. By means of such aid and trade with Canada, England, Japan, Sweden, Norway and part of Latin America, for four years now it has survived measures as harsh as were ever used by a great power against a small nation: broken relations, destruction of the tourist trade, the cutting off of all commerce, diplomatic pressure in all Latin America, in Europe, England, Canada, France, Italy, Japan, and armed aggression — all this in violation of treaties, the United Nations charter, and international law. In the face of such cruel and insane hostility, it has carried out tremendous agrarian, industrial, housing, hospital, educational and public recreation enterprises, the greatest reforestation program in the history of the world, has doubled its electric power use, has put up scores of new factories, and at the same time has become one of the most powerfully armed smaller nations of the world.

Whether we like it or not, more has been accomplished in four and a half years in matters basic for the peoples' welfare and for economic expansion (regardless of shortages — wartime always creates shortages — due chiefly to the cutting off of U.S. imports) than was accomplished in nearly sixty years of U.S. rule and the supremacy of the foreign-owned sugar plantation system.

7 ○ THE CHACO WAR AND THE BOLIVIAN UPHEAVALS

1

The most tragic aftermath of the Great Depression was the outbreak of the long simmering Chaco War between Bolivia and Paraguay over the possession of a vast border wilderness, an area almost as large as Italy. This enormous region consists of deserts (which could be irrigated by the huge rivers that traverse it), swamps (one nearly as large as Belgium), forests, scrub land. In it live untamed Indians, missionaries, imported Menonites, a few farmers, snakes, scorpions, wild animals, some quebracho cutters, considerable cattle.

One writer described the war as two bald men fighting over a comb. But the comb was toothed with oil-wells — nearby, in the Bolivian counterpart; and the Chaco itself was said to be floating in oil. In this long-disputed area recently, Paraguayan Dictator Alfredo Stroessner has given away forty million acres of potential oil-land to U.S. corporations. (Oil played a major role in the Chaco struggle.) Huge new oil concessions have been handed out in Bolivia also.

Not much U.S. capital had gone into Bolivia — until after an oil concession of some seven million acres was secured by William Braden (father of Spruille Braden, Latin American promoter, later diplomat and Under-Secretary of State).

The acreage was taken over by Standard Oil of New Jersey in 1921. This was promptly followed by the 1922 loan for $26,000,000, which gave the New York bankers complete economic control of the country: the national bank, railroads, all export and import duties, all mining and corporation taxes, all liquor revenues, and 90 percent of all profits from the government tobacco monopoly. U.S. capital then moved heavily into the tin industry — National Lead, Grace and Company, the Guggenheims and others — and gained toe-hold shares in the Big Three enterprises, the Patiño, Hochschild and Armayo interests, which with their lawyers, politicians, newspapers editors and hangers-on were known as the *Rosca* — *"The Screw"* — and controlled everybody from president to generals down to dogcatchers. Thereafter all public works, road and railroad building — what little there were — went to U.S. corporations. The stranglehold on the country was complete.

The third largest country in South America, with unsurpassed natural resources, Bolivia lacked the highways, roads and rail lines to knit the different regions together and enable the rich eastern Yungas and the low-lying fertile tropics to supply the highlanders — the bulk of the population — with necessary food, which had to be imported. The railroad lines were to extract mineral wealth to be shipped abroad across the Andes, down to the Pacific, through either Peru or Chile — for Bolivia had lost her sea outlet in Atacama in the terrible War of the Pacific with Chile at the end of the last century.

This great empire was peopled by a mere 3,500,000 people. Most were ragged starving Indians, who earned no more than fifty dollars a year. Wages in the 15,000-foot mines, cruel labor, ranged from fifteen to seventy cents a day for a fourteen-hour day. It was the Angola of South America.

When the Great Depression hit, the price of tin, tungsten, copper declined; tens of thousands were thrown out of work. And so they marched off to a war, two thousand miles distant from the capital, with no roads between. The highlanders could not live (or fight) in the lowlands; they died like flies; they died from Paraguayan bullets; they died because Argentina wanted to get hold of the Bolivian oil owned by Standard Oil near her border on the Bermejo River, and because the oil people wanted an outlet for their product through Paraguay.

2

Look at this magnificent, beautiful land. Held in the sharp prongs of gigantic snow peaks of the inner Andes, the gray-bronze plateau stretches south from the big sea of Lake Titicaca to the salt beds of Uyuni and the highland desert of Atacama. Here in this sky-high, bleak region — studded with barren hills, traversed by sharp cut canyons that lead down to the smiling, year-round springtime of the rich Yungas and the sugar-cotton-fruit-cattle country of Santa Cruz — live four-fifths of the country's population under skies often leaden and dour. More than half are Quechua and Aimara Indians, the rest cholos, men of mixed blood, plus a handful of upper-class whites — the tiny class that has ruled the land since Spanish Conquest days — the men of the Rosca.

On the bosom of purple Titicaca under the snow-peaks float the reed-bound boats and the painted matting sails — for two thousand years and more such craft have plied those waters. In ancient times the Quechuas and Aimaras of the integrated empire of the Incas, sought, time and again, to pierce the eastern mountain wall and descend into the fertile Yungas and rich tropics of the inner Amazon and on to the Argentine Pampa, to the desert coast. They finally succeeded in building fine roads down to the Beni River and elsewhere. Thereby the remarkable Inca culture knit this region into a prosperous highland unity that included mountainous Peru, an empire that stretched from Colombia to northern Argentina and Chile, an empire better cultivated, with better communications, with more social justice in spite of the caste system, than was in existence four centuries later at the time of the outbreak of the Chaco War.

With the Spanish conquest the great north-south and the highland-jungle highways of the Incas were abandoned, and Bolivia become isolated, sealed in by mighty mountains. Thereafter, when the "Second Conquest" came, the new lords and masters built roads and railroads down to the Pacific, so that the wealth of the interior — first silver and gold, later copper and tungsten, manganese and antimony, and tin — mostly tin — could be torn loose and shipped to the new imperialist powers of Europe and to the United States. The wealth flowed abroad; the people remained behind enslaved, driven under the lash, starving. A forgotten folk. For the railroads brought back in return few of the blessings of modern knowledge, equipment or luxury.

Seventy percent of the people were illiterate, not allowed to vote. Sanitation was almost non-existent. Infant mortality was probably the highest in the world. Their dwellings were and are mostly damp, dark, thatched adobe; sometimes, even in high places where blizzards sweep in, they are only of wattled walls.

Part of the progress these past three years — pointed to with inordinate pride by the U.S. government do-gooders on the scene — has been to induce peasants to buy glass — imported and expensive — to put windows into their caves.

Those who come close to the lives of these exploited people love them. They are at their best in remote mountain folds or in the warmer Yungas, where some cling to their pre-Spanish farming communidades and live by self-sufficient farming and handicrafts. Their folk art is the most beautiful anywhere, for these poor driven people have an aesthetic sensibility not found in so-called civilized countries where taste is no longer a creative, individual expression, but is imposed by mass production goods. Some were always independent — far more so now since the 1953 revolution, though they were always likely to be gouged by tax-collectors, looted by soldiers, or taken away by force to the army or to the mines.

Their quiet, abiding strength, an incredible poise and dignity, has helped them to persist proudly, even if, for centuries, it has never translated itself (except by sweat and tears) into the sort of power symbolized by the stamping smelters of Oruro, Catavi and Colquiri. With the same erect dignity, in their homemade woolens, their tall felt hats, their brilliant ponchos, their leather sandals (or more often barefoot), they walk the streets of La Paz, with its skyscraper apartment houses, office buildings, even a skyscraper university. They have even learned to ride airplanes which now zigzag over the land.

Recently I went by jeep over a horrible road (built with U.S. tax money and profiting U.S. contractors of the Point IV program) to the Colquiri mines, the oldest in the country, and there spoke to five hundred Aimara miners, who still, nine years after the revolution, earn less than a dollar a day. At least they need toil only eight hours a day now, and no children work any more. Stolid, with impassive faces, these people who still speak Aimara but know considerable Spanish listened to me talk about Cuba and Mexico and Colombia. It was discouraging, that broad round-faced statuesque immobility; then, after about fifteen minutes of appraisal, they accepted me and (apparently liking what I told them) broke into laughter and cheers that shook the rafters. Afterwards, they talked themselves and asked questions. Though more than half are still illiterate, they knew more about international affairs than the average New Yorker, certainly were more interested. They wanted to know all about Korea, Laos, the Congo, Algiers, the situation in Berlin, wages in Cuba, Mexico and the United States, land-ownership, the status of labor unions.

3

Repeatedly, the inept rulers who have swept into power every other year during Bolivia's long disturbed history have plunged the country into wars to attempt to conceal their own inadequacies. The outcome has always been disastrous. The nitrate fields and Pacific ports were lost to Chile; huge rubber regions were lost to Brazil. But no war was a worse fiasco than that launched to seize the Chaco. It lasted for more than five years and cost more than 100,000 lives.

At the start, in spite of the distance, the fantastic supply problems, it seemed like an assured victory. Bolivia had an army twice as large as that of Paraguay; it was well-equipped with U.S. and Chilean aid; it had help from Brazil; and it was well-trained by German General Hans Kundt — though, as it turned out, idiotically trained for desert and jungle fighting. For the armament makers of the world, the Chaco was a great boon, especially in the dark hours of the Depression. Presently Bolivia was provided with powerful U.S. bombers. Vickers of England also had a finger in the pie.

But Paraguay was not without help. It, too, was smarting from territorial dismemberment in the terrible Tripartite War with Brazil and Argentina, which had left only 25,000 male Paraguayans alive. Argentina seized all the Chaco lying below the Pilcomayo River; it seized the fertile province of Misiones, a long finger wedged between Uruguay and the chunk given to Brazil. Paraguay, to wipe out this bitter memory, was determined once and for all to cement its claim on the whole Chaco.

Following the Tripartite War, Argentine capital had moved into Paraguay; it owned all the river transportation and, like the United States interests in Cuba, soon came to own a lion's share of the land of the country; it produced much of Paraguay's quebracho, yerba mate, cotton, sugar, cattle. And the working conditions, the serfdom, as in Cuba under the recent U.S. sugar plantation system, was harsh, harsh as that in Bolivia. Argentina was now arming Paraguay, backing it to the hilt, just as U.S. oil and tin interests were backing Bolivia.

The immediate provocation came when Argentina closed its borders to U.S.-owned Bolivian oil. The rich fields of this area, plus potentially rich fields in Santa Cruz, were of little use except for local consumption, unless the oil could be gotten out; so production had been throttled down to a mere 26,000 metric tons. The central highlands could consume more, but to build a pipe-line with pumping stations would be inordinately costly. There was no railroad, and the Santa Cruz-Cochabamba road, which the U.S. government was proposing to build to help out, had not even been started. A pipe-line to Chile would also be very costly, and that country had shown no inclination to permit it. Standard Oil next tried to obtain a Bolivian free port on the Paraná River in Paraguay, to which a pipe-line could be laid down.

Under Argentine pressure, Paraguay, bitter anyway over Bolivia's steady advance into the Chaco ever since 1928, refused. Brazil, it is true, had provided Bolivia with the free Puerto Suárez further up the river and was pushing her transcontinental railroad to nearby Corumbá, also on the river, a road which eventually was to connect up with the Bolivian oil fields and the highlands; but Puerto Suárez was beyond the reach of ocean-going tankers.

The war broke out in earnest in 1932. On file in Paraguayan archives is a letter by a conscripted Bolivian student to his family in La Paz, describing the bloody Battle of Boquerón, when the Paraguayans first met and routed the cream of the Kundt-trained Bolivian army in September 1932.

The defeat brought violent disorders in La Paz. Another bad defeat followed at Saavedra in 1933. The ill-conditioned highlanders — conscripted, ill-clad Indians — were dying even when not fighting from the lowland climate, disease, parasites, lack of food and water. People at home were starving because of the disruption of the economy.

Popular fury kept mounting. Disabled or returned soldiers shouted the news of the incredible mismanagement and repeated defeats and death. University students, for almost the first time in history, began protesting, taking an active part in politics. Labor leaders for the first time got up enough courage to defy the government and the military and demand better treatment in factory, mines and field.

The United States, though it had provided armaments and bombers, was damned up and down, forward and back. Particularly was Standard Oil denounced, for by this time the Bolivian people were aware of behind-scene intrigues. But especially hated were the tin magnates and the Rosca (tin was 90 percent of all exports).

In 1934 President Daniel Salamanca toured the front to reanimate the battered Bolivian forces, to dress down the officers for the latest disaster at Balliván and to fire the commandant there, Colonel Enrique Peñaranda — not without reason, for he was one of the most uneducated, stupid, inept officers on the entire front.

But Peñaranda had two friends, Colonels David Toro and Germán Busch, and they seized Salamanca, holding him incommunicado until a military Junta had installed Tejada Sorzano in his place — with instructions to negotiate peace with the six-nation Inter-American peace commission.

A quasi-truce was patched up in 1935. Fighting between the

1. Carlos José Fernández, *La Guerra del Chaco II,* 14. "We were surrounded by dead bodies. Not a soldier who lifts his head above the trenches but he is shot down by the Paraguyans . . . The number of dead is enormous . . . (And later) "The names of the dead are being concealed from the people. In Villa Montes there isn't any more room anywhere for the wounded, nor in the field hospitals . . . The best trained and capable of the soldiers of Bolivia have disappeared. . . . "

exhausted contenders dwindled off, with Paraguay holding nearly the whole Chaco, at some points beyond.

Paraguay still refused to grant a river port, Argentina made
her stall on the final settlement until it could get Bolivian oil on
its own terms. The mastermind of this inner treachery was Foreign Minister Salvador Saavedra Lamas, long touted as the
United States' best friend in all South America.

In 1936, the same three colonels booted Sorzano out, issuing
a manifesto that they intended to lead the country "prudently
and gradually" toward socialism. David Toro took over the presidency in May. He fired fifty thousand civil servants to make way
for ex-combatants. The Rosca began shivering when a tax was
placed on absentee owners' profits and a currency reform deprived them of their more than 50 percent advantage in exchange rates enjoyed over everybody else. This had permitted
them to augment their already huge profits and send them out
of the country.

But what really sent ice down the spines of the corporations,
native and foreign, was Toro's bold confiscation of Standard Oil
properties, on the grounds that the concession-terms had never
been carried out. (This was a year before Cárdenas expropriated Mexican oil properties.) At the same time, Toro made a deal
to sell all surplus oil to Argentina. In turn Argentina agreed to
provide oil equipment and construct a railway to the oil fields,
on into Santa Cruz and eventually to the highlands. Argentina
then became quite agreeable to settling the Chaco dispute.

Bolivia lost all the Chaco, but it kept its existing oil fields and
was given Bahía Negra on the Paranà river and free zone rights
at Puerto Casado, where the river was deep.

The signing ceremonies were held with great diplomatic and
military pomp at the Casa Rosada in Buenos Aires. The *New
York Times* hailed it as a great "victory for the Hull policies."
But the man who settled the matter was Saavedra Lamas. Ironically, after having kept the war going three years longer than
necessary, he was awarded the Nobel Peace Prize.

4

Toro was in serious difficulties, under fire from both Left and
Right, from the Socialists and from the Rosca and U.S. interests.
Secret overtures were made to Busch by the Americans and

the Rosca. In July 1937, when Toro took the cure at a Yunga spa, on his return he learned that his good friend and compadre Busch had taken over the government.

With a foot in both camps — or better said, on two circus horses going in different directions — Busch could not possibly succeed. Toro had used a lot of suppression, and the people were briefly quieted now when Busch lifted censorship and allowed political parties to reorganize and hold elections. In 1938 he was duly elected "Constitutional President."

But within a few months, newspaper editors (most newspapers, especially the biggest, *La Razón,* were owned by the Rosca and dependent on U.S. corporation advertising) were called to Busch's office and dressed down — "hysterically" according to accounts — and numbers were jailed "in the best Berchtesgaden tradition" — i.e. in Nazi style. The reorganized parties were pushed back into the shadows, and individual liberties went up in smoke. Like Toro, Busch was soon without support except for the Army.

The Right, badly shaken, but now reorganized and strong, had no further use for him. The Left felt it had been badly betrayed. To meet the growing disorders, after consulting with the army chiefs, Busch issued a flamboyant manifesto, sent to the press with the tersely worded order scribbled on the copies, "Favorable comment only." The manifesto proclaimed a totalitarian state.

Busch stated that he had accepted the presidency at the behest of the Army and the Socialist leaders out of purely patriotic motives, but the press had been unruly, the traditional parties had tried to regain power, and so to prevent disorders he was obliged to establish a totalitarian state. Congress was dissolved, the Constitution set aside. All Nazi, Fascist and Communist activities were prohibited, including the wearing of foreign insignia and uniforms. (Black shirts had been parading.) Clearly — though he was now played up in the outside press as a tool of Hitler — his coup was Bolivian "totalitarianism," i.e. dictatorial provincial nationalism.

His new program became wholly reactionary. Unauthorized strikes were made crimes against the State. New ideas tending to upset the social order or to provoke panic in economic and financial domains were declared high treason punishable by death. He extended army regulations and law to every citizen; worker-employer relations were brought wholly under government regulation. As a sop to the Left, rents were frozen and food profiteering prohibited.

Actually Busch undertook previously and now many basic reforms in behalf of labor, imposed new taxes on the Rosca and threatened to nationalize the mines. His one dream was to build a tin refinery, the one way the country — without nationalization — could wiggle out of the clutches of the Rosca. His efforts in this direction were fruitless; he was turned down cold by New York banking interests.

Yet such a step, it was pointed out by Bernard Baruch at the prolonged Senate tin investigation in Washington, was vitally necessary for proper wartime defense of the United States. Tin was our most crucial strategic material, and the setting up of a refinery in Texas — as was eventually done with some financial scandal — would not solve the problem. In case of war, refined tin could be flown in from Bolivia, whereas tin-concentrate would demand valuable shipping, exposed to submarine attacks.

In any event, Busch was blocked — profits are always more important than patriotism — and in 1939 he committed suicide, or was murdered, or, as some claim, killed in a whorehouse brawl. His friends said it was at a party celebrating his sister-in-law's birthday. In any event his body was found at a late hour seated at his desk in the Palace; ostensibly he had been signing papers. The whole matter was very hush-hush and has remained a mystery to this day.

In 1940, the Conservatives took charge of the ballot boxes, with the aid of the Army, and Colonel Peñaranda, the third of the original military triumvirate, was duly elected president. Already he was tagged as a dutiful instrument of the Rosca, of U.S. corporate interests and the U.S. Embassy. This, *apparently,* was a lucky choice, with the European War going on; Pearl Harbor would soon occur, and with tin from most of the world then cut off, the tin of Bolivia was to became life or death for the U.S. war effort.

According to stories, Peñaranda's own mother was utterly astonished — he had been the dullest of her children — and exclaimed, "Had I ever had any idea he would become president, I would have sent him to school."

This, however, was remedied, when, after the terrible slaughter of mine workers, women and children by the army at Catavi, he journeyed to Washington to be kissed on the cheek by F.D.R.

and to receive a Ph.D. from that lover of high academic standards, Columbia University, ever ready to dignify the meaning
of its degrees by obliging political mice in Washington whenever a Latin American butcher shows up.

But Peñaranda's days after the Catavi massacre were numbered. No man, even with Washington support, could weather
the horror and protests and fury resulting from the brutal shooting down of three hundred unarmed men, women and children
in behalf of Patiño, the Tin Czar.

For this massacre, the U.S. chargé d'affaires — as has been well
documented — was largely responsible, due to his intense patriotic interest in maintaining tin production, freezing prices and
wages, though inflation since the Chaco War was up 1,500 percent. What that had done to fifteen cents a day or even the seventy cents a day wages a few received, can be easily figured
out. People were literally starving to death, revolution was in
the air, but the U.S. Embassy forebade Peñaranda to pass a labor law, blocked any rise in the pre-war price of tin it was paying and made the explosion — and the massacre — inevitable.

5

"Bolivia is Patiño" was the current saying. Patiño Mines and
Enterprises Consolidated, Inc. was incorporated in Delaware,
New Jersey. National Lead Company came to control 10 percent of the concern and was represented by several directors.
Controlling the best tin deposits in Bolivia, in 1941 it produced
21,000,000 kilos (46,000,000 pounds) of fine tin, about 50 percent
of the country's total export that year.

Nearly 11,000,000 kilos came from five companies controlled
by Mauricio Hochschild of Austrian-Jewish extraction, a naturalized Bolivian with two sons, one an Argentinean citizen, the
other Chilean, a choice made for diplomatic influence and protection.

From the Armayo Company, a Swiss concern, came 2,600,000
fine kilos. The rest of Bolivia's tin, over 8,000,000 kilos, came
from smaller mines, among which the Guggenheim and Grace
interests had holdings.

The Patiño interests, however, were world wide, and reached

from refineries in England and on the continent to mines in Asia. In 1939 Patiño took over the General Tin Investments, Inc. of Great Britain. On the board of both companies were Simón Patiño and his son Antenor, and Ricardo Martínez Vargas (a Patiño man). The British company owned thirty Malayan tin mines and had a large share of Consolidated Tin Smelters, Ltd. with large operations. In this company, Simón Patiño was president and a director. His son Antenor held directorship in all three concerns, likewise in the Arnheim Smelting Company of Holland and Thailand Tin Mines, Ltd. They dominated the International Tin Cartel, presided over by a British official, and the annual income of their corporations was far greater than the entire Bolivian budget. The Patiños had a complete stranglehold on the mining, refining and sale of all the tin in the world.

At the outset of World War II, the Germans seized all tin refineries on the continent; the Japanese took over refineries in Penang and Shanghai. If the Germans had succeeded in invading England, the United States would have had no place on earth to get refined tin, and the entire steel industry might have been put out of business, the country rendered unable to wage war. Even without such disasters, Patiño flatly refused to provide the United States with tin concentrate or ore from Bolivia or elsewhere (except via England), alleging prior contracts. He also had much of the ore of Hochschild and Armayo sewed up, so that the U.S. government refinery set up in Texas had to depend chiefly on low-grade Bolivian ores. These were soon greatly expanded.

Since Patiño had a monopoly on all the know-how of refining, there is indication that the Texas effort — quite apart from smelly financial aspects of its construction which involved high U.S. officials — was sabotaged in every possible way.

The United States could not afford any slow-up of Bolivian tin production, either by the Patiños or of tin purchased for the Texas refinery. It wished to keep the price down. Hence our zealous Embassy in La Paz, on Hull's instructions, pressured President Peñaranda to scrap proposed labor legislation.

The inevitable result was a strike by the starving Patiño miners. At Catavi, 15,000 feet high, where are located the two richest tin mines of the Americas, Lallagua and Twentieth Century, the company stores, the only source of food, were closed down.

On December 21, 1942, at 10 a.m., 8000 unarmed men, women and children moved on the mines en masse to plead that the stores remain open until strike issues were settled.

They were met by a Bolivian army force under Colonel Cuenca and raked with trench-mortars, machine guns and rifles. Hemmed in helplessly, they were intermittently fired upon until three in the afternoon, when they were permitted to gather up their dead and wounded and retire. The government said 19 had been killed; news reports set the figure at 400; labor members of the Magruder investigating commission, sent south by Sumner Welles in an effort to investigate the scandal, reported the number as probably about 300. How many were wounded is conjecture.

The United States, if not directly responsible for the barbarity, was seriously involved — not only because of the Embassy pressures against proper labor legislation (a matter soon to be aired), but because one of Nelson Rockefeller's five good-will coordinators of inter-American affairs was Joseph C. Rovensky, a vice-president and director of Patiño Mines and Enterprises. Another coordinator was also a Bolivian, an intimate friend of Mrs. Rockefeller. When I called on him in Washington about tin matters, for an article for *Harper's Magazine*, he refused to give me the slightest information.

Rovensky hastily took a month's vacation, then discreetly resigned. But there is little doubt that Rockefeller's good-will committee was the high fortress of the Bolivian Rosca in this country. Rockefeller investments in Bolivian enterprises were said to be large.

His hands still red from the blood of Catavi workers, President Peñaranda thus visited Washington to be entertained by Roosevelt and to receive his Columbia University degree. The spectacle of this jovial but bulky cholo and caudillo of Bolivia, almost illiterate, in gown and mortar board, getting the academic sash across his enormous shoulders, must have been edifying for faithful scholars of higher learning. Peñaranda's brow sloped back from his conical head. The bridge of his broad flaring nose was deeply sunk between piercing dark eyes; his wide bulky jaw jutted forth from a soft round chin acquired because of his great animal lust for sybaritic joys.

A touch of irony was further added by Vice-President Henry

Wallace's good-will visit to Bolivia in April 1943, in an attempt to get the Peñaranda government to declare war on the Axis. Peñaranda had done everything conceivable to further the interests of the Rosca, to accede to all Washington demands, and to give Bolivia's tin away at pre-war prices, while inflation zoomed and miners starved and Bolivia could get no goods in return; yet the country had remained neutral, afraid of the anti-U.S. sentiment among the people.

But Wallace aroused enthusiasm among the most ardent Bolivian anti-imperialists. Bolivia declared war on April 6, the very day Wallace was being made an honorary citizen of Cochabamba, the place where Simón Patiño was born, and where he delivered a speech telling the populace of the rights of man and freedom from want. Not far from there, the workers had been slaughtered and driven back to their toil at the point of the gun — with no improvement in their intolerable conditions. All over Bolivia, the mass of people — our new allies in the battle for human freedom — were little better than slave-laborers. They had never known any freedom and did not know any now.

It is true that in December 1941, the United States had sent down an economic mission, headed by Mr. Merwin Bohan, who had been raised in Mexico, spoke Spanish perfectly, and had unimpeachable integrity. But his chief instructions were to get new industrial, transportation and other projects started which would aid the war effort, not to promote Bolivian independence and welfare. The main thing was to buy all of Bolivia's mining products — at low prices — to keep them out of German hands. If this maintained full employment, it in no way improved conditions, quite the contrary; and once the war ended, inevitably Bolivia would be plunged into economic disaster.

As the Bolivian Ambassador in Washington, Luís Fernando Guachalla, pointed out mildly to the State Department on January 2, 1943 — right after the Catavi massacre: In "the maintenance and increase of Bolivian production of strategic materials," the chief concern had been "with the commercial, financial and technical aspect of the mineral production." Little attention had been given "to the human element . . . in such production or to the problem of improving living conditions."

Martin C. Kyne, C.I.O. member of the Magruder commission soon to go down, stated similarly: "The human resources of the

Bolivian republic and their role in the war effort have not received as careful and sympathetic scrutiny. The situation of the
Bolivian worker has awakened little interest. The ignorance of
the outside world of what is going on in the world is matched
only by the ignorance of the outside world of what is going on
in the remote mining camps of Potosí, Oruro and Lallagua."
The formula "war-tin versus human welfare" somehow had to be
converted into "human welfare plus more tin."

Explosive publicity over Bolivia was first set off by a letter to
Under-Secretary of State Sumner Welles from Ernesto Galarza,
chief of the division of labor and social information of the Pan
American Union. (This letter, by coincidence, was dated December 21, the very day of the Catavi massacre.) He accused American Ambassador Pierre Boal at La Paz of pressuring President
Peñaranda to prevent the passage of a new labor code which
provided for, among other things, prompt payment of wages,
minimum wages, the right of collective bargaining, and the
strengthening of mediation and arbitration.

"It is clear," wrote Galarza, "that the Ambassador's observa-
tions [to Peñaranda] were intended to diminish the possibilities
of passage of the labor code. The Ambassador clearly agreed
with the position of the large mine-owners that the new code
would impose disagreeable administrative expenses on the companies; that it was desirable not to pay earned wages on time
in order to compel the workers to remain on the job; that the
. . . code would compel the companies to demand higher prices
from the United States government for tin and other essential
materials; that collective bargaining would be detrimental . . . to
production. . . . "

"And," Galarza added, "democracy and production must go
up or down together. The contrary is the thesis of totalitarianism
. . . . The attitude represented by Ambassador Boal will lead
to further decline of production in Bolivia and other parts of
Latin America. The physical reserves of the Latin American
workers, especially in the vital industries, are already so low that
the systematic opposition to better housing, higher wages, adequate medical attention, official training, collective bargaining
and proper representation before public administrative bodies
will drive the workers to adopt every form of active and passive
resistance. Must continental solidarity . . . be bought at the price
being currently paid by the workers of Bolivia?"

Hull cynically denied Galarza's charges in a press statement. In a public letter, Sumner Welles also rebuked Galarza, saying his statements were false and groundless.

Galarza stood by his guns, offered to accept the verdict of any impartial tribunal, and demanded a Senate investigation. But he was obliged to resign, which in itself proved that the Pan American Union was not a bonafide alliance of nations but merely an office of colonial affairs.

On January 9, I. F. Stone, Washington correspondent of *P.M.* and the *Nation,* published excerpts from cables exchanged by Boal and Hull, when the labor code was being considered. Even then strike trouble was pending, and mining companies were strengthening their armed forces, buying machine guns and rifles. In a five-page cable Boal pointed out the inconveniences of a new labor code. In reply Hull ordered Boal to inform "the President or other appropriate authorities" of the U.S. government's "hope and confidence that no steps will be taken which ... would inhibit the full performance of contracts ... for the purchase of ... strategic materials, particularly tin, tungsten, antimony and rubber.... The uninterrupted flow of these items is essential to the optimum prosecution of the war. It is consequently hoped that no action will be taken which might jeopardize hemisphere security."

Debt, slavery, peonage, starvation apparently were not considered as jeopardizing continental solidarity or production. Hull had deliberately, brazenly, lied to the American public. So had Sumner Welles.

The labor code was now hurriedly passed, but simultaneously decrees were issued suspending the essential provisions, nullifying the code. Nearly all labor leaders not already shipped off to the Titicaca Island prison or to pestiferous jungle prisons were rounded up. The Magruder mission could not find a single one to interview, all were in jail or in exile; anyway the commission had been "forbidden" to probe into the Catavi massacre. This, however, was exposed in an independent pamphlet by the C.I.O. member of the mission.

And so, the scabrous matter was hushed up, Galarza was allowed to return to his post, and the report of the U.S. mission was given little publicity.

"Low wages are the rule," the C.I.O. report said. "The real wages of mine workers have declined; 41 percent . . . receive less than 20 bolivares [80 cents] a day." (This incidentally was the *maximum*. A large percentage received as little as 15 cents.) Most hacienda workers, the report went on, were held "in farm tenancy little short of feudal serfdom" and received "no cash wages... While the rubber workers of the Beni are typically paid a cash wage [40 to 60 cents a day] this is, for the most part, dissipated by the cost of necessary tools, fire-arms and supplies.... The rubber workers have derived little or no benefit from the increased price of rubber due to the war boom."

What the report did not indicate was that the rubber program was in the hands of U.S. government technicians (or supposed technicians). But even these miserable wages attracted such a flood of workers that hacienda owners were protesting because their serfs ran off to the rubber jungle. Later, of course, it came out that the U.S. government agents mostly had handed over their efforts, supplies and equipment to the traditional rubber *enganchadores* or exploiters of the region, who profited greatly by high rubber prices and by the sale at fantastically high prices of supplies — supposed to go free to the workers.

The Magruder report went further into social matters. There was an "insufficiency of medical, dental, hospital and nursing care." On haciendas medical care was "generally unavailable at any cost."

There was an "acute shortage of housing, and workers' homes generally are forlorn, overcrowded, unhygienic and lacking in elementary sanitary facilities." Company mine houses were "miserable, dark, one-room hovels unfit for human habitation."

The factories inspected in La Paz (the best in the country) showed "frequent lack of safety appliances and promiscuous use of child labor." Not a single safety engineer was employed in the entire country.

In the mines, the mission said emphatically, there is much "human wastage due to respiratory diseases... lack of safety appliances... violations of the child labor law." There was a "total absence" of collective bargaining, of the "straight-forward bargaining" as practiced "in modern democratic countries."

"Today," the report summed it up, "it has been estimated that the population of this country is at least 75 percent illiterate, that not over one-sixth of the children of eligible school age are enrolled.... Seventy-four percent of the students are without chairs or desks." The ill-paid teachers lacked proper training. Seventy percent of the rural teachers had never gone beyond the sixth grade.

Conclusions were positive; more sound legislation and labor freedom were recommended. "The best assurance the workers will receive a fair deal is a well-organized labor movement under responsible leadership." At the time, leaders not in prison could not go from place to place without a police permit; no labor meetings could be held without a policeman or government inspector on hand. No labor union could exist at all unless 50 percent of the workers were enrolled; the strike vote had to be 75 percent. The labor code which Boal had blocked, in itself wholly inadequate, had contained no "provision which would protect or enforce the rights [ostensibly] conceded to the workers."

Peñaranda did nothing whatever to correct the abuses told about in the report. In December 1946, riots and uprisings drove him out and brought in another Chaco war hero, Major Gualberto Villaroel.

8 ◯ RISE OF THE BOLIVIAN REVOLUTION

1

The Villaroel coup came about through a coalition of opposition groups, military and civilian. Villaroel represented the secret Santa Cruz military lodge, Radepa (Razón y Patria), closely affiliated with the Grupo de Oficiales Unidos (GO), the secret counterparts in Chile and Argentina. The Radepa was made up mostly of young officers up to the rank of colonel, super-nationalistic, most probably pro-Fascist or pro-Nazi, but neutralist; pro-Labor and reformist; in general anti-United States but realistic enough to conceal their antipathy.

Its chief civilian support was the MNR (National Revolutionary Movement). This organization, founded in 1941, was led by Victor Paz Estenssoro, a young professor, aided by Hernàn Stiles, a brilliant economist (son of a previous president), and Luís Peñaloza, also an economist, both of whom had split off from the Partido Obrera Revolucionario (P.O.R.), the strong Trotskyist organization.

In a secret late-night conference in a house on the corner of

Potosí and Socayaba Streets, not long before the coup against Peñaranda, Villaroel and an aide conferred with Paz Estenssoro, Stiles and newspaper editor Carlos Montenegro to form an alliance and get rid of Peñaranda.

The P.O.R. had been founded by Gustavo Navarro (generally known as Tristán Maroff, when he was an exile in Argentina during the Chaco War) as the Tupoc Amaru Lodge (after the Inca emperor). I knew Maroff before that, when he was in exile in Mexico, a tall, bearded, hilarious young man. He left to become the chief intellectual adviser of the Germán Busch regime.

Juan Lechín, who was to become the strongest labor leader in Bolivia as secretary of the Miners' Federation, followed the same Trotsky anti-Stalinist line, though never a P.O.R. member. Even so, the MNR had a big influence among the miners. Especially after Paz helped hide the general secretary of the Catavi miners following the massacre and promised to support their cause did Lechín come to occupy an important place in the Villaroel dictatorship.

Another important leftist group, founded in 1940, was the P.I.R. (Party of the Revolutionary Left) led by sociologist José Antonio Arce who called himself a Marxist but not a Communist. Arce ran as presidential candidate against Peñaranda and, surprisingly, carried a few important cities. By 1943 he controlled the chief labor organization, La Confederación Sindical de los Trabajadores, particularly the railway workers, though not many miners nor the rising COB (Confederación Obrera de Bolivia), which Juan Lechín was eventually to control.

After the Peñaranda election, Arce fled to the United States, where he taught briefly at the Jefferson School (Communist), then secured a job with Rockefeller's Inter-American good-will organization in Washington. He became influential and gained the confidence of the State Department. He soon followed the official U.S. line so slavishly that on occasion he was accused in Bolivia of being a sub rosa agent. Later in La Paz, he was a distinguishable figure at all U.S. Embassy parties.

Another group was scheming, the Falange Socialista Boliviana (formed in 1937). It was pro-Franco, pro-Church, close to the Rosca. But it was not to assume much importance until after 1952, when it worked against Paz Estenssoro and the MNR, and actually staged several armed revolts that were quickly crushed.

Following Paz Estenssoro's refusal to break with Castro's Cuba, there were indications that it has been secretly helped by our C.I.A. which, since Kennedy, has been very active in Bolivia.

In 1946 nearly everybody, right and left, but not of course the Rosca, joined to overthrow Peñaranda. On December 19, the Radepa seized key military positions and took Peñaranda prisoner. The MNR took over the telephone system and all radio stations. Bolivians woke up December 20 with a new government.

They were not overly surprised; in all of Bolivia's history, no government had ever been established by elections, only by conspiracy and bayonets. Arce demanded from Paz Estenssoro that a quadripartite coalition government be set up: Radepa, MNR, P.I.R. and the Syndicalist Confederation, controlled by the P.I.R. Paz rejected this, and Arce became a ferocious opponent of the new regime, suddenly discovering it was pro-Nazi.

It is likely that he influenced Cordell Hull to attack the new Villaroel government, although Hull and Welles were wrathful over the overthrow of their bumbling pet, Peñaranda (as they had been over the overturn of the De Cespedes regime in Cuba), and they branded the revolution "a Nazi plot" paid for by the German Embassy — "Nazi" being the smear word of the day.

Villaroel reluctantly kicked out the elements from his first cabinet not liked by Hull; he delivered all Germans to a U.S. battleship and otherwise supported the Allied cause, and actually produced more tin, with better conditions, for the miners. But Arce still screamed that these were merely ruses to conceal "pro-Nazi totalitarian terrorism."

2

The memorandum against the new government and its personalities circulated by Secretary Cordell Hull was one of the slimiest smears ever put out by this government, though with enough distorted truth to make it credible. Obviously, however, it was based on the concept that there was no room in the world for neutrality, national independence, and that anybody against U.S. financial imperialism was ipso facto pro-Nazi. Today, of course, they are labeled "Communist." Thus Hull said Villaroel had been an intimate friend of fellow-officer Major Belmonte

Pabón, who was considered — no documented evidence was presented — to be a Nazi agent. Actually the two men were not very close. At the inauguration of Dictator Morinigo in Paraguay, Villaroel, the Washington propaganda paper said, had stated that soon Bolivia, too, would have an anti-democratic military government. Why then was Morinigo flattered and decorated in Washington? Why, today, is his bloodstained successor, Dictator Alfredo Stroessner, so aided and favored?

Secretary Hull, as those before and after him, wished only yes-men in Latin America ready to give all advantages to powerful U.S. interests, whatever the injury to their peoples.

Those kicked out were MNR members: among them, Carlos Montenegro, Minister of Agriculture, and Major Jorge Calero, Minister of Education and Indian Affairs, editor of *La Calle,* the official MNR organ, which (without proof) Hull said had been receiving Nazi subsidies. Calero was responsible for Article III of the first platform of the MNR: "We affirm our faith in the power of the Indian Mestizo race; in the solidarity of Bolivians to defend their collective interest and in the welfare of the individual ..."

He also went on to demand agrarian reform and the nationalization of the tin mines.

But Secretary Hull did not try to force out the overt pro-Nazi elements of the Radepa. Apparently what he was really worried about was not Nazism or anti-Semitism or his charge that the revolution was a "a Nazi plot" against the peace of the New World, but that the new anti-imperialist regime might indeed jeopardize the output of raw products, might even regulate or expropriate U.S. corporation properties. One of the close advisers of Villaroel whom Hull denounced most bitterly was Dionisio Foiani, ex-Minister of Mines and Petroleum under Toro and Busch, who had drafted and enforced the petroleum law which had confiscated Standard Oil properties.

He was guilty, according to Hull, of having promoted closer trade relations with Germany, back in 1939. But so did we! One rubs one's ears that such a charge could be considered damning in an official U.S. document. In 1939 the United States itself was getting all the trade with Germany it could and was selling Japan fabulous amounts of scrap-iron, glad enough to find a road out of the Great Depression.

Also, Foiani, said Hull with a big shudder, had been a member of the German Club in Santa Cruz; likewise of the Cercle
Française, which was then pro-Vichy. Some other cabinet members had also been members. What he did not state was that
such officials are *always* made honorary members of such clubs,
that this therefore had no particular significance. Indeed, it was
a more democratic practice than in some local American clubs,
which in American mining centers carried such signs as "No Bolivians allowed."

When an American mine manager took me to a club with such
a sign, I declined to enter, and told him: "Sooner or later that
sign is going to cost your company millions of dollars, in fact
you will probably lose your properties entirely." He scratched
his head over that, and later the sign was removed.

In any event, Hull refused to recognize Villaroel's government
until he had dismissed "pro-Nazi" cabinet ministers, though just
how, after his denunciations, this purified Villaroel himself is
not clear. Statesmen never have to be logical. Bolivia also had
to promise to hold elections promptly to give the dictatorship the
aura of legality, however tarnished, so beloved in Washington.
At Washington's behest elections of a sort were held to legalize
the regime. The result, in spite of Radepa coercion at the polls
and to the dismay of Washington, was a smashing victory for the
MNR.

The MNR was in no way a rigid dogmatic movement. There
is little doubt that some members had Fascist ideas, that some
were anti-Semitic, perhaps due to world-wide Nazi propaganda or
the fact that Bolivia was being flooded by Jewish refugees
who had bought their way into the country illegally, thanks to
corrupt Bolivian consular representatives.

Hull had charged Paz Estenssoro of being directly subsidized
by the Nazis and of being anti-Semitic. Proof that he was a Nazi
was: he had declared himself opposed to "false and fawning
democracy."

Paz, forced out of the government, did not bother to answer
until he spoke to the Constituent Congress on September 12,
1944. "The National Revolutionary Movement is not Nazi; it
could not be Nazi; its position in international affairs has been
and will coincide with the fundamental interests of the Bolivian
Nation. . . . A country with a semi-colonial structure, such as Bolivia, in a revolutionary period and in accordance with actual

reality, must accommodate itself so far as is possible to a Socialist regime which will enable it to realize its own social advances in accord with its national policy. . . . We profess to nationalism, but it is not of European extraction, and even less an offshoot of German nationalism." He threw the charges right back; Nazi-Fascism had been the product not of underdeveloped countries but of supercapitalist countries. "Such countries . . . [are obliged] because of their industrial system, to seek political economic expansion by Nazi-Fascist programs which lead them fatally to policies of aggression and conquest."

After U.S. recognition and his own success at the polls, Paz was restored to his post, and both Montenegro and Calero were given less prominent positions. In fact they constituted the Bolivian delegation to the Inter-American conference in Mexico in which the United States sought to oblige the Latin American countries to recognize the Soviet Union in order to smooth the way for the first United Nations conference at San Francisco. But Calero by then had become a tool of the Rosca, and all was forgiven.

Villaroel, under Paz's influence, especially after armed disturbances by reactionary army elements supporting the tin interests, carried on a few reforms, which merely exasperated the "Oligarchy" and failed to win proper popular support. But exchange controls were put on the exports of tin profits, which previously had been given rates that had doubled their profits at the expense of the government and all other business; a big national peasant congress was held; the tin miners were permitted to organize and to strike. A million acres of idle lands were acquired for distribution. By incredible economies $36,000,000 was accumulated to launch a program of economic diversification, to construct a sugar refinery, an oil pipe-line to the plateau, to buy farm machinery and increase food production.

But the "Tin Curtain" was coming down again, and as opposition disorders increased, the Villaroel government, particularly Radepa elements, resorted to executions, jailing of newspaper men, and terrorism of every sort, alienating more and more elements.

"Freedom of the Press" at best was pretty much an illusion. The three big papers were *La Razón*, owned by the Armayo tin people, *El Diario*, controlled by Patiño, and *Ultima Hora*, owned by the Hochschild interests. The only independent paper of any importance that supported the government was *La Calle* (which had been damned by Hull) with only a 5,000 circulation, and actually its owner had secret ties with the Rosca. It was a solid chorus of denunciation.

José Fellman Velarde, in his book *Victor Paz Estenssoro* wrote: "Behind the scenes, imperialism pulled the strings. American agents arrived in Bolivia with concrete orders to help the conspirators. A large amount of arms were surreptitiously brought in by official planes and the big importing houses. The Communists on their part . . . sent in scores of proven activists."

The Communists "took over the management" of Arce's P.I.R. which was joined by outstanding reactionaries, a sort of reverse boring from within. The stage was being set: the Rosca, corrupt army elements, the P.I.R. (curiously enough controlled by the Rosca and the Communists), the Communists, the Students Federation (lately won by P.I.R.) and the railway workers (P.I.R.) made up the cast. But Villaroel's brutalities — at least those of Radepa — had become intolerable. And since there was no way to get more money for the tin exported for the war effort and orders had been curtailed, and the price of food from outside had risen so much that reserves were exhausted, the people were hungry and despairing.

3

On July 21, 1946, the unarmed populace of La Paz went up against the machine guns and tanks in front of El Quemado, the National Palace, climbed over their own dead and rolled on. A tank was captured. The revolters rammed it through the iron-barred palace doors into the great central salon, three stories rising to an enormous skylight.

President Villaroel was chased from room to :oom, finally was cornered and thrown out to the mob in the street outside. He and his aide were hung to a plaza light post. Other members of the government were captured and killed. Paz Estenssoro, the young professor, the guiding intellectual mentor of the dictatorship, head of the MNR, escaped to Argentina. So came to an end a regime that had ruled in the name of the people and had instituted many reforms for the people, but the resistance of the Rosca, the tin conspiracy, had kept the country in an uproar.

This new "victory" of the people was born of the Chaco War, it was born of the suicide of President Germán Busch, it was born of the Catavi Massacre, it was born of the intolerable price squeeze. It was born of inflation, at this time up 1,700 percent since the beginning of the Chaco War.

But the "victory" of the people in overthrowing Villaroel, who had killed so many people, who had murdered newspaper men, who, like his predecessors, had used troops against students, teachers, strikers, was sadly enough also a victory for the Rosca. It was a victory for *La Razón*, the great daily of the Rosca, which Villaroel had closed down. It was a victory to a new crowd of greedy army men. The people cheered, and the people lost again.

The great international tin monopoly did not simplify internal or international problems. The tin purchases of the United States at bargain-counter prices did not ease the economic squeeze. The development of oil had brought neither peace nor prosperity. The borrowing of fantastic sums abroad, on which the country could not even pay the interest, had strengthened and enriched dictatorial regimes without bringing new industry or constructive enterprise. The loans helped the munition merchants; they bred war. Despite millions from the United States to build the Santa Cruz-Cochabamba road, it was still unfinished. And under Villaroel, in the name of reform, Bolivia had been converted into a concentration camp of hunger and a charnel house of murder. His latest abuse had been to jail seventy newsmen (most were not worth weeping about, but they included the leading writers of the country). Then, as the situation worsened, he failed to give arms to the MNR, a step opposed by the Army and the police, and he was doomed.

In June a military revolt, army men, working with smaller industrial and business elements, seized the military airfield and La Calama, La Paz fortress. The movement was apparently provoked by the reactionary government of Peru. It was put down in blood within hours.

Soon there was a teachers' strike, a 50 percent pay raise demanded. They were controlled by the P.I.R. but their average pay was $30.00 a month, and food cost more than in the United States. Villaroel said he would man the schools with army sergeants. Time and again teachers and students were driven back with machine guns. They gathered up their dead and assembled again in front of the palace, again and again. On July 18 the teachers and students were joined by demonstrating railway workers, store clerks and others. The next day the trains would stop running. The railway workers were also P.I.R. people.

Just below the propaganda offices of the U.S. Embassy and the afternoon daily *La Noche* on Mexico Street, the machine guns mowed down grammar school boys, and among the dead was Antonio Gismondi, the most famous stained-glass expert in Latin America.

Magistrates deserted their benches, some in fear, others in protest. The stores closed down. There was no food. More workers began parading with the students. If the people want to starve, let them starve, was the answer, and the troops drove out the few Indian vendors who drifted into town.

Thursday night, July 18, snow fell, blanketing the city gardens and slopes up to the rim of the plateau, the plateau was white for a thousand miles. In the morning, the women tramped and gathered around the statue of Bolivia's first liberator. They asked that the killings cease, that they be given food.

The plaza buildings, the roofs about the Palace, the cathedral, the stores, bristled with machine guns. The soldiers, peering over the balustrades, out in the snow all night, looked like white rabbits. The machine guns opened up. How many fell, one hundred or three hundred, women and children, the stories differ, but the snow was stained red clear across the plaza.

The women did not break or run. They gathered up five of their dead and marched on through the city. At the flower-market they were machine-gunned again. They rang the door bells of all the important embassies and consulates in the city. They showed the diplomats their dead. And that day Villaroel, completely controlled at this junction by the Rosca elements in Radepa, asked for the resignation of the MNR members of his cabinet and installed a military government, mostly reactionary officers belonging to the Rosca conspiracy.

All day Saturday the students scoured the city for arms, shotguns, pistols, knives, clubs, table legs, any kind of weapon. That night little groups of students from grammar school up lay in wait at corners, attacked traffic police, *carabineros*, police, soldiers, and took away their guns. They hung around the barracks and raided the gun racks. Police and soldiers died. So did many young students.

At the Palace, the gang of worried militarists wrangled violently; Villaroel wished to resign. The Radepa refused to hear of
it and seized the other members of the cabinet at pistol point.

The students got hold of an ambulance and drove up to the
Palace with clanging bell. Villaroel received them but refused
to compromise. He did give them safe-conduct out of the building.

Saturday night was quiet, still as death. Sunday morning
dawned completely peaceful, the church bells ringing as usual.
Everybody went quietly to Mass. Villaroel's confidence revived,
but just in case, he had a plane waiting at El Alto, the aviation
school on the bluffs.

Not quite everybody was at Mass. The students had quietly
gathered in friendly homes nearest the plaza. Right after Mass
they sallied forth, mingled with the crowds, and everybody began throwing up barricades, carrying stones from buildings under construction, tossing planks and furniture down from windows.

Men, women and children, many not even knowing what was
being planned, fell to and helped. Indians trotting into town
with their wares dropped their loads and pitched in, they and
their women in their bright shawls and tall white hats. Conductors stopped their street-cars at strategic points and helped.

The first actual blow was against the city hall, several blocks
downhill from the Palace. Young students armed only with
sticks and stones were driven back by guards, but by a ruse some
got through a side door. Townsfolk gathered and got in. A small
stock of arms and ammunition was captured.

Several police stations were overpowered, more weapons obtained, including a number of machine guns and a small tank
of Italian vintage. At the National Police School they found allies, who flung open the doors and handed out military supplies.
At traffic police headquarters they wrenched off the iron shutters and streamed in. Commander Max Toledo had flown the
coop, but later he was shot through the head and hung from a
tree in Sucre Plaza.

The Panóptico, the national prison, seemed impregnable with
its outer and inner fifty-foot walls, with only one side entrance
other than the main doors. The defenders braced this side door
by wedging an iron lamp post against the cement stairs. Braving
a withering fire, the students hurled bottles of gasoline. The

doors caught fire, the smoke and heat drove the defenders back from the top of the steps. The attackers swarmed in.

Twelve government planes swooped down and attacked, but by then most of the freedom fighters were inside the prison, where a fierce battle was raging. Part of the garrison overpowered their officers and joined the students. Piles of tortured prisoners' bones were discovered.

By noon everybody was converging on the Plaza Murillo that sloped down to the Palace. They had to fight their way through the streets and clean out roof snipers. They had to clean out the Paris Hotel where Roberto Hinojoso, the dictator's press-agent, had organized armed defense. He finally fled across the rooftops to Indaburo Street, where he was cornered, killed and strung up to a lamp post. One by one, every building around the plaza was captured.

The troops still held steep, narrow Ayacucho Street beside the Palace. Across that street was the Intendencia, the main police station. The attackers, better armed now, fought fiercely there for control.

Inside the Palace, Villaroel, trapped now, wrestled with his soul, his fear and his cabinet. One minute he breathed brimstone and chili, the next in a blue funk proposed to resign. The next he schemed how to flee. The palace radio sent out a call to foreign embassies to send a car to save the president. He phoned outlying garrisons. The officers refused to move. He ordered tanks.

Meanwhile another rebel group was attacking powerful Calama barracks on Cavalry Hill, a battle that lasted several hours; at three-thirty the defenders threw down their guns and fled across the ridges. One hero was a tennis player who knew nothing of the trouble until he heard the firing. He found a disabled tank. Throwing his tennis racket aside, he got the machine going, ran out of gas, then was joined by others who pushed the tank ahead manually into the fighting, where the guns were used with good effect.

At the Palace Villaroel abolished Congress, then handed in his resignation, turning authority over to the general staff. Then he, his secretary, Luis Uría, already badly wounded, and his military aide, Balliván, hurried down back stairs to a dead-end room on the ground floor, overlooking Ayacueho Street, a secret meeting room used also for keeping the records of the inner cabal.

Ayachucho Street was still controlled by guns on the roofs of the Palace and the Intendencia. Villaroel tore off his military jacket and put on a camel-hair overcoat and turned the collar up to conceal part of his face. It was quite a drop to Ayacucho Street, but with luck —

On the second floor, the cabinet ministers and officers, now also frantic, battered through the thick rear wall, finally made an aperture three-feet square. Twenty feet below was the slanting tile roof sloping to the inner patio of a business establishment, a mean drop. But all made it.

Perhaps to cover these attempts of escape, police chief Major J. Escobar ordered the machine guns to cease firing and ran up a white flag. The attackers moved up trustingly, but the machine guns opened up, and the plaza was strewn with dead bodies.

This treachery sealed the president's doom. After that there would be no mercy. And by this time he was cut off, as the students in a pitch of insane anger tore through the withering fire and gained the Intendencia entrance. Inside they found the police piling up records in the patio to burn them, but fearing to be trapped by the flames and smoke, they had held off. Surprised, they fled to the second floor, soon surrendered.

After the surprise machine-gun attack, the defenders worked back into the plaza, set up their captured machine guns and a single artillery piece. The front of the Palace was gutted worse than ever, windows were blown in, iron bars twisted and blown loose, but the heavy iron-grilled entrance portals remained intact.

At this moment one of the tanks ordered by Villaroel rolled down from the high part of the city, spewing machine-gun fire. Once more the tide of battle seemed about to turn against the rebels. The tank rolled on toward the Palace.

Actually three tanks had responded. Two had already been captured. This third was being driven by its crew, with two students holding guns to their heads. As it approached the Palace going downhill it gathered speed and crashed through the entrance portals, on into the big entrance salon and across the thick red carpet under the stained-glass skylight. Behind it came a horde of attackers.

In the narrow between-stairs cubbyhole that served as the presidential barber shop, a single bullet cracked the old-fashioned washbasin. The presidential concert hall with its canary-colored fragile Louis XV chairs was riddled from all sides, from the doorways and from the street. The walls looked like a plowed field; the ceiling was pockmarked from end to end. But oddly two mirrors were not cracked, not a light bulb on the elaborate chandeliers was broken. And, though full of holes, the canary-colored chairs remained in a stiff circle about the grand piano as though a concert was about to begin.

An armed student at an upstairs gallery window saw Balliván standing by the wall in the secret downstairs council chambers and fired. The military man crumpled in a thick pool of blood. A rush was made down the back stairs. Balliván was tossed to the crowd below. Uría, badly smeared by his own blood, crouched unseen behind the desk. Villaroel was nowhere around.

They heard a sound in a closet closed by a spring lock. A student fired through the door and heard a moaning sound. Putting his hand through the jagged hole made by his gun, he unfastened the lock. Villaroel fell out on his face, badly wounded, unconscious. They tore off his overcoat and tossed him over the balcony where the crowd seized him and hung him in the plaza.

Uría groped his way groaning and bleeding along the wall. A bullet sent him writhing to his death. His body, too, was tossed out and strung up.

A student wrote on the wall in chalk over the first bloodstain "Balliván", over another "Uría", and drew an arrow pointing to the closet on a blackboard and scribbled "Villaroel."

Three days later the bodies were taken down and given Christian burial, a favor Villaroel had accorded few of those his government assassinated — indeed the bones of many were found in buried coffers in Panóptico.

At the moment Villaroel's skull cracked on the Ayacucho Street cobbles, Bolivia was without a central government. The Palace was a shambles. Crowds surged in the streets. Distant firing was still going on.

At eight o'clock Paz Estenssoro took refuge in the Paraguayan Embassy.

The news swept the country. Everywhere the citizens seized the public buildings and hunted down hated enemies.

We reached Villazón on the Argentine frontier the day of the revolution. Fighting was going on. The authorities left seven dead. The rest fled across the border into Argentina.

When our train reached Oruro (the strike had been called off the previous night), the Catavi mine workers were still fighting their armed guards. Four carloads of guards and police were blown to pieces by their own dynamite.

I talked to a tiny Peruvian mother who had come to La Paz to see her son who had been studying at the National University. When, over her protests, he had rushed out to join in the fighting she had wept. It was not her fight, she told herself, but she was on the side of her son. She hurried to the central plaza, snatched up a rifle from a wounded soldier, and was right behind the tank which crashed into the palace. She claimed to have felled two palace guards.

Major Jorge Eguino, one of the worst killers of the regime, was captured fleeing, disguised as a ragged Indian, near the Chilean border by a father who had just buried his son in La Paz. Eguino revealed how many of the citizens had been tortured and killed.

In the Palace, several days after the uprising and the hangings, the president of the student federation led me up the great marble staircase, just as half the bullet-shattered skylight crashed into the patio we had just crossed. From Villaroel's desk, he handed me as gift a fine album of photographs of Bolivia, dedicated to the fallen dictator. We went on to the secret room. A student who had been an eyewitness of the final death of the dictator told me all the grisly details.

Among the strewn papers in the bedroom of Major Antonio Ponce, the Minister of Public Works, I found notes and a letter in that official's own handwriting, in green ink. One was a note underlining the names of persons that should be liquidated by the Santa Cruz Lodge. The sheet praised Franco Spain and the Falange which he said was merely a front for the real rule of the generals. He advised talking "democracy" to the U.S. ambassador but using the slogan "Anti-Imperialism" to fool the people. That Ponce himself must have been disillusioned was revealed by his details of how the regime pretended to be against foreign interests; but actually was throwing all business and power to the Rosca. This same Ponce had shouted on Saturday, twenty-four hours before the uprising, that if necessary every student and professor in Bolivia would be killed.

While I was seated on the floor in the mess of strewn papers, a tall, rangy man entered so quietly I was not aware of him until he tilted a long cigarette holder up the side of his mouth and drawled in a whimsical tone, "Find something interesting?" He was Tomás Guillén, a former president of the Supreme Court, and, at the time we met, Provisional President of Bolivia.

I jumped up. "Please don't call me 'President,' " he said, with a little gesture of his cigarette holder. "Really I'm just a member of the new Junta, like everybody else. In a few months we will have elections and I will be back on the bench."

He gave me a long scholarly discourse about constitutional government. Obviously he was bored with his new responsibilities. He preferred the quiet life, though he had opposed Villaroel in case after case, had been a constant thorn in his flesh, particularly his habeas corpus orders for the release of prisoners.

"Come see me anytime," he said when we separated. "Just walk in. No silly appointments."

Guillén was a gracious but embittered, rancorous man, who for thirty years had been in and out of nearly every party in Bolivia. His cabinet revealed that this was not a government of the people but a counter-revolution. His first act was to close down half the rural schools. His next was to initiate secret negotiations with Standard Oil to turn over the national petroleum enterprise to them. Labor leaders were thrown out of jobs. Terrorism was launched against the peasant movement, and schools built by the peasants themselves were razed. Serfdom was re-established. The jails were soon full.

A "People's Tribune" held a session in the morgue in the General Hospital and condemned Villaroel's body to death.

Elections were held in January 1947. The MNR, the majority party, if not outlawed, was not allowed to present candidates. Only 44,000 votes were cast in the entire Republic; 13,000 of these were blank. The victor, Enrique Herzog, and his associaates were photographed in triumph "flanking the dry smiling figures of Charles Armayo," tin mogul, and the editor of Patiño's *El Diario.*

Almost Herzog's first act was to send the troops to massacre striking miners, some of whom were hanged to telegraph poles. Juan Lechín, their leader, though a Senator, was deported. Peasant massacres occurred in Ayopaya and Caquiaviri.

Whenever thereafter an MNR Congressman or Senator was

elected on this or that ticket, he was seized and deported. Numerous unsuccessful revolts broke out each year of the Six Year Rule of the Oligarchy.

In 1949, despite exile, jailings, inability to campaign, the MNR won the Congressional elections, despite official fraud and terrorism, by an overwhelming majority.

On the night of the elections an MNR victory demonstration in Plaza Murillo was mowed down with machine guns. This atrocity was followed within a few months by an MNR uprising which captured Sucre and Santa Cruz. Only after prolonged fighting and artillery bombardment was it put down. Military terror throughout the country surpassed nearly all previous proportions.

But the counter-revolution — "The Six Years" — could solve none of Bolivia's problems. Terror does not mine tin or sow corn and potatoes.

4

At certain times, a single U.S. official has been able to decide the fate of governments there, because in his hands has rested the fate of the tin industry, and on the tin industry has depended whether the miners got their fifteen or seventy cents a day or whether most of the mines shut down.

In 1951 that man was Mr. Stuart Symington, head of the Reconstruction Finance Corporation, and on his decision rested Bolivia's fate. He, as much as anyone else, was responsible for the overturn of the elected government of the country, another seizure of power by a military junta, the outbreak of the revolution led by Paz Estenssoro.

Symington was undoubtedly working for the best interests of the United States and not concerned with the fate of Bolivia. The matter turned on the price of tin, as usual.

"It was natural," a Bolivian official told me, "that Symington should be especially conscious of tin prices. Before he took the R.F.C. job, he had headed the largest stainless steel corporation in the world, and his Emerson Electrical Manufacturing Company (a company generously providing profit-sharing for its employees) had built up the largest airplane armament plant in the world. Both are big users of tin. The price interests him deeply.

He was a man of relatively modest means till war contracts made him into a multi-millionaire."

Bolivia was demanding $1.50 per pound as compared to the $1.12 offered by Symington. Actually Bolivia would get little benefit, for the profits mostly went abroad, but the Bolivian government would enjoy $10,000,000 increased revenues and slightly better wages for the workers. That small difference spelled the difference between labor peace or strikes, political stability or blind revolution.

"A low tin price," said a Bolivian treasury official, "is a yeggman that reaches in to rob the bread from our mouths."

Tin was life or death, 80 percent of all revenues, 90 percent of all dollar exchange. Now Symington embargoed Bolivian tin until the government would sign on the dotted line at the price he dictated.

He was engaging in the laudable operation of trying to reduce the Cartel price of $1.84 a pound, the highest in the history of the industry, though not as much of an increase as that enjoyed by most metals. Bolivia was the goat. The international Cartel, controlled by Patiño and U.S. interests, had a monopoly on all world tin refining, except for the Texas refinery built to handle chiefly low-grade Bolivian ores.

In contrast, the prices for machinery and supplies necessary for the tin industry had multiplied four times and more.

The prices of supplies for the tin industry had never been low for Bolivia due to long rail hauls, thievery in Chilean customs (so bad, no insurance could be secured) and special problems of high-altitude mining. And now equipment was wearing out, since it could not be renewed during or immediately after the war. The cost of such replacements would now be many times as much, and the price of tin little bettered. The Patiño mines, those of the Big Three, could get by, having the best ore. Their cost of production was now $1.09 a pound and less in Malaya. But at large and medium-sized Bolivian mines otherwise owned, the cost averaged $1.33 and in small mines $1.80.

The U.S. reply was that it was just too bad if the non-Rosca mines were marginal, unable to compete with richer ores in Asia and Africa. The Bolivians replied that even so the United States was still subsidizing with vast sums marginal production of silver, copper, manganese, nickel and other needed metals, that the marginal production on which so many Bolivians depended had been built up at the request of the United States during World War I when tin could not be secured from Asia or the Cartel. Without the annual 241,096 tons of wartime tin from Bolivia, the war effort would have been disastrously disrupted, and American consumers, in any case, would have suffered deprivations. The price proposed by Symington, it was argued, would return world control to the Cartel and destroy new-found U.S. tin security. As soon as Symington forced the impossible price down Bolivia's throat and competing mines were crushed, the Cartel would again send prices soaring, and Bolivia would not benefit. Bolivia had bitter memories of long-term contracts, with no escape provisions made with the U.S. government.

If Bolivia was going to starve, it might as well begin at once. Soon thousands of tons of Bolivian tin were piled up on the wharves of Chilean and Peruvian ports. The tin mines began shutting down. More starvation than ever stalked the bleak upland plateau in the shadow of the Andean snow-peaks.

In exile in Argentina, Paz Estenssoro was running for president, not allowed to return to his country and campaign. His movement had grown. His popularity had grown. He was remembered as the one man in the Villaroel set-up who had had no hand in the terrorism and had put across what few benefits the people had won. He campaigned on a two-plank platform: nationalize the tin mines; give the land to the people. Symington's tin policy, by arousing popular wrath against the United States, elected him.

The Army seized power to prevent Paz's return. And tin kept piling up. And the people were desperate.

The resultant upheaval was bloody. But successful. After six years in exile, Paz came back in triumph under great floral arches. Bluntly he repeated that his two major objectives were to take over the tin mines and to give the big estates to the peasants. He had hardly turned away from the cheering crowds before the Palace than he appointed commissions to work out the problems of nationalization and agrarian reform.

5

The agrarian reform was carried out on a nation-wide scale. Unfortunately it could not be accompanied, as was the revolution in Cuba, by the providing of the proper seed and tools, the building of houses and schools. The government had no money. The over-all picture, however, was brightened by the completion in 1954 of the Santa-Cruz-Cochabamba-La Paz highway. It has saddled the government with a $42,000,000 debt owed the Export-Import bank and nearly a million dollars worth of too costly road-building equipment, but it opened up a vast new agricultural region that immediately began to bloom and boom. This and the new roads to the Yungas have been very costly, for the most part badly constructed and unsurfaced, indeed inferior to the worst country roads in the United States; nevertheless they are one of the important keys to economic diversification and the ultimate elimination of the need for food imports. At present Bolivia must import rice, cotton, sugar, fats, wheat, all of which could easily be produced in excess of need in Bolivia itself.

But Paz's tin expropriation was and is a headache. For the outlet for tin is still the Cartel and the U.S. government. The economic squeeze still works, though profits from the good mines have kept the marginal mines going, have kept employment up, at too high a level, given present prices and demand. The work day has been cut to eight hours, but the wage increases have been scanty.

The key to the whole situation is for Bolivia to build a refinery. Neither the U.S. bankers nor the government has been willing to give the money to build one. The USSR has offered to do so, plus $150,000,000 credit, and to take payment in tin or other products. The refinery would belong to the Bolivian government, not to foreign interests. Paz has not dared accept this offer, especially as his general financial situation forced him to turn to the United States for more help.

The help was given, but only after eighteen months of negotiations which required Bolivia to introduce an austerity program which has since slowed up expansion, prevented proper wage increases, created inflation, driven many Bolivian enterprises to the wall. The United States as a price of its money also forced annual payments be made for the expropriated mines.

Thus, much of the new aid has had to go in payments to the old owners and to the Tin Cartel. No agreement could be reached as to the final price for the mines, but the Bolivian government is still forced to pay many millions each year, with no time limit, no final agreement. Another proviso was the cancellation of outside trade debts to the United States and the forced purchase of food and other products from her. There was little emphasis, except for road-building, on development programs.

In short, nothing really basic looking toward the economic emancipation of Bolivia. Not only did much of the aid money not reach Bolivia at all, but the Bolivian government had to match the funds with counterpart funds under control of U.S. administrators, so that Bolivia has been brought under the political and economic control of the United States. The government can hardly pay a dog-catcher without U.S. permission. This has slowed up the revolution, blocked most of its plans for the welfare of the people.

Part of the money was used to buy wheat and flour in the United States — The Food for Peace program — 365,000 tons, which were sold in the markets by speculators. How much the Bolivian government got from this money to be administered by U.S. Point IV agents has not been revealed. If Peru is a criterion, the percentage must have been small indeed. At the same time this dampened expansion of an incipient wheat-growing plan, even while Bolivia has great acreage well-adapted for wheat.

To a loan for monetary stabilization went $17,500,000. Such stabilization is, of course, impossible unless export of capital and exchange and trade are regulated. It merely means that Bolivia pays out good money and goes into debt in order to facilitate the *export* of capital. It cannot possibly work unless productive capacity is increased. Instead the country is burdened with just that much added debt and interest charges with increasingly less capacity to pay. As it is it must pay for what is stolen from the country plus interest—a triple or quadruple loss. Such shenanigans benefit only the international bankers and privileged groups; it weakens national credit and forces the country to seek more and more outside loans and aid. This was the program carried on in Nicaragua under the Marines. It has been followed in Bolivia by abdication of the revolutionary program.

To get still another driblet of gold, the government had to back down on its oil policy, and the country was parcelled out into four zones, covering nearly all potential oil lands, which were handed over to six U.S. oil companies to explore and put in wells. The contracts lacked time-limits, so that the companies have done little except sit on the reserves until the international oil situation becomes more propitious, which seems unlikely for years to come, if ever.

In all, the U.S. government has pumped about $200,000,000 into Bolivia. Mostly it has been to pay the Tin Cartel, or pay trade and other debts to bail the government out of immediate financial crises when payrolls have fallen in arrears. It has kept the government afloat, but has *contributed* little, has merely hopped from crisis to crisis, but this, unlike Eliza crossing the ice, has provided no haven of escape.

The dumping of tin on the market by the United States (1962) has cost Bolivia an enormous sum, has wiped out a large part of the benefits from U.S. aid, has created near catastrophe, just as our wheat dumping has meant catastrophe for Argentina. New U.S. capital has provided employment for 2,000 workers, but in the Bolivian and public sector — 80 percent of the industry — tens of thousands have been thrown out of work.

Bolivia has presented the first Latin American ten-year plan under the Alliance for Progress, largely worked out by Peasant Affairs Minister Roberto Jordán Pando. It calls above all for transport, power, new industry and agricultural aid. But the "Alliance" is wholly in U.S. hands, and thus far she has declined to aid state-owned industry or an agriculture based on peasant cooperatives. An ordinary government clerk makes about $25.00 a month in La Paz, half that much in the provinces.

It is hard to see where this vast sum of $200,000,000 has gone. It seems to have watered the desert — for Bolivia, except for its own land reform and the Santa Cruz development, shows little tangible improvement. In most ways it is poorer than it was twenty and more years ago. The aid money has corrupted U.S. and Bolivian administrators; extraordinary and shameful graft has been uncovered. The political skullduggery is tremendous. Much of the counterpart money is used for propaganda, to control the press, to subsidize local organizations to carry on an "anti-Communist" crusade, with the aid of the Church. Why starving people should be paying for and fighting in the cold war to promote U.S. policies is not clear.

To get more money, the government had to impose a U.S. designed austerity program. This created still more economic misery. President Stiles finally went on a hunger-strike in the Palace against the program! To get another small loan in 1961 not yet available, to rehabilitate the tin mines and provide replacement of worn-out machinery, Paz had to agree to freeze wages at less than a dollar a day and fire thousands of tin miners. They went on strike late in 1961, and were put down by force, their leaders arrested. This was blamed on Cuba, not the United States.

But the "plan" goes on. It has meant recession, the stopping of public works. It has made possible the shipping out of profits (while reducing exports and imports, including needed food) and has allowed native Bolivians and U.S. interests to get out of the country more money than the aid put in.

The government has tried to take up the unemployment slack by putting some miners and others into farm cooperatives. This has proved far from successful. Meanwhile this whole land grows poorer. The revolution, still alive in the hearts of the people, moves forward at a snail's pace. The country needs capital, lots of it, but not on U.S. terms. It is a rich country of hard-working loveable people, who if given proper access to that wealth, could within a generation make it into a garden spot of prosperity, instead of its being a garden spot for greedy U.S. do-gooders, bureaucrats, bankers and concession-hunters and C.I.A. agents — a burden for its people and for the U.S. taxpayer.

This is not to discredit a few hard-working well-meaning experts, but they are working on a small raft on a stormy sea. Some are busily teaching peasants to put expensive imported glass windows into their dark mud huts, and they drive you about pridefully pointing to this or that window, like small boys enthusiastically counting white horses. They also are ecstatic at the number of people they have induced to ride bicycles; quite a few thousand Bolivians now have been able to do so, though they cost several years income for most of the population. And what is worse, the present gradualism, even if honestly pushed, will require not a generation but about 2,000 years.

It is not likely that the Bolivian people will wait that long. Unfortunately the People's Militia, formed at the time of the revolution, under financial pressures has been deprived of assistance (though the miners remain well-armed). The regular army is now under the control of the U.S. Mission; and the old pro-Rosca officers, closely connected with the ousted land-holding class, are slipping back into the Army. They are favored by the

U.S. mission, they are the ones selected to be trained in the United States.

As one rides through this majestic, beautiful and difficult country, one sees the Bolivian herdsman seated on this or that knoll with his staff, his bright poncho, chewing coca and gazing off into space, in a cocaine trance. He may not have food, but for a few pennies he can get a wad of coca leaves to stick into his cheek and forget his hard and unprofitable life.

9 ◯ JUAN PERON AND HIS SHIRTLESS

1

At ten o'clock, the night of June 3, 1943, Colonel Juan Domingo Perón of the Argentine army dashed off in long hand a proclamation to the people: "There is no glory without sacrifice . . . ."

He and the eighteen other officers of the GOU (or GO) Group of United Officers were alerting their troops for the coup on the morrow to throw out the government of President Ramón S. Castillo. And so June 4, 1943, became "the Day of the Revolution." The tanks rolled. Castillo hid out on a river mine-sweeper. It was to take Perón two years of busy-beaver effort before he controlled the movement and "revolutionized the revolution."

From 1932 until this June 4, 1943, day of sacrifice and glory, Argentina had remained in the hands of the heirs of the General Uriburú Depression dictatorship, which had brought Yrigoyen's Radical Party rule to an end in 1930 by violence in the name "of the Constitution, God and the Holy Evangels." (Whenever a Latin American general or politician talks loudly about the Constitution, the Sacred Family, God and the Holy Ghost, one knows at once that he is bent on smelly business.)

His successor, General Augustín P. Justo, wealthy landowner and ex-cabinet minister, was installed in 1932 by the most brazen bayonet election in Argentina's history. "A gentleman's dictatorship," his regime was called. A government of foreign corporation lawyers and big landowners. Argentina was a British-U.S. colony. "We could afford to lose Canada sooner than Argentina," one British statesman remarked, perhaps after a meal of succulent La Plata beef.

But the United States and her financial interests were nibbling at the edges. From Justo's clever Foreign Minister Saavedra Lamas, adored by Sumner Welles and assiduously courted by Cordell Hull, American capital won lucrative concessions. But to the State Department's chagrin, the British, French and Belgians won more.

The British rushed over titled visitors, and in London, in May 1933, the Roca-Runciman treaty was signed, setting up rigid bilateral trade (anathema to Hull). It kept tariffs low on British goods and prevented Argentina from competing with British products or building any highways that might compete with British-owned railroads.

And so, when Hull came along with his Don Quixote free trade ideas in a world where free trade was dying and had to die, to insist that Argentina sign a reciprocity treaty, Saavedra, still in a duel with Standard Oil over the Chaco War and resentful as were all Argentines that the United States would not import the fine Pampa beef, said, "Nay, nay." Nasty words were exchanged, and a beautiful politicians' friendship went puff! Saavedra believed that the United States would buy few of his country's competitive products even if duties were lowered, whereas Argentina would be shelling out precious dollars to the United States for goods that logically should be bought in England and on the continent. It was Perón who was to say bluntly a few years later: "Free trade is a device used by capitalist imperialism to keep less developed countries in misery."

But faces in Washington brightened once more when in 1938 Roberto M. Ortiz was installed as president in an even more corrupt election. He began dishing out concessions to the United States and doing Washington's bidding, and the U.S. press called his regime "the outstanding democratic government of the continent."

However, he was soon desperately ill with diabetes and had to turn his office over to Vice-President Ramón S. Castillo, the very cream of the land-holding pro-clerical elements. He believed in "Hispanidad!" — a Fascist slogan. He called himself a "Christian Fascist"; a Falangista, Franco-style, he surrounded himself with ardent pro-Fascists, pro-Nazis, Italian and German propagandists. Clearly he was going to have no more truck than necessary with the "greedy and godless, atheistic Protestant-Jewish plutocracy" of the northern colossus.

After Pearl Harbor, sparks really began to fly, even though Castillo gave the United States, as he already had England, favored belligerency status. The Argentine people were passionately isolationist. But most of the Army, however, was pro-German and believed that Germany would win the war. Argentines were proud of their record, unmatched by any other country in the world, of seventy-five years of peace; they wanted no part of this war.

England was not displeased. Its policy was based on Realpolitik, not illusions, and it kept setting up more factories in Argentina to turn out munitions and other needed war supplies. After all, Argentine labor was more helpful turning out goods for the war effort than on the battlefields, and without Argentine meat and wool the British Isles might very well perish. Also, it was glad to keep Argentina from being dominated by Washington, the Pentagon and U.S. capital.

Except for Argentina, Bolivia, Chile, all Latin American countries had swiftly bowed to Washington's wishes and had broken with the Axis or had declared war. Several banana and sugar republics had in fact been quicker about it than the United States itself. But the United States had a phobia about continental solidarity; it was galling to have hold-outs not following the Washington line. Olney had stated back in the eighties the basic State Department attitude from that day to the present: "The United States is practically sovereign on this continent."

Continental pressure was brought by calling the Foreign Minister's Conference in Rio de Janeiro a month after Pearl Harbor. But Argentina did not budge, and Chile and Bolivia still followed her lead. A watered-down declaration everybody could sign but which changed nothing saved face, so Washington and the press could hail it as another victory for U.S. diplomacy.

Before the invasion of Africa, a member of the U.S. General Staff wrote me confidentially, "The General Staff believes that getting Argentina into the war is more important than a major victory on the field of battle. What should we do about it?"

Actually it would not have been difficult: a few bold strokes, a few rectifications of past U.S. blunders and aggressions against Argentina, and the entire Argentine nation would have clamored to come in with us. My report back was described as "the frankest, most helpful and intelligent of any report ever submitted to the General Staff." That was enough to insure that nothing would be done about it; and nothing was done about it.

Open and behind scenes pressures continued: Argentina was denied arms; Brazil was armed to the teeth, and U.S. money and advisers were poured into Paraguay and Uruguay, as presently they would be poured into Bolivia; concentrations of battleships were rushed down; fruitless, wasteful squadrons of army planes swooped southward — a silly, unnecessary policy of containment, such as had been practiced years earlier against Mexico. It merely served to fortify Castillo's position, especially as his country was booming with war orders for Argentine products at mounting prices.

Finally the O.S.S. — the Office of Strategic Services — predecessor of the C.I.A. in the pernicious international cloak-and-dagger business, went into high gear to drive out Castillo. Agents were subsidized. Undercover contacts were made with Argentine generals. Money was spilled out. Palms were greased. The chief base of operations was to be Brazil, which was given additional military aid and money for continental defense, the training of new units to be carried on at the Argentine frontier, ready at the drop of a hat, if the occasion required it, to invade Argentina.

Our golden-haired boy was ex-President Justo, the "gentleman dictator." He was honored in elaborate military and public ceremonies, flanked by Dictator Vargas and Ambassador Jefferson Caffery of Cuba-Batista fame. More U.S. warships galloped into Montevideo. But Justo, always the gentleman, was ungentlemanly enough to die, leaving the busy O.S.S. holding the empty bag.

Before the cloak-and-dagger boys could dig up a new candidate, a blow-up came in Argentina. Factories there were going full-blast, gold reserves were piling up, there was no unemployment, but imported goods were hard to get, inflation had reduced real wages. The vast prosperity had brought hardship to the people. Military coercion was irksome. The situation had grown unstable: not only were the people angry at their plight in the midst of plenty, but never had the plundering of public funds, the graft, waste and corruption been so great.

The O.S.S. intrigues, the bitter U.S. propaganda countered by equally bitter Nazi, Italian and Spanish propaganda, were dividing the people into hostile camps: pro-U.S., pro-Axis, pro-neutral, with various shades in between. Though a larger number swung over to a pro-Allied position, U.S. propaganda was not able to convince a majority that Argentina should abandon neutrality.

With the June 4 coup, what the O.S.S. and Washington got for their folly was something far worse than Castillo.

2

General Arturo Rawson was installed as provisional president; several days later he was replaced by General Pedro Ramírez, Castillo's War Minister. Washington shot off jubilant fireworks. The U.S. press hailed it as a victory for the Allied cause and the rights of the people. Even Waldo Frank, who should have known better, hied himself to Buenos Aires to cheer for the restoration of "democracy" in Argentina.

Surely some one around that lot in Washington should have known the score. Rawson and Ramírez were the most overt pro-Nazis in the Argentine army. Ramírez had served two years in the German army in Europe. He had used his influence in the Castillo regime to hold back on friendliness with the United States. Why he should be a god-send to the democratic cause now was a mystery. These two generals had organized a secret pro-Nazi cabal in the Army; they had organized youth and children's military units to goose-step and shout "Viva Hitler!" Their backers now were the militant pro-Nazis of the so-called Nationalist Party. And Nationalist Party thugs proceeded to break Waldo's skull, would likely have killed him had they not been interrupted.

Ramírez' first step down the noble road of democracy was to suppress Congress, to close up newspapers (particularly those subsidized by the U.S. Embassy and all Jewish publications), to jail or deport all critics, and to cancel the September elections. He declared, on the authority of St. Thomas Aquinas and Pope Pius XII, that the Argentines wanted justice not elections. His cabinet posts went to generals (except one), all of them strong Axis supporters. German agents had a free hand.

His Secretary of War, General Edelmiro Farrell, named fellow GO officer Juan Perón (who had been on his staff in an Andean post for several years) to head the secretariat. Perón had a free hand and began shifting generals and favoring friends. Colonels suddenly became generals. Generals found it convenient to resign.

Perón knew military matters well. He had been an instructor at the war college; he had written six volumes on military organization and tactics; he had looked over the armies of Europe for several years: in Germany, Italy, Albania, Hungary and Spain. Asked what he had learned, he replied, "What not to do." In Chile, as air attaché, he had earlier hobnobbed so much with the Chilean counterpart of GO and with exiles belonging to the Bolivian Santa Cruz Lodge, that he was accused of espionage by the Chilean government and sent home persona non grata.

In Spain he looked over the terrible destruction of the Civil War. "What has anybody gained from all this?" he wanted to know, and resolved that civil war had to be avoided in Argentina. If it were to be avoided, the bases of government had to be widened, counter-checks to army power had to be built up. He was looking far ahead.

On October 27, 1943, he got himself appointed to a coveted post where he could build up popular support: the Department of Labor and Social Welfare, not yet a cabinet department, merely a minor bureau in the Department of Interior. Though a batch of labor leaders were arrested the very next day, Perón declared he was the friend of labor, promised higher wages, better working conditions, social security, and energetically set to work to get non-unionized workers organized.

Up until this time there were only about 200,000 organized workers in all Argentina; there had been no important labor legislation since the Laws of the Indies set up by Spain in the sixteenth century. Labor reunions were illegal. Even executive committees could not meet without a police or army officer present. Strikes had always been put down with force. The peasants and farm workers, the peóns, had no rights whatever. They could not even vote, and all efforts to win rights or to organize had always been met with machine guns and death. This was just as true under Radical Yrigoyen prior to 1930 as under all subsequent governments. Perón made himself Labor's protector. He denounced "the false apostles who had gotten into the unions to trick the workers and betray the masses, or to lead them into agitations in the field of international politics and ideologies."

On December 1 he got his bureau raised to cabinet rank, and addressed a mass meeting of workers the following day. He spoke of the "extraordinary intuition of the masses when they are guided with loyalty and honor." "With the creation of the Secretariat of Labor and Social Welfare [Previsión] we have initiated the era of Argentine *social* politics. The epoch of instability and disorder in which were submerged the relations between employers and workers is behind us forever . . . . Private enterprises will be guaranteed that if they pay the wages and follow the healthy rules of human welfare, the state will recognize their efforts in behalf of the general economy and the engrandizement of the fatherland." The policy of his department would be based on "the highest principles of social collaboration, with the purpose of strengthening human solidarity, national economic progress, fomenting new private capital, increasing production and bettering the life of the worker."

His reforms came fast: an over-all wage increase, presently a month's pay as a Christmas bonus, eight-hour day, minimum wage, vacations with pay, accident insurance. His Ley de Peón set up the most progressive farm-worker laws in the world, far more extensive than any laws covering itinerant workers in the United States: an eight-hour day, rest periods, minimum food requirements, minimum wage, vacations with pay, proper housing, schools, free medical care for the worker and members of his family, the right to organize and enjoy all civil rights.

He began building hospitals and clinics all over the country; set up mobile hospitals on the highways and railroads. People who had never known medical care any more than had their forefathers, now had access to it. He started public housing, and worked out plans for building 100,000 workers' homes. Special statutes improved the condition of railway workers and newspaper men (pensions for one thing), actors and actresses, port workers, workers in the quebracho industry, nurses, schoolteachers.

Washington, soon disillusioned with the new regime, resumed its pressures, its threats and its battleship diplomacy against Ramírez. Finally Ramírez and his Foreign Secretary surrendered and, on January 26, 1944, broke relations with the Axis powers and suppressed *El Pampero*, the leading pro-Nazi newspaper.

The reaction in nearly all quarters was unfavorable, not merely from the reduced group of pro-Axis sympathizers but from Nationalists and isolationists; the mass of the people wanted neutrality, and they had been defrauded. The proud Argentines were shamed that their government had supinely bowed to the wishes of Washington. Anti-Americanism rose to a new pitch.

On February 15, Perón led a group of army officers to the Ministry of Foreign Affairs and forced the minister to resign. On February 24 Ramírez retired from the presidency and delegated his powers to Vice-President Farrell and on March 9 resigned entirely. People began asking whether Farrell had pulled Perón up with him, or whether Perón had pushed Farrell to the top.

Farrell announced his cabinet on February 26. Juan Perón, without relinquishing his cabinet post as head of the Labor and Social Welfare Department, took over the duties of Minister of War. By July 27 he was also Vice-President.

At once he began overhauling the military forces. On March 14 he abolished the GO by fiat and set up a favored "Colonels' Clique" in its place. When the generals protested at the new political preponderance of younger officers, Perón promoted seventeen colonels to the rank of general (April 6).

On May 1, he addressed a monster workers' rally, telling of the social accomplishments which had been effected since 1943 — in a single year, in fact in six months, the period he had been in charge of the Department and Secretariat.

"Every day thousands of workers come to the Secretariat of Labor and Social Welfare, workers of every branch of productive activity. Scores of delegations bring us their problems, their hopes and aspirations. On this classic Labor Day I promise that this confidence will not be defrauded."

3

At another rally June 10 — four days after the Normandy invasion began — Perón clarified his neutralist pro-Argentine position — what was to develop into his "Third Position." It was not important so far as Argentina was concerned which side won the war: the legitimate nationalist aspirations of Argentina could be realized only through vigorous diplomacy, military strength and organized unity.

At once Hull began applying diplomatic, economic and moral sanctions. This type of U.S. unilateral aggression merely strengthened the regime and enhanced Perón's growing popularity. Finally on September 29, Roosevelt denounced Argentina as the citadel of Nazi-Fascist influence in America.

It was soon discovered that Great Britain would not go along with U.S. policy. The aid from Argentina which she was getting was too important for her own war effort. The *Manchester Guardian* remarked facetiously, "We like the Argentine brand of Fascism as little as does Mr. Cordell Hull, but we also prefer Argentine beef to American pork."

On November 27 Hull resigned. His successor, Secretary of State Edward R. Stettinius, and Assistant Secretary of State Nelson Rockefeller took steps to conciliate the Farrell government. Hull's attitude toward Argentina had been condemned by numerous Latin American governments, and the demand for an inter-American conference made by Argentina in October had embarrassed the Roosevelt Administration, for it was apparent there would be less unity than at the Rio Conference. Washington at this juncture really needed the full support of all the southern countries, if not for the war effort, for the forthcoming United Nations conference in San Francisco.

The Soviets were threatening to refuse admission to the United Nations of all countries which denied her recognition, and only by having an almost solid block of countries from Latin America could the United States hope with assurance to control the proceedings. Because of U.S. pressure, most Latin American

countries, prior to the war, had broken with the Soviets or refused to recognize them. Now secret U.S. diplomatic pressures
were invoked to have all the countries tender recognition.

A back-door deal was cooked up with Argentina to save face
all around. The United States managed to exclude fellow-mem-
ber Argentina from the February Chapultepec conferences in
Mexico, but secretly arranged for her admission to that body
and the United Nations in return for a last-minute declaration of
war on the Axis, to be followed later by recognition of the Soviet
Union.

The truce was short-lived. In May 1945 Spruille Braden arrived in Buenos Aires as ambassador and began an attack, centered not so much on the government as on Juan Perón, and he
encouraged the oligarchy, business elements and the large hacendados to attack the work of the Secretariat of Labor and Social Security. He spoke on the platform of the most reactionary
landholders' group in the country, and there is little doubt that
he was behind the sudden bold joint attack of the Argentine
Chamber of Commerce and the Buenos Aires Stock Exchange
which charged that Perón's department was sowing economic
heresies and class hatred. It would not be long before Braden
would quit calling Perón a "Nazi" and brand him as a "Communist." You have your cake, and you eat it too.

No diplomat accredited to the United States would dare med-
dle in U.S. internal affairs in the fashion Braden did, but, though
he was more arrogant and flagrant than was usual, this has usually been the modus operandi of our diplomats in Latin America.
They are not so much diplomats as representatives of large corporations or pro-consuls (Braden was both); they take for granted the colonial status of the southern countries. As Ambassador
Smith, accredited to Cuba, told a Senate sub-committee, in attacking the Castro regime before the revolution, before Castro,
the American ambassador had as much to say or perhaps more
about the conduct of affairs than the president. In his mind, this
charge constituted a complete damning of Castro and all his
works.

But Perón was delighted. He warned Braden and the oligarchy that he now had a "labor army" of four million men who
would unhesitatingly accept the challenge made by their enemies. More than ever he was the champion of the neglected

masses. Their enemy, his enemy, was the hated Oligarchy and Yankee imperialism.

There is little doubt that Braden's activities, later his hostility as Assistant Secretary of State, helped spark the army uprising, led by pro-Nazi ex-President General Rawson, on September 14. Some militarists, deluded by their reactionary backers — as Perón had pointed out in the *Boletín Militar* ten days before — feared the new power of Labor. But Labor and the Army, he insisted, were the true pillars of Argentina; both were working patriotically for the good of the country.

The Rawson revolt was put down without trouble, but on October 9, another group of officers, led by General Eduardo Avalos, of the key Campo de Mayo garrison, reached the Casa Colorada and forced Perón to resign as Vice-President, Minister of War, and head of the Labor Department. Perón rallied the workers and told them he had drafted a wage increase and hoped that they would receive it.

He was arrested and sent on a naval vessel to the Martín García Island in the Rio de la Plata. The military heads wrangled ever cabinet posts, over ousting Farrell also. But while they fiddled, Rome burned.

On October 17 a monster mass demonstration of the workers poured into the streets and plazas, whipped up by Cipriano Reyes, head of the slaughter-house unions, Domingo Mercante, Perón's assistant in the Secretariat of Labor, and particularly by Eva Duarte, Perón's mistress and head of the radio and movie actors' guild. There on the balcony of the Casa Rosada to address the marchers appeared, as by miracle, Juan Domingo Perón. By his side was President Farrell.

Two years ago, "from this same balcony," Perón told them, he had said to a similar gathering that his three claims to honor were that he was "a soldier, a patriot, and Argentine's first workingman." Now he had resigned from the Army "to help revive the almost forgotten civilian tradition of Argentina and join with the sweating, suffering mass of laborers who are building the greatness of the nation."

He did not return to the cabinet, but the new members were his personal friends and supporters and pledged to his program of "social justice." He went further and resigned even his commission in the Army, and on October 21 he married Evita Duarte.

They went to live in the slums "with the workers."

He was as adroit as a politician during the campaign that followed as he had been as an army officer and an administrator. The Communist Party split four ways. The Communist Labor Federation was dissolved voluntarily, the members instructed to seek admission to the General Confederation of Labor, which Perón was soon to build up to five million members. The Socialist Party split wide open. Most of its labor unions deserted to the General Confederation; the younger members of the party went in droves into the Perón camp; one state organization went over en masse, leaving the older more dogmatic leaders isolated. The Radical Party, made up of some workers, most of the middle class and native business men, was already divided between a progressive group with an economic program and the old-guard which resorted only to platitudes. The progressive wing now supported Perón. The Conservatives also split badly, and if the hierarchy of the Church failed to support Perón, he won over a large part of the poorer clergy and the lay members, enough so, when the show-down came, he could carry several traditionally Catholic-Conservative states.

The fractured remnants of the old-line parties cooked up a "democratic" coalition; Radicals, Socialists, Communists and the Progressive Democrats (this last, in reality the most reactionary land-holding group in the country), the party of Spruille Braden. The coalition called itself the Democratic Union, but aside from a few phrases about freedom and democracy, it had no program except "Beat Perón!"

Perón's program was pro-labor, pro-peasant, pro-middle class, pro-native business, above all pro-nationalist and strongly anti-imperialist. He promised to nationalize public utilities and do away with the privileged position of foreign capital. He told of what he had done to organize and strengthen the Army; how for the first time in history the ordinary recruit was given good food, proper clothing, club rooms, and better pay. This, in fact, was why, when a showdown had come in October, the generals had not dared move against him.

If the democratic coalition had no program, no dynamic proposals, neither did it have a leader. Finally by the end of the year, it selected José Tamborini, a colorless creature, the only sort that could get past the bickering among the "democratic" factions. He was a sixty-year-old physician, a former deputy and

cabinet minister, and always a wishywashy turncoat. Turned cat-
tle-man, he spent all his time at the Jockey Club, the aristocratic
center of the reactionaries, on Florida Street, playing poker with
cronies. Perón was up at dawn or earlier. Tamborini rarely got
up until noon.

"Normalcy" was the "democratic" watch-word. Perón stood for
social revolution. He stood for the righting of ancient wrongs.
The "democrats" stood for the status quo; they wanted merely a
chance at public posts and spoils. They were confident of victory
up until the last for they were quite out of touch with the people and the new economic forces reshaping the country.

Perón continued to be aided by Braden's long-distance meddling (he was now in Washington) and his irritable pronouncements against the nationalist-proletarian leader. Two weeks before the election, obviously in order to help defeat Perón, he issued the State Department's "Blue Book on Argentina." It
damned the Farrell government, which had broken relations
with the Axis, as being "so seriously compromised" with the Nazi-
Fascist "enemy that trust and confidence could not be reposed
in that government."

It was mostly a McCarthy-type document; the evidence, in
spite of quoting many secret papers, was highly dubious, and
where no evidence existed, smear names were generously used.
It was a war-hysteria document besides, and many of the condemned Argentine relations with Germany and Italy were merely the normal intercourse between recognized governments.

It was already stale stuff. Already the German line had crum-
bled. U.S. troops had taken Manila, Iwo Jima had been captured,
the Yalta agreement had been signed.

What did seem particularly damning was an early Argentine
attempt to get arms from Germany. But since the United States
had embargoed arms to Argentina and was building up Brazil
and surrounding countries, it is difficult to blame Argentina.

Perón, of course, was singled out for special treatment. The
evidence, if examined in historical context, is laughably trivial
and unconvincing. The Blue Book did not mention that Perón
had actually been cashiered from the Army during the Castillo
period for his pro-Allied position. That he had grown more sympathetic to the Axis afterwards is also clear, but his basic position was pro-Nationalist, pro-Argentine, and at no time had he
come to love the ways in which the O.S.S., secret agents and dip-

lomats had meddled in Argentine affairs, nor the frequent spleen
of Washington and the repeated use of gunboat diplomacy.

In any event The Blue Book was a godsend for Perón;
it aroused the Argentines to bitter anti-Yankeeism; sunk whatever slight chances Tamborini ever had. Perón, during his campaigning, never mentioned his opponent by name. Now the walls
were plastered with posters reading "Perón or Braden?" and
"Perón Sí, Braden No." Perón won with 56 percent of the total
vote, a margin of victory larger than that of any U.S. President
since the Civil War. In the electoral college, modeled after that
of the United States, the result was overwhelming, for Tamborini
had carried only four states, and the vote was 304 to 72. Perón's
forces won two-thirds of the votes in the chamber and even a
larger majority in the Senate. On top of that it was the largest
vote — since the rural workers could vote for the first time and
because of aroused feelings everywhere – in Argentine's history — 50 percent larger — and though the opponents complained of pre-election intimidation, all admitted that otherwise it had been the most honest election the country had ever
known. Perón was one of the few presidents in Argentine's history not imposed by the Army — not that his "Colonel's Clique"
was not more than busy.

It was a dictatorship — with the support of the people, which
many another dictatorship, supported and praised by the United
States, did not have.

After the election, Perón told the country — with his handsome poise and easy eloquence— "There seems to be a feeling
in the land that the aims of this government are a dark dangerous
mystery . . . There is no need for anybody to be alarmed on that
score. There is no mystery whatever. I shall set up in the Casa
Rosada, the Executive Mansion, a big blackboard for everybody
to see, on which everything we propose to do will be chalked up.
. . . No one need fear we will go beyond that. As each thing is
accomplished, we will cross it off so all may see how well we
have lived up to our announced program and whether we have
been worthy of your confidence." All "honest Argentineans"
could help. He held out the olive branch to all, even his worst
opponents, who wished to work "for a greater, more prosperous
Argentina."

The blackboard was the five-year plan, which, in print, filled

128 pages. With respect to economic reorganization, it was basically the well-studied Federico Pinedo Plan (originally brought out by the Conservatives) brought up-to-date and revamped to emphasize social welfare, labor and peasant rights, and national defense. Its defect: it was too ambitious, likely to falter because of lack of money, machinery supplies, technical know-how and labor shortages. Perón admitted some aspects might require ten rather than five years.

The Plan included:

(a) Financial and banking reform. It gave rights similar to that of the U.S. Federal Reserve Board, something denounced by pro-Allied newspapers as "centralized Fascism." Actually it did not go as far, and even with these changes, Argentina was not up to its neck in government banking and loan-giving to the extent the United States was. What went beyond traditional practices was control over loans to see they were granted for enterprises desirable for the general economy. In practice, this same thing is done — though with no particularly patriotic interest — by the great government lending agencies in the United States. What was involved in Argentina, of course, was the effort to free the country from domination by outside banks and capital from Europe and the United States.

(b) The complete liquidation of foreign debt, to do away with interest charges going out of the country. This was quickly done by means of Argentina's vast monetary reserves and profits from government trading monopolies. A debt of $250,000,000 was eliminated.

(c) Government ownership of foreign-owned utilities and various basic industries. This was carried out expeditiously. All British and French railways were bought up, also North American and British light, power, traction and telephone companies. Standard Oil was left alone, but was required to sell all products to the government oil corporation.

(d) Promotion of essential industries, such as metal refining, automobiles, airplanes, railroad equipment (the first locomotives were turned out), chemicals, expanded rubber products, drugs, etc. Tin refineries and steel mills were set up.

The new steel mill in northern Argentina was not merely dedicated to industrial efficiency but to human efficiency. The location looked like a beautiful park rather than a drab industrial system; the workers' landscaped housing looked more like a Cleveland millionaire's suburb. Certainly no American steel worker has ever enjoyed such good housing in such a graceful setting.

The tin refinery was a "must." This meant saving enormous shipping costs and avoiding monopoly prices set by England. Previously tin ore had to be shipped to England, the tin made into cans, which were shipped back for Argentine's meat, which then had to be reshipped to England. The State Department, according to the press, was upset when in 1946 Argentina outbid the United States for half of Bolivia's tin supply.

(e) Government purchase and sale of wheat, wool, meat, hides, vegetable oils. This was handled by the Exchange Institute (IAPI) which in 1947 provided a profit to the government of two billion pesos (when the peso was still around five or six to the dollar) that was to be used for financing the industrial plan.

This was absolutely necessary, to face up to government buying from abroad. Argentina had long been gouged by joint British-U.S. government meat-and-food-buying agencies, which had abolished competitive purchasing. Now, for the first time, Argentina was able to get a fair price for its farm products.

Second, the trade administration provided an iron-fisted control over the big *hacendados* and *estancieros* who, with the help of the Army, had always run Argentina — keeping it underdeveloped, backward, badly exploited for centuries. The bitter war against Perón's administration was chiefly by these outmoded plantation elements (not by the new Argentine industrialists) who now fought him strongly in conjunction with the State Department and the large U.S. corporations. Now the landholders were brought to heel, and the government skimmed the cream off their profits.

Some aspects of this control were abusive. When Péron set up new government-owned farm machinery factories and created also a government farm-machinery importation monopoly, landowners showing open hostility to the regime were unable to get needed equipment. Political retaliation by previous governments in the hands of the feudal elements and foreign-corporation lawyers had been directed against workers, peasants and intellectuals. Now it was directed against the powerful Argentine-U. S. industrialists and latifundists, and their anguish echoed around the world.

Another promise of the five-year plan was better national distribution of industry on a regional basis (the government was heavily weighted with new men from the provinces). With this went a proposal to develop new resources, to carry on extensive highway and railroad construction, develop water power and electricity. (Sixty-nine major light, electric, canal and irrigation projects, expansion of the merchant marine, expansion of government and private air services, the building of new airports.) New immigration was actively promoted, the Argentine government paying transportation costs and $280 a head (to be repaid in forty installments). Public health and social welfare were advanced.

Perón strengthened his control over most institutions often in an arbitrary manner. He let his erstwhile enemies, the Socialists, hold their national convention — in which they denounced him up one side and down the other — in the Congress building while the lawmakers were in recess. But he purged the Supreme Court, as Roosevelt tried unsuccessfully to do. He intervened in the universities, as every previous president had done. Most professors had been against him. The rectorship of Buenos Aires University for instance was given to my good friend, Dr. Oscar Ivanassovich, a plastic surgeon and graduate of the University of California, and pro-Perón.

But the actual purging was mostly done by the faculty members themselves, by professors now anxious to climb on the Perón band-wagon — for that meant jobs, travel funds, research funds, exchange professorships and other advantages. Many notable professors bit the dust. Inferiors seized the chance to step into their shoes. One of the casualties was Dr. Alfredo Palacios, head of the Socialist Party. Perhaps this experience taught him how later to purge the Socialist Party, with the aid of Frondizi's police, in 1961.

Perón promptly bought out the British-owned railways, the British, Belgian, U.S.A. public utilities, including the properties of American and Foreign Power and I.T. & T., paying good prices, cash on the barrel-head. In the case of British properties, he was aided by the fact that about a billion wartime dollars owed Argentina were frozen in England.

He quickly built up the seventh largest merchant-marine in the world, even competing with large luxury liners, and took over the Dodero shipping which monopolized river trade with Paraguay. Argentine shipping soon carried a larger share of Argentine's trade than did that of any other nation.

Some of Péron's punitive measures were ill-considered. He seized *La Prensa*, Argentina's biggest newspaper, and turned it over to the workers. His motives were not so much press suppression, but because it was owned by one of the wealthiest landowning families in the country, and its columns were used, with slogans of "democracy" and "free enterprise," to denounce the Perón program.

New Perón laws favored Labor and the peasants. He continued to encourage labor organization, and membership rose to nearly 5,000,000 compared to a previous 200,000. An enormous peasant movement was born. Previously the Argentine peasants were mowed down with machine guns, had never been allowed to vote. They voted under Perón and have never lost that right, regardless of the manner in which later elections were manipulated or stolen under the "democratic" regimes of Aramburu and Frondizi.

Perón plowed full steam ahead with his labor and peasant reforms, and his reorganization of the economy that soon caused so many screams of anguish.

4

In 1949 the constitution was revamped by an elected Constitutional Convention (109 Perónistas, 48 Radicals). Despite the die-hard opposition of the Radicals, the new document established direct election of the president (abolishing the electoral college), women's suffrage, greater control over property rights. All foreign trade was put in the hands of the State. All minerals and most sources of energy were nationalized, "public services" were to be state-owned. It contained lengthy articles entitled "The Rights of the Worker," "Rights of the Aged." In some directions it went further than the 1917 Mexican constitution, in other directions was less progressive.

The incredible Braden policies were somewhat offset when George Messersmith was sent down as ambassador. He felt that Argentina should manage its own affairs, that the ineffective pot-shotting against Perón merely strengthened his hand and weakened the bargaining position of the United States.

"This is a revolution," he told me. "It is long, long overdue."

But his own Embassy remained a spider's web of intrigue against Perón. The cultural attaché, who mostly hobnobbed with sour-grapes Spanish industrialists, took me to a secret gathering of opposition elements: Socialists, Radicals, Conservatives, several military men. A worse bunch of shoddy bellyachers I have never encountered. The whole evening was spent in discussing what army generals could be utilized for overthrowing Perón. When Perón later deported the attaché, I knew the reason why. Washington sputtered, but Perón's charges were true.

Meanwhile Perón plowed ahead and boldly announced his Third Position, neither capitalism nor communism, but national independence, economic progress, human welfare.

It was Evita Perón who worked most indefatigably on labor matters, peasant protection, public housing, public health. She became the idol of the masses, and her jewelry and expensive minks did not seem to disillusion them. She also handled public relations and the press, subsidizing newspapers and building up a large pro-administration daily.

The perniciousness of this was obvious. But the U.S. Embassy was also subsidizing newspapers and writers, then, since, and now — now more than ever. The big dailies were also indirectly subsidized by advertising, which for them was life or death, from large U.S. corporations and exporting houses. Nobody breathes a word about this or the tremendous U.S. pressures, financial and otherwise, which were and are being directed against the independent press in various countries.

Perón was riding the wave of post-war prosperity. For many of the down-under countries, peace had been a disaster, as raw products dropped in price. But the world still needed Argentina's food badly, and Perón's trading methods brought better prices than ever. He was accused of being a Shylock, sucking the blood of the miserable of the earth. Nobody worried about the long-suffering Argentine workers, who had been squeezed so long to provide other countries with low-cost food, and who now had to pay three to six times as much for staples from the United States.

But inevitably the march of world events caught up with Perón and hit Argentina, as earlier it had hurt the rest of Latin America so disastrously. Soon enough, he was in financial difficulties: some due to his own blunders, but mostly because of the price squeeze which was taking more billions out of Latin

America by the industrialized powers than all the aid in the world, more than the Alliance for Progress can ever put back. As raw product commodity prices dropped and dropped, the cost of manufactured goods, of machinery, of replacements, of automobiles or farm-equipment, soared up and up, to many times wartime costs, and by the time they reached Argentina — what with freight, corruption, tariffs — the costs were doubled again, or tripled, even over the increased cost in the United States. Then three years of bad drought hit Argentina. Perón, not the weather, was blamed for the disaster.

Still, he handled it well, and the crisis would have been worse had it not been for the new cushions built into the economy, had it not been for the new industry he had implanted (by this time twice as many people were employed in industry as in agriculture) — the mixed-corporations he had set up, the new light-and power and highway developments, the wide-spread new mining operations. His nationalization policies had stopped the drain of at least $100,000,000 a year out of the country. At this juncture, he brought into his government the finest economist and financial mind of Argentina, Federico Pinedo. Soon, too, the Korean War gave a new shot in the arm, and Argentina moved back into the prosperity column.

In November 1951, Perón was re-elected by 65 percent of the vote. The Perónistas took every seat in the Senate, all but four-teen seats in the Chamber of Deputies. His party had been the only one to put up women candidates; now six Senators and twenty-three deputies were women. The Perónistas even carried Buenos Aires, always the Radical stronghold, by a large majori-ty. Even his opponents, though they claimed pre-election coer-cion, acknowledged that once more it had been an unusually honest election.

His controls were not as extensive or overriding as Democratic Party controls in much of the U.S. South; in Argentina every-body, not merely a white minority, could vote. Whatever Perón's methods, there was no doubt at all that he had the support of the majority of the Argentine people, a larger majority than he had enjoyed six years before.

The great blow to Perón and his system came with Evita's death from cancer. She was more popular than Perón himself, and all Argentina wept. Every taxi driver had her picture on his windshield alongside that of St. Christopher. In homes, Perón's picture might be absent; but it was rare not to see Evita's, framed like a saint.

After her death, he seemed to lose his magic touch and began to abandon his Third Position. On May 24, 1948, right after the disastrous inter-American Bogotá conference, he had declared "the best way to consolidate Pan Americanism" would be "to put an end to the spoilation of Latin America by capitalist-imperialism and trusts without a country." He was then able to boast that Argentina had eliminated its foreign debt; he would accept no aid from the "imperialist" powers; he would grant no concessions to foreign capital but intended to liberate Argentina from all alien rule.

Yet in 1953 he was stating that Argentina would have to have the collaboration of "capitalist-imperialists, or development would have to be indefinitely postponed."

There was no way to get around the price-differential between Argentine exports and imports necessary for industrialization — or for that matter, Argentina's ordinary needs.

International timing also worked against him. As long as Britain was on the scene and competing with the United States, they could be played off against each other; as they drew together, it had been possible to seek a new balance by playing off German and U.S. interests, as Vargas of Brazil did with skill.

But after the war England, reduced to a third-rate power, and economically retrenching, was herself becoming a U.S. satellite. Germany was crushed, her industry in ruins. Japan was crushed. Perón recognized the Soviet Union right after his first inauguration, and arranged a few trade deals (which caused Braden to relabel him "Communist"), but Soviet industry had not yet become a factor in world trade.

After the war the United States was the ruler of the world trade roost, and the squeeze on less developed countries — on Argentina — was cruel and implacable.

A new Argentine law now guaranteed the right of foreign investors to export profits up to 8 percent. After ten years they could also export their investment capital — up to 20 percent annually. The government would provide subsidies and grant exemption from customs duties.

As yet Perón had received little aid money from the United

States. The $125,000,000 loan in 1950 from the Export-Import Bank had merely paid off commercial accounts overdue in the United States itself. But now the way for a loan was cleared when he bowed to our oil diplomacy — so determinedly pressed for so long — and granted oil concessions to U.S. corporations. At one swoop he reversed his position, and he also reversed nearly half a century of stern Argentine policy — to retain control of her own oil reserves. This had been a passionate conviction with the armed forces, particularly the Navy. This move brought him into open conflict with the military and with labor, which staged strikes.

His personal conduct was not above reproach, and provided fuel for his enemies. He had set a young schoolgirl up in a fancy apartment as his mistress. Similar charges could be made against almost every political leader and general in Latin America, but Perón, in view of the vast popular love for Evita, and the hostility of the U.S. news agencies, was particularly vulnerable. Apparently, however, Perón loved the girl, took her with him when he went into exile, and finally married her.

His divorce law and full legalization of civil marriage, and his law to regulate and control prostitution, brought him into sharp conflict with the Church hierarchy. The law on prostitution was construed by the Church and the U.S. press to mean that Perón was actually promoting prostitution.

The underworld sex problem in nearly all countries has been handled in two ways: by the free-enterprise-police-graft-police-persecution method (as in the United States), or by state regulation — the French way, and in vogue throughout much of Latin America. The latter method requires the registration of prostitutes, price-controls and periodical health examinations. If found diseased, they have to enter a hospital at their own expense, or else a state-owned hospital to be treated free. In short, the Perón law represented a decided improvement, morally and health-wise, over Buenos Aires' existing wildfire vice, disease, and police corruption.

A small military putsch was easily put down, but the plotting by the Army and the Church grew serious. Perón assembled his *decamisados* and the people of Buenos Aires in a monster mass meeting. His great oratorical powers had not declined. The immediate result of his incendiary speech was the wrecking and burning of half a dozen Buenos Aires churches. He had a large national police force built up — another check on the Army. For the moment, it remained loyal. Too late, then, he began arming the workers.

But the Church roused the extreme pro-clerical clique in the Army and backed General Eduardo Lonardi, who took over the very pro-Catholic provincial capital of Córdoba by an armed coup in September 1955; other army units moved. The Navy, burned up by his oil concessions, moved, and Perón fled to Paraguay.

Lonardi assumed the presidency on September 23, with pious medieval phrases, and dissolved the elected Congress.

By this time the historical significance of the Perón revolution was clear. It had been first of all, nationalistic and anti-foreign. To establish Argentine political and economic independence, he created an alliance similar to that made by Calles in Mexico back in the twenties — native capital on the one hand, labor on the other. Strikes were directed against foreign, not native enterprises. Both groups were subsidized and given advantages, by means of special exchange rates, freight rates, tariffs, etc. At the same time he squeezed the juice out of the feudal landlord class by state control of trade.

He failed because he did not actually carry out an agrarian revolution, so that the most powerful groups, in spite of his coercive measures, were still able to plot against him. He realized this too late, and in his spleen sent his *decamisados* to burn down the aristocratic Jockey Club. The failure to cut the economic roots of the great landholders also made his industrialization plans unworkable. He could not build up adequate purchasing power fast enough merely by raising urban wages.

He purged the Army, but only part way. The officers shoved to one side, but not eliminated, nursed deep grudges, and they had arms— waiting for *Der Tag*.

In November, Major General Pedro E. Aramburu replaced Lonardi. One of Aramburu's first acts was to cancel Perón's ·oil-concessions — some of which had displeased major U.S. oil companies — but he did not close the door to new ones. Otherwise he followed the State Department and Pentagon line.

Washington considered the downfall of Perón a great boon, and the publicity in Aramburu's favor went into high gear. "Democracy" had been restored to Argentina; "freedom" had also been restored.

Aramburu's regime was out and out counter-revolution. He

represented, above all else, the landed aristocracy, for whom Perón had created so many difficulties; he represented that part of the business oligarchy allied with foreign capital; he was pro-Church. This represented a restoration to power of the traditional exploiters of the Argentine people, in which nobody else would have any part or say-so.

His economic policies — following all of Washington's suggestions — soon plunged the country into disaster. The various agricultural, industrial and trade bureaus were liquidated overnight. Exchange control restrictions, without which Argentina would be quickly stricken down, were lifted overnight. He was provided with some millions for currency stabilization by the International Monetary Fund — a curious contradiction to the new "Free Enterprise" being set up. It merely created insuperable difficulties. Argentina was forced to abandon bilateral trade treaties with eight countries. An unfavorable trade balance resulted.

Billions of dollars rushed from the country overnight. A lush free-enterprise looting of the land occurred immediately. Back trade credits were paid off without regard for the national economy. Profits were rushed out by foreign corporations. Argentine citizens sent vast sums abroad for safety. Imports now became luxury imports. New foreign cars blossomed on the streets, providing a false air of prosperity.

While street cars continued to fall apart, industrial production slowed down, employment declined by leaps and bounds, revenues fell off, public works had to be abandoned. Hundreds of thousands of pauperized people flooded into Buenos Aires. For three million of its seven million inhabitants, neither Aramburu nor his successor Frondizi were able to provide water, sewage facilities, electric lights, street paving, schools, hospitals — only police-stations. Buenos Aires, once a fine, clean, modern city, began to stink with human excrement and piled-up garbage, and still stinks. One suburban town council reported it had had to meet by candle-light. All this was blamed upon Perón and his disastrous policies.

The Army moved in on the labor unions, kicked out all elected officers. No Peronista was allowed. Wages were sliced. The great haciendas now flouted the Ley de Peón. Such was Argentina's New Freedom.

Unrest resulted, and as the economy went from bad to worse, attempts at armed insurrection were made. Aramburu righteously shot dissenters. This was a democracy — was it not?

As ruin stalked the land, U.S. corporations began buying up big estates and Argentine industries at bargain-counter rates. Soon great haciendas were stocked, not with fine-blooded meat cattle, but with new strains good for making corned-beef. As a result, within a few years the fine herds of the unfenced Pampa were ruined, and Argentine steak and roast-beef, once the best in the world, was no longer produced. By 1961 I found it impossible to buy a decent piece of beef in any restaurant, and actually broke two teeth gnawing on the best.

The sad career of treacherous Frondizi is too recent to need much recapitulation. After the election he promptly went back on his promises to the Peronistas, without whose support he would not have won — a betrayal that brought him strikes, protests, constant trouble and agitation. Whenever he attempted to conciliate the Peronísta demands, the Army moved in on him. Soon he became a mere puppet of the most reactionary pro-Catholic group in the armed forces. A cartoon in *Marcha* of Montevideo shows him being repeatedly yanked first by one ear, then the other, by hairy military hands — saying with gloating triumph, "But I survived, didn't I?" At what cost — to himself and his country!

Desperately in need of money, once more he gave away the country's oil resources. Cleverly he worked out a formula by which actual ownership would remain in government hands, but the outsiders would get the oil. Certainly, oil was a serious problem, for it accounted for the principal import drain on the treasury.

His deal brought him more labor strikes. There was even a threat of revolt by some of the armed forces, until the Army became more interested in suppressing the strikes than in protecting Argentina's oil.

By the end of his term, he boasted that his policy had made Argentina self-sufficient in oil. Perón's gas and oil pipe-lines to Buenos Aires had been completed, and helped greatly. Actually the increase in production was far below that which was expected or publicized. Practically no new fields were developed, the new U.S. wells were on property that was chiseled away from the existing fields under government oil administration. And the oil which the new companies produced cost from four to six times that from the government enterprises. The needed gas, benzine, and crude oil could have been imported as cheaply or more so. The price of gas and coal-oil, used by nearly all Argentines for heating and cooking, went up and up. Just before Frondizi's downfall there was another big hike, again after he fell.

José Norieja in *Presente*, August 16, 1962, put the total investment of Loeb Bank, Pan American, and Tennessee, including perforation and cost of extraction, at $53,000,000. On December 31, 1961, the government paid them $62,000,000 for 6,500,000 cubic meters of crude petroleum.

The oil deal netted Argentina big loans from the U.S. government totalling over $300,000,000. Costly oil indeed! To get more money, since over-all production was still declining, Frondizi had been obliged also to institute the austerity plan demanded by the United States.

The austerity plan, a typical old-fashioned bankers' concept, benefited the privileged class even more than the International Monetary Fund had. More than ever it stimulated the sending out of profits and the money of wealthier citizens, but it slowed down new investment and trade. Argentine capital was steadily reduced. Austerity was deflationary, to the extent that it froze wages, already sadly reduced by inflation. Broad inflation was not halted on food, clothing or housing. Living standards kept going down.

Nor did any of Frondizi's new tax-measures hit the big hacendados or foreign business; they were borne by small native businessmen, the middle class and the poor. A 300 percent tariff surcharge was placed on nearly all imports, except on supplies needed by U.S. enterprises.

The crisis deepened. More factories closed down. More workers joined the ranks of the unemployed. Government revenues declined. And so for eight years Argentina has been pushed toward a declining economy. There was a slight pick-up in 1961, but there was also the worst unfavorable trade balance in Argentina's history.

The decay has not been confined to the closing down of factories — the bankruptcies, which in 1961 were the greatest in Argentine history, some two and a half billion pesos, still continue — it starts in the interior itself. In 1962, the area under cultivation in the Pampa, according to the most recent farm reports, was 27.2 percent less than the 1936-40 average. And not only that but the output per rural inhabitant in 1961 declined 40 percent, even though the population of the Pampa has gone down 6.4 percent from that in 1947, while the over-all population of the country, mostly crowded starving in cities, has increased.

In spite of the Alliance for Progress' brave stand about Agrarian Reform, land monopoly has grown worse. According to economist Nicasio Salas, the Monetary Fund has been putting heavy pressure on the government to wipe out all the chacras or small farms, on the grounds of inefficiency. Yet until the barbarous, inefficient, feudal land-holding system of Argentina is broken, the country can achieve little progress. The countryside cannot support its sons; the large cities become cancerous, overcrowded slums, rife with misery, bitterness and political instability.

The steady decline in farm exports has been paralleled with a decline in the home consumption of food. In 1940 Argentina's share of world exports of wheat and flour was 36 percent (U.S., 53 percent) but by 1955 this had dropped to 15 percent (U.S., 60 percent). Partly this has been due to the dumping of U.S. wheat abroad, either at low prices or as gifts. Brazil was one of Argentina's leading markets for wheat; the U.S. destroyed it; and 1961 witnessed the incredible coals-to-Newcastle spectacle of U.S. wheat being delivered by the Food for Peace program to northern Argentina itself.

In spite of the considerable increase in population, because of unemployment and sagging wages, the consumption of eggs, meat, bread, milk, potatoes has declined, according to Silenzi de Stagni, 33 percent from the high points of a decade ago.

This is reflected in the closing of schools and greatly reduced enrollment in both primary and university re-enrollments. Illiteracy is growing, and in a few years Argentina promises to be on the level of the Central American banana republics. Hospitals have been closed, the mobile auto and railroad clinics established by Perón have been withdrawn, and once more practically the entire rural area of Argentina is without medical care.

The program of what was being done to the country and what

was going to be done by the government at the behest of the international bankers was finally disclosed by Frondizi on December 29, 1959.

The government was bound to balance its budget by not later
than the end of 1960 (the budget today is more out of balance
than ever) and by 1959 to reduce the number of government employees by 15 percent. This meant an increase of unemployment at the time industry was closing down, thus reducing demand, thus causing still more shutdowns.

Two billion pesos were sliced off public works. Projects were
left unfinished, often with complete loss, and no new ones were
initiated.

Railroads tariffs (the plan was to prevent inflation) were upped
150 percent. More than a hundred thousand railroad workers were
thrown off their jobs, costly strikes lasted for months.

At the behest of U.S. experts, more than 6,000 miles of railroad
have been abandoned, and more than 8,000 miles more are to be
abandoned as not economical. This is a long ways from the free-
enterprise days of Minor C. Keith in Costa Rica, who, when his
railroad did not pay, started new industry to make it pay.

The narrow U.S. concept of efficiency ignores broader problems of political stability and possibilities in a country which has
incredibly vast undeveloped resources. What Argentina needs is
not fewer miles of railroad but twice as many as she now has.
As it is, large areas of the country will be left isolated with no
contacts except possibly by air. Argentina, which has had the
largest rail network of Latin America and is the second largest
country in Latin America, will be stripped to bare bones. Why
should the United States impose its own railway decline on Argentina which has such a great potential for growth?

Electric rates were to be substantially increased, as it turned
out, 50 percent on ordinary users, none on larger users. A consumers' strike resulted.

Petroleum products' prices were increased 200 percent — a
grievous burden, for most Argentines heat their homes and cook
with coal oil.

Internal revenue taxes were to be increased by three billion
pesos, a tremendous percentage, and actually were increased
much more. Farm products had to pay from 10 to 20 percent export duty, further restricting exports. Tariffs were upped from 40

to 300 percent. New taxes for the consumer on gasoline and coal oil were to provide six billion pesos.

The Central Bank was taken out of the commercial credit business, allowed to make only long-term loans and could not loan to other banks. The amount of cash on hand by all banks as backing for deposits was raised from 20 to 30 percent. Ostensibly this was to halt inflation; actually it failed to do so, and merely made money tight in an economy needing more money not less, and contributed to the rising tide of bankruptcies.

While a temporary price-freeze was made on ten articles of public consumption, this resulted in some of them being held off the market almost entirely, and bootlegging increased at higher prices. Wage increases were arbitrarily limited to 15 percent, though previous inflation had reduced real wages 50 percent or more, and additional inflation continued.

To maintain the peso's price in international exchange, the Monetary Fund set up a reserve which had disposable in 1959 about $171,000,000. These funds came from the Argentine government, the U.S. Treasury, the U.S. Export-Import Bank, U.S. Development loan funds, and private banks. This intricate process, which displaced Argentina capital export, exchange and trade controls, and for some peculiar reason was called "free exchange" or "free enterprise," merely substituted an outside monetary authority. The result has been a tragic failure. Argentina is saddled with nearly three billion pesos of debt, with nothing to show for it but dishing out to financial speculators abroad, nothing in the way of new factories, new enterprise or better living conditions. The country has lost all effective financial controls over money, investments, trade commercial loans and new investments to an agency of the U.S. government.

Yet Secretary of the Treasury Douglas Dillon told the Punta del Este Alliance for Progress delegates that Argentina was the bright example of wise and progressive economic policies. He should have gone over to Buenos Aires and sniffed the smells of that ill-lit, pot-holed, declining city.

Frondizi dared not as yet take an open stand against Cuba, dared not break with Cuba, knowing the storm that would raise in his country. But gradually he shifted ground. The United States and the Army demanded it. And that was the price for the additional $150,000,000 loan he was *promised* late in 1961 —

and he paid that price.

Quite misjudging the temper of the country, he persuaded the militarists to permit the Peronista Party to participate in the 1962 state and congressional elections. The result was a smashing victory of the opposition, in Buenos Aires itself four to one, and in Salta and Tucumán seven to one. The only entity Frondizi carried was the bleak Territory of Tierra del Fuego, where his candidates had a scant 250-vote lead, due largely to the soldiers and guards at the Ushaia prison on the Beagle Canal. The Peronistas won the governorships of ten states and led all other parties in the number of elected Congressmen.

Those army elements, known as "the gorillas," close to the U.S. military mission, moved in on Frondizi and ordered him to set the elections aside. He put in military governors in five states, but partly resisted, knowing it would precipitate civil war.

The Army deposed him, jailed people right and left, cracked down on labor leaders, suppressed newspapers.

On pressure from the U.S. Embassy and threats of cutting off financial aid unless an appearance of legality and certain control were maintained, the Army installed the head of Congress, José María Guido, as provisional president, but only after he had signed all army demands on the dotted line. This miserable creature thereupon dissolved the national Congress, dispersed Congressmen by bayonets and tear-gas, and set up an all-military council so the newly elected deputies could not be seated.

Dr. Alvaro Alsogaray — actually a military officer — was successful in getting a new loan of $200,000,000, in spite of our sudden repugnance for military dictatorship. The terms included continuation of the austerity program. He had just suppressed a terrible scandal over falsified imports by an American concern and had handed one of the operating oil companies a juicy check for 400,000,000 pesos. Also he had masterminded the U.S. oil concessions secretly behind the back of Congress, which many Argentines believe to be illegal and unconstitutional. He was received with open arms in Washington.

For weeks on end prior to his departure, he had been talking over TV as to the money he would get from Washington, how he would solve the tragic Argentine economic crisis, and his display of financial pyrotechnics was dazzling indeed. They tell the story in Argentina that one evening an unexpected delegation of workers appeared on the screen, having gotten in by some ruse. They told him, "We agree to cooperate in everything and not to strike if only you will quit talking on TV. *That* we cannot endure any longer."

The $200,000,000 will save Argentina's military dictatorship for a few months or years. It can do little to save Argentina from its political or economic disaster. It wouldn't even put Buenos Aires on a decent going basis.

Proud Argentina really has joined the ranks of the Central American banana republics.

10 ◯ THE OIL KINGDOM — VENEZUELA

1

Dr. Carlos León, a Venezuelan educator exiled in Mexico, was one of the youngest men I have ever known, though he was in his sixties. A lawyer with progressive leanings and considerable following, he had refused the post of minister of education under Dictator Vicente Gómez. A few days later, he was tapped on the shoulder by a gendarme and tossed into La Rotunda, the torture prison of the dictatorship, and held there without charges or trial for more than eight years, wearing eighty-pound leg-irons. He was released only because he was expected to die.

He reached Mexico where he presented an almost boyish, eager, much-freckled face to the world, and his enthusiasm and energies were incredible, as if he were trying to compress the lost years into those that remained.

In the eyes of Latin America he soon became one of the heroes. He issued propaganda against Gómez and organized at least one armed invasion against him. He also saw that freedom for the Venezuelan people could not come about except as part of a greater movement for Latin American liberation, and he organized UCSAYA, the Union of Central and South America and the Americas, to fight Marine invasion in Nicaragua and the Caribbean and to rouse the continent to resist such aggressions. The organization started a continent-wide boycott of U.S.A. goods, and already, before the Great Depression hit, this was drawing blood and alarming Washington — thanks to Dr. León and Dr. Zepeda, a Nicaraguan exile, dedicated to the Sandino cause.

On a boat trip, somewhere, sometime, I met another notable Nicaraguan, Rafael de Nogales, a soldier of fortune in many parts of the world, and a bitter enemy of Gómez. One twilight I saw him with a book in his hand leaning over the rail and took him to be a bull-fighter, because he was wearing bull-fighter slippers and his hair had a longish bull-fighter's cut. As soon as I told him my name, he gave me an enthusiastic *abrazo*.

His fantastic career is partly told about in his book *Four Years Under The Crescent*. He led German and Arab forces in World War I in the Middle East, and was decorated personally by the Kaiser. An aide of Allenby's once told me that of all the English general's adversaries, Nogales had given him the most trouble. "That man is so modest and has such a fantastic imagination, he couldn't bear to tell all about his real exploits. The whole truth about them is even more incredible than what he tells in his book."

Afterwards he went to the Dominican Republic during the Marine invasion, then to Nicaragua and was with Sacasa in Puerto Cabezas. He made his way through the jungles to Moncada's army. His *The Looting of Nicaragua*, an indispensable source book, is in part devoted to an account of brutal Marine massacres in Santo Domingo.

Once he landed in New York without money. In a shabby hotel in a few days he dashed off four stories for *Adventure Magazine*, went down and sold them for a handsome sum. He was never at a loss in any situation.

He was doing everything he could to expose Vicente Gómez and break down the false legend built up about him in U.S. publications.

It was really dangerous, Nogales told me, to fight for the liberation of Venezuela, for the oil companies had a plot to set up a separate oil kingdom in case of revolution. "Except for the oil companies, backed by Washington, Gómez' frightful tyranny would not last a week."

Over the years I met hundreds of exiled Venezuelans. Some, among them one of my best friends, later died in unsuccessful armed expeditions to overthrow him. Some returned to Venezuela after his downfall, and several became important.

One of the most prominent was Gustavo Machado, a handsome, intense but good-natured young man, even then a Communist. After the downfall of Gómez, he returned to Venezuela and became head of the Communist Party, which during the depression had about 50,000 members. In June 1962, following the naval revolt, he was arrested as he stepped off a plane from Moscow.

But the most important exile, Rómulo Betancourt, I did not meet, though he was active in Costa Rica when I went through that country in 1928. He had been a Communist, then a Trotskyite. He returned to Venezuela right after Gómez' downfall, organized Acción Democrática, and wrote extensively during 1937 to October 1939 for *Ahora*. Exiled anew, in Santiago de Chile, 1940, he published his articles as a book, entitled *Problemas Venezuelasos*. He sent me an inscribed copy on March 4 of that year.

Betancourt returned to Caracas in 1941 and founded a daily paper. His articles showed a deep grasp of his country's economic problems and needs. He bore down heavily on the methods, profits and effects of the oil industry. He advocated starting a government oil corporation. His book had several withering descriptions of Nelson Rockefeller's visits to the country and ridiculed his noble press interviews about the new social welfare role private capital should play. Actually, Betancourt said, he had gotten the pension and profit-sharing provisions of the Venezuelan labor law set aside, and had arranged the confirmation of a big oil-land concession of doubtful legality, that dispossessed thousands of Venezuelan families.

2

Gómez "El Bagre," the Cat-Fish, died in 1935 at the age of seventy-eight, dictator since 1908. He left behind more than a hundred children, legitimate and otherwise, squabbling over the inheritance. News of his demise brought the populace raging into the streets of Caracas to plunder and burn his houses and those of his sons and henchmen. After several days, they were driven back in a hail of bullets that left many writhing in blood in the plaza.

The dictator's Minister of War, Eleazer López Contreras, though suffering from t.b., took over. Political prisoners were released, some freedom of the press was allowed, a few reforms and a three-year "plan" of public works were started.

Presently the crack-down against the people came again. Forty-seven persons were deported as "Communists." Few actual Communists were touched, for they had made a deal for immunity for their support in the 1940 elections of General Isaias Medina Angarita for president.

Medina's rule from 1941 to 1945, if not remarkable, was efficient, progressive, featured by a degree of political freedom. The strongest party to emerge was Betancourt's Acción Democrática.

It attracted a group of young officers, the secret military Patriotic Union, and when it became likely that Medina would reimpose López Contreras as president, a plot was hatched and plans laid for a military coup in November.

But on October 18, one of the plotters, Major Marcos Pérez Jiménez, was arrested, and the others had to move in at once. López Contreras was seized, and President Medina fled from yellow-walled Miraflores Palace as the rebels entered. Even so there was fierce fighting for three days, most of it by the Communists against the take-over. The crowds broke into the arsenals and roamed wildly through the streets, looting and burning. Not until October 21 did the joint military-civilian junta gain control of the city — after 500 deaths and thousands wounded.

The junta was headed by Betancourt, and though the future dictator, Pérez Jiménez, was not a member, the latter's new father-in-law, Major Carlos Delgado Chalbaud, was one of its moving spirits.

A new constitution was adopted, which provided for social legislation, the right to expropriate oil properties, agrarian reform and direct election of the Executive. Foreign companies and big landholders were alarmed, though Betancourt indicated he would not take over oil properties.

Nelson Rockefeller soon revisited Venezuela and, despite Betancourt's earlier caustic comments, they became friendly. A pipe-line concession long held up was promptly granted. One newspaper ran a caricature of "Rómulo and Rockie" dancing in bathing suits underneath a spilling geyser of oil.

Revenues from oil were "plowed" back into developing the country's long abandoned interior and to grow enough food to end food imports — doubly costly for Venezuela, for oil tankers were a one-way shuttle, taking out but bringing nothing back.

Rockefeller had also brought "welfare capital" to Venezuela, subsidiaries to carry on enterprises which the Venezuelans, after a certain number of years, were to be allowed to buy. The big, hill-top, modern hotel had been previously put up by a Rockefeller company on this basis, but no local buyers at the price asked came forward.

Rockefeller had been buying up haciendas, going into the cattle, milk and truck farm business. Presently he had a monopoly on all milk production in the country. He also secured a monopoly on fishing and fish-marketing. Another line was the establishing of self-service chain stores.

The only papers whole-heartedly laudatory were mostly subsidized. His chain-stores were denounced by small businessmen and the Chamber of Commerce. Venezuelans, they claimed, were capable of selling goods themselves; he was injuring native business. Because of bulk purchasing abroad, he could obtain goods cheaper than could native businesses; he had tariff advantages not enjoyed by Venezuelans; via the oil companies he had a big advantage in monetary exchange operations.

To offset such hostility, Rockefeller offered to provide any native competitive business with experts and to sell it goods at the same cost as to his own stores.

What most riled Venezuelans — at least it became a patriotic issue — was his purchase of the coffee plantation that had been the birthplace of Liberator Simón Bolívar, which was looked upon as a national shrine. The "big Gringos" moved in with bulldozers, ripped out the coffee plants, pushed aside the native houses where some families had lived for centuries, and started an up-to-date truck-garden farm.

There was much criticism that the higher-priced Rockefeller milk was being mixed with imported powdered milk and that the price had gone up sharply. It was explained that this was a temporary expedient until supplies could catch up with demand.

Rockefeller cattle plantations did much to improve the breed with bulls from Texas and Africa, able to withstand the climate and parasites. New types of grazing grass were introduced, and Venezuelans were taught how to conserve, improve, and extend their pasture lands.

But large landholders were worried by the new mechanization — machinery they could not afford, either to buy or operate. Venezuela, though an oil country, had no oil refinery (the companies had fought this for many years) so gasoline and oil were higher priced than almost any place else on earth.

The fish enterprise turned out the worst. The fishermen made somewhat more because, with motors, their individual catches were larger. But so were costs, due to the imported motors and imported gas. The fine refrigeration plants, the refrigerated trucks for getting the fish to the market, ran the price of sea food up to about a dollar a pound — a price only well-to-do city folk could afford. Most farm workers did not earn a dollar in a whole day.

Behind all this was the problem of all underdeveloped countries: how to produce better modern products more efficiently. This meant more costly processes and larger overheads. But both machinery and imported articles were too expensive. It was difficult, because of the limited market, to set up native industries. This was the problem Perón had faced in Argentina, that the Mexican revolution faced, that Rockefeller's do-good enterprises also faced.

3

The Betancourt reforms were fought bitterly by the oil companies and the large landholders. But he managed to install Rómulo Gallegos, the well-known novelist and most beloved of Venezuelans, as president, by an honest election in 1947.

Gallegos tried to arm the Acción Democrática members, which angered and frightened the military. Ten months later a military Coup, led by Colonel Delgado Chalbaud, seized power. Among the signers of the manifesto of the new military junta was Colonel Pérez Jiménez, and the head of the Navy, Captain Wolfgang Larrazábal. Both Gallegos and Betancourt, driven into exile, accused the oil companies of being behind this coup, though typical military ambition seems sufficient to account for it, plus the arming of Acción Democrática.

Although the Betancourt-Gallegos regime had been the first in Venezuela's history to permit full civil liberties and political freedom, the new military junta justified its coup as concern over "democracy" and the menace of Betancourt's "communism," from which the country had to be saved.

At once the brass-hats imposed censorship, jailed opponents and labor leaders without trials, put down protesting students with tear gas. The development of the interior, the Indian program, crop diversification, agrarian reforms were abandoned. Labor did receive a few favors, but strikes were ruthlessly suppressed. The dictatorship was not beneficient, it was cruel, but it was "progressive," it got many new things done: urban development, basic industry and foreign enterprise were promoted.

The regime was quickly recognized by the State Department, and in the years that followed it got much aid and many favors, and thanks to big oil revenues, the junta, in spite of constant revolts, was able to hang on to power for four years. In 1952 they risked a fig-lead election. All parties except the UDR Democratic Republican Union and a small Catholic party had been outlawed.

Thanks to secret Acción Democrática organization, the government party was swamped by the UDR and the Catholics. The ousting of the two members of the junta was followed by the mysterious assassination of Pérez Jiménez' father-in-law, Delgado Chalbaud. (Later, in 1958, his widow filed murder charges against Pérez, who by then was in exile in Florida.) Pérez took over the junta completely, governing with a false-front civilian provisional president.

Two years later, he, too, risked elections. When the vote began going against him, he stopped the elections, declared himself victor, and assumed the presidency. His leading opponent in the elections was arrested and deported. Early in 1953 he had a hand-picked constituent assembly confirm him as president for a five-year term. Once more "democracy" was saved.

Marcos Pérez was a truly ugly creature, short, fat, who resorted to uniforms so showy he was a comic opera figure, about the worst skulking dictator in the history of the Americas. His excesses of food, drink and women were titanic, and sometimes his hysterical outbursts were lurid. He was a paranoid megalomaniac, unpredictable, lightning fast in his thought, and when not in a fog-like torpor could act murderously. He always had to have the sensation of absolute power, and the slightest frustration would send him on a smashing spree — dishes, furniture, any heads that happened to be around.

Though by this time Pérez had sired four girls, his orgiastic exploits became the legend of the continent — but did not seem to perturb U.S. officials, as did Perón's infatuation with a schoolgirl, and he was decorated. He had many palatial retreats for his excesses. His Orchilla Island mansion is said to have cost more than $2,000,000 and was provided with a private airfield. It was inaugurated by a grand slam-bang party, for which the dictator's "sexual minister," a wealthy businessman, flew in two hundred beautiful women of the demi-monde for the three days of revelry. On another occasion girls were flown in from Havana, Santiago de Chile and elsewhere.

4

These were boom times in Venezuela. The demand for oil due to the Korean War and other international crises was large. Daily 1,800,000 barrels were taken out, 45 per cent of it produced by Creole, subsidiary of Standard Oil of New Jersey.

A big concession was made to the Bethlehem Steel Company for iron ore near the Orinoco River, and by 1951, 2,000,000 tons a year were already being shipped out. U.S. Steel also entered the scene with the discovery of new, enormously rich deposits. A 5,000,000-ton production was projected by 1954, and soon thereafter 10,000,000 tons. Iron has become the country's largest export.

To Pérez' credit, he started building a steel mill — something that the oil companies had long blocked — and he promoted an oil-refinery which brought prices down for the Venezuelan consumer. Though perhaps short-sighted, American capital likes dictatorships, and floods of U.S. capital flowed in, new oil wells, new pipe-lines, auto assembly plants, factories of many sorts.

Government revenues rose. Pérez promoted vast public works, road building and above all the beautification and modernization of the capital, into which flocked at least 300,000 paupers, dispossessed from the land. Some money was also spent on schools and public health. But how many hundred millions he pocketed personally is not known. What is known are the thousands he tortured, exiled or killed.

His security chief, a bloodthirsty reader of French philosophy and of De Sade, was Valenilla Lanz, but actually Pedro Estrada did the work. Their headquarters were in a great five-story gray building on Calle México, and they maintained a vast espionage service in all Latin America. Many of the cruelties and murders of the regime must be laid at Estrada's door. The F.B.I. and C.I.A. who shared space there were enchanted with him; he was vociferously anti-Communist (though he protected Communists in Venezuela and used them as informers). He headed an enormous corps of gum-shoes, degenerates, sex-deviates, psychotics and ex-criminals. Prisoners were brought into the intricate honeycomb of underground cells where they were tortured in the most intricate sadistic fashion. This building was stormed during the uprising against Pérez, and four hundred emaciated, tortured beings, scarcely human any more, stumbled out of the flaming building.

In May 1957, fellow dictator Rojas Pinilla was kicked out in Colombia, and Marcos Pérez, preparing to extend his own term for five years, did not sleep as well at night. Suddenly he was hit by a pastoral letter by Archbishop Rafael Arias Blanco, which spoke of the evil economic system that condemned the majority of Venezuelans to live in sub-human conditions and in an atmosphere of corruption and spiritual bankruptcy. It was the tack in his heel that stopped Pérez' onrush to more power.

Elections were announced, but no opposition candidates. There was no opposition "leader on the scene" except Rafael Caldera, head of the Christian Democratic Party (COPEI), and he was held in one of Estrada's underground dungeons. People could merely vote whether they wanted Pérez to remain in office. "Yes" and "No" ballots were handed to each voter, and woe betide the voter who could not show a "No" card after he had exercised his electoral privilege. An 80 percent "Yes" vote was announced within thirty minutes of the closing of the polls.

An underground coalition of Acción Democrática, UDR,

COPEI and the Communist Party was formed — the Patriotic Junta — headed by newsman Fabrica Ojeda, organized like the Cuban A.B.C., so that few knew the identity of others in the organization.

A few days after the election, a student protest was broken up by police, and the dictator closed the doors of the university. To try to calm things down, he released Caldera (who went to New York).

The dictator staged a magnificent New Year's party, but hardly had he gotten to bed in the wee hours than bombs began going off, jet planes flew low over the Palace, the anti-aircraft guns crashed into his sleep and into his aching skull.

But it was a badly planned coup, and by noon the next day, all rebel ground troops had surrendered. People were swept into Estrada's dungeons like autumn leaves. Five were priests, and the archbishop threatened excommunications.

The generals were making demands now — chiefly that Pérez dismiss Valenilla and Estrada. Not until January 9 did Pérez give in to a final army ultimatum, handed to him by his Chief of Staff, General Rómulo Fernandes. But first the dictator, in one of his frustrated rages, slapped Valenilla Lanz in the face for his having promoted the silly plebiscite that was still causing so much uproar. He also called in officers courtmartialed for the New Year's day revolt, and tore off their insignias. Fernandes was made Minister of Defense. Everything seemed under control. But on January 3, when the latter was driving to the Palace to ask for the dictator's resignation, he himself was seized and thrown out of the country!

It split the armed forces down the middle, then into splinter groups. By then the patriot junta was in close contact with army officers. Students, women, workers, lawyers, physicians and engineers were staging demonstrations that grew worse and badly frightened the dictator, who alternately huddled in dark corners of the Palace or went on smashing sprees. The Palace was ringed about with tanks, armored cars and elite guards.

On January 21 a general strike was called, and half the city swarmed into the Caracas streets, smashing stores that failed to close, setting buses and autos on fire. The crowds reassembled all over the up-and-down tilted city faster than the soldiery could disperse them with machine guns.

The next day the navy and army heads ordered Pérez to get

out at once. He was given a few hours to leave, and he and his entire family were escorted by army cars to La Carlota airport and put on a plane bound for Ciudad Trujillo.

Crowds roared through the streets, and the Security Police building was attacked, its defenders killed, the place burned down.

5

Caldera from New York, Betancourt from Puerto Rico, Gallegos from Mexico hurried back. The underground parties and their leaders, sobered by the long twilight of dictatorship, all the violence and bloodshed, agreed to honor an honest election and to support whoever was chosen.

The provisional junta, headed by Admiral Wolfgang Larrazabal, attempted in every way to satisfy the people. Anti-American feeling was tremendous, because of the close punitive alliance of U.S. secret agents and the secret police. The close alliance of the Pentagon and State Department with Pérez, the financial aid given him, the honors heaped upon him, had aroused fury throughout the land.

One of the early acts of the junta was to up Venezuela's share of the petroleum take to 60 percent, and protests from Washington, vastly relieved that the industry had not been expropriated, were faint. Larrazábal, UDR candidate for president, accepted the support of Gustavo Machado's fifty thousand Communists. Against him was Betancourt of Acción Democrática, who had pretty much lost the support of urban workers, but was still strong in the back country. Against him also was Rafael Caldera of pro-Catholic COPEI.

It was into this turbulent lion's den that "Daniel" Richard Nixon ventured. His very name to Venezuelans was a red-rag. He was anathema, a symbol of McCarthyism and witch-hunting. His beaming, go-getter, glad hand manner seemed to typify everything the Latin Americans find most repelling in Yankees. He was insulted, stoned, spat upon, all but lost his life. Eisenhower started parachuters moving to the closest bases to rescue him, which further angered the Venezuelans. But he was stealthily hustled out of the country before anything worse could occur. With dignity and considerable insight, showing no resentment, he warned the Venezuelans that such lawlessness would cost them their liberties and bring back a dictatorship. He blamed it on the agents of the ex-dictator; later, on Communists.

The elections were close, but Betancourt's well-organized Acción Democrática nosed into the lead. This was a bit humorous. For several years he had been denounced, particularly by newscasters, as being a Communist, chiefly because he had been one once upon a time, and was trying to undermine the dictatorship. Now the tune changed, and overnight he became a paragon of democracy, the truest friend of the United States, especially after Fidel Castro emerged.

The various parties stood by their promises, and all, per previous agreement, were given cabinet posts in a coalition government. Larrazábal, to avoid becoming the center of more radical elements in a trying moment of political reorganization, accepted the post of ambassador to Chile. He is to be a candidate again in Venezuela's 1963 elections.

Betancourt quickly established strong, popular, orderly government. On the side he aided the anti-Trujillo and anti-Batista exiles and provided money, arms and airplanes for the overthrow of those dictators.

After the revolution succeeded in Cuba, Castro's first tour out of the country was to visit Venezuela and thank Betancourt for his aid. The two revolutionary governments, Castro announced, would stand together impregnably.

Betancourt had other ideas. He needed U.S. money badly, and he already knew the price he would have to pay to get it.

Little by little he began harassing Castro Cubans and pro-Castro Venezuelans, until the day came when he threw all pro-Castro Cubans out of the country, suppressed *Prensa Latina* and openly favored the old Batista crowd. More and more he was hailed by us as the ideal "democrat" of the continent, distinct from dictatorships of the Right or Left. This was the Washington line, and the mass magazines and most smaller liberal publications followed it implicitly.

By April 1961, the picture had changed decidedly. Betancourt had been faced with a number of serious army revolts, but at the faintest smell of any reactionary plotting, the people surged into the plazas. Twice his regime was saved by such loyal demonstrations.

But suddenly he called upon the Army to suppress students, workers and other demonstrators, particularly those favoring Cuba. It was evident he had received his orders, or wanted U.S. loans; but overnight he thereby threw away his popular support. He had gone the way of all flesh, like Frondizi in Argentina. Having started to crush popular parties, which were soon outlawed, his only sure support became the Army, the landholders and the Church — though none was wholehearted. They tolerated him because he was anti-Communist and anti-Castro. He became, and still is, largely a prisoner and puppet of the Army.

At the time of his break with Castro, he received a new U.S. loan within days. But this cost him still more popular support. He was left with only the reduced segment of his own party, the Catholic COPEI and the military as the mainstays of his rule — a very small minority.

More and more he has had to resort to all the devices and injustices of dictatorship, force and coercion. The dissident parties withdrew from his cabinet; several were outlawed, and any demonstration in favor of Cuba was now met with machine guns. All Cuban literature was banned and newspapers were forbidden to publish any information about Cuba, except denunciations. Numerous papers were suppressed entirely. But in U.S. magazines, he is still the bright star of free democracy.

Pablo Neruda, the Chilean poet, perhaps expressed the truth when he said: "He had time for everything but being a man."

6

President John F. Kennedy's flying two-day trips early in 1962 to Venezuela and Colombia, the U.S. oil kingdoms of South America, were to buttress up the dubious regimes in both countries and advertise his Alliance for Progress.

These are the key countries of the great North American dollar empire of Latin America, accounting for nearly half the total U.S. investments — in oil, iron-ore, crucial war materials. Venezuela has the highest U.S. investment per capita of any foreign land. Hundreds of millions are drained out annually in profits.

During the Suez crisis, had it not been for rush oil shipments chiefly from Venezuela, the European economy would have toppled within weeks. But lately, much to Venezuelan indignation, oil imports to the United States are restricted, and this at a time when Venezuelan exports to Argentina have largely ceased and other markets have been lost, including Cuba, because of cheaper Soviet oil.

The major reason for Kennedy's jack-in-the-box morale building in the two "democratic" countries, so shaky they were under martial law, was the Cuban revolution. The Foreign Ministers' Conference, scheduled for January 10 but postponed till February, called by Colombia to harass Cuba, needed heroic support if it was to drum up sanctions of support for new invasion. The outlook at that moment that a majority vote could be obtained in the conference looked gloomy.

Though Alliance for Progress money had purchased the breaking off of relations with Cuba by Colombia, Venezuela and Panama as previously done by the Central American countries and Peru, Venezuela got an additional $25,000,000 (the going price for this operation) within forty-eight hours of the rupture — there was no assurance that even Venezuela would go along with any proposals for intervention.

That break, brought about by U.S. dollars, propaganda, the Catholic Church, the large land-holding families which now control the Betancourt government, was not popular. The Venezuelan Labor Confederation, since purged by army force, cabled its support to the Cuban Labor Federation just prior to the rupture. The communiqué denounced the Minister of Foreign Relations, Marcos Falcón Briceño, whose financial connections are well known. The Unión Democrática Republicana (UDR), headed by Jovita Villaba and Luís Ignacio Arcaya, had withdrawn from the governing coalition, giving up cabinet posts, because of Betancourt's anti-Cuban policy. The President's own party split three ways. Cesar Rondón Lovera, head of the party's foreign policy-making and also of the Congressional Foreign Relations Committee, staunchly opposed intervention in Cuba and insisted that rather than breaking off relations, they should be improved. Even more outspoken was Raul Ramos Jiménez, head of the powerful Centrist group of the party, who expressed deepest sympathy for Cuba. Bitter recriminations flared between him and Betancourt.

Six thousand students gathered in the university — Communist-inspired, of course — to denounce the U.S. "imperialists" and the "dictatorial puppet regimes" of Guatemala, El Salvador, the Dominican Republic, Paraguay, Honduras and Nicaragua for selling out to the "Colossus of the North." For three days they protested in the streets and were hammered by army, police and the national guard with guns, clubs and tear gas.

Tanks and machine guns were massed about Miraflores Palace and in the streets; they were still there when Kennedy entered behind a wall of bayonets so dense he could scarcely see the school children ordered out to greet him. The same was true in Colombia — tanks, soldiers, bayonets.

At least he got a quick glimpse of Caracas, a magnificent city of more than a million inhabitants, a seventh of the total population of this vast land equal in area to France, England and West Germany combined. He was whirled down wide avenues and over dramatic concrete viaducts, past the new skyscrapers of U.S. corporations and tall multi-tinted apartment houses.

This seeming wealth and progress actually symbolizes the sickness and despair of the land, for this top-heavy concentration of people has been driven here chiefly by land monopoly. If Mr. Kennedy chanced to lift his eyes toward the skyline, he must easily have seen the wide circle of Hooverville shacks encircling the city on every hill.

In these filthy, improvised slums live nearly half the population in hovels, without streets, transportation, electric light, water, mostly without even outhouses. The stench, excrement and sickness drip down on the magnificent palaces. Caracas has built its filthy, leaking toilets right over the banquet rooms.

Did Mr. Kennedy ponder that merely to convert this city into a decent and viable community would require the better part of one year's appropriation of the so-called Alliance for Progress, leaving nothing over for the interior to correct evils of land monopoly and lack of industry, nothing for the nineteen other countries of the continent?

Perhaps he may ponder the fact also that even if this vast outlay were to be spent honestly, without the waste and corruption that has featured U.S. aid throughout the continent, it would be a futile effort; for even if public housing and running water and sewers and electricity and schools were provided, people earning $100 a year in a land with higher living costs than the United States could scarcely utilize them, for they could pay no rent, pay no light bills nor even buy the clothing necessary for this modest change in status. Besides, 200,000 of the city's workers are now unemployed in this richest of oil lands. Nor can Venezuela or the other countries afford the added permanent upkeep of such charity welfare projects.

Already Venezuela has received more dollars per capita than any other country. Are not U.S. dollars supposed to improve living standards so that people will not be obliged to turn to communism? Of course, this is only one side of the picture. The American dollars cannot halt the population explosion, the refusal of the Catholic Church to promote birth-control, nor wave a wand to do away with feudal land monopoly — even were private investors or official meddlers interested in doing so. Even so, the whole thesis of dollar aid per se needs to be re-examined, for the Venezuelan people are worse off than they were a dozen years ago; they are among the most poverty-stricken and miserable of all Latin Americans — and a great many people, with fatal results for U.S. prestige at home and abroad, are going to be sadly disillusioned.

Ideas of what dollars can and cannot do are sadly jumbled by us, but perhaps nowhere are they more jumbled than by much of the intelligentsia of Venezuela, be they lackeys or not of the U.S. propaganda-and-money putsch. With the present drain of money and resources, the even greater loss each year because of the growing gap between the prices of raw materials and exported coffee, cacao, sugar and tobacco on the one hand and manufactured goods and imports on the other, Venezuela grows steadily poorer, losing billions. The expected U.S. aid in Latin America will hardly begin to cover these perpetual losses.

Tax reform has been demanded as a sine qua non of further aid. But the group which owns the land and which pulls the strings of government will not permit any sound tax reform — and the United States cannot point with any pride to its own tax structure and methods, or for that matter to the need for agrarian reform elsewhere when its own farm management is in an unholy mess. Nor is it likely that proper tax reform can be imposed because of existing terms in concessions. The oil companies and mining companies are allowed to bring in all supplies and machinery almost tax-free, whereas the duty on bread is three times the original cost-price. To pour more money into the voracious

feudal system of Venezuela, once more in the control of the oligarchy, the military and the Church — the very elements supported most heartily by U.S. propaganda — is to aggravate not improve basic conditions, it means helping the sharks eat the
sardines.

Venezuela has carried on, under Betancourt, what it calls land
reform, and some 35,000 people have supposedly benefited. Possibly it is not land reform at all, but resettlement on government
land. Were this land much good or capable of development with
present transportation, it would have been grabbed by the big
landholders ere this. Even if a living can be made on it, the small
farmer will be at the mercy of the big landowners, the warehouse
people, the concession merchants and the middle man. No basic
change has been made in the land ownership structure, the
feudal rule of the big owners, and Venezuela remains chained to
a helpless raw-product role, a U.S. colony — a producer of oil and
iron, coffee and sugar, for export. Not even its own food supply.

Kennedy participated in this farce, journeyed to a prepared
show-place and handed out a deed for a nineteen-acre plot.
Practically all the land given out in the uplands to the peasants
is unfertile land and worthless without water which is not available. Who was Kennedy fooling by this type of Catholic charity?

The instrument for this renewed betrayal of the Venezuelan
people is President Betancourt, who began as the idol of the people, who up to two years ago was still the idol of the masses for
his overthrow of the bloody but pampered dictatorship of General Marcos Pérez. But in so short a time, the policies of Betancourt show little difference from those of Pérez whom he helped
overthrow. But not till then did the official circles in Washington
consider him fully trustworthy, not till he abandoned the people
and his supporters and became an anti-Cuban agent.

He has indeed fulfilled the prophecy of the great liberator,
Simón Bolívar, a century and a half ago: "The United States
seems destined by Providence to plague America with miseries in the name of liberty."

Kennedy flew in by helicopter to El Arbol de la Morita settlement, a special show-place for the Betancourt land program,
on a hacienda confiscated from Vincente Gómez' estate. Here
well-dressed kids in neat homes — thanks solely to Kennedy's

visit — were provided with refrigerators, T.V. sets, and signs on the wall in English, "Welcome Kennedy." The peasants who own such equipment in Venezuela in any province can be numbered on the fingers of two hands.

He was then helicoptered to nearby El Toro and there behind a wall of national guardsmen that kept back all but a handful of well-dressed peasants, he handed out a land title for nineteen acres and piously renamed the place Alianza Para el Progreso. The day after, it took back its old name — "Bull."

In most places provided for the peasants, the acres are sterile, without water, and can provide only a worse living than the hacienda wage of $1.00 a day or less (living costs higher than in the United States). Otherwise they get land nobody wants or can properly use in far off jungles.

From his scant acres, the benefited peasant is supposed to pay annual installments, which amount to more cash than most of them have ever seen or will see. If he wants a house (8,000 have been built so far, 700,000 are needed) a worker or peasant must earn $530 a year. The average peasant income is $177 a year, less than 50 cents a day, and only a few better-class urban workers make as much as $530.

Thus the peasants, for the most part, even with their meager land reform, cannot possibly emerge from misery; they cannot provide a market for goods if new industry is set up. His subsistence farming (a more backward way of life than the hacienda system) cannot provide the diversified food products necessary for the modern urban centers, and food must be imported at high cost, mostly from the United States. The government cannot afford to help him properly with seed, tools, credit or technical training. Few schools have been built, and 70 percent of the people are illiterate.

There are 400,000 peasants still landless, and 4 percent of the landholders own 80 percent of the land. The bulk of government rural credit goes to the big landowners. Actually, all effort to keep up with the land program was abandoned late in 1961 — about the time of Kennedy's visit.

Venezuela, the "great democracy," was then and is still under martial law. Two-thirds of Betancourt's own party has turned its back on him. Opposition middle, leftist and Communist parties have been outlawed. He is the mere puppet of the Army, the Catholic Party, and the Alliance for Progress, which is trying to bail him out of his predicament, with a *promised* $600,000,000 in addition to the money paid to him right after he broke with the Cuban government.

A new military dictatorship is in the making.

11 ◯ THE BOGOTAZO

1

All modern Colombian history pivots on the "Bogotazo," the up-rising in April 1948, during the Ninth Pan-American Conference, which wrecked and burned half of Bogotá, the capital, and left piled up dead bodies. Better said, the pivot was the assassina-tion of Jorge Elicer Gaitán, head of the Liberal Party, and the idol of the people— a deed which precipitated the mob violence and aroused the frustrated rage of the masses all over the country.

The horrible events of April 9 and the days immediately fol-lowing did not advance the cause of freedom or provide Colom-bia with the social and political reforms which might by now have helped create a more stable, progressive country. Instead it provoked a brutal counter-revolution which according to offi-cial admissions has taken the lives of 300,000 Colombians, sav-agely slaughtered by the Army — more than the total of U.S. casualties in the Korean War, the most deadly of all U.S. wars.

Two of the Conservative leaders hiding out from the inflamed mob that April day and night and who were hanged in effigy on the lamp posts of the Plaza de Volévar were Laureano Gómez, head of the most murderous regime in Colombia's history, and Guillermo León de Valencia, a rigid, dogmatic pro-clerical, who became president, elected in an utterly meaningless fig-leaf plebiscite, in May of 1962.

The fifteen years since the Bogotazo were also crowded by the rule of army officer Gustavo Rojas Pinilla, who crushed the 1948 upheaval in Cali and Buenaventura with blood and steel, and continued the process in all Colombia as dictator. Thus, since the Bogotazo, the Oligarchy (I use the current Colombian expression) is still in the saddle, and the country is still divided, seething with strikes, peasant uprisings and revolt. Civil war continues.

The awakening of the people began with the Great Depression. Following Roosevelt's "Rape of Panama," the country had relapsed into economic misery and defeatism and hatred of the United States, which, if since softened, has never died. Five years after World War I, the Congress of the United States authorized a heart-balm payment of $25,000,000. This had been proposed by Secretary William Jennings Bryan seven years earlier, a sum much less, even so, than the money paid over to the defunct French canal company and their almost worthless concession rights. The money, however, was not paid to Colombia until the government was ready with secret documents to turn over oil and other reserves to U.S. corporations.

In 1912 only $2,000,000 of U.S. capital was invested in Colombia. By 1930 when the Great Depression hit, there was $250,000-000. By then Colombia was taking 41.42 percent of her imports from the United States and was selling to this country 61.4 percent of her exports, seemingly an advantageous situation, except that most of the money for oil and numbers of other exports remained abroad as profits, so that in the ten years from 1950 to 1959, Colombia's actual trade balance showed a deficit of $537,-000,000. The $718,000,000 worth of petroleum sent abroad during that period represented profits not returned to the country; wages and taxes were mostly covered by the petroleum sold within the Republic.

Thus Colombia is part of the great international U.S. oil empire, next to the Middle East and Venezuela an oil kingdom par excellence and most profitable, for the royalties to the government are small compared to those in other parts of the world. Of Colombia's 444,000 square miles, an area greater than France and Germany combined, 108,000 square miles are actually or potentially oil-bearing. Of this vast area, 90,000 square miles — more than a fifth of the entire country and an area nine times the size of Belgium — are owned by foreign oil corporations.

Another large part of the national territory is owned by the United Fruit Company. There are large U.S. investments in platinum, gold and silver mining, in coffee and sugar lands. Railroads and public utilities are largely in U.S. hands.

Under the recent administration of Alberto Lleras Camargo vast new concessions were awarded, and a big Peace Corps, an organization headed by a relative of President Kennedy and an ex-C.I.A. man, now operates in Colombia, doing good, it is claimed, for villagers having little or no land. To help drain a swamp or set up a few outhouses are beneficial but scarcely have any bearing on Colombia's basic problems. Many Latin Americans suspect that the Peace Corps personnel is trained as additional C.I.A. agents.

Nearly all the land of the country is owned by a few families, and the going wage for farm workers ranges from 15 cents a day up to as much as $1.00 a day near Bogotá. The American companies employ relatively few Colombians so that the sending of natural wealth abroad benefits the country but little. Illiteracy runs well over 60 percent. Under President Alfonso López, the second Depression President, some feeble attempts were made at land reform, and sharecropping was abolished, without provision for settlement, so that a vast influx of rural people flooded into Bogotá and other cities to starve. Those that remained behind were reduced to peonage.

The only way to maintain stability under such circumstances is through armed force and repression, plus political chicanery. At present the Oligarchy is in complete control of the Army and governing apparatus, but there are at least four independent Guerrillero or Peasant Republics in the interior — which the U.S. military mission is preparing to crush, against which constant warfare in any event must be waged. Strikes are incessant and are settled by government-controlled wage-boards nearly always in favor of the foreign companies, or else are suppressed by the Army. Thus political instability is endemic.

A review of the careers of several of the presidents and a large share of the cabinet ministers show them to be lawyers, even officers of oil, fruit and other foreign corporations. Newspaper men are subsidized by U.S. companies or U.S. government agencies.

The more private capital comes in, the more Colombia slips behind in her balance of payments, the more the mass of the people are ground down, the worse the national economic situation becomes. To bridge the gap, to prevent more Bogotazos, the various governments, beginning with the early disastrous Kemmerer financial mission, have dutifully followed the mandates of the International Monetary Fund and the Export-Import Bank's old-fashioned programs of austerity, Budget Balancing, "Belt Tightening," etc. Now the imbalance between the price of Colombia's raw products, particularly coffee, and the cost of imported goods is so great, that it takes more than twice as much today to pay for the same amount of goods as it did eight years ago. Merely the drop in the price of coffee has drained more money out of Colombia than the Alliance for Progress can return. And this new money, of course, will be administered by the present Oligarchy in power. Thus money sent to Colombia means, in spite of good efforts, a worsening economy, more misery, more dictatorship, and tends to promote rather than prevent communism.

2

In 1929 coffee dropped below cost of production, and by 1930 the value of imports had fallen off more than one-half, exports by 20 percent, and in terms of quantity far more. Universal unemployment, bankruptcies and discontent resulted. In the confusion, the Conservative Party, which had ruled for fifty years, split and the Liberal Party took over, without bloodshed, but with vast crowds in the plazas.

As arch-Conservative Rafael Azula Barrera has put it: "The tremendous and universal economic crisis of 1929 . . . in all America . . . produced a dramatic series of political changes." In Colombia, "disciplined and violent minorities seized power, with torrential mass demonstrations in the big cities. In a few hours, the dikes of order and the Christian structure of society were broken, like a cracked wall."

The Conservative Party, of course, represented the Catholic

hierarchy, the old-time feudal hacendados, the bureaucracy, and the more pious rural masses. The Liberal Party was more truly the oligarchic party, anti-clerical by tradition, made up of the owners of newer plantation agriculture, native industry, the lawyers, newspaper editors, much of the middle class; it largely controlled also the lumpen proletariat and the organized labor of the cities. It was less sleepy-eyed, more progressive.

Liberal President Olaya Herrera (1930-34) followed a mild New Deal pattern, with some stress on economic nationalism. There were no more foreign credits, loan payments could not be met, and rigid exchange and trade controls had to be set up. The outflow of capital was severely restricted.

The situation was ideal for the "totalitarian" powers. Japan set up her first legation in 1933. Germany flooded the country with new immigrants and new enterprises, and by barter deals Colombia's coffee, cotton, sugar, vegetable-ivory, rubber and platinum began to move. For a time Germany came close to setting up a world-wide coffee monopoly, and Colombian beans went first to Hamburg, then New York. SCADTA (Colombian-German Aerial Transport Company), the oldest commercial airline then in existence, with new push behind it, expanded and provided service to every corner of the sprawling country, the Andean valleys and cities, the vast jungles — 4,000 miles of air routes.

"The Oil President," as Olaya Herrera came to be called, faced terrific pressure from the State Department. In 1928 the previous Conservative administration had annulled the Barco concession in Santander province near the Venezuelan frontier, allegedly for non-fulfillment of contract. This had come into the hands of the South American Gulf Oil company. The State Department was now pressuring the president to re-grant this concession to the Colombian Petroleum Company, a subsidiary, which already held leases on a million acres. This was a complicated deal: a pay-off to the original concessionaires, and intricate wheels within wheels involving Tide Water Oil, Atlantic and Gulf West Indies Steamship Company (who were to turn over development work to the South American Development Company, participated in by British and American concerns and by Standard Oil of Indiana).

Olaya Herrera faced a 1930 debt of $30,000,000, and early in the year began negotiations with the National City Bank for a loan of approximately $25,000,000. Ambassador Jefferson Caffery (of later Brazilian and Cuba-Batista fame) sat in on the discussions. The loan was made contingent on customs reorganization and other tax and financial laws, a phosphorous monopoly, but particularly on ratification of the Barco concession. The last was political dynamite.

The government staggered along for a year, finally was able to force Congress to approve the concession, to which was added a pipe-line concession (Law 80). This law ignored existing statutes limiting such contracts to thirty years; the new contract was for fifty years. By 1960 the Barco concession was producing nearly 10,000,000 barrels a year.

"The country has been saved!" Olaya reported. In short, obligations due six months earlier had been covered, but not a cent was left to carry on the government program, and the loan and interest charges had to be paid off. For this dubious help the country lost one of its finest oil fields.

The deal aroused great anti-American, anti-imperialist feeling. A story of concession-hunting in Colombia sent just prior to the negotiations by a UP correspondent caused Senator William Borah, head of the Foreign Relations Committee, to sound off. This "Bolshevist" Borah upset the banking people very much, for his words were a bombshell in Colombia. To placate them, UP president Karl Bickel told me at lunch one day he had agreed to let the bankers see and O.K. or suppress all news reports to and from Latin America.

The following year, the Senate Finance Committee's investigations into the whole loan racket, which had cost American investors so much and the people of Latin America even more, turned a brief spotlight on the Colombia deal. But Jefferson Caffery — ours being a democracy — was not allowed to testify. Again anti-Americanism mounted in Colombia.

Increasingly as the depression deepened, punitive official and non-official action was taken against U.S. companies. The labor movement, previously almost non-existent, grew and became militant. Leaders were sent off to Mexico to study the revolution there. Bloody strife occurred in the banana and oil fields and in mines. American overseers had to flee the country for their lives. Student riots occurred. Peasant revolts shook the countryside.

In such an atmosphere, President Alfonso López (1934-38)

took over on a wave of reform almost revolutionary. He instituted many changes, some sound, some mild, some radical: a moderate land program, old-age pension, workers' compensation, the eight-hour day. The United Fruit Company, hit by bad strikes, resulting in deaths by armed guards, was sternly regulated, and an official was arrested on charges of wholesale bribery and theft of judicial documents. Here was a new attitude that alarmed the State Department and U.S. business, as well as Colombian reactionaries.

The trend culminated in the 1936 constitution, which, over the embattled protests of Eduardo Santos, Liberal editor of *El Tiempo*, placed social needs above private interest and made possible government participation in all industrial activities. It could own such enterprises outright, establish quotas, prices, wage levels. Governmental control over all national resources was the goal.

The Church, alarmed by the possibility of confiscations, transferred many of its properties to American Catholic corporations, the Candelaria Church, for instance, to the American Endowment Fund, Inc.

Education was taken out of the hands of the Church, which ceased to be the official religion. Even the word "God" was eliminated from the preamble, "a return to the thinking of the French Encyclopedists." For the first time, education for women was provided in all schools, including the university.

Both private business and the State Department sought incessantly to break down nearly everything progressive in the program, to get defaulted loan and interest payments resumed, to knock out exchange controls so profits could more easily be shipped home, to set aside labor legislation and all new economic and social regulations.

Eduardo Santos, who took over as president in August 1938, proved amenable. A Conservative writer (though a Liberal in politics), he was appalled by the popular trends, and as soon as he was elected, scurried off to Washington in the style of all good satraps. He was royally feted by business elements which had suffered from the López legislation. At the Starlight Roof at the Waldorf, the guests at the main banquet table, besides U.S. officials, were, among other corporation bigwigs, the high moguls of the International Telephone and Telegraph Company, Electric Bond and Share, Pan-American, Grace Airways, Texas Oil, United Fruit, W. R. Grace and Company, et al.

To get elected, Santos had criticized the United States but now told the world he had been converted to a new view of our lofty purposes, our nobility of outlook, our complete disinterestedness and unselfish concern over Colombia's welfare.

U.S. planes flew down to participate in Santos' inauguration, a martial display that aroused fury in the common heart, and Spruille Braden, promoter, close to oil interests, was made U.S. ambassador. He was fresh from laurels in securing an armistice in the Chaco War. Perhaps, as some declared, he had imposed a settlement that benefited the oil companies (it didn't stick), but any outlet for land-bound Bolivia, regardless of the desires of Argentina or whoever owned the Bolivian fields (originally secured by Spruille's father), was beneficial; and peace at any price was preferable to the senseless and bloody strife.

The Rockefeller Foundation now came into Colombia to wipe out yellow fever, without which eradication oil and banana exploitation could hardly be successful — or, for that matter, could people be kept from dying, whether exploited or not. Likewise Santos arranged for the F.B.I. to help run Colombia's secret service. And so Colombia, with only a slight deviation, was safely back in the orbit of U.S. Caribbean controls.

López came back into office in 1942 — but an even more chastened López, who followed the new line of collaboration with the State Department and foreign business quite tamely.

He could not compete with the energy, oratory and radical program of a new rising star of the Liberal Party, Jorge Elicer Gaitán, who overnight had become the idol of the Colombian workers and peasants. He was variously labelled a "Communist" or a "Nazi," the latter being a favored smear-word of the hour.

A secret service report (C.I.A.) to Washington on the eve of the Bogotá Inter-American Conference accused him of receiving money in the guise of party contributions from a leading Communist. Unfortunately the matter was not documented. "Those boys have to earn their money," remarked one official. The person accused as a Communist was actually a Liberal, a leading educator and rector of the National University. The Communists themselves launched bitter diatribes against Gaitán for his nationalistic philosophy and his refusal to enter a popular front with them. He was hated far worse than outright reactionaries, to such an extent that many have conjectured he may have been assassinated by the Communists rather than by the Conservatives.

Before the 1946 elections, the Liberal Party was split three ways. López had become so unpopular he had resigned, turning the presidency over to Alberto Lleras Camargo, a frank collaborationist with Conservatives, a number of whom he installed in his cabinet.

In the Liberal Party's nomination convention, from which Gaitán remained sardonically aloof, López tried to impose as candidate his close adviser and alter ego, Darío Echandía, but Gabriel Turbay, backed by Santos, was named. Turbay was the son of Lebanese parents. He dressed in a dapper, doll-like manner and wore an eternal thin-lipped smile. He was more of a political schemer than a leader.

Gaitán called his own Liberal convention and ran against Turbay and the Conservative candidate, Mariano Ospina Pérez. López and the "Oligarchy" of the Liberal Party, angered at both Turbay and Gaitán, threw their support to the Conservative candidate. The result was a Conservative victory, with Gaitán a close runner-up to Turbay.

Even so, Ospina came in with only a little more than a third of the total vote and faced an overwhelming Liberal majority in Congress. Civil war threatened. On Inauguration Day the Army had to drive back ugly demonstrators.

Ospina was aware that his mandate to govern was exceedingly flimsy, and at once he offered half the cabinet posts to the Liberals — though refusing to negotiate with them as an organization. He selected leaders from the López-Santos Oligarchy, the extreme right of the party.

Nevertheless, Ospina was faced with a long stubborn petroleum workers' strike, which sporadically caused sympathy strikes of varying duration. At one moment the capital was almost paralyzed for lack of gasoline and oil, and mobs began growing in the streets, which the general in charge seemed unable to handle. Once, when given definite orders, he did nothing. Lolling in a chair in the Palace, he said, "Those are my boys; I can't shoot them down." Finally federal troops were brought in, supply and distribution were taken over by the government, and since strikes on public services were prohibited by law, the strike crumpled overnight.

Meanwhile preparations were being made for the Ninth Pan-American Conference — soon to be renamed the Inter-American Conference. These were under the direction of Laureano Gómez, titular head of the Conservative Party, who would also serve as head of the conference. It was a bitter pill for the Liberals and Gaitanistas. Gaitán, whom Ospina wished to include as a Colombian delegate, was kept out by Gómez, and began rallying his hosts and making demands on the government.

The choice of Gómez was unfortunate for the prestige and tranquility of the forthcoming conference. He had been the ultra-pro-Nazi of the continent, tied in with Franco, German and Italian propaganda, had constantly baited the United States and its "Protestant-Jewish plutocracy," had openly avowed his admiration of Hitler. He represented, above all, the fanatic pro-clerical elements. The rumor spread, too, that General George C. Marshall, head of the U.S. delegation, was particularly keen on having Gómez as president of the sessions.

Ospina used the conference as an umbrella to sweep out his "National Union" government, throw all Liberals out of the cabinet, and boldly seat the much-hated Gómez in as its head and Foreign Minister.

At once Gómez pushed punitive measures against the Liberals. Their meetings were broken up by police and army, many killed, several in suburbs of the capital, though the big mass-meetings of Gaitán in Bogotá were not molested. A drive also was made against Protestants; and gangs, led by priests or army officers or both, burned down a score of Protestant churches and chapels. Protestant ministers lost their lives. It was also part of Gómez's ambition to become president. Gaitán, of course, was the great obstacle to that ambition. Turbay had gone to Europe and had died. Santos and López went into exile. There was no doubt that in an honest plebiscite, Gaitán would be overwhelmingly elected in 1950.

Several months before the conference, he spoke to a rally of 100,000 people. "Mr. President, we are not here to present economic or political demands. All we ask is that our country desist from the line of conduct that puts us to shame in our own eyes and those of foreigners. We ask this in the name of mercy and civilization. . . . Put a halt, Mr. President, to violence. All we ask of you is the guarantee of human life, which is the least a country can ask."

But the death toll continued to mount throughout the land. Colombia was close to erupting. Much of the angry propaganda was directed at the Inter-American Conference.

The Communists were particularly vociferous, calling it a bureau of colonialism and imperialism. The Liberals were increasingly anti-American also, but their chief target was the honors being heaped upon "the Nazi," Laureano Gómez, while those who had been the friends of the United States during the war were being increasingly shoved aside, not only in Colombia but all over the continent.

3

In April 1961, thirteen years after those horrifying events in 1948, I stood at the spot marked by a red cross and circle, across from the offices of *El Tiempo* (today one of the most reactionary newspapers on the continent), where Gaitán was assassinated, and bought a small newspaper called *Gaitán*.

It was published and edited by his daughter, Gloria Gaitán, whom I was to meet a few days later at a luncheon, where I sat between her and Alfonso López Michelson, son of the former president, soon to be the 1962 Liberal candidate in one of the most futile, strangest elections — if it could be called that — in Colombia's history: one in which less than half of the people voted.

Gloria is a beautiful girl, who has been fighting ever since her father's death to carry his message to the people — the ideas for which he lived and died. Anyone reading his collected speeches cannot but appreciate that here was a truly great mind and a noble spirit. His Emerson-like capsules of wisdom, that reveal a profound knowledge of human relations, individual, economic and social, will live on, like those of Martí of Cuba, as imperishable gems in Spanish literature.

In June 1962, Gloria founded a new weekly — *The Battle of the People* — as an organ of her nation-wide organization, Frente Unida de Acción Revolucionaria (FUAR), which many former Jegas or Gaitanists have joined, and to which adhere many of the labor and peasant organizations of the country. Gloria is a fine, moving speaker, a clear, incisive writer, and she has much of the same drive and magnetism of her father.

Gaitán himself, though some of his political maneuvering during and just after the 1946 elections seems less worthy of praise, nevertheless was the nearest that Colombia has ever had to a true leader of the people since the days of the Venezuelan liberator Simón Bolívar. He will live on as one of the greatest citizens of his country.

After getting his law degree, with some sacrifice by his school-teacher parents, who earned no more than $50.00 a month, he went abroad, studied under famous Enrico Ferri in Rome and wrote a book on penology. After witnessing Mussolini's march on Rome, he returned to Bogotá and set up a law office. He was a brilliant criminal lawyer, and in spite of his heretical ideas, his waiting room was soon full of wealthy clients. But he loved ideas and controversy and often would let them sit there while he talked inside with poverty-stricken artists and writers, discussing literature and world affairs. "I could have made a fortune at my profession," he once remarked, "but the emotions of art and life meant more to me."

He dreamed of a crusade to establish Colombia's political and economic independence. His great inspirations were Mariátegui and Haya de la Torre of Peru and the early doctrines of Aprismo. He studied and admired the Mexican revolution long before President Kennedy made it respectable. He based many of his political ideas and tactics on Ortega y Gasset's *Revolt of the Masses,* though he did not share that author's rancid hierarchical philosophy. He was particularly fond of the Russian novelists, of Proust, and numerous modern writers from all lands. His call to action and greatness came in the epoch of the Popular Front, Roosevelt's New Deal, the Spanish Republic, and he moved in harmony with those trends.

His emergence as a national figure came after he went down to view a banana strike and saw workers mowed down by company guards and the Army. In a great Bogotá mass meeting he denounced the Army as "the Praetorian Guard of foreign capitalists." Overnight he gained the leadership of the labor movement and the dispossessed.

He was elected to Congress, then for years was Rector of the Free University, the only center of higher learning not dominated by the Catholic Church, and with the largest enrollment of any in the counry.

Bogotá was overwhelmingly Liberal, a difficult city for a Conservative president to control, a city prone to frequent student and labor demonstrations. Ospina Pérez cannily appointed Gaitán mayor.

No man worked more assiduously, from dawn till late at night. He pushed public works, built schools, hospitals and clinics, made it the cleanest city on the continent. Then came the big blunder.

His passionate desire to create a fine modern city, a smart city, caused him one good day to order all public taxi-drivers to wear uniforms. They staged an angry strike at once. Gaitán refused to budge. The city grew unruly and the police fired upon and wounded many strikers.

Liberal boss López, back in the country from the United States and Europe, demanded his resignation. He refused. President Ospina fired him, and the mobs celebrated. For the moment Gaitán's luster as leader of the masses was dimmed. But he quickly restored it by his orations at his weekly mass meetings, which he had instituted at the university, at city hall, later in the plazas.

4

In the 1947 Congressional elections, the Jega (Gaitanista) candidates took a 100,000 lead over all other candidates. The party still controlled nearly two-thirds of the vote of the country. There was no doubt now but that Gaitán would be elected president in 1950.

Shortly before the inter-American reunion, Gaitán visited President Betancourt in Caracas, and this later led to wild charges that the president of the neighboring country had organized the whole Bogotazo, that they had planned the Liberal uprising, not foreseeing that one of them would first be assassinated.

Certainly Betancourt had organized a big pressure claque to influence the deliberations of the conference. Student leaders from all over the continent first visited Caracas, among them one Fidel Castro from Cuba, before going on to Colombia. Betancourt sent in planeloads of students, newsmen and labor leaders, five hundred of them, and arrived himself overland with a big cavalcade of bullet-proof autos and two ambulances.

For the Conservatives of Colombia, Betancourt in those days was a "Communist," a backer of the revolutionary Legion of the Carribean, and a blood-brother of those other "Communists," Arévalo of Guatemala, Figueres of Costa Rica, Prío Socarras of Cuba, Lombardo Toledano of Mexico, Jiménez of Panama. How Jiménez, a staunch Conservative, got on the list is hard to figure out, except anyone eaten by a bad anti-Communist bug quickly discovers that anybody with any new idea is a "Red." Even Eisenhower! And President Prío was a great grafter, not a Communist — indeed he purged all Communists out of the Cuban Labor movement.

On March 24 Gaitán accused the Communists of "planning disorders for the Pan-American Congress in order to blame me and the Liberals." The following day he was even more explicit. "They want to make a play behind my back." They had approached him and other prominent Liberal leaders to try to get them to participate in hostile demonstrations. "I believe I have stopped those crazy people, who merely want to compromise me with their absurd adventures."

The Inter-American Conference convened March 30 in the Egyptian Room of the Capitol. Laureano Gómez was acclaimed its president, and speeches were made by Ospina Pérez and the Brazilian delegate. Nothing happened, though the atmosphere was tense.

The delegates had ridden through streets plastered with posters denouncing the "anti-democratic and anti-nationalist" purposes of the gathering directed "by the imperialism of the north." They called for "tireless efforts by the people to defend themselves against foreign oppression" and, more specifically, "against the Marshall Plan being fabricated to combat freedom in the Americas." As for "rationalization of raw materials," i.e. price supports, which quite a few delegates wanted, the posters said this would "merely consolidate the economic domination of the capitalist oppressor by means of dollar diplomacy."

The Communists at that time totalled about fifty thousand party members. They controlled many labor unions. The chief aim of the conference, they charged, was to launch the American states on a crusade against communism and to promote military missions throughout the continent. Part of their accusation was based on the fact that the United States was now backing all the notorious pro-Fascists and Nazis throughout the continent, men like Gómez in Colombia and Dutra in Brazil, who, thanks in good part to the meddling of Ambassador Adolf A. Berle, presently would take over the presidency there while Vargas went temporarily into eclipse.

The Latin American delegates were interested in getting some form of economic cooperation, some orderly plan of development and price protection for raw products. The second matter being pushed with some militancy was the question of freeing European colonies in the New World.

At the previous Rio Conference of Ministers, it had been agreed that any colonies of governments overrun by Hitler's armies would be administered by the Latin American countries. This had been grossly violated by the United States which had put the Dutch colonies under British rule. Washington was incensed when De Gaulle in person boldly raised the banner of the Resistance over all French New World possessions.

The freedom of European colonies was not a theme the United States wanted discussed, and Marshall and Gómez quickly squelched discussion. Economic matters were also pushed aside by the promise of a special economic conference to follow. This, it so turned out, was to be postponed many years. Marshall — this was after the Bogotazo — made a pathetic schoolboy speech which was certainly in the economic field. After advising the countries they could expect no aid — though we were pouring out billions to our other wartime allies — except a few millions through such agencies as the Export-Import Bank and the World Bank, he advised them they would have to depend on private capital, and so it behove them to establish climates which would attract U.S. enterprises.

This was listened to in stony silence. It showed no understanding of the nature of economic thinking in Latin America ever since the Great Depression. This was going back to the old stand. Quite apart from the economic problems created by absentee capital, the continent was all too aware of what American capital had done in Cuba, in Mexico, in Central America, and the dollar diplomacy and Marine invasions that it had brought about. Latin American had expected great things from this conference, and the delegates included the outstanding economists and jurisconsuls of the continent. Marshall's speech struck them, quite apart from its unpleasant suggestions, as too elementary to warrant respect. It was, of course, tuned perfectly for the American mind, but not for this learned body.

The concessions that the other delegates did wrench out of the reunion was a change of name to Organization of American States instead of the overlordship title of Pan-American Union, and the election of the president, instead of his being automatically the U.S. Secretary of State. They wished to rotate the headquarters rather than have them in Washington always under the thumb of the American government, but this did not seem practical.

Also they wrote into the new charter the outlawing of armed intervention and the promoting of invasions from neighbor territories, the outlawing of all economic aggression, and they made recognition of any established government, regardless of how it came into being, mandatory within three days, a proviso that was meant to prevent the previous use of non-recognition as practiced by the United States as a means of coercion. How little binding these provisions were was demonstrated by the armed overthrow of the Guatemalan government, by the Cuban invasion, both brazen violations of both the spirit and the law of the inter-American system, and the withholding of recognition to the Peruvian military junta in July 1962.

Apparent calm hung over the city following the first session, but tension mounted. When the head of the Ecuadorean mission paid a courtesy visit to the president, his car was mobbed and he had to be rescued by the police. A few nights later the lights went out in the Egyptian room during the session, throwing the delegates into wild confusion.

Other incidents occurred. It was rumored that there had been an attack on the American delegation when they came out of one session. The president and the Palace people were alarmed. Gómez brushed their fears aside. "The size of the military patrols have been doubled; vigilance has been doubled. There won't be any trouble, not anything important."

"The main thing is, take care of yourself," the chief of secret police warned him ominously.

On April 3, Fidel Castro and another Cuban student, Rafael del Pino, were removed from the balcony of the Colón Theater for tossing down leaflets calling for the liberation of European colonies. They were ordered to present themselves at secret service headquarters the following Monday, but did not do so and vanished from their quarters.

While the Inter-American Conference was going on, Gómez' successor in the cabinet, Angel Eduardo Zuleta (who was later to call the Punta del Este conference in order to outlaw Cuba), was cleaning out the elected Liberal governors in the states and municipalities, putting in military men as violence continued throughout the country, a wave of bloodshed and imprisonments on every hand. (Zuleta's brother and business partner was and is a vice-president of the United Fruit Company.)

On the morning of April 9, the President attended the inauguration of the Agricultural Fair. That afternoon the National Museum was also to be inaugurated, and officers of the merchant marine, the Gran Flota, were giving a reception. Whether the president would attend was not known.

The head of the president's office, Rafael Azula Barrera, and various cabinet ministers went home to lunch. Some would go to the ceremonies in the afternoon. Most did not intend to return to the Palace.

The inter-American session lasted until well after one o'clock.

Gaitán was in his office in the Augustín Nieto Building on Seventh Street, across from *El Tiempo,* talking with friends until about one o'clock, telling them about his defense of a certain Lieutenant Cortés. The trial had lasted until 4 a.m. and thanks to Gaitán's eloquence the accused had been freed.

"It was the greatest triumph of my penal career," exulted Gaitán.

One of those present, Plinio Mendoza Neira, who had managed Turbay's campaign but had since joined up with the Jegas, invited Gaitán out to lunch.

"Accept," said Gaitán. "But I warn you, Plinio, it will cost you dearly."

Knowing of Gaitán's appetite and tastes, everybody laughed.

On leaving the building, Plinio took Gaitán's arm and they walked ahead of the others. "What I have to tell you is very brief ... " Plinio began.

Gaitán jerked back, covered his face with his hands and tried to return to the building. Three shots had rung out, after a minute a fourth one. Gaitán fell to the pavement.

U.P. correspondent Guillermo Pérez heard the shots and dashed across from the Tivoli bar.

Plinio, who later told the story, bent over him, anxious and frightened, not quite realizing that anything serious had happened. "What's the matter, Jorge?"

He did not answer. His eyes were half open, a bitter grimace on his mouth; a thread of blood flowed under his head.

His friends got him into a taxi and rushed him to the general hospital. He had been shot three times, and by an excellent marksman who had placed the shots in the traditional death triangle, the bottom of the skull, the lungs, and the liver. Miraculously he still breathed; he did not die until an hour later. Even before that, all hell had broken loose in the city.

The assassin, smoking gun in hand, was disarmed by police agent Carlos A. Jiménez, who thrust him into a drugstore to try to save him from the anger of the gathering crowd. The store employees rang down the iron shutters.

Presently the crowd tried to break down the door, so it had to be opened. The throng avalanched on the killer. A lottery ticket vender struck him and grabbed his hair. Another dived into his legs and threw him down. Various shoe-shiners beat him to death with their little boxes, battering his face to a pulp. His bloody clothes, a cheap gray suit — all but his blue, red-striped tie — were stripped off. A rope was tied about his neck and he was dragged out.

"To the Palace! To the Palace!" the assailants cried, waving his bloody clothing as banners. And so his battered, naked body, one eyelid flapping, the other eye half bugged out, was dragged toward the plaza where stood the Capitol, Carrera Palace, and the cathedral.

He was an insignificant little man, with a pale, angular, hungry-looking face, unshaven, a big mat of hair. Later he was identified as Juan Róa Sierra, but nothing much was learned about him, except that he was a Conservative in his convictions, a drifter who lived by odd jobs and on money from an older woman.

The populace believed from the first instant that the crime had been engineered by the government, if not by President Ospina, most certainly by Gómez.

On their side the Conservatives, as soon as they could be heard, moved heaven and earth to prove that it was perpetrated

by (a) Communists, or (b) by Liberals contrary to Gaitán, or
(c) by President Betancourt of Venezuela, or (d) by the Cuban
students, Fidel Castro, Rafael Ovares Herrera, and Rafael del
Pino, reportedly seen near the site of the killing about the time
it occurred. (They had had a midday appointment at *El Tiempo.*) Another theory was that Róa was not the killer at all, an
idea suggested by Rafael Azula, who stated that Róa's .38 revolver was not capable of producing the precise wounds revealed by
the autopsy.

Most of the evidence about the Cubans was *manufactured*
long after the event and rests chiefly on secret-police Agent no.
6's report — the author was never identified. Actually all police
records were destroyed during the Bogotazo. Azula Barrera, who
in 1956 wrote the best eye-witness account of events in the Palace,
does not use any of this questionable post-date police testimony
nor the apochryphal document by Agent 6, even though his
whole book tries by inference to prove that the macabre affair
was the joint effort of "Betancourt and the Communists."

It has been well-established that Castro did not contact any
Communist leaders though, according to Security Chief Nuño,
he was in contact with Antonio García and Gerardo Molina,
who Nathaniel Weyl in his *Red Star over Cuba* declares "worked
closely with the Russian Legation."

The political history and affiliations of these two men are perfectly well known. García was the most prominent leader of the
Socialist Party. Gerardo Molina was the rector of the university and an outstanding leader of the Gaitán wing of the Liberal
Party; in fact he, along with other leading Liberals, became a
member of the emergency Revolutionary Junta set up by the
Liberal Party after the rioting began.

Whatever the truth and whatever the events of the next few
days, a hero had died, a great man had been killed. The people
sought vengeance.

5

From mid-afternoon, all through the night, central Bogotá was
reduced to a shambles. The police joined the rioters and passed
out guns. Buildings were razed, burned, gutted, looted. No other
city in history has ever suffered from the fury of the populace

as Bogotá suffered that November 9. The devastation of downtown Bogotá was more complete and horrifying than that of San
Francisco by earthquake and fire. Numerous old colonial
churches were destroyed.

Yet in the end, little was done to rectify the abuses that lay at
the root of this insane demonstration. In the end, the answer
became merely more force, more bloodshed, more ruthlessness
by the rulers of this tragic country, a blood bath that kept up for
ten years and which is far from being terminated.

The President, after leaving the Farm Fair — he was apparently not yet aware of the tragedy — ordered an immediate return
to the Palace, though it was not his custom to do so until four
o'clock. Suddenly, he ordered his chauffeur to take him to the
airport, for he wished to look at a new monument he had put up
there which had aroused derision for its ugliness. But then, after
a few blocks, he again told his chauffeur to take him to the Palace.

He was astonished at the crowds, though used to impromptu
demonstrations in the streets. At the Palace there was a great
mob and considerable shooting. Those who lacked guns were
brandishing clubs and machetes. His car managed to get through
the iron gates just as he was recognized, and they clanged shut
in the faces of those who surged forward.

Similarly his Executive Secretary Azula and various other
cabinet ministers managed to get into the Palace. But one minister, caught in the swirling tides in the center, had to hide out
among the coffins in a mortuary establishment all night.

The mobs in the plaza surged into the capitol across from the
Palace and while the delegates of twenty-one sovereign nations
huddled terrified in the big salon, proceeded to demolish furniture, light fixtures, desks and records. The delegates — though
some, including Marshall, had already left — dashed through a
hail of bullets to the Palace barracks where they paced or huddled or slept on the floor all night.

There were only a score of guards and they had no rest at all.
One guard, who had been at his post forty-eight hours, said, "I
fired more than seven hundred rounds. I left heaps of dead in
the plaza. The mobsters climbed right over the dead and kept
trying to enter."

Those delegates who managed to get out of the center held
an impromptu meeting in one of the outlying embassies. Every-

body wanted to lift the sessions. General Marshall stood out against this courageously, saying it would mean a victory for the Soviets and a loss of prestige by the New World nations. Argentine delegate Bramuglio said his government was sending planes to evacuate its seventy-man delegation. He himself would stay on as long as anybody else did, but he would not risk the lives of the others. Decision on whether to call off the conference or adjourn it to some other country was postponed for three days.

Laureano Gómez, whom the crowds and all the Liberals blamed for the assassination, had hid out in a friend's house, but toward morning he made his way to the Ministry of War where the leading generals were gathered.

Obviously this was no coup d'etat à la Trotsky. The Trotsky blueprint for the seizure of power had been to make no frontal attack on public buildings (except the post office and telegraph offices) or on barracks, but merely to isolate them by cutting off all communications and services until the powers-that-be withered on the vine.

But the Bogotá rioters, those not smashing and looting and burning, centered all their efforts on the Palace. And even there, the telephone service was never cut, nor was the central exchange ever seized. This enabled the president to keep in contact with the military forces and the governors all over the country, to rally troops at Maracaibo and other nearby points to come to his rescue. Light service was not cut off until toward morning. Water supplies were never cut.

Those in the Palace begged President Ospina to leave. "We have enough men to get you to the airport. A plane is waiting."

"I shall not leave the Palace," he replied tersely.

His wife, rifle in hand, declared, "We remain here until the last cartridge is gone."

It seemed hopeless, a little group of top officials, some employees and a tiny garrison obliged to fight all day and night without relief.

At seven-thirty, the Liberal Revolutionary Junta showed up to see the president and hand him an ultimatum. Hastily appointed, they were trying to turn the uprising to their own political advantage. But they, too, were dazed by the turn of events.

Washington was utterly at sea. The Communists likewise apparently had been taken by surprise, but being better disciplined than any other element reacted quickly to take advantage of the situation. It was said they seized the radio stations right off. Perhaps true, but the stations broadcast the names of the Liberal Junta and clamored for a Liberal, not a Communist, take-over of the government.

As the Liberals entered the president's office, a girl secretary said, "Here come the crows."

By then it was raining hard, and they were disheveled, perspiring and soaked to the skin. Their outstanding leader was Darío Echandía, former supporter of López and the architect of the more radical measures of his first administration, sometimes referred to as his Rasputin.

The president sent everybody out and received them alone. The radio was going. At this moment Azula received a telephone message that the National Radio Station had been recaptured. Somebody there asked, "What shall we broadcast?"

"Say the situation is controlled by the government, that the revolt has collapsed, that the Liberal leaders are in the Palace at this moment offering their patriotic help to the president to save the country."

Presently the president called him in. Carlos Lleras Restrepo, one of the outstanding Liberals of the country, shouted angrily that the National Radio was saying they had come to the Palace to aid the government. "That is not true."

Azula replied smoothly, "All I said was you were in the Palace."

"Write down the purpose of your visit," said the president sharply. "The country should know what it is."

The Liberals, confused, talked long-windedly at cross-purposes.

"What do you indicate you would like me to do?" the president cut in.

After a considerable silence, all spoke at once. Lleras Restrepo broke in, "Señor Presidente, the city is in ruins. There are hundreds of dead. The government cannot survive more than a few hours."

"The government did not start this massacre," Ospina replied. "The Army is merely doing its duty in upholding the constitution."

At this moment sharpshooters on adjacent roof-tops broke windows. The delegation jumped up and suggested they adjourn to a safer place.

"If you wish. But I am quite comfortable here. This is the seat from which I have been administering the government, and naturally I prefer to remain right here."

Mendoza Neira broke in nervously. "We must take quick measures, every moment is precious, and each moment makes it more difficult to save the country."

"What you want to say, is it not, is that you wish the president to retire from office? Is that not so?"

"It is an interesting point," cried Lleras Restrepo, overjoyed. "We must consider it at once."

Ospina said, "It seems most interesting to me also. I did not seek this post and would have preferred to live tranquilly with my family. . . . But I was elected by the Colombian people to direct the country's destinies, and I would go down in history as a traitor if I abandoned my post. Furthermore I would be accused of a crime I did not commit. The six provinces that have rebelled will soon be brought back under control. If you insist, we shall face civil war."

Mendoza Neira launched into a long discourse about the death of Gaitán. Lleras interrupted brusquely. "Señor Presidente, the matter of your resignation is the one important point. We should define that."

"We shall define it. . . . My irrevocable opinion is that the constitution obligates me to remain in my post, without regard to personal dangers I may face.

"Don't fool yourself," he went on. "My resignation would not simplify matters. It would merely bring bloody civil war. In department after department, the Conservatives are preparing to march on Bogotá. Even if the Palace should fall in these moments and those who defend it, including myself, should perish, the situation for the country would be more disastrous if I were to desert my manifest duty. At least, on my dead body, it would be possible to reconstruct legality and save Colombia from anarchy. A dead president is worth more than a fugitive president."

He excused himself to answer the telephone. The Liberals milled around. The windows were red with the rising flames of the burning city.

"This can't go on," said one, pointing outside. "It cannot be controlled without a complete change of government."

Ospina sent word by Azula that he was going to call a meeting of his cabinet.

"That is absurd at this late hour under such circumstances. A minority government cannot continue to rule this country. We must have a rapid decision before it is too late," they told Azula.

"The real country is not a mob," replied the Executive Secretary, and went out.

The president left them sitting there biting their nails.

The night wore on. A telephone call came from Laureano Gómez at the Ministry of War. Cabinet head Zuleta Angel took his message. In a moment he slammed down the phone angrily.

"What does he say?"

"He's crazy! All he can repeat is 'Junta militar. Junta militar. Junta militar.' "

"That will not do," said Ospina. . . . "However, we might be thinking of what military names could be added to the cabinet."

The waiting Liberals, on hearing from Zuleta about a proposed military junta, protested violently. "That is insane. It would destroy the civil tradition of the Republic at one blow."

Zuleta Angel returned to the president. "Please, Señor Presidente! Say something to the delegation. They are angry at your failure to give them a clear and final answer. They are threatening to leave."

"Let them go. I didn't invite them — I have nothing to promise them, other than my determination at all costs to remain in the presidency. No other patriotic solution is possible."

Zuleta left to tell them, and returned quickly. "They are going. You ought not to let them go. . . . Tell them something, for God's sake! That's a requirement of simple courtesy."

"I am sorry they are going. They came here of their own will; I have nothing to say to them. Have General San Juan show them out."

They stalked out stiffly. At the foot of the staircase, an officer of the Guard said, "Be very careful, Señores. The firing continues. Two persons who left here a few minutes ago never got across the street."

All rushed back upstairs and sank into the big leather armchairs in the reception salon. They were served food and drink and settled down for the rest of the night.

They were supposed to be the leaders of the mob outside; their chief interest was to save their own skins, and to gain power, even though they were too cowardly to act.

Dawn came, tinged by the yellow and red flames of the burning city. All night Gómez had been phoning insistently. At eight
the generals arrived.

"I am at your service," the president said.

The general of the highest rank and longest service spoke.
"Señor Presidente, the situation is extremely delicate."

"I have the impression that we have gained ground during the
night."

"Perhaps not as much as you imagine. At this moment, the
wife and daughter of Gaitán and a big band of women are bringing his body to the Palace. They cannot be stopped except by
the most brutal methods; yet, if they are not stopped, it is possible
that the defense of the city and of the Palace will collapse."

"What do you believe to be the solution?"

"We are all ready to give our full cooperation, but we must
have the responsibility, if we are to act with the greatest safety
and efficiency."

"In what way, Señor General?"

"By the formation of a military junta."

"And what will be the role of the president in such a junta?"

Another general spoke up. "Señor Presidente, we will give Your
Excellency, your wife, and all of yours absolute protection."

"It is not a matter of protection for me or my wife. What is
fundamental is the protection of the Fatherland. Your solution
is not possible, it will not be constitutional, and at all costs
I intend to uphold the constitution." Before they could reply, he
added, "What do you say, gentlemen, if we consider the possibilities of a military cabinet?"

"Señor Presidente, that is no solution. The most important generals would be dispersed among the ministries and, at this complex and decisive hour, they are needed to command the military forces."

"And it is also my place to remain at my post and continue
acting as president of the country."

Disconcerted, the generals swore to defend him and the government.

"You may all leave and take up your duties," Ospina said crisp-
ly. "You, General [Germán] Ocampo will kindly remain here in
the Palace."

The generals stopped to speak to the Liberal Junta. Trying to

get awake, some members were stretching, others pacing to get
the kinks out of their bodies. When they heard that a military
junta would *not* be formed, they brightened visibly.

Presently the president strode in. "Doctor Azula, kindly make
out a decree making Ocampo the new Secretary of War. I have
just named Darío Echandía, the Ministro de Gobernación, as
head of my cabinet. Régulo Gaitán will act as Chief of Police.
Within three hours I will advise you concerning the other Liberals I shall appoint to the cabinet. As previously, before the
National Union broke down, half the posts will go to the Liberals. Above all, I shall appoint a Liberal to head the Ministry of
Justice, with special powers to investigate the execrable assassination and to leave no stone unturned to discover if others are
involved."

By phone Ospina offered to restore Gómez to the Ministry of
Foreign Affairs. Aware that his presence in the cabinet would
provoke disorders and difficulties, visibly upset because his
scheme for a military junta had not brought results, he declined.

Shortly he was put on a plane "for his own safety" and sent
off to Spain.

7

During the final two years of Ospina's administration, in spite
of the Liberals in the cabinet, their party was scourged by fire
and sword, a crescendo of terrorism that prepared the way for
the assumption of power by Gómez.

Returning for the 1950 campaign, he called the Liberal Party
"a basilisk, a monster having the head of one animal, the face
of another, the arms of still another, and the feet of some de-
formed creature, all together forming a creature so frightful
that its mere glance causes death. Our basilisk moves with feet
of confusion and stupidity on the legs of brutality and violence
which propel its immense oligarchic belly; with a breast of wrath,
with Masonic arms, and a tiny, diminutive Communist head . . . "

The government's terror was carried from the provinces into
the halls of Congress, where Conservative deputies shot down
Liberal members, killing one and wounding another, a distin-
guished scholar, who was left incapacitated for further public
life. The assassin was honored at a banquet by Gómez a few days
later.

The Army and the police rounded up non-Conservative citizens and passed out cards to those considered "safe":

"The undersigned President of the Conservative Directorate certifies: that Señor . . . . , bearer of card No. . . . . has sworn that he does not belong to the Liberal Party. Therefore his life, property and family are to be respected.

Alfonso Orrego, President."

On November 9, all members of Congress were driven out of the Chamber by the soldiery, the edifice seized and martial law declared throughout the country. All sessions of state legislatures and municipal councils were also suspended. All public meetings were forbidden. Censorship was established, and the Secretary of War was empowered to suspend any publication. Powers of the Supreme Court were restricted.

Terror, brutality, assassination, mass massacres swept all Colombia. The Liberal candidate, Darío Echandía, was shot at by Bogotá police officers on Thirty-first Street, and his brother and five others were killed.

Two days later "elections" were held. Laureano Gómez was elected by "unanimous" vote.

President Ospina addressed the nation that night. "The electoral campaign and the tranquility with which the election was carried out are proof that the authorities took measures to insure complete neutrality. . . . I give thanks to Divine Providence, which so manifestly continues to watch over the nation's destiny."

During those last two years of his administration, probably 50,000 Colombians were murdered to insure Gómez' victory. American Ambassador Willard L. Beaulac in his memoirs, *Career Diplomat*, heaps praise upon President Ospina, but has no word of reproach for the terrorism he unleashed upon the country.

The wholesale killing was to get worse and continue for years. The life of anyone known to be a member of the majority party, the Liberals, was not safe. Tens of thousands of refugees flooded into Bogotá for safety, and many starved. Two whole provinces the size of Nebraska were razed from end to end by massacres, burning, aerial bombardment. Those who did not obey army orders to get out were shot or bayoneted to death — men, women and children. Army officers forced owners to deed over their properties at the point of the gun. During the last two years of

Ospina's government, of Gómez and of Dictator Rojas Pinilla, it has been officially admitted that 300,000 Colombians perished, a terrorism not yet surpassed in the Americas. Yet Gómez, the worst of the killers, Marshall's ally at the fateful Bogotá conference, was accepted as an ally in the Korean War.

When things reached a crescendo of terror in 1953, a general, Gustavo Rojas Pinilla, noted for his ruthlessness around Cali at the time of the Bogotazo, seized power. For a short time he restored civil rights, but soon was shooting down students and strikers, soon was carrying on the same war of extermination in the provinces. He outlawed *both* the Liberal and Conservative parties and, imitating Perón, established what he called "The Third Force," both nationally and internationally.

Thereby he also created a curious mésalliance between the heads of the Liberal and Conservative parties, which still persists — at least so far as the top echelons, "the Oligarchy," are concerned.

8

The new dictator looted the country as it had never before been looted, and when a military junta threw him out on May 10, 1957, the country owed $450,000,000 in short-term obligations alone. By then inflation was breaking the back of the country. Farm and industrial production was down — in good part because of the continuing guerrilla warfare in the interior. It still goes on.

There is no need to recapitulate the story of those bitter years, or the student riots that began in Cali on May 2, 1957, and spread across the country, braving tear-gas, firehoses and bullets. On May 9 women and children were bayoneted to death in a manifestation in central Bogotá, which by then had risen from the ashes. On May 10 Rojas Pinilla was ousted by the generals and put aboard a plane bound for Spain.

It cannot be said that the new regime remotely represented the popular forces of the country, though it did provide a formula for peace, and for that everybody thirsted. A general spirit of good will and hope prevailed. Even the peasants, the so-called Guerrillas, surrendered their arms, only to discover all too soon that they had won only the right to be killed more easily. They have been re-arming ever since. One prominent Colombian told me, "Things are so ticklish that everybody in Colombia is armed, expecting a blow-up. Perhaps it's just because everybody is armed that it has not occurred yet."

The new political arrangement — and this was written into the constitution — was for the Liberal and Conservative Parties to rotate in power every four years and share posts in the government and in Congress. Thus automatically, every other four years, the president would be a Conservative, but would have only one-third the electoral strength of the country behind him, unless opinion shifted. Thus all other parties and groups were stripped of their political rights. Even if they put up a candidate and he won, he could not take office.

The bigwigs of the two parties who cooked up this incredible scheme were the highest members of the Oligarchy. The Liberals of the Left were led by Alberto López Michelson (son of former president López). Though he had a great following, even had he won the endorsement of the whole party or run as an independent and received a majority of the votes, he could not have become president in 1962. Thus elections were a meaningless farce. A North American was boasting to a Colombian about U.S. voting machines. "Why, we know who is to be our president within half an hour after the polls close." The answer: "We know that a year ahead."

The first president would be a Liberal. The candidate nominated under this farcical system, who would automatically be president whatever the vote-count, was former president Lleras Camargo. He had always collaborated with the Conservatives and in 1946 had treacherously paved the way for the Liberal defeat which brought Ospina Pérez into power.

During his first term, even more so during the second, Lleras was a dutiful hand-maiden of Washington. Lleras led the fight to call the Punta del Este conference to oust Cuba from the Inter-American Organization. As a reward for breaking off relations, he was furnished with a $70,000,000 loan. He rated a bit more than the Central American governments, or Peru, where the pay-off was from $14,000,000 to $25,000,000, or Haiti, content with $3,000,000. This aid money filled many a hungry Liberal pocket during the last months of his administration.

The mastermind of this maneuvering was the same Eduardo

Zuleta Angel, a Colombia-type Birchite, who had played a leading role in the period of Ospina and Gómez, at times heading
the cabinet. Though a Conservative, he became the trusted agent
of foreign affairs for Lleras — and for the United States. In the
1962 make-believe election, in which more than half the registered voters did not go to the polls, the Conservative candidate Guillermo León Valencia enjoyed a vote of only 25 percent
of the total electorate.

The president-elect, big-jowled, balding Guillermo Valencia,
hastened to make the usual hegira of obeisance and money-beg-
ging to Washington.

9

1963. Word has gone out that Colombia is a good place for
Americans. In few places in Latin America these days can one
find a larger, more varied assortment of U.S. aid officials, technicians, experts, Peace Corps youths and do-gooders, speculators
and business men than at the luxurious Hotel Tequendama in
Bogotá.

The most insignificant typist of the U.S. missions earns twice
as much a year as the peasant he is expected to help will receive
in an entire life-time. Even a self-sacrificing Peace Corps youth
aiding village peasants without land will get more in a year than
such a peasant will earn in twenty years.

The speculators and business men, perhaps some of the aid officials, if the example of what has happened in Peru is repeated
here, are not concerned with the true welfare of the Colombian
nation, about which they know blessed little, but with making
a fast buck. Bogotá is mostly a gloomy, chilly capital, because
of the climate and because next to Quito it is the shabbiest capital in all South America. But the gloom does not depress these
Don Quixotes of the dollar. The Tequendama makes good drinks,
and the Yanks are buoyed up by the sunshine of President
Kennedy's "great adventure of our century," the Alliance for
Progress, which means that plenty of shekels will be floating
around for sticky palms.

When not in the Tequendama bar, these busy beavers can be
encountered in government offices, where they are given red-

carpet treatment by suave officials. The latter, for the most part, are highly educated gentlemen, connoisseurs of the world's great art and literature — that is a long-nursed tradition in this country, even though for a generation now it has produced little literature worth writing home about.

The great danger for poets in Latin America is not that they will be scorned or ignored as in the United States, but that they will be named cabinet ministers. But the ex-poets and go-getters are brothers under the skin and see eye-to-eye on the proposition that Colombian resources would be better off in the hands of practical, uncouth Gringos. The officials — though in the cafés they rant about Yankee imperialism, commercialism and lack of culture — are also eager to make a fast buck. Nor are they asking the big cut demanded by the Batista and Trujillo entourages to do business. Latin American politicians are wont to sell themselves cheaply, but few come cheaper than the Colombians.

The oligarchs in power have reason to be grateful — not merely for loan money, but for the large military aid "for hemisphere defense," which aids the government to keep the people in their places, and keeps on killing revolting peasants. Even today there are scores of dead each clock-around; and four large areas, one in the capital province itself, in Tunja, in Los Llanos and near Cali, are practically independent — the so-called Red Republics. The U.S. military-aid mission has been making aerial maps of these areas, presumably trying to overrun them by a military putsch. The old terror will soon be back in full force.

Vast sums have also been spent on propaganda, subsidizing newspapers, buying or subsidizing radio stations. A terrific verbal bombardment of Cuba was carried on prior to the Colombian rupture. Walls were placarded with huge signs: "Colombia is a Christian country: break relations with Godless Cuba." A new Catholic "educational" radio has been set going, and two Cubans of Batista vintage, said to be C.I.A. agents, for secret service men are thicker here than prairie burrs, attack Cuba from dawn to dark.

All persons who favor the independence of Cuba or non-intervention are thrown out of jobs. Efforts to purge the Free University failed, but leading professors have been thrown out of the National University and other schools for their independent views about Cuba. All independent radio programs have been stamped out. Nearly all independent publications have been suppressed.

And so the terror, if not so blatant now (news of it is suppressed), made Kennedy's trip a visit to a land under martial law. As in Venezuela he arrived behind a wall of bayonets and tanks. Colombia is a land on the brink.

12 ◯ THE CRIME AGAINST GUATEMALA

1

It was wartime. And Guatemala was an occupied country. It was occupied by the army of Dictator Jorge Ubico (1931-44), beloved friend of the United States, and it was occupied by U.S. troops; and as usual the Rockefeller Foundation was on the job stamping out malaria, which was a commendable thing. It saved the lives not only of Guatamalans but of many G.I.'s.

A Guatemalan writer, Rafael Arévalo Martínez, once said that "a malarial country could have only a malarial government, viz. dictatorship." Perhaps the ending of malaria gave the people enough energy to throw out their malarial government. In any event, the revolts of 1944 and 1945 occurred during the greatest influx of dollars Guatemala had ever known and in a period of flushed wartime prosperity.

Soon the change-over was considered to be a dangerous "Communist" revolution. But are not dollars supposed to prevent Communist revolution?

The U.S. troops were in the capital city, the provincial cities,

in the ports, along the Pan American Highway. Their presence
in Guatemala City — had they not been so easily visible — could
have been surmised by the big signs in the center of town some
blocks away from the Red Light district and the big whore-house
known as "the French Legation," where the buying of champagne
was compulsory — signs announcing prophylactic stations where
the G.I.'s had to go after swarming through the streets of joy;
otherwise, if they got any venereal disease, they would be courtmartialed.

There were other signs of alien activity. U.S. engineers and
tractor drivers and blade-men were working feverishly to complete the Pan American Highway. The stench of the colossal
graft would shortly be exposed by Congress, but the matter
would be politely ignored in the U.S. press, though it was glee-
fully set forth by Fulton Lewis, Junior on the air — chiefly because he hated Roosevelt and the New Deal.

There was a big coffee-buying agency, ostensibly Guatemalan,
but run by U.S. officials. Coffee is the mainstay of Guatemala's
export trade, other than bananas, and the plantations were mostly in German hands. But all the Germans were on the State Department black-list, to trade with them was treason. The blow to
our good ally Guatemala was catastrophic — no coffee sales, no
revenues — and to save the dictatorship, the silly fakery was set
up to buy the coffee from the black-listed Germans, then for
the U.S. government to buy it from the intermediary agency.
Not a bad idea — a lot of extra people made a lot of extra money out of the shenanigans.

The other export staple was bananas, but these were not moving either, because F.D.R. had commandeered the United Fruit
Company fleet for war-purposes, thereby cutting off goods needed in the Caribbean and Central American area. There were
terrible food riots in Caracas and various West Indian islands.
Even in Cuba food shortages were acute.

Other U.S. agencies were at work hither and yon in Guatemala. Henry Wallace was setting up a big quinine industry, a
bit belated, since cheaper and better synthetic drugs were becoming available.

In Guatemala City we began building the huge Franklin D.
Roosevelt Hospital, the largest in Latin America, to be a show-
piece of all our benevolence and good-will. It would have every

modern scientific equipment and facility. It seemed a bit extravagant, though it was greatly needed, for Ubico had never built a hospital or a school for that matter, and the existing general hospital was a rat hole where most of the patients had to sleep on the floor. But there were not enough doctors in all Guatemala to man this new institution; most had no proper training in the use of modern medical equipment.

The sensible thing would have been to have used these many millions to build small clinics up and down the land, for rural Guatemalans had never had the services of any medicos except Indian witch doctors.

Other U.S. teams were building airports and modernizing the seaports. All the later were owned or controlled by the United Fruit Company — and so tightly that in all history no other steamship line and no European line had been able to set up regular service to the country. Goods from overseas had to be transhipped in New York, Havana or Panama and sent forward in United Fruit bottoms.

All these Santa Claus activities created an unparalleled labor shortage, and the Army was busier than ever rounding up Indians in the villages to work on the plantations and in the cities — the old Spanish *mitmae* system. They were brought down from Los Altos, the northern highlands, in long queues with ropes around their necks to the hotlands where they sickened and died or got diseases because they were separated from their wives. Often they did not receive the customary fifteen cents a day, for this was handed over to the military officers by the grateful hacendado, and when, after six months or a year, the peon was permitted to hoof it back to his village, he might be handed a few *quetzales* for food along the way.

But now the labor demand was pushing wages up a bit, and the hacendados were furious. On the Pan American Highway work the Americans were paying thirty-five cents a day or more; peons were running away to get on the work gangs, and the hacendado workers were growing rebellious. Finally our good friend Ubico sent us an ultimatum to cut wages back to customary levels, or he would supply no more labor. When the Americans refused to comply, he blocked off needed labor and sabotaged operations in other ways; mysterious mishaps occurred, operations languished; and the road never was completed.

Other grievances arose. U.S. workers received more a year than most Guatemalan peasants would earn in several lifetimes. Tractor drivers got more than a Guatemalan army officer or cabinet minister.

Guatemalan army men grew sullen. Under-officers received less pay than a G.I.; and the ordinary ragged, barefoot Guatemalan soldier, Indian conscripts from the hills, observed that the alien soldiers were well-dressed and had proper food. Resentments grew. The G.I.'s were able to get their pick of women, and bloody bouts occurred.

Guatemala City got paved, but inflation was bad, and competition for living quarters was great. Even wealthy Guatemalans, unable to pay the soaring rents or compete with even lesser U.S. agents for quarters, had to move into near slum dwellings. Resentment grew on *all* levels.

The whole economy was out of kilter. Never had such glaring class differences intruded as between the "invaders" and well-to-do Guatemalans. Local taste was being corrupted by such things as Coca Cola and American cigarettes and whiskey. Vast supplies of goods flowed in duty free and were blackmarketed, making the proper collection of customs almost impossible. The government was unbalanced in every direction.

We finally persuaded Ubico to confiscate all German properties. This was a war-measure, but it destroyed the basic principle of the sacredness of private property. The simpler-minded Guatemalans could not understand why U.S. property was more sacred than German property. Why not also expropriate the United Fruit Company and U.S.-owned public utilities?

Guatemala was prosperous, it was busy, it was booming, but somehow the more dollars that came in, the more miserable the people became. Except for top government swindlers, all classes of society became unhappy. Revolution was inevitable.

When the revolution became increasingly socialistic, when parts of the vast United Fruit holdings *were* confiscated, when the revolutionary governments began building their own light plants, when they started a highway to the coast to free themselves from the high rates of the banana railroad, when they began building a truly Guatemalan port that would be available to all ships and all nations, the charge of "communism" was leveled, especially against Arbenz. *Time* and *Look* magazines let loose with all barrels blazing.

We blamed the revolution on the Communists and their dreadful propaganda. Yet when the revolution came, you could have counted the number of Communists on the fingers of your two hands. A party was not organized till some years later. Actually, the cause of the revolution of 1944-45 was Guatemalan bitterness against the two occupying armies, that of Ubico and that of the United States. U.S. dollars, U.S. enterprise — "benevolent," but misguided and irksome — created the Guatemalan revolution. The revolution came also from the original evils of the land — one of the most beautiful in all Latin America but ruled by harsh, long-term dictatorship ever since the independence — and it came also from all the tampering and despoiling, so even the middle-class and upper-class elements joined hands with the young officers and the lepers and the ragged to get rid of the hurt.

2

The revolt, led by students and young officers, forced Ubico to hand over the government to a provisional president, who was ousted the following year. Prompt elections were held, and a professor, Juan José Arévalo, in exile at the University of Tucumán in Argentina, author of three books on pedagogy, became president for a five-year term.

I visited him at the National Palace in 1946. A quick, intense man, but with a monumental serenity, he answered all questions without the slightest hesitation or reserve. He described himself as a Christian Socialist. His obligation, he believed, was to help the Guatemalan people emerge from their centuries of misery.

Several things I had already noticed in contrast to my previous visits when the country was under dictatorships. For the first time the capital was scrupulously clean; it had become the cleanest city I have ever seen in the world — so clean I hesitated to throw a cigarette butt into the street. The market, which had always been a stinking place, was scrubbed morning, noon and night, and no flies crawled over the meat.

The attitude of the people was different, too. There was no soldiery on the streets, except in the vicinity of the big new barracks and police-station — the largest edifice in the country, built by Ubico with U.S. aid money. Indeed, though Ubico built no schools, all over the land he had put up, thanks to our help, enormous new barracks. The people had always walked the streets fearful and cowed, almost as though they were in an alien place. Now the street throngs were at ease, people were gay and smiling and playing music. Even in the old days, no Latin Americans were quite as charming as the gentle, courteous Guatemaltecos; but now it was truly a pleasure to be in their land.

Already, in a year's time, Arévalo had done tremendous things: a new road and free port, blue-prints for new power plants. A land settlement program was being carried out in distant Petén, the northern jungle region, so rich but never developed, and with the confiscated German estates.

The new constitution decreed that no land owned by the government could be alienated, and the confiscation of German plantations had provided the government with a large part of the developed arable land of the country. The estates were now being worked in new ways: a few had been leased, but most were being administered by the government agricultural department or by new peasant cooperatives, and several by the Army.

"Guatemala is too poor," Arévalo told me, "to be able to afford any parasites. We now have a working army, not a lot of idlers gambling and drinking in the barracks. Already our soldiers are self-sustaining."

Four magnificent new agricultural schools had been completed. An Indian policy had been started, with pupils being taught in their own Quiché tongue, spoken by a large proportion of the Guatemalan people. Newspapers and magazines were being published in Quiché. Native-language broadcasts were being provided over the radio.

The labor and peasant movements were encouraged and already had hundreds of thousands of members. Teachers were organized and taking an active part in government programs. Women could now vote, and women's organizations, charitable, political and recreational, were blossoming on all sides.

A minimum wage of thirty-five cents a day brought screams from the remaining plantation owners, and it also worried the United Fruit manager. Though UF workers were earning that or more, he feared wage advances would result. He was bucking the new government.

A rural housing program was under way all over the country. The new constitution obliged hacienda owners to put in proper housing, and Arévalo was enforcing this. Three types of housing had been worked out — for the hot country, for intermediary elevations and for the high country. The government supplied materials, concrete, lumber, at cost, and, if necessary, provided a low interest, long-term loan.

Every reform made the U.S. ambassador, Richard Patterson, groan, and he fought them in every possible way. He was a retired, millionaire, variety theater owner who had paid the requisite campaign contributions. His lack of comprehension was responsible for much of the tragedy that later overtook Guatemala and the super-tragedy of its present nightmare existence. Even his staffers were appalled by his furious antagonism.

Presently he discovered eight Communists on government payrolls, and sent a peremptory note to Arévalo to fire them. Arévalo sent back word it was none of his business whom the Guatemalan government employed; whoever did his job properly could be assured of tenure.

The ambassador then succeeded in halting work on the skyscraper hospital, leaving it a shell without windows, doors or equipment. All U.S. aid was cut off.

Arévalo had never been much interested in the hospital, which he considered a white elephant, instead had been building small clinics around the city and across the country.

Shortly after this, I was talking with a Point IV man back from Burma. Some money had been left from their appropriation. The Burmese officials were consulted as to what new project should be undertaken.

"How about a hospital?" our aid man asked.

"Nay, nay, anything but a hospital."

"Why not a hospital?"

"You start a hospital, then like in Guatemala, you stop in the middle because you don't like our politics."

That was the first the aid man had heard of it. But all the rest of the world knew about it.

Nor was Arévalo overly preoccupied about the loss of aid money, for he believed that Guatemalans, though so poor, had to learn to do things for themselves, and that since it is one of the richest countries in resources on the continent, it could with effort and direction soon become prosperous and independent.

But this rupture was really tragic; the gap grew wider, and as U.S. pressures increased, the spirit of stubborn independence grew among the Guatemalan people.

The straw that really broke good relations was Arévalo's new labor code. A mild decent code, it provided for the eight-hour day, minimum wage, proper working conditions, certain fringe benefits. When a strike hit the banana railroad and the labor board ruled in favor of the union, the lid blew off, and every form of pressure, including slanderous propaganda, was resorted to. The United Fruit Company instituted a boycott against Guatemala, which they were able to enforce through monopoly control of ports and shipping, so for more than two years the country could procure goods from abroad only overland via Salvador and Mexico.

This strike was serious. For the lawyers for the fruit company railroad were of the old Cromwell firm, which had so enriched itself at the time of the "Rape of Panama," and of which John Foster Dulles was now a member. Before long he would be Secretary of State, and his brother, Allen Dulles, a United Fruit Company lawyer, head of C.I.A.

The tariffs on this railroad were said to be the highest in the world. It cost more to ship goods two hundred miles from Puerto Barrios to the capital than to ship from Europe or the United States.

Simultaneously, with the United Fruit boycott, all U.S. arms shipments to Guatemala were cut off; the government was unable even to buy side-arms for the police.

The C.I.A. and the Pentagon had already become alarmed at the growing militancy of the peasants, clamoring for land. A number of land seizures had occurred, a secret report to the Pentagon said that the "Red menace" was rising in Guatemala, that there was danger of agrarian revolution. The only way to forestall it was to strengthen the military hand.

And so, behind the president's back and in violation of all international law (it is done frequently all over the continent), the U.S. Army flew in guns from the Canal Zone to interior landing strips for trusted officers of the Army. Humorously enough, their chief white hope was a general named Jacobo Arbenz. To him went the bulk of the shipments. The C.I.A. was really on the job!

3

Arbenz was elected for a four-year term in 1950. U.S. enthusiasm for him began to wane when he became the favored candidate of Arévalo, and U.S. electoral assistance was switched to a rival military candidate. But he was ambushed and killed. With his demise also vanished a lot of U.S. taxpayers' money secretly expended in his behalf.

Arbenz not only carried on Arévalo's program, but he pushed through an agrarian law, whereupon the charges of "communism" began to be leveled at him in full fury. Yet it was a wise moderate law. Hacendado owners were allowed to retain all the land they could cultivate and were given a year or so to expand acreage under cultivation. Large-scale commercial plantations were also permitted to retain land necessary for future expansion.

Payment for land was based on the assessed tax evaluation. Perhaps this was unfair; if so then the landowners had not been paying the taxes they should have been.

The United Fruit Company, the biggest owner in the country, had vast stretches, mostly uncultivated, to which no access had ever been permitted to landless Guatemalan peasants, though most of it had been obtained originally at practically no cost by government concessions. Some had been secured from Congress only after that august body had been surrounded with bayonets and after criticizing newspaper editors had been killed.

The State Department did not deny Guatemala's right to expropriate, but demanded proper payment in cash, not bonds. The proper payment in Dulles' opinion was what the United Fruit Company said their land was worth — some $15,000,000. But if the company had paid the taxes over the years on the price they themselves set, then instead of now receiving any remuneration, they would be owing the government millions of dollars.

Arbenz patiently pointed out that exceptions could not be made in favor of foreign owners. The government had perhaps gone beyond the law already in allowing the company acreage for future banana expansion. Even with the most fantastically imaginable expansion, the United Fruit Company had been left enough land for future uses for the next hundred years. Also, the Guatemalan government was paying double the original cost, though none had been developed or utilized.

More than ever, charges of "communism" were tossed at him. Was there any truth in them?

4

Just prior to the C.I.A.-promoted invasion, the State Department held its usual brow-beating session of inter-American states, this time at Caracas, and all but Guatemala, Mexico and Argentina fell dutifully into line. It also issued its customary White Paper. Naturally it built up every possible shred of evidence that Guatemala had a Communist government.

One needs merely to wade through the White Paper, shot through with McCarthy-like smear verbiage and illogical deductions, to appreciate that the charge was utterly false. The White Paper was Hitler's Big Lie, all over again. The matter is all the more absurd because the number given in the White Paper of Communists or supposed Communist employees in the entire Guatemalan government was infinitesimal compared to the number McCarthy had charged were being harbored by the State Department itself. No member of the cabinet was a Communist.

Besides guilt by association, criteria for declaring a person a "Communist," other than having registered as a PGT voter (Guatemala Workers Party), were: having membership in a peace organization or signing a peace petition, opposing atomic testing, believing in the poison gas warfare charges in Korea, attending the International Peace Congress in Uruguay, attending international labor congresses, visiting the Soviet Union or China, favoring Roosevelt and the New Deal, organizing a labor or peasant union, shaking hands with a Communist, etc., etc., in a descending scale of pettiness and old-maid snooping.

Guilt by association is used throughout the paper. "His brother was a member of the PGT, the alleged Communist Party in Guatemala." Ergo, the government employee in question is a Communist. Several persons are called Communists because they once registered as members of PGT, the "first names were different, but probably they are the same person." Another was called a Communist, because a friend said so many years back. The report depended heavily on the newspaper *Espectador*, and followed its Fascistic line in considering persons who supported Roosevelt and the New Deal as being Communists.

As an indication of the Know-Nothing tricks of the State Department's paper, it declared that all teachers, since they were well-informed as compared to the bulk of the population, must be considered suspicious. They were contemptuously referred to as *"ladinos"* — though nearly all Guatemalans, except pure Indians, are ladinos, people of mixed blood. The miserable snooping document has a nasty racist tinge.

It was an even more shameful and distorted document than that of Spruille Braden a few years before, which had had to prove that Perón and the Bolivian leaders were Nazis or Nazi agents. It did a great deal of harm to many Guatemalans who, on the strength of the suspicions raised by the White Paper, were later jailed or killed or had to flee into exile.

Nearly all civic organizations in Guatemala were branded as Communist because most had one or more Communists, suspected Communists or crypto-Communists on their executive committees. The secretary general of the labor confederation (CGT) actually was a Communist, and there were seven more among the forty-one officers. A leading student organization was called Communist because one officer had visited behind the Iron Curtain. The Arbenz government subsidized political newspapers (as does every government in Latin America and the U.S. government and U.S. corporations also); ergo it followed (no proof was given) that the PGT newspaper, *Tribuna Popular,* could not be successful without direct or indirect support of the public treasury, that this would require Arbenz's approval. Furthermore, he defended the right — as he did of Catholics and all others — of the Communists to organize and engage in politics as an authentic domestic party. So how about France? Italy?

The White Paper did not point out that a Catholic Party, largely led by priests, held meetings throughout the country, that the leading priest was allowed to speak regularly over the government's own radio. Such a party could also be labeled as part of an international conspiracy, the cliché used in the paper for the PGT. The military clique and the organizations abetted and financed by the C.I.A., a fact known to the Arbenz government though not publicized until later, were also an international conspiracy.

The consummate *proof* of Arbenz' pro-communism was his denunciation of U.S. atomic tests in the Pacific. Yet his statement was mild compared to that of Eisenhower a few years later. The Democratic candidate for President, Adlai Stevenson, made that same position a key point in his campaign.

The White Paper was obliged to admit that among the two-score officers of the National Confederation of Peasants (CNCG) there was not one known Communist, though one "probably" was (since his brother was a PGT voter), and though the peasants' confederation was affiliated, not with the PGT but the pro-Arbenz party (PRG), it was an organization under Communist influence.

The trickery of the White Paper was to designate every proposed reform supported by Communists as a Communist measure, ergo anybody in favor of such reforms becomes a pro-Communist or Communist even when he is anti-Communist. In this way it was possible to brand the whole agrarian reform as pro-Communist and run by Communists. Thus the paper finds it "significant" that seven of the large number of government farm-inspectors (not an administrative post) were "identified" as Communists.

All this seems sickeningly trivial now, and if I have dealt with it at length, it is to indicate the sort of tripe that can be used and is still used to befuddle the American people and lead them down the road to injustice, aggression and war.

No consideration is given in the White Paper that the agrarian law was a careful document drawn up after looking into various land-laws of Europe, after consulting all sectors of Guatemalan opinion (including the Communist), that it was one of the wisest, mildest laws ever promulgated by any government, that it was absolutely necessary to provide justice and economic security to Guatemalan life. Had such a law ever been put into effect in Cuba, there would never have been any Castro revolution.

As Dr. Jesús de Galíndez of Columbia University (later kidnapped in New York and probably assassinated by the Trujillo dictatorship) wrote: What was the U.S. government trying to do? "To prove to the Guatemalan people that reform is impossible in the social-economic structure of their country unless the Communists triumph?" (Quoted by Gregorio Selser in his *El Guatemala-zo, La Primera Guerra Sucia.*) And he added, "Guatemala and many of the Hispanicamerican countries need a social revolution. Only if the democratic parties first do this can the Communists be prevented from taking charge." He quoted the liberal Archbishop Sanabria of Costa Rica: "We should have the courage to approve good measures even if they are carried out by people we think are wicked; and disapprove of everything bad even though done by people we consider good."

On the basis of the White Paper's slanted findings, the United

States is obligated to overthrow most of the governments of the world. Even "Our Boy" in Cuba, Batista, who had just run for president after a military coup, had openly accepted the support of the Communist Party (thanks to corrupt opportunists in that party) and he later rewarded their help with fine positions in the government. Among those who accepted jobs under Batista was the poet Juan Marinello, now Rector of the University under Castro.

Leading Communists were given jobs in the Benavides dictatorship in Peru. They had participated in the Medina government in Venezuela. Many, until shortly before this, had been employed by three Chilean governments. In fact all those governments had been elected in a popular front — with the Communists. The number of CP Congressmen there was six times that in Guatemala, where there were only four. Communists also sat in the Congresses in Uruguay, Bolivia, Brazil and Costa Rica. There were many more Communists, actually and percentagewise, in the Congresses of France and Italy. The British Government had survived their presence in the House of Commons. No country can rightfully call itself free or democratic so long as any group, Communist, Fascist, Negro or Catholic, is denied his rights or free speech and lacks the right to form unpersecuted organizations. In this respect Arbenz of Guatemala was more "democratic" than the United States. "As long as a single citizen is oppressed," Francisco de Miranda told the Revolutionary Tribunal in France in 1794 when he was threatened with the guillotine, " . . . if a single citizen is oppressed, every citizen is oppressed — and I am oppressed."

In the United States of course, Communists were and are being persecuted and jailed. In all the world, only in the more backward, openly Fascist countries and a few Latin American satellites, were Communist Parties outlawed; such countries as Trujillo's Dominican Republic, Somoza's Nicaragua, also in Spain, Portugal, Formosa, Pakistan, the Philippines, South Korea and South Vietnam.

Arbenz did not even have diplomatic relations with most Socialist powers, though presently, since he could get no arms from the United States, which had also blocked purchases in England, Switzerland, France and Italy, and was faced with a buildup of C.I.A.-promoted and Pentagon-armed invasion forces in

Honduras and Nicaragua, he secured a shipment from Czechoslovakia.

Actually, the trumped-up anti-Communist invasion of Guatemala was motivated by only one really important factor, the expropriation of part of the land owned or claimed by the United Fruit Company. It was naked criminal aggression against a neighboring people and its government. Years later I talked with Arbenz in exile. "Our great mistake was: we failed to arm the people."

Smarting from the charge that it was a United Fruit Company war, as set forth in the entire Latin American press, the U.S. government hurriedly instituted an anti-trust suit against the United Fruit Company. This was a dust-in-the-eyes maneuver which fooled very few. The charges have never been pushed.

4

In December 1953, after appealing in vain to the Organization of American States, Arbenz sent a voluminous documentation to the United Nations and asked for protection against the violation of the sovereignty of his country and international law by the C.I.A.-promoted invasion preparations in neighboring countries.

The documentation, which the United Nations filed away and ignored — and this remains one of the worst blots on the record of that organization — included proof of the build-up of arms on United Fruit and other big plantations and the hiring of U.S. ex-army officers. It included bills of lading of arms shipments. It proved among other things that Luís Somoza, President of the Nicaraguan Congress and son of the then-dictator, now president himself, was acting as arms purchasing agent for the Carlos Castillo Armas rebels, except of course for arms air-lifted by the Pentagon to Nicaragua and Honduras.

An article in *The New York Times Sunday Magazine* gave a résumé of Ambassador John Puerifoy's tactics in carrying out his assigned task of overthrowing the Arbenz government. (1) Brand it as Communist. In this effort no magazines did as much as *Time* and *Look*. *Time* even went so far in 1953 as to print a column giving the gist of Arbenz's Labor Day speech which was completely apocryphal and contained only three words remotely connected with the original address. (2) Force it, by propaganda, economic boycotts, threats, to accept support from the Communists in order to survive. (3) When opposition was built up in and out of the country, be ready to move in with an overwhelming armed force.

He did not, in this article, mention the suborning of Guatemalan army officers, though he appeared in their midst after Arbenz fell, pistol strapped about his middle, to impose the desired provisional regime on the country.

Shortly before the armed coup, the *Progressive Magazine* (after stopping the presses and removing an article of mine) inserted an article giving full credence to the U.S. official propaganda lie and line. The author of the substitute article stated that Ambassador Puerifoy himself had informed him that Arbenz was an active Communist; he gave the secret number Arbenz used on his communications with the Party. Actually this was but the number he used on customary inter-departmental memos for government administrative purposes.

I wrote Puerifoy about these statements, and just before he was killed in the Far East, he answered that he had never made any such declarations to any correspondent, that he never had believed Arbenz was a Communist and knew very well he was not a Communist.

By then the whole question had become academic. In May, Washington flew more arms to Nicaragua and Honduras to support the rebel movement. Presently the attack was launched and planes, flown by American pilots, bombed ports and Guatemala City; a British vessel was sunk. These bombings were not — as official statements declared — of military objectives — but of open cities. Some were aimed at the historic National Palace in Guatemala.

And so, the strange little puppet — Carlos.Castillo Armas — was seated in power.

5

Castillo Armas had headed the Army Academy, had been arrested for attempting an armed coup financed by big landholders, and had escaped abroad. The C.I.A. picked him out of a bar, a little worse for wear, in Mexico City and flew him south to head up the revolt. He was a small man, who affected a Hitler moustache and had always had a photograph of Hitler on his desk.

Though a number of members of the Arbenz regime were shot immediately after his troops reached Guatemala City (one a Honduran exile, named by the White Paper as probably a Communist), Castillo was not a blood-thirsty dictator. He let the numerous refugees in the foreign embassies depart, jailed all Communists or supposed Communists, dissolved the labor federation, the peasant federation, the teachers' federation, even the Masons, and permitted only the small Catholic Party to survive. All public reunions or political activity were prohibited.

He stopped the pro-Indian program, closed up the agrarian schools and many other schools, stopped the government light and power project, the road to the Atlantic, the new free port, kicked fifty thousand peasants off the land, restored the properties of the United Fruit and the large hacendados, sold the wartime expropriated German *fincas* at great profit to favorites of his regime. The clock was turned back, and the 2 percent of the people owning 70 percent of Guatemala's land were back in the saddle; the Army was in the saddle; the landed aristocracy were in the saddle once more; the Church — though Castillo did not overly favor it — was soon to become the mentor of the subsequent Ydígoras regime.

Presently Castillo held bayonet elections. Even before they were held he quarreled with and persecuted the only opposition group, the pro-Catholic party. The booths were in charge of the Army, and citizens were required to vote yes or no, viva voce. Further to safeguard this election, Castillo disqualified, on the grounds of illiteracy, nearly 80 percent of the voters. Not in the history of the Americas — except perhaps the French viva voce vote in Mexico used to seat Maximilian or that held by the Marines in Haiti — not in the entire history of the Soviet Union or other members of that bloc, had such an incredible doctored and coercive plebiscite ever been held.

The United States, oddly enough, was slow at first in shelling out money to its caudillo, and Castillo was obliged to up taxes on the big estates, suddenly finding himself denounced by those for whom his so-called revolution was fought. He got no added popular support thereby.

He abolished Congress, suppressed newspapers. Seventy-five thousand people — everyone who had held a job under Arbenz, or who had ever helped organize a union, or had ever signed a peace petition, or had accepted land under the farm program — were on a secret army-police list and were picked up systematically, held in jail for three to six months, and even if released or tried and acquitted, could be picked up the day after and held another six months without trial. Naturally, since "our man" and not Castro were doing these things, they were never criticized in the United States. Democracy had been restored to Guatemala!

A year later Castillo Armas was assassinated. Not even the government accused the Communists; the matter was hushed up, though hints were thrown out that — curiously enough — implicated Dictator Trujillo of the Dominican Republic, who later tried to kill Betancourt of Venezuela and who tried to hire an American aviator to bomb the Cuban Palace and kill Batista. Reciprocally, Batista tried to assassinate Trujillo. It is too bad neither succeeded.

6

Any one who visits Guatemala these days can observe for himself what a sweet democracy we have established in that forlorn country. A helicopter flies overhead every day, radioing information about any groups of people on the streets — three, I believe, is the legal limit — then an armored car hurtles forth spewing tear gas almost indiscriminately; passers-by have to duck for doorways. This car is followed by bullet-proof autos loaded with machine guns, which race to any suspected point. Tear gas and machine guns have laid low, with much loss of life, student demonstrations, labor demonstrations, many innocent citizens. This is part of the C.I.A.-U.S.Army training on how to control public demonstrations.

Go anywhere in Guatemala, and the soldiery will repeatedly stop you for your travel documents — not politely either. Every public building is heavily guarded. When you enter or leave the country, your passport must be stamped by the military commandant. The government operates behind a wall of bayonets.

Behind that wall function swarms of C.I.A. agents, U.S. officials, U.S. do-gooders, U.S. Army men, and some, not many, U.S. business men, United Fruit men behind the added fences of barbed wire, and, of course, the Guatemalan people — except

they do not function; they spend most of their time hoping
not to be arrested; others — officials — spend time worrying how
long their mastery of the land will last. Such a regime cannot possibly survive except by using more and more force, murder, and
dollars — not even then.

Behind that wall, also, are the seven secret bases used by the
C.I.A. to train the anti-Castro mercenaries (more are now being
trained under Pedraza, one of Batista's worst killers). A good
share of the first batch languished until December 24, 1962 in
Cuba's prisons, from where troubled spirits Eleanor Roosevelt,
Walter Reuther and Milton Eisenhower tried to extract them.
Those brave incarcerated fighters for freedom — i.e. for the
restoration of United Fruit properties — who brought death to
the peaceful shores of the Bay of Pigs surely merited the grati-
tude of important U.S. citizens. The good samaritan group decided they were worth a little over $2,000,000 or about $2,000
a head. That's more than Haitians killed by Trujillo a few years
back were worth. But Castro considered them worth more than did
the good Americans; he held out at that time for $30,000 a head.
Cuban patriots had died defending their country. Castro was
also upset by the damage to the Cuban beaches, the pavilions and
houses built as homes and for the recreation of the people, who
prior to him never had any access to the beaches.

In answer to a remark by Castro, Mr. Kennedy remarked ir-
ritably that Castro knew better than to believe that the U.S.
government could ransom those "fighters for freedom." In Cuban
talk they were "mercenaries shipped there by him and the C.I.A.
in a vain, bloody absurdity." Yet surely the U.S. government owed
something on the bill, quite a few millions in fact. Prior to the
aggression, the mercenaries received high C.I.A. salaries; they or
their dependents were guaranteed large sums. Did our government stop their pay and benefits because they had the foolish
ness to get imprisoned instead of killed?

The Cuban government certainly has a big claim against the
Guatemalan government, which nursed the viper in its bosom.
Why doesn't Ydígoras ransom them?

Ydígoras kept shouting then and since that Cuba planned to
invade Guatemala. He sent the U.S. fleet scurrying after every
little fishing boat sighted off the coast. He keeps U.S. cruisers
bravely hunting mysterious submarines. His own forces bombed

a fleet of Mexican fishing boats, creating an ugly international incident. More recently he accused Mexico of permitting Cuban revolutionists to train for Guatemalan invasion on a farm near the border owned by former president Lázaro Cárdenas — another brazen falsehood, or maybe he is just the cry-baby of the Americas.

Miguel Ydígoras was a god-send for the State Department and the C.I.A., not merely for training mercenaries, but for granting secret bases in violation of the laws of Guatemala, the charter of the Organization of American States and the United Nations, among other international regulations. He carried the torch for the propaganda against Cuba when the rest of Latin America would not yet do so. He made it possible to pressure the rest of Central America into line.

Like Castillo Armas, he was elected by a tiny minority of the Guatemalan people, a much smaller minority. As before, the bulk of the people were disqualified from voting; but the balloting was secret this time, and opposition parties were permitted to put up candidates. It is doubtful if Ydígoras held his mandate with more than 10 percent of the people. Even so, he *lost* the election; therefore he annulled it and installed a military junta to hold a second one, which he won but, even with soldiers nudging the voters, only by the skin of his teeth.

More recently, the Congressional elections of late 1960 were so fraudulent, revolts broke out in the capital and all over the country. In preparation for that election, he reported that grenades, packed in Cuban pineapple tins, had been planted on the shores of the country. Apparently, however, nobody but the State Department believed this tall tale.

For months after the Cuban invasion and long after the truth had been spilled in the United States, Ydígoras continued to deny that Guatemala had had anything to do with the invasion.

On September 7, 1961, five months after the invasion, he told Paris *L'Express* correspondent K. S. Karol categorically that Guatemala had had no hand in the attack. If there were foreign mercenaries on his soil (they are training there again), this, Ydígoras said, was Guatemala's right and privilege. They were training wholly for defense. That Karol even brought up the matter, the President said, revealed how badly he had been "brainwashed" by the Cuban "Communists."

The next morning the police marched Karol over to the army-police Bureau of Immigration, headed by Arturo Aguirre Matheu, Ydígoras' right-hand man, one of the biggest landowners in the country, for prolonged questioning. (Matheu will have the say over Alliance for Progress money for land-reform!)

But Ydígoras declared he was running a "democratic" country and believed in "free enterprise." Proof was tangible — the gift of oil reserves, with a minimum of benefit to Guatemalans, to U.S. companies. It was one reason, it has been suggested, that Ydígoras qualified for much U.S. aid.

Ydígoras declared, "I listen to all the complaints of my compatriots [and many get into prison thereby]. Anybody can come here to see me." His words have a familiar echo.

On January 29, 1962, he deported the leaders of all the opposition parties.

Only once was the State Department visibly annoyed by its protégé. Early in 1962, he complained that the United States had not kept its promise to repay his aid for the Cuban invasion (till then he had denied it) by helping him recover Belize, British Honduras (pried loose from Guatemala, despite the Monroe Doctrine, in the last century). The State Department was upset. These days Belize smells of oil-concessions, granted not long ago to British and U.S. companies in violation of the present Belize colonial government's rights, and the State Department denied Ydígoras' statement point-blank. It did admit, however, that such a promise *might* have been made off the cuff by some C.I.A. officer involved in the Cuban affair!

As for Belize, a plebiscite is pending to let the people vote on independence, annexation by Guatemala or to remain a colony. Large sums, it is alleged, have been given (by the C.I.A.?) to the Christian Democratic Party (Catholic) which is in favor of colonial status, i.e. continued British rule.

In November 1960, a bad revolt broke out in Guatemala, in which two companies of soldiers in Matamoros joined the rebels, who also took the important port of Puerto Barrios. Ydígoras blamed the uprising on the Communists, the Partido de Unión Republicano (non-Communist) and Mario Méndez Montenegro, former candidate for president, who had to flee to the United States. The revolters were put down with the aid of U.S. battleships rushed to the scene. But guerrillas headed by Marco Antonio

Yong Sosa are still operating in the hills with nuclei of army revolters.

They have been trained and have U.S. arms, Ydígoras complains sadly, "so it's hard to put them down." On August 9, 1961, the president of the Association of Secondary Students was seized by the police and tossed out of a car forty-eight hours later on a country road ten miles outside of Guatemala City, after having been brutally tortured to try to find out the whereabouts of guerrilla leader Yong. One of his captors was a Cuban, who, a Mexican magazine conjectures, was probably a C.I.A agent.

The problem is more difficult than that. The rebels are inspired by a desire to end the dictatorship; they have the support of the people. They must fight not only the Guatemalan dictatorship but C.I.A. mercenaries currently being trained again for the invasion of Cuba. To these have been added paid French and Spanish Foreign Legionaires, sent, the press has announced, by Catholics in Europe. Here is an obvious "violation of the Monroe Doctrine," an "international conspiracy" scarcely "compatible with the American system." But Kennedy speaks only of aggression by Cuba against Latin America. The only serious armed aggression in the Americas thus far has been perpetrated by Guatemala and the United States against Cuba. For a hundred years the only armed aggression, except for South American wars, that has been perpetrated against Latin America (usually in the name of the Monroe Doctrine) has been perpetrated not by European powers but by the United States. The present dictatorship in Guatemala is precisely a direct product of that type of aggression.

13 ◯ THE HOLY ALLIANCE

1

Philosopher Alfred North Whitehead once said that it required a thousand years for a new basic concept of human relations to take hold of the mass mind and become powerfully operative in society. When we listen to most Senators and Congressman, particularly to racists from the South, we are convinced that Dr. Whitehead was over-optimistic. At this writing they are terrifically upset about God and prayers in public schools, yet it is obvious that Christianity has caught up with few of them.

In contrast to some of their fire and brimstone utterances, our Executives have sustained a loftier tone. We recall President Eisenhower's glowing good-will statements about peace and freedom, ending poverty, promoting economic growth in Latin America. The same sentiments have been parroted by Kennedy, with ever more emphasis on "freedom," but accompanied by additional aid in dollars for the countries to the South — and also armed aggression.

More and more as the years of this century speed by, the new role of the United States in pursuing Realpolitik in a world-wide power struggle have made the words and deeds of our Executives ever more contradictory. Damn sin on Sunday, but get down to good tooth and claw on week days. Indeed noble utterances and actual conduct are hardly on speaking terms any more within the same soul. It is part of the schizophrenia of our world, the terrible menace in our world from the weapons of destruction, the continuous use of propaganda for power purposes, not for truth.

This is not unique with heads of state in this country, it is even more marked in many Latin American leaders, most of whom seem to be mounted on circus horses going in different directions. Their dilemma grows worse as the economic conditions in their countries inevitably deteriorate — a deterioration that Alliance for Progress money cannot hope to stem, which is more likely to be accentuated and which, together with long standing malpractices in the southlands, plus all the secret money, arms, intrigue and propaganda, plus military and police-controls we are utilizing throughout the area, will at best promote a recrudescence of militarism and dictatorship rather than freedom or an evolutionary process.

Unfortunately modern government in the United States has become a vast secret process. A government of secrecy in the long run becomes more destructive of human rights at home and abroad than an overt dictatorship. Governments, as well as individuals, must have their corners of secrecy, but today the agencies in our government that absorb most of our money, that have the power and the real say-so over policies, are no longer properly controlled by our elected officials. There is only a remote connection between the people and either operations or decisions, and the people anyway are controlled by a vast and stultifying propaganda apparatus. We are in the age of push-button government, but what elements — and some of them are ignorant, selfish, power-mad and sinister, I feel — will actually push that button? Eisenhower warned us on leaving office of the danger of trusting our fate to the overwhelming power of military-corporation rule. It is apparent that civilians, citizens, professionals, intellectuals have less control over our military than the Japanese had over their war-lords, little control over the vast power of corporate wealth. The heads of steel corporations cannot, like ordinary citizens, be tried for contempt of Congress. Today our politicians have become window-dressers, shielding secret operations from view, operations they can do little to modify. There need be no surprise, therefore, that their moral and intellectual abdication is so great, their ideas so inadequate and rancid, their egotism and selfishness so colossal — no surprise that the people are bemused. Latin Americans are wont to explain, "The United States is a big hoof without a brain," or as one writer has put it, "a dinosaur with a pin-head brain."

This moral and political bankruptcy is nowhere more vividly displayed than in Richard Nixon's "six crises" book. One crisis came when Kennedy in his campaign came out in favor of the abetting, training, financing and arming of Cubans to engage in an attack on their homeland. At the time, Nixon set forth statesman-like reasons for opposing this: the folly of such a violation of inter-American rights and treaties, all the ill effects it would have on the rest of Latin America and our prestige in the world. But in his recent book, he admits *with pride* that he was utterly insincere, that he was obliged to take this lofty position in order to conceal the impending attack on the island being prepared by the C.I.A. and the Pentagon under the Eisenhower administration of which he was a part. This is Machiavellian cynicism with all the stops out.

Naturally these processes that have so corrupted our government and our leaders, plus a stultifying catch-as-catch-can cold war, plus a wholesale grabbing for the wealth of the world, are at work all over the globe and, in spite of the bright slogans, nowhere more perniciously than in Latin America. Secret manipulations and lavish use of money have corrupted every government there, have blocked normal political, social and economic evolution — supposed to be the basis of our fight against Castro — and have made inevitable the rise of brutal governments, diaphanously veiled with false phrases of "democratic freedom." The fact is the alliance between backward feudalism and outside capitalism has never been closer or more relentless.

This process was well under way even before the advent of Castroism, but the Cuban developments have turned our whole secret apparatus into a monster which, quite apart from inexorable economic factors, everywhere converts the Holy Alliance for Progress into an instrument of political coercion, despite fine words about agrarian reform and social welfare. Our charity pills are little likely to save Latin American health, are more likely to damage Latin American freedom and social growth. The facts are far different from the rosy picture presented to the public.

The visible front of all international relations is, of course, the diplomatic corps — at least up until our generals became our chief spokesmen. It can be truthfully said that the caliber of our representation in South America has steadily improved over the years. Fewer wealthy meat-packers, copper men, oil men, country gentlemen and what have you are appointed to pay back campaign contributions; more career men forge to the front, quite a few know the language and are more efficient and adroit. This does not mean that they follow or can follow correct or honest policies. In colonial areas, willy nilly, they are obliged to act like pro-consuls rather than bonafide representatives to a sovereign nation. The day comes when they are secretly instructed to block labor legislation, agricultural and tax laws, to put estimable intellectuals on the black list, and work in behalf of concession seekers and large corporations. Diplomacy is like an iceberg, most of it below water. These days the part above water is only a little suds above the waves.

Above all, secret duties involve dollar diplomacy, never more omnipresent than today. How many Americans are aware, for instance, of all the secret oil diplomacy carried out for a generation or more? As yet it has not broken down Mexican oil sovereignty, except for controlling some derivatives; it has failed in Brazil, though President Truman sent down a notorious oil speculator as his representative. Chile persists in drilling her own wells. But Argentina and Bolivia have been induced, through constant pressures, loans and other devices, to reverse their long-standing position that their oil was an inviolate national patrimony. In Peru even Haya de la Torre became an instrument for pushing concessions to U.S. oil corporations.

Added oil-lands have been secured in Ecuador, Colombia and Venezuela. Stroessner of Paraguay has given away most of the Chaco, over 40,000,000 acres. The U.S.-imposed dictatorship in Guatemala has granted concessions in the Petén. In Belize, the new constitution and self-governing parliament and premier were bypassed to grant concessions to British and American corporations. Haiti, said to be rich in oil, granted a concession cov-

ering most of the country. It coincided with loan money and the
increase of the military mission. In Colombia the scandal over
the million-acre Barco concession still haunts our relations: State
Department pressure prevented loan-money being granted to the
Olaya Harrera government until the concession was put
through Congress there. Then the money was handed over within days.

Oil is an industry that needs a small personnel and hence returns little in wages to local people. Nearly everywhere operations have been dogged by bribery, concealment of actual shipments, subversion of military officers and officials, dollar diplomacy, even threats of intervention or war. In Venezuela, however, fearing confiscation, the oil companies have sweetened
the pill with schools and scholarships, housing, public welfare. It
costs them only a fraction of a percent of profits and has vastly improved their public relations. In most places oil companies
now carry on a continuous Madison Avenue type good-will campaign, get favorable matter published by heavy advertising, and
even own newspapers.

In a recent world-wide study, the British government's Anglo-
American oil company, looking for new fields abroad, reported
that were it not already mostly monopolized, the most favorable
would be Venezuela, where the costs of exploring for and producing oil could be recovered within *three* years. In Argentina
the oil companies have taken out in one year more than their
total outlay for development and operation.

2

Secret diplomacy constitutes only part of the embassy duties.
Theoretically the U.S. ambassador is responsible for all aid and
other programs, secret or otherwise. Often the secret operations
are so extensive, the ambassador himself has only a hazy idea
of what is going on. Other government departments are involved, those of Health, Education and Welfare, Commerce, Labor, Agriculture, the Information Service, the Pentagon, F.B.I.,
C.I.A., and various executive agencies. Even the army, navy and
air missions don't always know what another branch is doing.

Last year I asked an embassy attaché in Mexico City if he knew
so and so in the Embassy. He threw up his hands. "No, it would

be only chance if I did. We are a small city. There are more than five thousand employees, more than the entire staff of the Mexican Foreign Office, and often I hardly know what fairly close associates are doing."

Obviously such an operation goes far beyond the traditional relations between sovereign nations. A hundred and one activities are carried on that affect the life, politics, newspapers and government of the country. They affect nearly all fields of human endeavor, and they add up to power and control. In its September 1, 1962 issue, *Politica* of Mexico complained bitterly about the false and vicious anti-Cuban films being shown throughout the country by the U.S. Embassy. The U.S. Information Service has trucks that deliver its foolish propaganda bulletins by tons, oddly enough to the most reactionary elements.

In his recent book on India, John K. Galbraith remarks that policy-making by agents of another country is always harmful and may often be disastrous. This is twice as patent in the case of a rich powerful country wielding, directly or indirectly, controls inside a weaker country. Certainly this represents an advance over former military invasion or overlordship, yet in the long run this more subtle, relentless type of imperialism, with pseudo-respect for foreign sovereignty, may prove more pernicious. Let us proceed to elaborate on these generalizations.

3

Military control in the southern countries has been pushed assiduously. We now have more than seventy military missions in the south, many secret bases as far south as Argentina, and our militarists exercise a great influence in training, techniques, arms purchases, and policies of the southern armed forces — and the governments.

This expansion was not accomplished with entire smoothness. Mexico has resisted accepting military missions, but secretly granted a "Guantánamo." In many places there was much popular resistance before arrangements could be made for military missions and the so-called neutral defense pacts. In Brazil, where congressional opposition was originally led by João Goulart, now president, the treaty could not be put across until that body was purged by Vargas and the sessions surrounded by bayonets.

Of course the missions to Cuba were tossed out because of assistance given to Dictator Batista. At one time, Trujillo threatened to do the same because a U.S. military academy refused to give his son Ramfis a diploma on the basis of his success with Hollywood actresses.

The treaty arrangements establishing these missions consist of a known contract and secret agreements unknown to the people of either country, which are supposed to relate to secret bases and possible armed take-over of the given country in case of extra-continental attack or seizure of power by Communists. What the local authorities or the Pentagon may label "Communist" is, of course, just about everything and everybody fighting the regime in power — unless, of course, it is the local military.

The visible contracts provide that the government desiring the services must pay the salaries (U.S. scale) in dollars, pay transportation of the members of the mission and freight on their household goods to and from the United States, provide adequate living quarters, and make available to the head of mission a free car and chauffeur. All mission officers have precedence over all local officers of similar rank. Everything imported by the mission, including personal goods, are exempt from duties.

This latter clause, which applies to all diplomatic aid, and technical missions also, has led to fancy black-marketeering and profit-taking. A new car can be imported every two years, and since in some countries, as in Brazil, there are restrictions and high tariffs on car imports, there such a car can be sold for a profit of from $8,000 to $10,000. Many coveted luxury items are black-marketed, a wholly legal graft from which the invaded country makes nothing, but which runs into hundreds of millions annually.

But what caused some countries to balk at mutual security pacts was the small print which gave the United States the prior right to purchase any or all of strategic materials produced, and the term "strategic materials" at any time can be stretched to cover almost everything.

Naturally the United States does not have enough money to purchase all the coffee or sugar or copper or metals available, but it does provide a leverage with which to stymie deals with

other countries. Thus Colombia worked out a deal with Czechoslovakia to put up an ore refinery to be paid for with refined
metal over a period of five years, after which the installation
would belong to Colombia. This was a sweet deal, better than
could be made with any private U.S. company, which would
want to retain ownership permanently; but the government was
informed that this was a violation of the mutual security pact,
that Colombia could not make such an arrangement which involved a strategic material.

Though military aid in material and money has probably
equalled or surpassed other forms of aid, it has also resulted in
a steady increase of military budgets which none of the countries can afford. Last year they totalled nearly a billon and a
half — up in a few years from 100 to 500 percent — more for
such unproductive purposes each year than the Alliance for Progress is expected to provide. This is an intolerable burden. At
least in the United States, with the greatest military outlays in
quantity and percentage-wise of any nation in history, militarism
promotes production, the setting up of vast munition plants that
provide employment and wages. Most of the Latin American outlays are spent for goods in this country, provide little native employment. It is good business for us.

Actually, as Edwin Lieuwen has pointed out so cogently in
his *Arms and Politics in Latin America,* it may be good business but the effort has little meaning for continental defense.
The armies and their equipment would be of little use in a new
world war. Thus, the countries mostly serve as a dumping
ground for cast-off U.S. armament, which, deadly though it is,
would not stand up for two days against a modern-style attack.
It is all play-acting at war. But it provides lucrative outlets for
munition makers, lucrative posts for a vast military personnel,
and a leverage on the very mainsprings of political control.

This, according to an article by Paul P. Kennedy in the *New
York Times* of September 30, 1962, was set forth brazenly by
Lieutenant General Andrew P. O'Mears, chief of the Caribbean
command, who admitted that Latin American forces were no
longer being trained to fight against "external pressure" but in
"techniques of dealing with clandestine movements, guerrilla
fighting and anti-constitutional attacks." Five U.S. training
schools are maintained for this purpose in the Canal Zone. Anoth-

er school has been set up, the Jungle Warfare Training Center, which includes police-training to handle popular demonstrations.

The program also envisages the use of soldiers in public works, such as the building of feeder roads, potable water supplies, irrigation systems, sanitation works and school construction. The major projects are now being carried on in Ecuador under U.S. military supervision. This is supposed to gain "civilian coopera- tion and respect." It also means that U.S. military intervention reaches out to all key points and provides a blanket network for colonial control.

The army authorities admitted that the new program was based on internal defense and the protection of governments. The nature of those governments was not discussed; our Defense authorities admitted that some of the armed forces of the con- tinent are not contributing noticeably to constitutional processes, but once the new trainees would gradually gain authority, things would be different. . . .

Yet the dictatorships of Nicaragua, Haiti, the Dominican Re- public, and to a degree elsewhere, have all emerged from the ele- ments trained by the United States. Their training enabled them to maintain dictatorships successfully for a generation.

The whole process adds up to providing instruments with guns in hand for keeping the people down and blocking bonafide rev- olutions against tyrants, blocking the whole democratic process, peaceful or otherwise. The armed status quo becomes the only criterion. But actually it does not halt military coups, which are on the increase. Militarism in Latin America, which is being so greatly augmented in power and influence, has been the worst cancer of all the republics. The armies, as in Argentina, Ecua- dor, Brazil, Peru, Salvador, Venezuela, are increasingly asserting their rights to set aside elections, to overthrow governments, to exercise control over political life and international policies. In other countries, they already rule. The armies everywhere are particularly jealous of labor unions and peasant organizations, which they fear may mean a curtailment of their monopoly con- trol, as occurred under Perón, and naturally a complete liquida- tion of the established army, as has occurred in Cuba, makes them hyper-sensitive lest any popular movement make headway. Thus army-rule everywhere, everywhere now on the march, means turn- ing back the clock and the obstruction of normal political evolution. In this miserable process, the U.S. military plays an ever-expanding role.

Yet Adlai Stevenson's brightest suggestion on his tour last year, after consulting with Colombian leaders, was that the military strength of the armed forces of the continent needed to be augmented. It was all too clear, uttered in a place like Colombia where the peasants are still struggling against the Army for their rights and for land reform, that this was not for continental defense but to keep the people in their places. During the recent administration of Lleras Camargo, it is estimated that 10,000 more peasants were killed by the Army. And things are worse now under Valencia. The bugaboo — the possible loss of estates by the big landholders who hold such countries as Colombia to backwardness and incredible poverty — is Cuba, is communism.

The Pentagon, naturally, has been training local military men to be put at the head of local bureaus to detect and punish Communists. This is mostly a species of exported McCarthyism. When I was in Nicaragua the Conservatives indiscriminately called all Liberals (Somoza is a Liberal) labor leaders, Protestants and everybody in opposition "Communist." Most South American dictatorships brand all opponents automatically as "Communists." In Brazil, Vargas even applied the epithet to Catholics, leading business men and reactionary newspaper editors who opposed him. Later on, ironically, when Ambassador Adolf Berle, Junior, demanded more "democracy" from him, Vargas freed Communist leader Carlos Prestes, after holding him in prison eight years, and made a deal with him to support the *Queremista* ("We Want Vargas") movement.

In Cuba too, the results were not those quite expected by the Pentagon. The Cuban general put in charge there under Batista did gather great dossiers about Communists (and also about many other citizens), but since Batista had a sub-rosa agreement with the Communists and had given leaders good jobs, the general, only for appearance's sake, periodically rounded up a bunch of Communists, served them drinks, scolded them a bit, then released them.

More recently, at the behest of the United States, a "Committee of Swords" has been set up by the O.A.S. at Punta del Este. It has the reverberating title of Committee on Security against Subversive Action of International Communism. It has available the F.B.I. and C.I.A. blacklists, which include more non-Communists than Communists. This means that any opponent of any existing government is automatically so labeled, anybody who has ever criticized U.S. policies, etc., will be subject to far-reaching persecution. It is a thought-control and police-control organization, a witch-hunt of everybody not in favor of the status quo.

Professor Ronald Hilton, editor of the excellent *Hispanic American Report*, wrote (May 1962), "Had this committee consisted of moderate civilians of high repute, it might have enjoyed international prestige. It is made up instead of army officers (with the possible exception of the Costa Rica delegate)."

Naturally, Pentagon-trained men and generals of the Stroessner dictatorship in Paraguay, Somoza in Nicaragua, Ydígoras in Guatemala, Rivera in Salvador, Duvalier in Haiti, the military governments of Argentina and Peru, of Arosemena in Ecuador, of the new "gunboat government" of the Dominican Republic have their generals on the committee. Ironically some of those generals have been the worst subversives of their respective lands, have assaulted and wrecked civilian governments, not in behalf of the people but for the greater glory and power of the military caste.

This latest move has aroused great anger throughout the continent, and it has reinforced the current concept that the Organization of American States has reverted to a U.S colonial office once more, that it does not represent a bonafide alliance. Thus have Cold War pressures dropped another black curtain over the southern continent.

4

Supplementing the work of the military missions are the F.B.I. and police missions which now operate in nearly every central police headquarters and secret service organization in Latin America. In some countries they are honeycombed through the provinces as well. In Mexico they even peer over the shoulders of immigration officials, to seize any suspected Cuban literature. Recently a leading Mexican physician returning with a diplomatic Mexican passport from Cuba, where he had been giving a specialized medical course, had taken from him the collected works of Jose Martí (the Cuban liberator of sixty years ago), medical reports, technical works, and the poems of Nicolás Guillén. Recently a shipment of books from Argentina to Cuba was illegally confiscated in transit on the pretext that several were Marxist. If so, this was an amazing carrying of coals to Newcastle.

In all countries the F.B.I., installed in all the police offices of the continent, compiles long lists of alleged subversives, not merely Communists, but Socialists, leftists, labor leaders, peasant leaders, student leaders, teachers, any and all pro-Cubans, all anti-imperialists, all peace advocates, all persons who may at any time have breathed some criticism of U.S. policies — such persons thereafter cannot secure visas to the United States, and are often hounded in other Latin American countries.

Writing from Santo Domingo in the September 2, 1962 *New York Times,* Tad Szulc noted that the government there isn't doing much to establish democracy. But U.S. representatives are pitching in to speed the process. For example, he reports, "At the Police Academy, an expert from Miami and two Los Angeles detectives are busy organizing riot-police squads and teaching the men to use truncheons instead of rifle bullets on disorderly crowds." Ain't civilization great!

In the last Chilean elections, the Center-Leftist coalition, which in times past had elected three Chilean presidents, came within two thousand votes of carrying the country. Yet no one of any rank in those parties, I was told, can now get a visa for the United States. The saying in Chile is: "You know, if somebody gets a visa, he's either a stooge or a lunkhead." What good this sort of diplomatic McCarthyism will do us, it is hard to see. Rather, it widens the influence of the Communists; it builds up anti-Americanism among the most intelligent and influential people of the continent, those who tomorrow may be running their countries.

Among recent exclusions was Carlos Fuentes, leading Mexican novelist, scheduled to discuss the Alliance for Progress with the State Department Assistant Secretary in charge of Latin American Affairs over the Columbia Broadcasting System. Another was the son of ex-President Cárdenas, head of a new independent Mexican party with a large following. By such stupidities are we alienating the intellectuals of the continent.

It is hard to see what benefit accrues to us by the exclusion

of Senator Pablo Neruda, the leading poet of the continent, even
if he is a Communist, or to molest him by stationing agents outside his house in Santiago de Chile and checking on everybody
who visits him. He is a world figure, and I considered it an honor
to be invited to have lunch at his house, so that day did the
leading news columnist of the country. At one time we subsidized him to visit the United States, and it is not on record that
the pillars of government ever quivered when he passed by to
lecture at universities, or that those institutions were harmed by
his vast erudition. . . .

And the same goes for Nicolás Guillén, the grand poet of Cuba,
known everywhere the Spanish language is spoken and beyond.
He, too, is a Communist. About a year ago he told me, "I can't
get a visa to go to your country, but the world is big and round
and most of it's more interesting and alive and less boring."

5

More super-secret, with unlimited funds and swarming everywhere in the countries south, are the C.I.A. agents, many of them
Cuban counter-revolutionaries. They are deeply involved in electoral contests. The customary phrase for the preferred candidate is "our man."

December 25, 1961, C. L. Sulzberger wrote in the *New York
Times*, "The C.I.A. threw support to presidential nominees in
more than one country and not all its choices are successful.
In a land I shall call 'Banania,' a relatively recent election ended
with defeat for the C.I.A. candidate. However, he contested the
result. Consequently a U.S. military aircraft arrived, containing
a gray-haired gentleman who preferred to be identified only as
'Joe.' 'Joe' instructed his principal contact in 'Banania' to arrange
that the defeated nominee be given a choice of $300,000 in ex-
change for withdrawing his opposition. This was done. 'Joe' de-
parted."

"Our man" in British Guiana was roundly defeated by Cheddi
Jagán, the latter's third resounding victory, even though U. S.
agents of Dr. Schwarz's bigoted Christian anti-Communist crusade were brought in to work against him. Presently George-
town had its Bogotazo, a good part of the city was torn down,
looted and burned in protest over tax reform. This time, except

for Senator Thomas Dodd's belathered denunciations, it was not laid at the door of "Communists" (the party is unknown in British Guiana). Everyone, rightly or wrongly, lays it at the door of the C.I.A. and of several large foreign corporations who have been putting out big money to beat Jagán.

In other words, subversion and sabotage — and this means arson, bombing, railroad and bridge demolition and lawless terrorism against regimes or parties not liked — is a frequent aim of the C.I.A.

Principios, the famous journal of equally famous Leonardo Barletta, the Argentine dramatist, reported that the sudden shift to support the U.S. position by the Uruguayan delegate at Punta del Este, a betrayal of his own government's instructions, was obtained by the offer of a $10,000-a-month job with an international bank. *Principios* was suppressed and Barletta went to jail.

The F.B.I. and C.I.A. blacklists mean that as soon as a military regime takes over, the people on the lists are swept up in a police dragnet. This happened in Argentina in May 1962 when Frondizi was thrown out. (It has just happened in Peru.) The leading intellectuals, writers and editors in the country, those not actually jailed, were taken down to the police-station or to the barracks and kept there all day or longer, often not being given even an inkling as to the why of the indignity.

The Haitan delegate at Punta del Este was bluntly asked what he wanted for his country to change its vote. He came cheap, a $3,000,000 loan.

"Our boy" in the recent Peruvian elections ("Cuban" agents swarmed all over the place) was Haya de la Torre, head of APRA. Once he was considered a dangerous "Communist," though he was always attacked by the Communists, but over the years he abandoned all his principles, and though this has caused much defection and of late the rise of the strong splinter movement "APRA of the Left," he still has considerable glamor among the masses. Incidentally, the head of APRA of the Left was badly beaten up by the APRA Bufalos and is in prison in Trujillo, where he has been held now for some years. But what endeared Haya most to our Embassy was his shift to an anti-Cuban line. (The Bay of Pigs expeditionaries consulted with him prior to the invasion.)

It is generally believed that the C.I.A. procured the downfall of the first military-civilian junta in Salvador following the ousting of President Lemus, because it was "soft" on Cuba, and has helped the present Rivera dictatorship in the recent one-candidate election. Salvador today is a land of arrests, deportations and terror.

In Argentina a Cuban agent published texts of certain documents allegedly stolen from Cuban Embassy archives, to prove that the Cuban government was launching a subversive movment in that country. These were published during Frondizi's visit to Washington, to try to provoke a rupture with Cuba. The Argentine government proved that the documents were forgeries. The agent fled to Miami.

Even so, Frondizi later broke with Cuba, then was ousted himself by the military, and Congressmen trying to get into the capitol were dispersed with tear gas.

The chief drive of the C.I.A. these past few years has been against all who support Cuba: newspapers have been suppressed, people have been arrested, harassed by police, thrown out of jobs in government and private companies.

Every effort has been made to drive news of Cuba out of newspapers and off the air. In Venezuela, the independent *El Nacional*, with the largest circulation in the country, persisted in trying to present impartial and pertinent Cuban news. The effort cost it more than $300,000 in advertising in one year, the government finally suppressed mention of Cuba. The owner and editor, Miguel Otero Silva, a prize-winning novelist, is now in exile in Italy.

Nowhere can any large newspaper afford to go against the wishes of U.S. agents – a black nod would mean the cancelling of their advertising from U.S. corporations or distributors. Genaro Carnero Checa's fine newsweekly in Peru was smashed in this way. The Embassy ran ads accusing him of being a Communist. Newspapers are practically obliged to use U.S. Information Bulletins as news. A representative calls on the editor in person to inquire why not.

Even so, one large Mexico City daily, *Novedades*, could not resist observing satirically that one bulletin announced a Catholic Action anti-Communist rally. Catholic Action hastened to deny it had anything to do with the bulletin.

The U.S. Bulletin in Paraguay is particularly vicious, giving much space to falsehoods about Cuba put out by counter-revolutionary publicity centers. In Uruguay the Information publication is, in contrast, so utterly inane nobody bothers to read it.

The corruption of the press and distortion of free expression is fomented by lavish subsidies or jobs to writers, cartoonists, editors, newsmen. Many C.I.A. agents pose as American or local newsmen, sometimes are. Many U.S. newsmen these days see nothing improper in taking money on the side. Post-revolutionary search of the Cuban archives showed that a number of employees of the big U.S. news services were on Batista's payroll, one as a commercial attaché.

Other paid agents started false-front anti-Cuban organizations, usually consisting of two or three names. Half a dozen such were unmasked in Costa Rica during the elections early in 1962, with plenty of money to put out anti-Cuban propaganda or to praise the Alliance for Progress. Student goon squads are organized to stir up trouble, break up meetings. When I was in Uruguay, "Catholic students" were paid to tour the countryside to attack Cuba, the same ones involved in the recent knife-branding of Jews. Naturally, violence was stirred up. In Santiago de Chile, a Jesuit priest hand-in-glove with the U.S. Embassy has organized a claque of students to create disturbances at student gatherings. They come primed with false anti-Castro documents, cite laws that do not exist, etc.

In Chile, the head of the National Library denied the use of the auditorium to a combined meeting of the leftist and rightist writers' associations, previously scarcely on speaking terms, which had invited me to speak on contemporary U.S. literature. His excuse was, he received aid from the Embassy and was not sure my talking there would please his benefactors.

In Colombia much propaganda is carried on by the "Black Hand," a group of wealthy hacendados and U.S. corporation lawyers, one close to the foreign office, whose brother engineered the final Punta del Este meeting. They are spending five million a year on anti-Cuban propaganda, and have plastered the country with signs: COLOMBIA IS A CATHOLIC COUNTRY. BREAK RELATIONS WITH GODLESS CUBA.

They have bought up or otherwise suppressed nearly every independent publication and have forced all independent programs off the radio, substituting Cuban pro-Batista exiles as commentators.

The Catholics have reaped a bonanza out of the anti-Communist, anti-Cuban crusade. U.S. money has been poured out to their writers, editors, newspapers, publishing houses, educational and charity organizations. In Peru three million dollars were turned over by our aid officials to the Catholic charity organization. Much U.S. money has gone to the Paraguayan department that pays the salaries of priests and promotes Catholic schools. In Colombia, in the guise of aiding education, a new six million peso Catholic radio station was set up. Its education consists of Cuban counter-revolutionary agents denouncing the Castro regime around the clock.

In Mexico, the country has been cut up into zones, each with a new U.S. radio station or programs. In Bolivia a radio station is maintained in La Paz, and radio time is bought elsewhere. While I was in Bolivia, *La Nación*, the daily newspaper of MNR, the official government party, which had been giving pertinent news about Cuba, was purged and an entirely new staff put in. The first issue after the change-over showed the new editor and the U.S. Information Service attaché smiling at each other. That day *La Nación* ceased to be an independent newspaper. No more news about Cuba. At that moment, the government was on its knees for a new loan for the tin industry.

This vast continent-wide outlay of money, the pressure on press and radio, the incessant propaganda have had their effect, particularly in government quarters. Cuba is now less popular among many middle-class groups than before. Besides, the punitive action against everybody favoring the Cuban revolution or opposed to outside intervention has become terrifying. And so, the effort to quarantine Cuba, not merely economically, but propaganda-wise, has made headway. However, it may turn out that Latin American, not Cuba, has isolated itself from the big wide world.

Fortunately the Cubans still try to present their case, and there are many breakthroughs. In 1961 such fine magazines as *Bohemia, INRA, Cuba, Olivia y Verde* were still available on newstands in Ecuador, Brazil and Uruguay. Now they are gone from Ecuador. Elsewhere they are seized by the authorities, as in Puerto Rico and the United States itself, at the behest of U.S. agents. But individual copies, official bulletins, the fine reports of the cultural center Casa de las Americas still circulate individually through the mails. At least a million copies of Fidel Castro's vivid account of the Playa de Girón invasion have circulated over the continent. British and French publications, which give a more truthful account of Cuban affairs than can be read in the United States, still come in. Most potent is the new powerful Cuban radio that can be heard clearly everywhere on the continent and is listened to avidly by friend and foe. The burning sparks fly over the high wall of power and suppression.

No country, however mighty and wealthy, however much it tries to prohibit information and free travel and maim the rights of man, can shut out all facts, either printed news or that on the air. The Spaniards tried it two centuries ago, and the problem was much simpler than today. Nor has it been entirely successful with the politicos who genuflect to us, who have betrayed their sister republic. Nearly all have a bad case of schizophrenia: fear of the Cuban revolution mixed with hopes of easy northern lucre, versus intense pride that the island has been able to defend itself against the aggressions of the Colossus of the North.

The process of converting Latin America into a closed trade empire, to make all the governments subservient to U.S. foreign policy and military might, to impose upon them our concept of the Cold War, to open and control a vast zone for the expansion of private U.S. capital, and to create a condition and attitude which would make that capital safe against what happened in Cuba, goes on implacably. The whole diplomatic-military-F.B.I.-C.I.A.-Information Service machinery has been mobilized in this incessant effort: the Cold War and the isolation and destruction of the Cuban revolution. The effort has been extended to the entire world: pressures on Japan, Canada and England and the NATO countries to break off trade relations; threats to Morocco of cutting off aid money unless it quits buying Cuban sugar.

6

New agencies and programs, less secret and cloaked in pleasant phraseology, have been added — Food for Peace, the Peace Corps, the Alliance for Progress.

Food for Peace, the dumping of surplus food, unfortunately, has not meant food for the people, but mostly food for speculators. It has meant the dumping of American soil, labor, technical efficiency, science and tax-money abroad to ease the consequences of the blundering in our own agricultural-government system. But it has sometimes injured agriculture abroad. Cotton dumping has hurt badly the industry in Mexico, Brazil, Argentina and Peru, not to mention Egypt long since. Ecuador declined to receive Food for Peace for this reason — it feared damage to its own farming. Argentina wheat-growers were chafed by the ruin of their big Brazilian market; and U.S. wheat has even been dumped into northern Argentina, something that hardly makes sense in the biggest wheat-exporting country in the world. In Brazil, Army, police and speculators have had a field day stealing the stuff and shooting it into the black market. The theft of food in Peru, even before Kennedy dreamed up the new name, was fantastic. Of $14,000,000 worth of grain sent down for drought victims, only about $200,000 reached the drought area, and this was handed over to the hacendados — so some at least was used to feed animals, not human beings.

The Peace Corps provides another holy medium for meddling inside the countries. It all adds up to power and control. To help backward villagers in petty ways is most laudable. But it is social slum welfare work, not a solution of any basic problems or needs. And it would be more encouraging if we had reciprocal Peace Corps contingents from Latin America, Asia and Africa working here in such backward communities as Mississippi and Louisiana.

The Holy Alliance for Progress represents a still more grandiose undertaking to blanket all Latin America: twenty countries having a common culture but each extraordinarily different, each with varied conditions and problems and at widely varying stages of development.

The Alliance was not created by the Latin American countries but by President Kennedy, who laid it down from Mount Sinai at a pin-stripe gathering in Washington, and it was heralded throughout the continent simultaneously with flamboyant posters and Madison avenue "Oomp," showing Kennedy's smiling countenance and teeth and pseudo-Harvard crewcut.

It was a rehash of the trite recommendations of Milton Eisenhower and of President Kubitschek's broader plan for "inter-American cooperation," but with most vital things left out. It was a rehash of General Marshall's statements at the Bogotá conference back in 1948 when he had urged the southern countries to make themselves safe for U.S. capital. The new note was that, for the first time, money would be available for social welfare, public housing, land reform and certain government-owned enterprises.

During the campaign, Kennedy had tentatively outlined this program in connection with his attacks on Cuba and his threat to back invasion. Thus it owes its origin to the Cuban revolution as much as anything else. Without the threat of that revolution to the rest of the Americas, likely it would not have been put forth with so much fanfare and urgency. Thus it can equally be said that it was "Made in Cuba" as well as "Made in the U.S.A." As one southern diplomat remarked: "We have Cuba, and Cuba alone, to thank for whatever aid we get from the United States under this program." Still, it will be U.S. money that goes south.

The Holy Alliance for Progress is a bit like the Holy Roman Empire, neither Holy, nor an Alliance, nor for Progress. What little is visible of its application indicates that the money has been used and will be used to force further aggressions against Cuba, breaking off of relations, trade boycotts, and, above all, to maintain the status quo everywhere. The land settlement programs thus far put across indicate that they are tailored to preserve the feudal hacienda and big land-holding system, to make the system more palatable, not to change or destroy it.

Also, the timing and launching of the program, followed by new punitive moves against Cuba and the issuing of the White Paper, indicated that it was a well-thought-out maneuver to justify the forthcoming April 1961 Bay of Pigs invasion, to make that aggression more palatable to the rest of Latin America.

The storm that the Playa de Girón invasion aroused throughout the southern countries must have had at least a slight sobering effect. The Punta del Este conference to set up the Alliance had to be postponed. Even before the Alliance, the Inter-American Conference scheduled for Ecuador (which had broken its financial back preparing for the gala event) had to be suppressed because of anti-American feeling, and because it would have coincided with the planned aggression against Cuba.

I was in Guayaquil, Ecuador, when the news came through of the U.S. bombing of the Camp Liberty (Camp Colombia) scholastic center and other places on the island. The inhabitants poured into the streets in angry and mighty protest.

I was in Lima when the actual invasion started, and watched

the great workers' and students' demonstrations day after day, which were beaten back by the police and soldiery, with clubs, guns and tear-gas, and the still bigger demonstration of rejoicing when it was known that the U.P. and A.P. dispatches had all been wrong, and that the invaders had been destroyed.

The invasion unleashed the worst wave of anti-Americanism ever to hit the southern countries — far greater than in the days of the Marine interventions or the invasion of Guatemala.

Even before the police tear gas and the smoke of the burning of Kennedy in effigy and of U.S. flags had drifted away from the anti-American demonstrations, Adlai Stevenson was rushed down over the broken glass, with his tarnished liberalism and his lips still tingling from his United Nations lies about the Cuban invasion, to try to bolster up the wavering dictators and pseudo-dictators to the South. Everywhere he had to go behind a wall of bayonets, and he left in his wake protests, riots, arrests, hundreds of wounded, many dead.

In Brazil, where Janio Cuadros refused to fall into line on his anti-Cuban preaching, Stevenson gave the president a little jab in the ribs — perhaps a portent of the military ousting soon to follow; he tried to soften universal criticism of his visit to the graveyard dictator of Paraguay by suggesting the country needed more democracy. It was like an old lady of the SPCA patting a jackal on the head and telling him to be a good boy and eat no more carrion.

His greatest praise was for Foreign Minister Pedro Beltrán of Peru, the wealthiest landowner in the country, owner of *La Prensa*. There the United States has put millions into land and housing schemes — money corruptly squandered and stolen. In Colombia, where the army terror has never been worse, he suggested that what Latin America most needs is to augment its military establishments.

In 1959 Beltrán tripled the gasoline price and upped the prices of other oil products 100 percent under pressure from the International Petroleum Company, and in 1960 blocked a radical new oil bill. A $53,000,000 package loan was arranged to coincide with the debate on his own bill favoring the I.P.C. This the State Department paid off in behalf of Standard Oil. Beltrán was a man any good U.S. statesman could understand.

The Uruguayan conference could not be held in Montevideo under the eyes of the people, for feelings were too intense, and it convened in Punta del Este, the isolated, winter-dreary spa of the chief Uruguayan gambling casino. Even with this isolation, large hostile demonstrations occurred all over the continent, and in spite of the monopoly of South American news distribution by the great U.S. news agencies, the hero was not Douglas Dillon (related to the banking firm which has had so many deals in Latin America), who held the purse strings; it was the voice of Che Guevara, the Cuban delegate, which echoed across the continent.

It has long been the custom of U.S. politicians to cite the words of the Founding Fathers, though these days that can be dangerous, but with true *noblesse oblige* Dillon quoted Cuba's own George Washington, the early patriot Jose Martí, though there is little evidence that he has ever read or pondered the warnings of that martyr in the cause of Cuban freedom against the dangers of foreign economic penetration for the new Republic. "Americans," quoted Dillon, "are one in origin, in hope and in danger."

It was a gross reading out of context, for Martí was referring to Hispanic Americans.

Che was thereby given a golden opportunity to puncture the contention that this was purely an economic conference, that the Alliance had no relation to the efforts to quarantine Cuba (a ticklish subject at best). All the delegates knew better, but any one who hinted at "politics" was, so to speak, breaking wind at a tea-party.

"Let us quote from the true Martí," Che suggested. " 'Whoever says economic union, says political union; the country that buys, commands; the people who sell, serve.' "

A committee of experts, headed by Felipe Pazos, ex-President of the National Bank of Cuba, dismissed by the Castro government, soon discovered that an adequate sanitation program for the continent, one of the goals stressed, would alone eat up the entire proposed outlays. Merely to provide three million of the inhabitants of Greater Buenos Aires with a sewage system, instead of the present stinking ditches and vacant lots, and a water system, would eat up at least half of a year's allotment designed for the entire continent, not to mention other great cities, not to mention towns and villages and rural people, not to mention simi-

lar bad conditions in nineteen other countries. The stop-gap solution – one ever beloved by U.S. experts in backward lands –
would be to provide sanitary outhouses.

People who can earn a decent living don't need that kind of
help. It was a laughable anti-climax. "Why," Guevara asked sardonically, "do you not speak of dollars for machinery? Why are
there no dollars to convert under-developed countries into developed countries? ... You are putting the outhouse ahead of
economic development. Why do none of these documents speak
of industrialization?"

His words must have chilled the money-hungry delegates. Certainly many of them soon preferred to spend most of their time
at the gaming tables.

Che added, "We are sorry we no longer have Dr. Pazos' able
assistance. Cuba by now could boast of being a nation of outhouses
instead of the schools and factories of the revolution."

More specifically he pointed out that the Alliance program
stood everything on its head: houses and primers and pure water
for people who lack the means to earn bread. Public housing
for people unable to buy clothes or pay utility bills.

Actually the figures of aid promised were puffed up for publicity purposes. The total included funds already available annually from the Export-Import and World Banks. The rest was
to be put up by yesterday's villains, German and Japanese capitalists (how Dillon could be assured of this was not divulged),
and by private U.S. capital, the latter to the tune of $300,000,-
000 a year. Yet in 1961 U.S. corporations had invested only $97,-
000,000 – had taken out a billion in profits. The amount invested has been dwindling ever since the Cuban revolution and is
expected to go lower. Thus what Mr. Dillon really offered in new
money was less than a billion a year.

The program called for a 2 1/2 percent increase in production
per year. When it was pointed out this would not even keep up
with the 3 1/2 percent a year population increase, it was amend-
ed to mean 2 1/2 percent per person. Nothing in the program indicated how this could be done or, if done, that the increase would
be properly distributed to the people who at present get such a
small part of overall production. It was patently absurd: $50,-
000,000 a year per country would not begin to make a dent even
if used for new production facilities instead of mostly for social
welfare. Merely the new Connecticut Turnpike across that

little state cost $400,000,000. New York City sometimes spends nearly $150,000,000 merely for snow-removal each year.

Technical help for farmers was stressed. But peasants even if given land and given machinery free could not begin to pay for the replacement of parts or the gasoline to run it. Machinery and parts cost double or triple what they do in the United States. Thus this type of proposed technical help is likely to bring more disaster. We have made a peculiarly brilliant mess and corruption of our own agricultural system, so that it has cost the government as much as $8,000,000,000 a year. To augment the production of existing Latin American crops, which must compete in a glutted world market, can mean only economic tragedy, lowered prices, more unemployment; nor do the southern countries have the funds to support prices (which would create greater hardship at home) or pay for expensive warehousing.

Take Paraguay. Much U.S. money has gone into promoting a brand-new coffee industry there. Why, in God's name, coffee — even if Paraguay does have excellent *tierra roja?* Coffee is running out of the ears of the world; it is piled up, a year and a half supply ahead for the entire world merely in Brazil, not to mention Colombia and Central America. Coffee is being burned and dumped in the sea. The depression in coffee prices has cost Colombia hundreds of millions a year; Brazil half a billion. The countries have lost more in a few years than they have ever gotten or are likely to get in U.S. aid.

Paraguay has one of the greatest iron deposits on earth, but no one talked of creating a steel industry there, which could make the Paraná Valley the Ruhr of the New World, the heart of a great industrial complex. Perhaps manufacturing steel does not make people happier, but it makes more sense than growing coffee and starving.

What that country basically needs, what all the countries need, is the overthrow of the existing land-system. In Paraguay twenty-five persons own almost half the entire area of the country, which is many times the size of England. Ninety percent of the rural people are without access to the soil except as peons earning a few cents a day. Those twenty-five owners run the country, they run the Army, they run the government. Stroessner, whom we support with so much money, and who has driven 300,000 into exile, is their man — and "our man."

The Alliance for Progress has made no provisions for the money to go into honest hands. It will go everywhere into the hands of those who own the land, who exploit the peons, who have no interest whatever in land reform, though to get their fingers on the kale they will give land reform lip service, as indeed Stroessner is doing at present.

His picture is plastered on the walls heralding *his* land reform for 6,000 peasants a year. But what land? The sterile lands of the Chaco; the inaccessible lands of the jungle; the stony land of far-off hills. And at that, it would take half a century to begin to bring about such resettlement. This, of course, is not land reform at all.

Thus the Alliance for Progress merely entrenches the status quo. We are putting the wolves to guard the sheep we are supposed to be saving. But as sure as God made little kittens, Paraguay is going to have a thorough-going land revolution, and it is not going to be a peaceful one.

8

Mr. Kennedy, visiting Mexico, amid throngs, flowers and speechmaking, cited the revolutionary origins of both the United States and the present Mexican regime, but did not mention that both revolutions were prolonged, bloody contests. Unfortunately none of the objectives which changed Mexico from a feudal, military nightmare into a more modern capitalist state could have been accomplished peacefully. No power elite gives up the fort peacefully, and that is why a new revolutionary era is at hand in Latin America. It is a moment in history when the whole structure of their societies must be changed if they are to meet the challenge of today and tomorrow and the people are to be liberated. That this change be peaceful is highly desirable. Unfortunately the whole process of U.S. military, police, economic and political intervention is against the necessary changes; there is nothing in the Alliance for Progress, except for words, which will bring about such revolutions, peaceful or otherwise, for everything it promotes promotes the status quo, promotes military dictatorship, prevents the rise of the very forces, which if strengthened, might bring about a peaceful transition. The Alliance program is a beneficent (?) counter-revolution.

Nor did Kennedy on his Mexican visit, in praising the agrarian revolution, indicate that this, too, cost a generation of strife and bloodshed, and that its methods and aims were the same as those which have moved Cuba more recently. He did not mention that the leader who carried through the major part of the agrarian reform, ex-President Lázaro Cárdenas, is now feared and circumscribed by the present Mexican government and by the United States, and with such petty spleen that just prior to Kennedy's visit, his son, also a political leader, was denied admission to the United States.

Nor did Kennedy note that other outstanding leaders of the agrarian revolution, David Siqueiros, the world's outstanding painter, and Filomeno Mata, Jr., long-standing fighter for human rights, are now in jail, were held there for two years without trial, then were sentenced for eight years more, for "social dissolution." Their crime was that they formed a civil-rights committee in behalf of the swarms of political prisoners — the labor leaders and teachers and students and agrarian leaders now in jail under the López Mateos regime.

Nor did he even hint that all over Mexico at this hour, as the *Wall Street Journal* pointed out at the time, mass demonstrations are demanding fulfillment of the agrarian law — hunger marches, pitched battles between peasants and local and federal police. Dozens have been killed, and many, even as Kennedy spoke of freedom and the good life, are in jail throughout the Mexican land.

In May, a month before his visit, Juan Jaramillo, a notable Morelos peasant leader trying to block the ousting of peasants from land favored by a new irrigation project, was taken along with his wife and children by secret-police and army officers up to the ruins of Xochicalco and there all were assassinated. Two weeks before Kennedy's visit, the names of the killers were given to the authorities by a grown son who escaped and were published in the May 15 issue of *Politica*, but no arrests were or have been made. And *Politica* was suppressed in honor of Kennedy's "freedom visit."

In the last year dozens of other Mexican peasant leaders have been jailed or murdered. In May 1962, the white guards of the big Carlos Bermudez La Elena Hacienda, in collusion with the authorities, burned down a whole village, which was demanding enforcement of the agrarian law. Shortly before this the village of Huanal in Vera Cruz was destroyed by army and police for the same reasons. Such atrocities are frequent in these two states and many other places, and are increasing in number.

Nor did Kennedy indicate that 53 percent of all Mexican farmers belong to *ejidos*, the ancient Aztec system of collective farms, similar to the Cuban cooperatives, except that on that island the percentages are reversed: there 54 percent of the peasants own their own farms, more than ever before in the history of the country.

Perhaps Kennedy could also have generously pointed out that Cuba has done in two years with relatively little bloodshed what it has taken Mexico fifty years to do with torrents of bloodshed. Even now it would take Mexico at least twenty more years to complete its land program, but that hope has been destroyed.

Unlike in Cuba, the Mexican farmers have had less technical help, seed, tools and credits; Kennedy's good-will loan, therefore, of $20,000,000 to be used for rural credits, if sadly inadequate, was highly laudable charity. Or was it? The money was not given to the regular rural credit agency but turned over to the banks. The Kennedy *noblesse oblige* loan is for forty years, the first ten years interest free, then bearing a modest 3/4 of a percent. But the banks may charge 6 percent. Thus the beneficiaries will pay back to the banks $48,000,000 besides the principal. Strings are attached. It cannot be loaned to *ejidos*, the age-old land communities, which represent 53 percent of the rural farmers, or to cooperatives, only to individual owners or corporations. It cannot be loaned for corn or bean cultivation, carried on by 80 percent of all Mexican farmers — lest this create a surplus that could be exported to Cuba. In short, it can go only to the large haciendas — many of them in violation of the laws — producing commercial crops such as sugar, cotton, coffee, bananas. Cotton production last year was down 200,000 bales because of U.S. dumping on the world market.

As a result of Kennedy's visit, López Mateos has rushed through a farm bill breaking up the *ejidos* and handing out millions of individual titles. This was tried by the Juárez government more than a century ago and made possible the creation of the Díaz land-monopoly system. The peasants are not able individually to stand up against the great processing and distribution corporations such as that in the henequén industry or Anderson Clayton who have a stranglehold on all Mexican cotton. In short

Kennedy has struck a deadly blow at the Mexican farm system, a destructive counter-revolution. The jeweled hilt was encrusted with $20,000,000. Cheap enough!

Mr. Kennedy visited a fine new public housing project and praised it. But it would take *all* the $1,000,000,000 Alliance for Progress money for ten years — and more —to solve Mexico's housing problem. There, in spite of fifty years of revolution, 60 percent of all families, according to the latest census, still live in one room—and they have large families—85 percent have no more than two rooms. Of all Mexican dwellings 83 percent have no running water. A vivid account of the Mexican underprivileged is given in Oscar Lewis' *The Children of Sánchez,* one of the truly great books of recent years. In the last eight years the government has put up 7,666 houses in all Mexico. Luis Quintanilla, head of the National Institute of Housing (INV), declared on August 2, 1962 in a talk at the Lion's Club that Mexico urgently needed 3,000,000 new houses. Actually 5,000,000 are needed now and by the end of the century many more. At the present rate, which, even with Alliance for Progress money, cannot be greatly accelerated, it will require 70,000 years to take care of the housing needs of Mexico, even if the population were to remain stationary .At present growth rates, the population will be 100,000-000 by the end of this century.

Of course, the poor cannot even afford to live in the housing provided. Obviously the solution does not reside in charity housing, which benefits a handful of the middle class, but in expanding the productive capacity of the country, which likewise is not keeping pace with the population growth; not only that, the share of increased production for wages and salaries has been steadily declining. The Mexican government recently suppressed a magnificent book, *La Magnitud del Hambre en Mexico* — "The Magnitude of Hunger in Mexico" — by Ana María Flores, the head of its own Department of Statistics. Here are some of the findings. There are 5,000,000 Mexicans suffering from acute hunger. In 1958 the rural population spent 84.89 percent of its income on food; urban dwellers 64.97 percent. Rural dwellers eat only about 1,000 calories a day; urban dwellers average under 1,200 calories. The consumption of meat, milk and eggs is insignificant in large areas.

The Alliance for Progress proposes to wipe out illiteracy in ten years. After due deliberation, the amount to be spent on education was cut down to $150,000,000. There are at least 150,000,000 illiterates in Latin America, so that this provides $1.00 a head. There are nineteen countries, so this means less than $8,000,000 per country. This will not begin to teach even the A.B.C.'s let alone build schools, increase the pitifully low teachers' salaries or provide training for teachers. The New York public school system, catering to a population about equal to that of Venezuela, spends nearly a billion a year on its school system, and even so many of its school buildings are ancient rat-traps and fire traps.

The Alliance for Progress will not even add enough school money for Latin America to keep pace with the population growth. Argentina, once the brightest spot on the continent, has been slipping backwards during the past eight years. There is likely to be more illiteracy ten years hence, even with Alliance aid, than at present. The fact is, the people who will handle this money have no interest in such an effort. They preside over a system which has had four hundred years to abolish illiteracy. Their own literacy is part of their privileged position.

Yet Cuba, which under Batista had a 40 percent illiteracy rate, wiped it out in a single year. How was this accomplished?

It was not merely the building of more schools than in all the previous history of the island, so that every child now has a classroom, not merely the crash program of training new teachers, not merely the implantation of new short-cut methods in advance of those in U.S. schools, not merely money — but esprit de corps. Teachers volunteered to work double time. Brigades of students went to the remotest corners, more of them than the total number of U.S. Peace Corps emissaries for all the world, thousands upon thousands of them. Labor brigades of doctors, lawyers, bank clerks, electricians, hotel cooks went forth. Neighbors helped neighbors. Every man in the militia who could read and write was mobilized for the crusade. Even a new pencil factory was built. A paper mill was expanded.

Such a spirit can exist only when a people believe their government really has their interests at heart. Only governments who do have the welfare of their country at heart can carry through such a transformation.

The Mexican Revolution briefly developed this esprit, and in the spurts and starts with which the illiteracy curse was attacked, the percentage in the country was cut down from 80 to 40 percent, where it has stayed.

It is thus doubtful if the injection of a piddling — or even an enormous — amount of dollars into the present outmoded educational pattern and the present military-feudal set up of the countries to the South can do away with illiteracy.

Naturally any permanent construction, housing, schools, hospitals, dams, drainage systems, roads, even if they mostly benefit the people who need help least, represent permanent national assets, even when put up with extravagance, waste, theft of moneys — characteristic of so much of our effort to the South. Naturally to build an irrigation system, as at great cost in Peru, which has no water supply to feed it, or to put a road through barren country ending up against a mountain — the famous Smather's Road — or to build a five-building normal school where, because of lack of proper drainage, the classrooms are under water, does little except for the meager wages paid out and the profit-taking on materials; nothing certainly for U.S. prestige.

Actually U.S. money, and now the Alliance money, has been and is directed toward maintaining the status quo, toward creating a closed-trade empire for investment of U.S. capital, to further the aims of the Cold War and to denigrate the Cuban revolution. This has meant not the growth of democracy but the increasing spread of militarism, a reversion to the dictatorial methods of early this century.

At the second Punta del Este conference, which saw Cuba ejected in violation of the Charter and statute provisions of the O.A.S. itself, President Oswaldo Dorticós of Cuba said: "The purpose of the Alliance for Progress and of this gathering is to isolate Cuba from the Western Hemisphere family of nations. But Cuba can never be isolated. It belongs to the Western Hemisphere. It is a vital part of its culture, and we wish Latin America to grow as we are growing. But the measures being taken here to divide the continent will merely bring more economic injustices, more suppression of the people, more brutalities." Part of his prophecy seems to be on the road to fulfillment. Bolivia recently seceded from O.A.S. conferences.

9

Though this is presumably an Alliance, conditions have been laid down by the United States before any country can qualify for handouts. These are, among others, Austerity, Tax Reform, Agrarian Reform, etc. In none of these fields has the U.S. government shown any brilliant achievements at home.

Austerity is not a new idea. It has been sought in Latin America by U.S. missions for half a century and invariably with funereal results, for it is not patterned to the needs of the peoples or the countries. It is an old-fashioned bankers' concept. It was the program in Nicaragua under Marine rule — balance the budget, pay off the bankers — and it left the people in misery and under cruel dictatorship that has lasted down to the present. It was tried in Ecuador, and a decade of political and military disorder resulted. It was tried in Colombia — the so-called Kemmerer Mission — and there is no doubt that it was in good part responsible for the rise of Gaitán, the Bogotazo, and the slaughter of the people that has followed and continues to this day.

The recent experiences in Argentina have been lamentable, even though Mr. Dillon praised it as the prize example of progress and democracy on the continent. Actually the Argentine economy has been going backward. Its production has decreased nearly 10 percent in eight years; in 1961 it had the worst trade deficit in its history. The program calls for the freezing of wages, already at a low ebb, already hit by inflation, and at the same time raising the price of food stuffs to cut down consumption. Real wages under the Monetary Fund and the austerity program have dropped, not 10 percent but 30 percent. Social welfare, educational budgets, public services have been cut back drastically, while military expenditures have steadily mounted. Austerity has insisted upon the removal of all monetary and exchange controls — presumably a free-enterprise concept — the result being that billions of dollars have fled the country and there has been also a quick, disastrous outflow of profits on foreign investments. At the same time the enforced deflation has meant lowering exports, putting Argentine products on the market at a price not competitive with the rest of the world. It has caused factories to close down, an increase in the amount of unemployment. With this increased bankruptcy, foreign capital has been able to buy up enterprises at bargain rates, and the hard-pressed government has had, in the face of Argentina's long tradition, to give away its oil resources on infamous terms, in order to qualify for loan money.

As Harvey O'Connor has summarized it in his new book, *World Crisis in Oil:* "The Monetary Fund's advice always is 'austerity.' This is achieved by balancing the budget at the expense of health, welfare and education; by tightening the belt around shrunken bellies; by sharply increasing the price of food to cut off consumption (a device more cruel than the well-fed in the United States and Western Europe can readily imagine). The result is economic stagnation, rising unemployment, falling living standards. While the Monetary Fund's experts are dictating 'austerity,' they are scouting the terrain for any potential wealth that needs development by foreign capital. These sharp-eyed gentlemen can smell oil ten thousand feet under the ground. This must immediately be exploited — and guess by whom?"

And so it was that the nationalization of oil in Argentina and Bolivia came to an end, even though the revolution in Bolivia had greatly increased oil output. Bolivia is the only country where I have been a millionaire: my week's hotel bill there came to nearly a million sucres. The sucre under the Monetary Fund control is now worth 12,200 to the dollar.

The girl receptionist in the president's office in Quito nodded at her desk. She explained to me that she had to work nights at another job, because she was making less than $40.00 a month, and she was probably the highest paid woman employee in the National Palace.

Our imposed austerity has also reduced Chile to stagnation. There are few signs of new enterprise either in the capital or the countryside.

It is not likely that tax reform proposed by Kennedy and the Monetary Fund is meant to press down properly on foreign corporations, which often work tax-free and pay no import duties, and whose profits often run to 30 percent of their capital investment each year. The idea is to extract more money from payrolls and the struggling middle class. Theoretically it is meant to make the big landholders pay more of their share. But this can be suicidal at the present moment of depressed world prices for farm and mining products. Instead of altering the power structure, tax reforms have led to disorders and threatened revolts, not merely by the masses but by the land-holding groups as in Salvador and Guatemala, by business groups in Guiana stirring up mobs. There are some who lay Castillo Armas' assassination at the doorsteps of the owners of large coffee fincas, when he tried to increase their taxes at U.S. behest, while we withheld needed loans to our own puppet until he gave concessions for oil on half the territory of the country.

"Land Reform," as already indicated, merely means a costly type of land resettlement, not the break up of large estates or their conversion into cooperatives of the peasants. This resettlement puts peasants, supposedly benefited, on submarginal lands ' or undeveloped lands, a process costly for the government, for the peasants, and often benefiting the large holders. At best it can provide only a subsistence type of farming, out of step with modern needs and urban development. It is more backward and less in the national welfare than the present feudal set-up. In Peru under the regime of Prado and Pedro Beltrán, so admired by Adlai Stevenson, the peasants have been driven off more land than they have received in jungle areas in the hot lands. In our own country, we are doing nothing to stop the colossal theft of lands in Alaska from the Eskimos and Indians, a cruel policy of human extermination going on right now. It would be surprising if we were concerned with similar land-stealing in Chile, Peru and Colombia.

10

The Alliance, even if it meant what it says it means, faces other mountainous difficulties inherent in the present economic system of the Western and satellite area. Mr. Kennedy, however much he may be valiantly trying to preserve that system, and with considerably more flair and fine words than did Eisenhower, did not make the forces that obstruct his program.

(1) The present drain of U.S. private profits from absentee capital invested in Latin America totals at least a billion a year above reinvestments. In 1961 the take was over two billions. Most of this investment is in raw materials and in public utilities, not into manufacturing or consumer goods industries. Such investments dovetail with the U.S. economic empire, not with the productive life of the countries where they operate. Indeed they warp the entire national economy and actually often block the creation of a rounded economy corresponding to popular and national needs. That and land monopoly create a gangrene of swollen urbanization. The more capital that goes in, the greater

the subsequent drain becomes. If a certain amount of benefit is provided through wages and some tax returns, these are paid for out of local income to the corporation, sales within the country, not out of the materials and profits sent overseas. The drain of capital constantly going on throws the foreign exchange picture out of kilter faster than the International Monetary Fund can keep it in line, thus creating added debt, chiefly for the purpose of aiding the export of the national wealth for the profits of alien companies.

In many enterprises the original capital investment is recovered within three to five years. Not that there is any great risk, for much of it is guaranteed and insured by the U.S. government itself, as are the new oil enterprises in Argentina, which in less than three years have more than recovered their original investment and operating costs.

Every dollar invested in Freeport Sulphur, which had big interests in Cuba over the years since its founding at the time of the First World War, has ballooned into eight thousand dollars in dividends and stock splits, without considering possible compounding of interest. The scandal of its Cuban operations is now coming to light in the Senate investigation of stock-piling. Americans see nothing very wrong in this, even applaud it, but where the enterprise is located abroad, this means that profits are taken *out* of the country. They are not reinvested to any extent, but go to an *alien* land, i.e. the United States. In highly developed countries, in Europe or Canada, this drain is compensated for in many ways, since the investment is more likely to be in manufacturing enterprises and provides new wealth, not merely extraction of wealth. But the Latin American countries simply cannot afford this drain of money and resources. They are hit by repeated economic crises, and new development is held to a minimum, or production may actually decline.

President Hoover nearly forty years ago, when he headed up the Department of Commerce, pointed out that sooner or later Latin America would want to own and would come to own its own resources. He intimated that this should be the goal of U.S policy, not forcing more investments upon them. Our reward would come with greater good-will and greater trade.

Instead, U.S. policy, backed by all the weight of the State Department, doubly so since the ill-starred Bogotá conference, has been to pressure countries to keep wages low, to avoid new labor and social laws, in order to make conditions attractive for more U.S. capital. Though the State Department insists on tax reform, invariably it has sent angry notes whenever increased taxation has affected U.S. investors. This policy means the inevitable continuation of sweat-shop practices, and augmented subserviency to the U.S. economic empire.

Perhaps we should be seeking some formula for quick liquidation of all such investments, as Rockefeller hoped to do with the money he sent into Venezuela and Brazil into the retail store, cattle-raising, milk, fish and truck gardening and corn storage enterprises (but not oil). It is precisely why the putting up of factories by the Soviet Union, China, Czechoslovakia, Poland and East Germany is so attractive to the Latin American countries, because the installations become the property of the countries where they are built and do not remain perpetually in foreign hands.

(2) With the lifting of exchange controls by the International Monetary Fund, even more money, perhaps several billions, is sent abroad each year by wealthy families preferring for safety or other reasons to invest in Europe or the United States or merely to stash the money away in Swiss banks. The sum is greater by far than is being restored by the Alliance for Progress. It has been estimated that since the Cuban revolution at least $9,000,000,000 has fled from the southern countries.

(3) Enormous sums are shipped abroad, not merely in tithes but in bequests and gifts, to the Vatican. Yet some countries, like Paraguay, must still pay for the upkeep of the Church, now of course with U.S. aid.

(4) The seventy military missions have caused a large increase in military expenditures and the purchase of military equipment in the United States to the tune of nearly a billion dollars, a non-productive outlay to say the least.

(5) But the biggest drain is from the differential between the low price of raw materials and farm exports as compared to the high cost of manufactured goods. This unfavorable relationship has grown worse, the gap has widened for the past eight years. Today from 20 to 300 percent more raw product goods must be exported to get back the same amount of imported goods as eight years ago. This drains out billions every year and forces starvation wages to even lower levels. It prevents the accumulation of home-grown capital.

No alleviation by seeking to buy competitively elsewhere rather than in the costly U.S. market is permitted. The Austerity program with Argentina has required that country to abandon barter or unilateral trade agreements with most of Europe and the Socialist countries. The few that remain are to be terminated when the contract period expires. The pressures of U.S. capital investment, of treaty arrangements, etc., force the southern countries chiefly to buy from us. Congressional clauses force them to spend 80 percent of all aid moneys in the United States, which in itself automatically reduces the amount provided them. Against this closed-empire system, the Japanese, German, Czech, Soviet, and Swedish governments (and others) have managed to make some slight headway, but not enough to alter the overall picture or to appreciably change the imbalance between the prices of exports and imports.

Thus the rising prices of processed goods from abroad versus the lowered prices of Latin American products — coffee, copper, wheat and meat and wool, zinc and lead, tin and bismuth and tungsten — have cost the countries more than they ever have gotten or will get out of the Alliance for Progress. This price chasm widens because of the periodic erratic dumpings by the United States — which has brought countries to their knees, created crises and bloody revolutions — of such materials as wheat, cotton, tin, lead, silver. The Food for Peace program — far from benefiting the hungry, since it goes into the hands of speculators — is a colossal dumping operation which has been disastrous for many countries. (Even potatoes to Peru, the leading potato land of South America!) The lead, zinc, silver policies have all but broken the back of Mexican mining prosperity. Lead, the second mineral exportation item, and one of the ten leading export items of Mexico, has been going down for years and in 1961 — thanks to sudden U.S. dumping — dropped to 6.31 cents a pound, 50 percent less than the market price at the time. This alone meant a loss to Mexico greater than any aid money that year. Such destructive price differentials, coupled with the fantastic population growth, mean misery and deterioration, an explosive revolutionary situation everywhere, which has little to do with communism or any other ideology.

Economic conditions continue to go downhill. All the countries are worse off than they were ten years ago, in spite of much urbanization. It becomes increasingly evident that the Alliance for Progress is a mere spit in the ocean, that it cannot possibly accomplish what it promises; the disillusionment is going to be tremendous, the reactions dangerous indeed.

11

Nowhere has industrial growth been greater than in Brazil, an exception to most of the continent. Yet curiously this has mere-ly intensified the misery of the people until today in few places in the world is poverty so great and getting worse. For no agra-rian reform has been carried out. Though boom conditions in São Paulo, to a lesser extent in Rio de Janeiro, prevailed briefly and the new manufacturing drained off many discontented peas-ants to the city to try to get jobs, so that unrest was temporarily held to a minimum, the bright hopes have faded.

A big inrush of U.S. capital, considerable German, French, Italian and Japanese capital, contributed to the boom, but the pace of new investment slowed down and the drain on finances is creating new strains.

The interesting thing about the original impetus toward indus-trialization was that it began mostly with native initiative, and though native capital has expanded, relatively it has now been overshadowed by foreign capital, which has wrapped its tenta-cles about much of the indigenous enterprise. Thus the drug in-dustry, which a few years back was almost entirely Brazilian, is now 80 percent foreign-owned, and likely will be lost entirely. Partly this has been due to dubious national policies, which stim-ulated the setting up of new drug laboratories and plants by en-couraging foreign enterprise to come in on a tax-free basis, and the right of non-payment of duties on supplies, benefits not ac-corded native entrepreneurs, who were soon unable to compete and could not match the vast laboratory research carried on in the United States. Doubtless in many ways, Brazil has benefited by this introduction of new knowledge and processes, even if they are made guinea pigs for new dangerous drugs. Certainly the American companies sell drugs down there at a fraction of what they charge American consumers. But in other lines such advan-tages are less apparent, as native enterprise is choked back.

The process of strangulation has been slowed down, in part because of the Cuban revolution, which has frightened off foreign capital, and more recently by the expropriation of U.S.-owned public utilities in Rio Grande do Sul and elsewhere. On various pretexts, chiefly the attempt to impose unsatisfactory conditions, aid money has also been held up. Conditions recently laid down by our Congress with regard to expropriation procedures may cut it off entirely.

Somehow our dollars and our technicians do not seem to match up to realities, even less in moments of crisis. Thus in northeastern Brazil, traditionally a region of droughts that periodically cause a diaspora of the people, sending them into the back country or far afield into the Amazon areas, a peasant movement arose more than fifteen years ago and has now become militant, making worried U.S. news pundits talk about the menace of communism. There have been land seizures, clashes with the police and Army.

In addition to special military supplies rushed to the area, we have sent in a small army of American bureaucrats and experts, with a gushing well of additional dollars, to try to stem the danger (?) of an agrarian revolution.

According to my own investigations on the spot, a great deal of waste, ostentation and graft seems to be involved, especially with Food for Peace (mostly bootlegged). In addition the do-gooders and saviors of democracy are bemused by their own theories of the "American way," which are not attuned to the unstable situation.

The health work, the supplying of food, schools here and there are admirable undertakings; many people are grateful, but quite as many are resentful. Charity is not always easy to swallow. This type of social welfare assistance throws into sharper relief the fact that the peasants do not have the means or opportunity to maintain a decent life. Perpetual charity is obviously no solution.

The bulk of the U.S. effort is now going into more basic enterprises: water-supplies, irrigation systems, dams, roads. But we dare not and cannot, even should we try, alter the land-holding system which is at the root of all the misery, or shake loose one acre for the peasants from the properties of the big owners, who will ironically be the major beneficiaries of our present efforts.

And so, with every dollar we put in, partly because of those dollars, the northeast movement continues to grow and to spread and become more militant. This is a mighty good thing, though that is not the purpose for which we are pouring in so much cash and help.

We are obsessed not so much with human values as with technical proficiency, with getting more and more production — in the case of Latin America mostly the wrong kind of production, and much of it merely institutionalized charity. Our efforts rarely gibe with the over-all national needs or with popular needs. The more we give, the more we go along such misdirected lines, the more the people see the discrepancies between word and deed, the more they are defrauded of what they could obtain or what they think they should have. We help create the very unrest we deplore and strive to allay.

Sometimes we arouse derision. We do everything with such blatancy, with such colossal waste and munificence, all of it so far out of scale with local means and local habits. We put the piano right in the pigpen where it won't play, forgetting perhaps the pigpen is more important.

What is efficiency to us often turns out to be the worst inefficiency in an alien setting. For efficiency, like everything else, has to be organically and intimately related to the whole, and that whole includes the entire cultural life and tradition and habits of a people, the history of a people, the defeats of a people, their victories and hopes. That whole includes race and religion, geography, flowers and animals, copulation and prayer. Even the most insignificant work-habit cannot be altered without far-reaching ramifications that may make fissures in the entire social structure. We need to know these things, and we do not know them. We scarcely know them in relation to our own culture, because we have such a large cushion of comfort, so why should we know them about other peoples? But efficiency, like democracy, is something that has to grow out of the soil and cannot be artificially implanted, cannot be produced abruptly over night. And there is no real proof that the American way is more efficient, either in immediate or in over-all and far-reaching applications.

In a curious way, our power elite have ceased to be realists; they have become the most arrant romanticists. Their pragmatism with regard to wealth and power has made them unrealistic and non-pragmatical with respect to human relations. They are as dogmatic in their way, and quite as rigid in their mental processes for all the technical efficiency they demand, about the superiority of the American way of life (about which they hold only imaginary concepts) as the dogmatic Russian Communist is about his concept of what Russia is and what the world should be like. If anything, the U.S. dogmatism, even if it also uses many grandiose clichés about human welfare, includes little sensitivity to the emotions and thinking of other peoples, little comprehension of their history and tradition and culture.

Our efficiency is presumed to be born of free competition, but it rests also on the greatest waste and corruption in the history of the world. Most countries cannot afford either our kind of competition or our extravagance. For many peoples, the concept of economic competition along our lines is a concept of slavery, not of freedom. They consider competition means freedom when it lies in the fields of cultural endeavor, not in battling dog-like over the bones. The privileged carry on that competitive war with money and intrigue for governmental favors. The under-privileged compete with their sweat and their bellies. They know the debasing features of that sort of competition all too well.

And so our efficiency in South America, since it is largely divorced from comprehension of social processes, is mostly self-defeating. Our imposition of austerity and belt-tightening which means more starvation, of curious tax-reforms which safeguard the wealthy, our falsely-labeled agrarian reform have already ruined several countries and will ruin more. Even were such measures desirable, in the uncomprehending manner in which they are applied, without due regard for national idiosyncrasies or the opportune moment, they are arousing so many resentments in so many quarters we shall reap the whirlwind. Even were they projected in full good faith and carried through without theft and corruption, they still spell out meddling, and whatever generosity is contemplated or whatever doses of good deeds and valid accomplishments are injected, that meddling adds up to power, not the freedom we like to prate about. The good deeds run counter to our whole secret power-apparatus throughout the continent. They are little sparkles in the darkness of imperial power. They are conscious or unconscious false-fronts for that power — little show-places for the gullible.

Efficiency, not people. It was understandable that in the stress of war-needs, we did the terrible things we did to the Bolivian tin miners. But our failure to heed even now the anguished appeals of the miners, our failure to appreciate that a starving man can produce little and does not really augment output – such failures cause violence and revolt and the collapse of many governments.

It was understandable that Mr. Symington should want tin more cheaply, but it was on a basis decidedly punitive and unfair for Bolivia, and that too set in motion new revolution, which to date has cost us about $200,000,000 in aid money that has mostly gone down the drain or into the pockets of the Rosca, corrupt bureaucrats, U.S. interests and officials. Certainly it has done little to benefit Bolivia.

An Embassy official was quoted as saying: "We do not have a damned thing to show for it. We're wasting money. The only solution to Bolivia's problem is to abolish Bolivia. Let her neighbors divide up the country and the problems." The result was the stoning of the Embassy, the evacuation and hiding-out of the diplomatic personnel by the Army to save their lives, and the complete destruction of the U.S. Information Office.

It is understandable, now that the Bolivian tin industry is foundering because of low prices, because of the previous development of marginal mines to satisfy our wartime needs, because of the lack of costly machinery and replacements for which there is no money, that in the name of efficiency we have forced the firing of thousands of miners – the price of our aid to the industry. But Bolivia is not a place where they can find other employment, and this, too, has led to bloodshed and violence, which was blamed on Cuba! Yet we ask no sacrifice whatever from the old owners, who are no longer contributing anything, but ruthlessly keep on extracting the pound of flesh – a larger sum than we are providing – for expropriation payments. These must go on even if the miners starve, even if the pockets of the American taxpayer are picked.

The ruinous differential between the prices of exported raw materials and those of imported manufactured goods extends also to the differentials in the salaries of U.S. agents administering aid money and counterpart Bolivian funds and their Bolivian employees. Thus, the executive secretary of MNR told me,

the head of the road-building enterprises in Bolivia was receiving more than $2,000 a month, though he was an ex-veterinarian,
whereas the competent Bolivian engineer who actually did the
work received only $200 a month — and of course lesser employ-
ees are lucky if they earn $50.00 a month.

This particular U.S. official became so furious at a sign at
archaeological excavation work at the Tiahuanaco ruins which
read THIS IS STRICTLY A BOLIVIAN UNDERTAKING that
he ordered a conduit, used to drain off waters which had flooded the diggings because of the building of a new road, to be
torn out.

Even in the most bonafide undertakings, the person who gives
of his techniques and shells out the money (even though it comes
from the taxpayer) is in a superior position, and, given our almost universal attitude of Caucasian self-assurance, can rarely
help acting superior even if be believes all men are brothers under the skin. It is the rare individual who can appreciate that the
barefoot Indian facing the sports coat and flannel trousers may
be a nobler human being or even more intelligent, though possibly defrauded of the proper use of his intelligence because of
illiteracy and poverty. It is difficult for the ordinary U.S. office
secretary on the job, and some earn as much as $7,000 a year,
not to feel superior to local clerks earning $25.00 to $50.00 a
month. But if there is one thing the Latin American, even if he
wears no shoes, cannot forgive, it is condescension. And so the dollars, however wisely used, often do more harm than good, and almost always corrupt in one form or another.

But perhaps the biggest part of the trouble with the Holy Alliance is that it is not sincerely for the benefit of the people, regardless of the fine phrases. It is poisoned by the State Department's concern over U.S. properties and its strenuous efforts to
assist in obtaining new concessions, particularly oil.

We back up this effort by handing out loans at the psychologi-
cal moment and this aid is poisoned by the Cold War and a Mc-
Carthy-type, anti-Communist crusade. Aid to Latin America
cannot be successfully funneled between those gray grim walls.

It is poisoned by our hatred and fear of little Cuba. It seeks
to create difficulties everywhere for Cuba. It seeks to isolate,
quarantine, boycott, damage and destroy the Cuban revolution.
The Alliance money is paid out on the basis of this brutal cam-

paign. Countries which have resisted our policy with respect to
Cuba have whistled long for aid; money already allocated has
been held up in diverse ways. Countries which have broken with
Cuba have received many millions within days. Never in the history of our relations with the southern countries has dollar diplomacy been so blatant, so ruthless or so shameful! Do not imagine that even the recipients of our apparent largesse do not
resent these things.

It is poisoned by our efforts to block and hinder diplomatic,
cultural and trade relations with all countries — except the United States; in short, to create a closed system. With respect to
education, public housing, sanitation, expansion of electric power, proper management of forestry reserves and reforestation, the
development of diversified agriculture and industrialization, it is
pretty obvious that the Alliance will not accomplish in ten years
the things that Cuba has already achieved in a few short
years, in spite of constant harassment and the continuation of
sabotage, arson and airplane terrorism and punitive sea-raids,
which the Cubans claim are fomented by the C.I.A. The U.S.
people get echoes of Castro's "caterwauling" about invasion —
we rarely get his full or pertinent statements — and say "nuts."
But from the Cuban standpoint, they have every reason to fear
and to believe the worst. Our denials do not help. Adlai Stevenson lied even when armed forces were landing on Cuban shores.
Why should Cuba have any confidence in his subsequent declarations that the United States does not intend to invade?

President Kennedy, a few days after the ill-fated Bay of Pigs
invasion, as much as said another attempt would be made. He
said the same in Miami on December 28, 1962. He has
stated that no invasion is planned *at the present moment;*
he and he alone will decide when *he* thinks the moment is required. The fate of the continent is in his hands — the peace of
the world, the fate of the world. His administration is using every effort of diplomacy, economic boycott, warlike demonstrations, airplane violations, improper buzzing of shipping to coerce
and terrorize the Cuban people. A U.S.-based Cuban group
brashly bombards Havana with U.S. surplus war materials that
cannot be purchased unless their use is known. The perpetrators
violating the U.S. neutrality laws have not been punished; indeed one of these violators is busy speaking over national radio
hook-ups.

There is a constant chorus going up from American Senators to blockade the island, to send in troops — to hell with international law, to hell with treaties and agreements. If you were a Cuban, such announcements could hardly `soothe you into not fearing a new invasion. Even now new C.I.A. contingents are being trained in Puerto Rico, Guatemala, Panama. To them are being added ex-French and Spanish legionaires. Photographs in our magazines show such potential invaders training near Miami. If the newspapermen can get such photos, the authorities could easily arrest the law-violators. Now Cuban exiles are being directly trained in separate units in the U.S. Army. At night when Cubans see the lights of U.S. war vessels anchored offshore a little ways beyond the three mile limit — numbers were there shielding the recent Havana bombardment — can they believe they are there for peace and understanding? Or are they there for the purpose of terrorism? Or will they open fire?

Obviously the Cuban government must arm to the teeth, be prepared to kill every Yankee and mercenary Cuban who tries to set foot on Cuban shores, and be prepared to die themselves.

The following is the complete text of Fidel Castro's September 1 statement replying to the U.S. charge that Cubans fired on a U.S. Navy plane.

"The Government of the United States issued yesterday afternoon the following declaration: 'Two small boats, which are believed to have been Cuban, shot at an airplane of the U.S. at 2 p.m. Cuban time, August the 30th, 1962. The attack occurred approximately 15 miles north of Cuba on international waters, while the airplane made its routine flight of instruction. It was occupied by three reserve members of the Army on active provisional service. In case a similar incident should again occur of shooting at airplanes or ships of the U.S. on or in international waters, during peaceful actions of the functions of the Army of the U.S.A., we will use all the necessary means for our own defense and will assure the free use of said waters. The Cuban Government has been informed by the appropriate channels.'"

Dr. Castro continued: "We categorically affirm that the statement of the North-American Government is absolutely false. It is a pure invention, a method in which Yankee politics have much experience. It is not at all strange that after the embarrassing and criminal attack on the city of Havana by armed boats which left from Florida and which returned there, the Government of Washington should now turn to this cynical and un-scrupulous recourse. Neither a naval craft nor airplane of Cuba has ever committed a hostile act of any kind in any form against the airplanes, ships, installations, or waters of North-America. Instead, military ships and planes of the U.S.A. have violated hundreds of times our aerial space, our own waters, and har-rassed our ships with low flights. Their guards at the Guantánamo Naval Base, usurped territory of the Cuban nation, almost daily shoot towards our land. In addition to all this, countless times airplanes proceeding from the United States have set fire to our sugar cane crops or dropped arms and explosives over our Na-tional Territory. The pirate ships that proceed from that country have attacked ships, industrial installations and residential zones, before and after the criminal invasion of Playa de Girón (Bay of Pigs). This was all recognized and confessed by the President, the Pentagon, the C.I.A. and the Yankee State Department. At no time has Cuba answered the provocations with another pro-vocation. Hundreds of times our rights have been violated and always, invariably, we have responded with a public protest and denouncement before the international organizations and world opinion. We have been denouncing the U.S.A. for prepar-ing an aggression against our country. The cynical, unscrupulous and shameless invention of this incident, which presents Cuban ships as shooting against a Yankee airplane in international wa-ters, coincides with the belligerent campaign and the hysterical anti-Cubanism which has been let loose during these days, con-firming the justness of the warning which Cuba is making to the world of the dangers which are involved for our country and world peace from the adventurous and war-like politics of the Government of the U.S.A. In its statement the Government of the U.S.A. threatens that 'in case a similar incident should again occur, their armed forces will act.'

"Real incidents provoked by Cuba shall never occur, but in-vented incidents, truculent, criminal, forged with means of ag-gression against our country will possibly occur. The Govern-ment of the United States is devoid of all scruples. But do not believe that Cuba can become intimidated with the brutal threats. If the armed forces of the U.S.A. attack Cuba, they will have to come disposed to die in the battle.

"Our country or death! We will win!"

It is the American people who have had the wool pulled over their eyes, not the Cubans. Perhaps if Cuba buzzed our shipping coming into New York, if her planes flew over and burned our fields, and dropped propaganda, and landed invading troops; if our vessels were attacked and sunk, perhaps we could understand why the Cubans remain alarmed and on the alert.

On top of that we read false stories of internal revolt, of industrial collapse and food shortages. What is sad about this is that once more, as before the Bay of Pigs invasion, our officials are beginning to believe their own fake propaganda. Rationing is due, not so much to shortages (which have occurred chiefly because imports have been cut off) but because the Cuban people are eating more than they have ever eaten — and they eat all year long now. Shoes and clothing are rationed — ergo, failure of production. Formerly 60 percent of the Cuban population went barefoot and wore only rags. Actually shoe factories and textile mills are working around the clock. They have been expanded, new ones have been built, and production is greater than in Cuba's past best years. Factories, needing parts available only here, have broken down for periods. Now most parts are being made in Cuba. Hundreds of new factories have been built, and a thousand new ones are rising, including a gigantic steel mill to make use of Cuba's vast iron resources, heretofore merely owned, never developed, by a U.S. corporation.

There has been an enormous increase in light and power production, which for the first time provides service to every corner of the island. Pinar del Rio and Oriente provinces, except for a few cities, were formerly in darkness. No longer.

What shall we say about the reforestation program, relatively the largest in the history of the world — 7,000,000 new trees in one year merely on one small southeastern peninsula?

There is little need to recapitulate the extraordinary statistics about public housing, public schools, hospital building, health care for all. A new Cuba is rising. We may not like its doctrines, but we are indeed a deluded people if we do not look, observe, and understand. The wool is over our eyes, not those of the Cubans.

Compare all this with the Alliance for Progress — and believe me Latin Americans are doing it — with its economic and political coercion, its outside meddling, grandiose pretensions beyond anything the Alliance can possibly do, its failure to meet the problems of international trade, of production, of political freedom. It is a costly adventure that may end not only by ruining Latin America but ourselves as well. The Alliance makes pie-in-the-sky promises for the future, promises which can never be carried out, whereas the Cuban Revolution thus far has produced results in the here and now. This is a fact, even if we detest its political and economic system. That is a challenge we have not met — except by armed threats.

It is nice to talk of gradualism, of a peaceful evolutionary process, but unfortunately the bases for this scarcely exist; the pressures are great and governments keep tumbling and more are going to fall, and the more we try to buttress up the status quo, the more dreadful will be the outcome. Inevitably persecution and tyranny and violence are going to sprout and grow and overwhelm. We are out of step with the Zeitgeist of our age; we are out of step with the moving forces and hopes of Latin America.We have money and weapons and swarms of experts, mostly carpetbaggers who do not even know the languages and must depend upon low-paid local assistants. The face of the Ugly American is by no means confined to the Oriental meadows.

Even were we free from our present-day super-militaristic nationalism and chauvinism, even could we rid ourselves of our smug superiority, even were we free from our peculiarly materialistic philosophy and aims and our belief in our God-given right and ability to manage the affairs of all peoples, and even if we could rise above the hates and fears which have become the mainspring of our national conduct and our international policies, it would be a tremendous task, but a rewarding one, to penetrate the secret of the alien cultures at our doors.

How little interest we have shown in their social habits and customs, even when we try to run their affairs! How little we are interested in their literature, their art, their music, their danceforms! When I was in Costa Rica, the new U.S. cultural attaché, who spoke no Spanish, did not even know who J. García Monge, the greatest intellectual figure of the land and a towering continental figure, was: a writer, head of the National Library, an editor and publisher, who was a beacon of light for the entire Spanish-speaking world, who did more in his lifetime to create a continental interchange of knowledge and literature than almost any other intellectual leader of Latin America. Our second cultural attaché in Costa Rica was ordered to avoid him because he had once favored the Sandino cause in Nicaragua and had opposed our Marine interventions. It is generally believed that our pressures caused him to be thrown out of the National Library and brought about the effort (unsuccessful) to suppress his fine literary magazine *El Repertorio Americano*.

When he died several years ago, I could find not the slightest mention of his name in any U.S. publication. I wrote a brief piece about him and his vast erudition and accomplishments, but could find no magazine that would print it. What a vast interest that displays about the peoples for whom we insist on playing big brother!

Even if we do not like the ideas or the methods of Castro — and I am sure most Cubans and most Latin Americans don't like our ideas and our methods either — we should be interested in them, and it is important because of their growing influence on the creative minds of Latin America, the great cultural outburst that has accompanied the Cuban revolution: the new painting, the thousands of new books (and none were published under Batista and our ruling slave plantation system there), the new theater and playwriting, the new movie industry (films have already received prizes both in the Socialist countries and in Australia). The new art exhibits are thrilling experiences, and they travel to Europe but not to the United States, to Latin America but not to Georgia, to the Far East but not to Mississippi. And they travel all over Cuba. Today there are little theater and music groups in every town in Cuba, and in nearly every labor and peasant organization. Over the island there are today 427 singing choruses merely in labor unions; 146 dance groups; 267 theater groups. In all there are more than 800 such labor groups. The street-cleaners have their choir; the slaughter-house workers have set up a theater; the cooks and waiters are staging plays in the Jewish Community Center. The new Free Havana School for Instructors in July 1962 graduated its first class of 380 young people as instructors in the theater, dance and music.

Instead we have tried to throw a dark curtain about everything Cuban. Not all the walls of shame are made of concrete and barbed wire. There stands the Wall of Shame we have erected around the little island of Cuba. We have tried to shut out the light. Our only instruments have been coercion, aggression, war and international lawlessness. We have refused all negotiation. We cannot accept the postulate that Cuba is now an independent country, free to have relations with any countries, free to trade with the countries she can trade with. And as long as the Holy Alliance rests upon this narrow platform of hate, it cannot hope to prosper. Until we find more civilized ways to deal with Cuba, our efforts will be wasted.

"Vested interests in the U.S., certain elements in the Pentagon and Cuban counter-revolutionary groups in their pay are seeking by every means to provoke a war between the U.S. and Cuba, no matter what the cost," declared Richard Gibson of the Fair Play for Cuba Committee recently. "There is no 'Cuban problem,'" he added. "There is only a very serious problem of convincing U.S. statesmen that this nation must learn to live in peace with its neighbors, no matter what their political, economic and social systems."

There are many constructive things that can be done. If we do not like to be called "aggressors," we can abandon aggression and return to the norms of international law. If we don't like to be called "imperialists," we can restore the stolen Guantánamo base to its rightful owner. If we don't like Soviet influence and trade with the island, all we have to do is to buy Cuban sugar and tobacco and to sell her the machinery, oil and goods she needs. Rather than trying to keep Americans in ignorance of Cuba, we could lift our embargo on newspapers and magazines and books; we could restore tourist travel, and let Americans see for themselves, and thus become the free creatures they are supposed to be. If we do not like an unfavorable balance of payments, why did we wipe out a billion dollars worth of trade with Cuba each year? Instead we preferred to go hat in hand to West Germany for help. Instead we ask Japanese industrialists to set up factories in the United States.

The Cuban revolution, whatever its subsequent course has been, has represented a great moment of truth — in Cuba, in Latin America, in inter-American affairs. We have comprehended none of it. The answer is not to be found in dollar diplomacy or armed aggression, unless we really wish to lose the whole of Latin America — perhaps sooner than we imagine.

Perhaps we should shut off, if only for a few months, our Voice of America programs, our raucous day and night shouting of propaganda into the hurt ears of the world, and listen, listen closely and patiently to the Voice of Latin America. We shall hear, all too often, "Yankee, Go Home." But we shall also hear about the life and hopes of other peoples.

If would be of great help to us also if the efforts should be reciprocal. Is it not strange that Latin America is not trying constantly to propagandize us, to get hold of military bases, to send us Peace Corps, to invade our peace and complacency, to dig oil wells in our back yards, to dig out our uranium and copper and tell us how to treat our Negroes, or to practice austerity or to run our dilapidated railroads, or to reform our messy tax structure, or to get us out of our blundering agricultural fiasco, or do away with our unemployment, or solve our crime problem, the worst on earth?

It may turn out that Latin American cultural contributions to the world, if we permit them to survive, if we ourselves survive, may prove far greater than our own. Ethnically the southern lands represent a more complete melting pot than the United States; there lives what José Vasconcelos has called the "Cosmic Man." Free from the racial prejudices and suppressions that exist in the United States, which block off or destroy so many of our human and cultural resources, their composite culture can draw freely on the great cultures of their Indians, their Negroes, their Asiatics as well as on the cultures of Spain, Portugal and Western Europe.

Ere long — it is inevitable — the people in the rest of our hemisphere, who already outnumber us and will have twice our population by the end of the century, will discover their freedoms, their true potentialities, and follow their own paths to glory and defeat and glory again. Those paths, we repeat, do not lie between the narrow prison walls of the Cold War, are not going to be shaped by any ephemeral and distorted anti-Communist or anti-Cuban crusade; they are not the paths of the United States or the paths of Soviet Russia. Their destiny does not lie in Washington or in Moscow or in Peking. Nor will it be the capitalist democracy as we know it, nor the communism as Moscow knows it. We can slow up, we can distort and even briefly ruin their achievement of cultural greatness, their political independence, their social evolution, as we are now attempting to do in the name of "freedom" with such grievous results. But in the end their contributions will be great; and it behooves us to tread with humility, not with our present arrogance, our attitude of superiority.

These are critical years. Great changes, even castastrophic changes are at hand. Latin America is a world in revolution. No King Canute in Washington or anywhere else is going to stop that rising tide. Unless we are able to comprehend the other peoples of this hemisphere, unless we are able to act generously, our loss in Cuba will seem small with the losses we will soon sustain. We cannot solve the continental problem by perpetuating injustice and military dictators, by attempting to grab more and more wealth and power.

The first thing we have to learn is to recognize the complete independence of all the countries regardless of their form of government. That we cannot force them blindly to follow our policies. That their peoples need economic freedom and are going to fight for it, with or without our understanding and help. Unless we can arrive at this simple minimum of understanding, the Alliance for Progress can only bring evil and trouble in its train. As it is, even our finest efforts are being sunk in a dismal and dark swamp of futility.

That need not be so. But who will reverse our headlong plunge into military capitalism and war? Who will restore our economy to a sane condition in which we are no longer slaves, as Hitler was, to ever bigger wartime expenditures without which greedy feeding the economy would collapse? Who will extricate us from our hysteria, our fears and hates, from our inordinate lust for wealth and power? Who will bring about a moral and spiritual rebirth in this country? Who will create just and equitable economic relations with the other countries of the world? Who will put into practice that peace tenet laid down by Franklin Delano Roosevelt — one of his four freedoms — free access to the raw materials of the world? Instead we observe only monopoly by private corporations backed up by diplomacy, battleships, and broken relations with half the world. Who will replace our bland arrogance and smugness with more human qualities that can make possible the true cooperation of the peoples of the world? Alliance by the fist of wealth and power is no alliance at all.

But until that comes about we shall not, as a country, be able to accomplish anything that will promote the freedom and progress of Latin America and its people. For Latin Americans the only salvation at this juncture is to fight against our overlordship, to fight for a neutral position. Their destiny is their own, not ours, to dictate.

SELECTED REFERENCES

ENGLISH

GENERAL

Arciniegas, German. *The Green Continent.*
————. *The State in Latin America.*
Arévalo, Juan Jose. *The Shark and the Sardines.*
Beals, Carleton. *America South.*
————. *Lands of the Dawning Morrow.*
Herring, Hubert. *A History of Latin America.*
Lieuwen, Edwin. *Arms and Politics in Latin America.*
O'Connor, Harvey. *World Crisis in Oil.*
Plenn, Abel. *The Southern Americas.*
Szulc, Tad. *Twilight of the Tyrants.*
Slominsky, Nicolas. *The Music of Latin America.*

CARIBBEAN AND MID-AMERICA

Arciniegas, German. *Caribbean: Sea of Destiny.*
Beals, Carleton. *Banana Gold.*
Blanchard, Paul. *Democracy and Empire in the Caribbean.*
Brown, Wenzell. *Angry Men — Laughing Men: The Caribbean Cauldron.*

Kepner, Charles David and Soothill, Henry Jay. *The Banana Empire.*

Roberts, W. Adolphe. *The Caribbean: The Story of our Sea of Destiny.*

Wilson, Charles M. *The Caribbean: Challenge and Opportunity.*

ARGENTINA

Jefferson, Mark. *Peopling the Argentine Pampa.*

Weil, Felix S. *Argentine Riddle.*

White, John W. *Argentina. The Life Story of a Nation.*

Whittaker, Arthur P. *The United States and Argentina.*

BOLIVIA

Alexander, Robert G. *The Bolivian National Revolution.*

Marsh, M. H. *The Bankers in Bolivia.*

BRAZIL

Azevedo, Fernando de. *Brazilian Culture.*

Da Cunha, Euclides. *Rebellion in the Backlands.*

Freyre, Gilberto. *Brazil: An Interpretation.*

Nash, Roy. *The Conquest of Brazil.*

Pierson, Donald. *Negroes in Brazil.*

Price, Willard. *The Amazing Amazon.*

Wythe, George; Wright, Royca A. and Midkiff, Harold M. *Brazil: An Expanding Economy.*

CHILE

Beals, Carleton. *The Long Land.*

Bowers, Claude G. *Chile Through Embassy Windows, 1939-53.*

Galdames, Luis. *A History of Chile.*

McBride, G. M. *Chile: Land and Society.*

COLOMBIA

Parks, E. T. *Colombia and the United States, 1765-1934.*

Rippy, J. F. *The Capitalists and Colombia.*

Whittaker, A. P. *The United States and South America: The Northern Republics.*

COSTA RICA

Bieranz, M. *Costa Rican Life.*

CUBA

Beals, Carleton. *The Crime of Cuba.*

Buell, R. L. et al. *Problems of the New Cuba.*

Foner, Phillip S. *A History of Cuba.*
Frank, Waldo. *Cuba: Prophetic Island.*
Huberman, Leo and Sweezy, Paul. *Cuba—Anatomy of a Revolution.*
Jenks, J. H. *Our Cuban Colony.*
Marzani, Carl. *Cuba and the C. I. A.*
Sartre, Jean Paul. *Sartre on Cuba.*
Szulc, Tad. *The Invasion of Cuba.*
Taber, Robert. *M-26.*

DOMINICAN REPUBLIC

Hicks, Albert C. *Blood in the Streets.*
Knight, Melvin M. *The Americans in Santo Domingo.*
Ornes, German E. *Trujillo: The Little Caesar of the Caribbean.*
Welles, Summer. *Naboth's Vineyard.*

ECUADOR

Blanksten, George. *Constitutions and Caudillos.*
Franklin, Albert. *Ecuador.*
Von Hagen, Victor Wolfgang. *Ecuador and the Galápagos Islands.*

GUATEMALA

Kelsey, Vera and Osborne, L. J. *Four Keys to Guatemala.*
LaFarge, Oliver. *Santa Eulalia.*
————. *The Sparks Fly Upwards.*
Raine, Alice. *Eagle of Guatemala.*

HAITI

Herskovits, M. J. *Life in a Haitian Valley.*
Montague, L. L. *Haiti and the United States, 1714-1938.*
Rodman, Selden. *Haiti: The Black Republic.*
Vandercook, John W. *Black Majesty.*

HONDURAS

Squier, E. G. *Honduras.*
Stokes, William S. *Honduras.*

MEXICO

Beals, Carleton. *House in Mexico.*
————. *Mexico: An Interpretation.*
————. *Mexican Maze.*
————. *Porfirio Diaz.*
Bell, Edward I. *The Political Shame of Mexico.*
Bulnes, Francisco. *The Whole Truth about Mexico.*

Calderón de la Barca, Frances. *Life in Mexico.*
Covarrubias, Miguel. *Mexico South: The Isthmus of Tehuantepec.*
Flandreau, Charles MaComb. *Viva Mexico.*
Gruening, Ernest. *Mexico and its Heritage.*
McBride, G. M. *The Land System of Mexico.*
Plenn, G. M. *Mexico Marches.*
Reed, John. *Insurgent Mexico.*
Roeder, Ralph. *Juárez and his Mexico,* 2 vols.
Simpson, L. B. *Many Mexicos.*
Toor, Frances. *Mexican Folkways.*
Turner, John Kenneth. *Barbarous Mexico.*
Valliant, George C. *The Aztecs of Mexico.*
Veríssimo, Enrico. *Mexico.*
Wolfe, Bertrand. *Portrait of Mexico: Rivera.*

NICARAGUA

Belt, Thomas. *The Naturalist in Nicaragua.*
Cox, Jocelyn Isaac. *The United States and Nicaragua.*
Nogales, Rafael. *The Looting of Nicaragua.*
Scroggs, William O. *Filibusters and Financiers: The Story of William Walker and his Associates.*
Squier, E. G. *Nicaragua.*

PANAMA

Bunau-Varilla, Philippe. *Panama.*
Ealy, Lawrence O. *The Republic of Panama in World Affairs.*
Harding, Earl. *The Untold Story of Panama.*
Kembell, John Haskell. *The Panama Route.*

PARAGUAY

Box, Pelham H. *The Origins of the Paraguayan War.*
Burton, Richard F. *Letters from the Battlefield of Paraguay.*
Warren, H. G. *Paraguay: An Informal History.*

PERU

Alegría, Ciro. *Broad and Alien is the World.*
—————. *The Golden Serpent.*
Beals, Carleton. *Fire on the Andes.*
Kelley, Hank and Dot. *Dancing Diplomats.*
Mortimer, W. Golden. *Peru: History of Coca.*
Prescott, William H. *Peru.*
Toor, Francis. *Three Worlds in Peru.*

SALVADOR

Martin, Percy F. *Salvador of the Twentieth Century.*

URUGUAY

Hanson, R. H. *Utopia in Uruguay.*
Hudson, W. H. *The Purple Land.*

VENEZUELA

Ludwig, Emil. *Bolivar.*
Rourke, Thomas. *Tyrant of the Andes.*
Von Hagan, Victor Wolfgang. *The Five Seasons of Manuela.*
Ybanez, R. T. *Francisco Miranda.*
————. *A Young Man of Caracas.*

SPANISH

GENERAL

Arévalo, Juan José. *El Antikomunismo en América Latina.*
Blanco Fombona, Horacio. *Crímenes del Imperialismo Norteameri-
cano.*
————. *El Conquistador Español.*
Carnero Checa, Genaro. *El Aguila Rampante.*
Fabela, Isidro. *Los Estados Unidos Contra la Libertad.*
Pereyra, Carlos. *Breve Historia de America.*
Saenz, Vicente. *Hispano América Contra el Colonaje.*
————. *Rompiendo Cadneas.*
Sánchez, Luís Alberto. *Historia de la Literatura Americana.*
————. *Vida y Pasión de la Cultura de América.*

CARIBBEAN AND MID-AMERICA

Krehm, William. *Democracia y Tiranias en el Caribe.*

ARGENTINA

Bunge, Alejandro. *Soluciones Argentinas.*
Fernández, Alfredo. *El Movimiento Obrero en la Argentina.*
Gálvez, Manuel. *Vida de Hipólito Yrigoyen.*
————. *Vida de Juan Manuel de Rosas.*
Güiraldes, Ricardo. *Don Segundo Sombra.*
Ingineros, José. *La Evolución de las Ideas Argentinas.*
Leguizamón, Martiniano. *La Cuna del Gaucho.*
Lugones, Leopoldo. *Historia de Sarmiento.*
El Movimiento Universitario, *Vol. I: Argentina, 1918-1940.*
Mallea, Eduardo. *Historia de la Pasión de Argentino.*
Manzi, Francisco. *El Viejo Taragüy.*
Mitre, Barolomé. *San Martín.*
Palacios, Alfredo. *Nuestra América y el Imperialismo.*
Perón, Juan. *Discursos.*

Romero, Luís. *Las Ideas Políticas en Argentina.*
Sánchez, Viamonte C. *Historia Institucional de Argentina.*
Solari, Juan Antonio, *Administración Pública Argentina.*
Strasser, Carlos (ed.). *Las Izquierdas en el Progreso Político de Argentina.*
Ugarte, Manuel. *Las Mejores Páginas de.*
Viñas, Ismael. *Orden y Progreso: El Era del Frondizismo.*
Ygobone, Aquiles. *La Epopeya Patagónica.*
—————. *La Patagonia.*

BOLIVIA

El Hombre y el Paisaje de Bolivia. (Anthology)
Loaiza Beltrán, Fernando. *De Penas 4,000 Metros Oteando.*
Molíns, R. Jaime. *El Estaño. Fundamento Vital de Bolivia.*
Moncayo, José Flores. *Derecho Agrario Boliviano.*
Paz Estenssoro, Victor. *El Penasmiento Revolucionario de Bolivia.*
Programa del Gobierno del Movimiento Nacionalista Revolucionario.
Vellarde, José F. *Victor Paz Estenssoro.*

BRAZIL

Amado, Jorge. *Gabriela Cravo e Canela.*
—————. *Obras Completas.*
Bastide, Roger and Fernandes, Florestán. *Brancos e Negroes em São Paulo.*
Cardoso, Fernando H. and Ianni, Octavio. *Cor e mobilidade Social en Florianópolis.*
Cavalcante, Paulo. *Eça de Queiroz, Agitador no Brasil.*
Couto de Magalhães, General. *Viagem ao Araguaia.*
Pinheiro Filho, João. *Problemas Brasilieros.*
Tapajos, Vicente. *Historia do Brasil.*

CHILE

Blest Gana, Alberto. *Durante la Reconquista,* 2 vols.
—————. *Sus Mejores Páginas.*
Domingo Silva, Victor. *El Cachorro.*
Edwards, Alberto. *La Fronda Aristócrata.*
Edwards Bello, Joaquín. *Valparaiso (Fantasmas).*
Eyzaguirre, Jaime. *O'Higgins.*
Guzmán, Nicomedes. *La Sangre y la Esperanza.*
Latorre, Mariano. *Chile: País de Rincones.*
Marín, Juan. *Viento Negro.*
Neruda, Pablo. *Poemas.*
Petit, M. *Don Diego Portales.*

Rokha, Pablo. *Antología,* 4 vols.
Sepúlvedo, Villanueva Hector. *La Revolución que Chile Espera.*
Yankas, Lautaro. *Rotos.*

COLOMBIA

Arías Trujillo. *Risaralda.*
Azula Barrera, Rafael. *De la Revolución al Orden Nuevo.*
Caballero Calderón, E. *Historia Privada de los Colombianos.*
Cartagena, Donaro. *Una Semana de Miedo.*
González Martínez, Manuel. *Llanura, Soledad y Viento.*
Gutiérrez González, Gregorio. *Obras Completas,* 11th Edition.
Isaza, Eduardo Franco. *Los Guerrillos del Llano.*
Salamanca, Guillermo. *Los Partidos en Colombia.*
Socarras, José Francisco. *Viento de Trópico.*
Vargas Echavarría, José. *Nos Roban el Petroleo.*

COSTA RICA

Acosta, Aguilar. *La Zafra.*
Fernández Guardia, Ricardo. *Morazón en Costa Rica.*
García Monge, J. *Novelas y ceuntos.*
Quijano Quesada, Alberto. *Costa Rica: Ayer y Hoy.*

CUBA

Bastista, Fulgencio. *Respuestas.*
Benítez, Fernando. *La Batalla de Cuba.*
Bravo, Marcos. *El Segundo "Asalto" al Palacio Presidencial.*
Bueno, Salvador. *Antología de Cuentos en Cuba.*
Camacho, Panfilio D. *Marta Abreu.*
Castro, Fidel. *Playa Girón.*
—————. *Discursos.*
Cepero Bonilla, Raul. *Politica Azucarera.*
Cruz, Manuel de. *Episodios de la Revolución Cubana.*
—————. *Estudios Históricos.*
—————. *Literatura Cubana.*
—————. *Pasión de Cuba*
Grillo, David. *El Problema Negro Cubano.*
Historia de una Agresión.
Humboldt, Alexander Von. *Ensayo Político sobre la Isla de Cuba.*
Lizaso, Félix. *Místico del Deber.*
Martí, José. *Obras Completas.*
Núñez, Jiménez, A. *Geografía de Cuba.*
Ortiz, Fernando. *Contrapunto de Tobaco y el Azucar.*
—————. *La Hampa Cubana.*

—————. *Los Náñigos.*
Portel Vilá. *Narciso López y su Epoca.*
Roig de Leuchsenring. *Los Estados Unidos Va Contra Cuba Libre,*
    4 vols.
Saco, José Antonio. *Historia de la Esclavitud en las Américas,* 4 vols.
Torriente, Lola de la. *Mi Casa en la Tormenta.*

DOMINICAN REPUBLIC

Galíndez, Jesús de. *La Era de Trujillo.*
Jiménez Grullón, J. I. *Luchemos por Nuestra América.*
Mosco Puello, F. *Cana y Bueyes.*

ECUADOR

Barrera, Isaac J. *Historia de la Literatura Ecuatoriana.*
Efrén Reyes, Oscar. *Breve Historia General de Ecuador.*
Gallegos, Gerardo. Eladio Seguro. *El Puno del Amo.*
Garcés, Victor Gabriel. *Idigenismo.*
Icaza, Jorge. *Cholos.*
—————. *En las Calles.*
—————. *Huasipungo.*
Jaramillo Alvarado, Pío. *El Indio Ecuatoriano.*
—————. *La Nación Quiteña.*
Pareja Díez Canseco, Alfredo. *Historia del Ecuador,* 2 vols.
Saenz, Moisés. *Sobre los Indios Ecuatorianos.*
Salvador, Humberto. *Noviembre.*

GUATEMALA

Alemán Bolaños, G. *Vida Agrícola de Guatemala.*
Arévalo Martínez, Rafael. *Ecce Pericles!*
—————. *El Hombre que Pareciá un Caballo.*
—————. *La Oficina de Paz.*
—————. *Manuel Aldano.*
—————. *Los Tormentados*
Arévalo, Juan José. *La Democracia y el Imperio.*
Cardosa y Aragón, Luís. *La Revolución Guatemalteca.*
Chavarría, Flores, Manuel. *Tezututlán.*
Juárez Muñoz, J. Fernández. *El Indio Guatemalteco.*
Popol Vuh.
Ríos, Efrain. *De los Ombres contra Hombres.*
Santa Cruz, Rosendo. *Cuando Cae la Noche.*
Selser, Gregorio. *El Guatemalazo: La Primera Guerra Sucia.*
Toriello, Guillermo. *La Batalla de Guatemala.*
Wyld Ospina, C. *La Tierra de las Nahuacas.*

HAITI

Gallegos, Gerardo. *El Embrujo de Haiti.*

HONDURAS

Durán, Rómulo E. *José Justo Mella.*
Izaguirre, Carlos. *Bajo el Chubasco,* 2 vols.
López Pinedo, Juan. *El General Morazán.*
Mejía Nieto, Arturo. *El Chele Amaya y Otros Cuentos.*
Navarro, Miguel. *Lecturas Nacionales.*
Ramos, Miguel Angel. *La Reconstrucción Nacional.*

MEXICO

Azuela, Mariano. *Los de Abajo.*
Cabrera, Luís (Blas Urréa). *Obras Políticas.*
Cruz, Sor Juana Inés de la. *Poemas.*
Fabela, Isidro. *La Tristeza del Amo.*
Frías, Heriberto. *Tomochic.*
Fuentes, Carlos. *La Región mas Transparente.*
Galindo y Villa, Jesús. *Geografía de la República Mexicana,* 2 vols.
Gamio, Manuel. *Forjando Patria.*
Gil, Mario. *Nuestros Buenos Vecinos,* 5th Edition.
González Blanco, Edmundo. *Carranza y la Revolución de México.*
González Obregón, Luís. *México Viejo.*
————. *La Inquisición y la Independencia de México.*
Guerrero, Julio. *La Génesis del Crimen en México.*
Guzmán, Martín Luís. *La Sombra del Caudillo.*
Jíménez Rueda, Julio. *Historia de la Literatura de México.*
Pensador Mexicano, El. *El Periquillo Sarniento.*
Mendizábal, Miguel. *La Influencia de la Sal.*
Menéndez, Miguel Angel. *Maya.*
Muñoz, Rafael F. *Santa Anna.*
Palavicini, L. G. *Historia de México,* 4 vols.
Payno, Luís. *Los Bandidos del Río Frío,* 2 vols.
Romero Flores, Jesús. *Leyendas y Cuentos Michoacanos,* 2 vols.
Rubén Romero, José. *Apuntes de un Lugareño.*
Saenz, Moisés. *México Integro.*
————. *Morelos y Bolívar.*
Silva Herzog. *La Revolución Mexicana,* 2 vols.
Taracena, Alfonso M. *Mi vida en el Vértigo de la Revolución.*
Urbina, Luís G. *La Vida literaria de México.*
Vasconcelos, José. *Bolívar y Monroismo.*
————. *Breve Historia de México.*
————. *La Tormenta.*

—————. *Ulises Criollo.*
Závalo, Lorenzo. *Ensayo Histórico de las Revoluciones en México.*
Zea, Leopoldo. *Apogeo y Decadencia del Positivismo en México.*

NICARAGUA

Alemán, Bolaños, Gustavo. *Un Lombrosiano Somoza.*
—————. *Sandino: El Libertador.*
Calderón, Salvador. *Alredador de Walker.*
Calderón Ramírez, Sebastian. *Ultimos Días de Sandino.*
Calero Orozco, Adolfo. *Sangre Santa.*
Cantón, Alfredo. *A Sangre y Fuego.*
Chamorro, Pedro Joaquín. *El Ultimo Filibustero.*
Cuadro, Manolo. *Almidón.*
Escobar, Estibán. *Pedro Joaquín Chamorro.*
Orozco, José Román. *Cosampa.*
Saenz, Vicente. *El Canal de Nicaragua.*
Selser, Gregorio. *El Pequeño Ejército Loco.*
—————. *Sandino, General de Hombres Libres,* 2 vols.
Somoza, Anastasio. *El Verdadero Sandino.*
Soto Hall, Máximo. *Nicaragua y el Imperialismo Norteamericano.*

PANAMA

Beleño, Joaquín. *Gambóa Road Gang.*
Castiller R., Ernesto J. *Historia de Panamá.*
Garay, Nicolás. *Panamá y las Guerras de los Estados Unidos.*
Garcia, Ismael. *Medio Siglo de Político Panamena.*
Jurado, Ramón. *Desertores.*
Méndez Pereira, Octavio. *Antología del Canal, 1914-1939.*
Moscoso, Antonio. *"Buchi".*
Olmeido, Alfaro. *El Canal de Panamá en las Guerras Futuras.*
Ozores, Manuel. *Playa Honda.*
Zarate, F. and Dora, Pérez de. *La Décima y la Copla en Panamá.*

PARAGUAY

Chaves, María C. L. de. *Río Lunado.*
Fernández, Carlos José. *La Guerra del Chaco,* 2 vols.
González, Natalicio. *Ideología Guaraní.*
Guasch, P. Antonio. *El Idioma Guaraní.*
Morales, Ernesto. *Leyendas Guaraníes.*
Radeglia, Vittorio Félice. *Trás la Cortina de Corned Beef.*
Stefanich, Juan. *El Paraguay Nuevo.*

PERU

Aquirre Morales, Augusto. *El Pueblo del Sol.*

Alegría, Ciro. *Los Perros Hambrientes.*
Basadre, Jorge. *La Iniciación de la República,* 2 vols.
——————. *La Multitude: La Ciudad y el Campo en la Historia del Perú.*
—————— *Perú: Problema y Posibilidad.*
Belaunde, Victor Andrés. *La Realidad Nacional.*
Belaunde Terry, Fernando. *La Conquista del Perú por los Peruanos.*
——————. *Pueblo por Pueblo.*
Benavides Corréa, Alfonso. *El Petroleo Peruano.*
Buse, H. *Huarás-Chavín.*
Díez Canseco, Maria Rostworowski de. *Pachacutec: Inca Yupanqui.*
González Prado, Manuel. *Bajo el Oprobrio.*
——————. *Propaganda y Ataque.*
López Albújar, Enrique. *Los Caballos del Delito.*
Mariátegui, José Carlos. *Siete Ensayos Sobre la Realidad Peruana.*
——————. *Colección Obras Completas,* 20 vols.
Moreno Segundo, Luís. *La Música de los Incas.*
More, Ernesto. *Reportajes con Radar.*
Ramírez Nova, E. *La Farsa del Panamericanismo.*
Semana de Arqueología Peruana. Antigua Perú: Espacio y Tiempo.
Tello, J. C. *Arqueología del Valle de Casma.*
——————. *Chavín.*
Valcárcel, *Etnohistoria del Perú Antigua.*
——————. *Tempestad en los Andes.*
Vásquez, Diógenes. *Tierra Regionalista y Regionalismo Peruano.*

SALVADOR

Barbereña, Santiago I. *Historia de El Salvador.*
Salarrué. *Cuentos de Barrio.*
Martí, Julio Alberto. *Vernáculas.*
Quijano Hernández, Manuel. *En la Montaña o El Alma del Indio.*

URUGUAY

Abril, Xavier. *Vallejo.*
Amorím, Enrique. *El Caballo y su Sombra.*
——————. *La Carreta.*

——————. *Corral Abierto.*
——————. *El Paisano Aguilar.*
Gravina, Alfredo Dante. *Del Miedo al Orgullo.*
——————. *Fronteras al Viento.*
Pereda Valdés, Ildefonso. *Negro Rioplatense.*
Pinto, Francisco R. *Historia del Movimiento Obrero del Uruguay.*
——————. *Historia del Uruguay.*

Pivel Devoto, Juan I. *Historia de la República Oriental del Uruguay.*
Quiroga, Horacio. *Los Desterrados.*
Rama, Carlos M. *Las Clases Sociales.*
————. *Ensayo de Sociología Uruguayo.*
Sánchez, Florencio. *Colección de Obras de Teatro,* 5 vols.
Solari, Aldo. *Sociología Rural Nacional.*

VENEZUELA

Betancourt, Rómulo. *Los Problemas Venezolanos.*
Breceño Iragorry, Mario. *Tapices de Historia Patria.*
García Chuecos, Hector. *Siglo Dieciocho Venezolano.*
Gallegos, Rómulo. *Doña Bárbara.*
Otero Silva, Miguel. *Casas Muertas.*
————. *Oficina No. 1.*
Picón Salas, Mariano. *Crisis, Cambio, Traición.*
Rumazo González, Alfonso. *O'Leary.*
Schad, Werner. *Negros Blancos: Fuego Tropical.*
Tello, Arturo Hellmund. *Leyendas Indígenas Guajiras.*
Uslar- Pietri, Mario. *Letras y hombres de Venezuela.*

INDEX